Better Homes and Gardens®

AMERICA'S

BEST-LOVED COMMUNITY RECIPES

BETTER HOMES AND GARDENS® BOOKS
Des Moines, Iowa

BETTER HOMES AND GARDENS® BOOKS
An Imprint of Meredith® Books
President, Book Group: Joseph J. Ward
Vice President and Editorial Director: Elizabeth P. Rice
Managing Editor: Christopher Cavanaugh
Executive Editor: Nancy N. Green
Art Director: Ernest Shelton
Test Kitchen Director: Sharon Stilwell

America's Best Loved Community Recipes
Editor: Shelli McConnell
Contributing Editor: Lisa Green
Associate Art Director: Lynda Haupert
Production Manager: Douglas Johnston
Electronic Production Editor: Paula Forest
Test Kitchen Product Supervisors: Marilyn Cornelius,
Maryellen Krantz
Food Stylists: Lynn Blanchard, Janet Pittman,
Jennifer Peterson
Photographers: Mike Dieter, Scott Little

Developed by Phoenix Marketing Group Ltd.
V.P. and Editorial Director: Candace N. Conard
Managing Editor: Chris Mellor
Contributing Editors: Phyllis A. Baeker,
Kim Gayton Elliot
Assistant Editors: Carol B. Nolin, Melissa B. Parsons
Production: Serena Torrence Fox, Susan Slabicki
Design: The Q Design Group, Ltd.
Initial Photography Styling: Michael Heintz Studios

On the cover: Tomato-Peach Barbecued Ribs
(page 239)

WE CARE!
All of us at Better Homes and Gardens® Books are dedicated
to providing you with the information and ideas you need to
create tasty foods. We welcome your comments and suggestions.
Write us at: Better Homes and Gardens® Books,
Cookbook Editorial Department, RW240, 1716 Locust Street,
Des Moines, IA 50309-3023

If you would like to order additional copies of any of our books,
call 1-800-678-2803 or check with your local bookstore.

Our seal assures you that every recipe in *America's Best-Loved
Community Recipes* has been tested in the Better Homes and
Gardens® Test Kitchen. This means that each recipe is practical and
reliable, and meets our high standards of taste appeal. We guarantee
your satisfaction with this book for as long as you own it.

INTRODUCTION

The dishes in this book are truly *America's Best-Loved Community Recipes.* These community classics represent America—coast-to-coast and all points in between—from Manchester, Connecticut to Salida, Colorado. What's more, these recipes originally appeared in community cookbooks that benefit a wide range of groups and institutions, from the New Orleans Museum of Art to the Central Presbyterian Church of Saint Paul, Minnesota.

While the recipes and their histories are diverse, all have one important thing in common: Each one has met the highest standards of the Better Homes and Gardens® Test Kitchen to earn the Better Homes and Gardens® Test Kitchen Seal of Approval. That means each recipe has been individually tested for quality and flavor. Our Test Kitchen professionals have added tips and hints along the way to help make your preparation of these recipes easy and successful.

Your family and friends will surely enjoy sampling a taste of favorite foods from all over the United States, just as much as we at Better Homes and Gardens® have enjoyed bringing *America's Best-Loved Community Recipes* to you.

CONTENTS

Vegetables

When your harvest is bountiful, these dishes will make the best of your garden produce. The Scalloped Carrots with Mustard-Cheese Sauce will add pizzazz to any meal. Fresh Asparagus with Orange Hollandaise Sauce provides a new spin on a springtime classic, and Spaghetti Squash Tomato Toss is a fun main dish your kids will love. When zucchini and tomatoes are more than plentiful, prepare the Ratatouille, and you won't have to worry about leftovers.

GREEN BEANS WITH TOMATO

Makes 6 Servings

1	pound green beans, washed, trimmed and cut diagonally into 1-inch pieces
¼	cup butter *or* margarine
¼	cup finely chopped onion
1	small clove garlic, minced
1	tablespoon brown sugar
1	tablespoon lemon juice
½	teaspoon salt
½	teaspoon dried oregano, crushed
⅛	teaspoon pepper
2	medium ripe tomatoes, cut up

♦   ♦   ♦

The Junior League of Mobile has published two cookbooks that have gained national recognition, Recipe Jubilee! and One of a Kind. Green Beans with Tomato hails from One of a Kind, a marvelous cookbook with a wide range of topics. The League members have included sections on microwave cooking, wine selection, "Things Mother Never Told You" and special menus. Profits from cookbook sales help to fund League projects.

Mrs. Caine O'Rear, III
One of a Kind
The Junior League of Mobile
Mobile
ALABAMA

1 In large saucepan, cook the green beans in a small amount of boiling salted *water* for 18 to 20 minutes or until crisp-tender. Drain the green beans and set aside, keeping warm.

2 Meanwhile, in a large skillet, melt the butter or margarine. Add the onion and garlic; cook and stir over medium-low heat for 3 minutes.

 TIPS FROM OUR KITCHEN

Sliced Italian plum tomatoes, halved cherry tomatoes or yellow tomatoes can be substituted for the tomatoes in this recipe.

For a change of pace, use other bean varieties in this recipe. Try yellow wax, Italian, Chinese long and purple beans. Cook the Chinese long beans for only 3 to 4 minutes.

If fresh green beans aren't in season, use 2½ cups frozen green beans.

3 Stir in the brown sugar, lemon juice, salt, oregano and pepper. Add the tomatoes. Heat through, stirring occasionally.

4 Add the tomato mixture to the cooked, drained beans. Gently toss. Transfer the mixture to a warm serving dish and serve immediately.

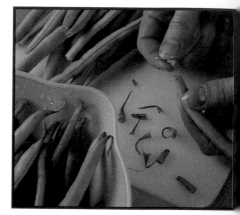

Wash fresh beans before you store them. Place the beans in an airtight plastic bag and refrigerate for 3 to 4 days. Remove the ends and strings and cut them diagonally just before cooking.

Nutrition Analysis (*Per Serving*): Calories: 113 / Cholesterol: 21 mg / Carbohydrates: 10 g Protein: 2 g / Sodium: 263 mg / Fat: 8 g (Saturated Fat: 5 g) / Potassium: 317 mg.

FRESH VEGETABLE DISH

Ripe tomatoes plus a hint of oregano, brown sugar and lemon juice turn ordinary green beans into a
dish that deserves a second glance—and a second helping!

SCALLOPED CARROTS WITH MUSTARD-CHEESE SAUCE

Makes 6 Servings

- 3 cups sliced carrots
- ¼ cup finely chopped onion
- 1 tablespoon margarine *or* butter
- 1 tablespoon all-purpose flour
- ⅛ teaspoon salt
- ⅛ teaspoon dry mustard
- ¾ cup milk
- ½ cup shredded cheddar cheese (2 ounces)
- 2 teaspoons snipped fresh dill *or* ¾ teaspoon dried dillweed
- ⅛ teaspoon celery seed

Dash pepper

Fresh dill (optional)

✦ ✦ ✦

Each March, the Geneseo United Methodist Women host a dinner to greet their new members. These meals have provided many of the recipes included in the group's fund-raising cookbook. Two recipes for Scalloped Carrots—submitted by Kay Taylor and Ferna Vanderheyden—were so similar, the committee decided to publish just one recipe credited to both women.

Kay Taylor
Ferna Vanderheyden
<u>*Geneseo UMW Cookbook*</u>
Buckingham
IOWA

1 In a large saucepan with a steamer rack, steam the carrots for 8 to 10 minutes or until tender.

2 In a small saucepan, cook the onion in the margarine or butter for 2 to 3 minutes or until the onion is tender. Stir in the flour, salt and dry mustard. Stir in the milk. Cook, stirring constantly, until the sauce is thickened and bubbly, about 5 minutes. Stir in the cheddar cheese, dill, celery seed and pepper. Cook and stir until the cheese is melted.

3 Toss the carrots with the sauce. Or, arrange the carrots on a platter and top with the sauce. Garnish with fresh dill, if desired.

TIPS FROM OUR KITCHEN

Although Kay and Ferna teamed this rich sauce with carrots, we found it to be tasty on green vegetables, too. Take your pick of steamed broccoli, green beans, cabbage or cauliflower.

Once the water is boiling, lower the vegetables into the steamer basket with a large spoon. Cover and steam.

To steam vegetables perfectly every time: Add water to a saucepan with a tight-fitting lid until the water level is just below, but not touching, the steamer basket. The vegetables should never touch the boiling water.

Nutrition Analysis (*Per Serving*): Calories: 120 / Cholesterol: 12 mg / Carbohydrates: 13 g / Protein: 5 g / Sodium: 202 mg / Fat: 6 g (Saturated Fat: 3 g) / Potassium: 286 mg.

SAUCY COMBINATION

An old favorite made fabulous by the addition of a creamy cheese sauce. We think that this carrot dish from Kay Taylor and Ferna Vanderheyden of Buckingham, Iowa, makes a perfect counterpoint for everything from roast beef to baked chicken to grilled fish.

VEGETABLES

417

BRAISED BELGIAN ENDIVE

Makes 8 Servings
4   heads Belgian endive
2   tablespoons butter *or*
     margarine
2   tablespoons chicken broth
2 to 4   teaspoons lemon juice
½   teaspoon sugar
½   teaspoon salt
⅛   teaspoon pepper
Paprika *and/or* snipped fresh
     parsley

◆   ◆   ◆

This recipe is a simplified version of Mary Hill Caperton's cousin's recipe for Braised Belgian Endive. Mary says that she usually includes both the parsley and the paprika and suggests trying vermouth or white wine in place of the chicken stock for a flavor variation.

Mary Hill Caperton
SPCA Cookbook
Abermale SPCA
Charlottesville
VIRGINIA

1 Preheat the oven to 350°.

2 Wash and drain the endive heads. Halve the endive lengthwise; cut out and discard the cores. Place the endive in a 2-quart rectangular baking dish.

3 In a small saucepan, melt the butter or margarine. Stir in the chicken broth, lemon juice, sugar, salt and pepper. Pour the mixture over the endive.

4 Cover and bake in the 350° oven for 35 to 40 minutes or until the endive is tender.

5 Using a slotted spoon, transfer the endive to a warm serving dish. Sprinkle with paprika and/or parsley.

TIPS FROM OUR KITCHEN

Belgian endive also is known as French endive or witloof chicory. The individual heads are small and cone-shaped with 5- to 6-inch-long, tightly packed leaves that are creamy white with pale yellow tips. The flavor is slightly bitter. After purchasing, store endive in a plastic bag in the refrigerator up to 3 days. Since it is usually imported, Belgian endive can be expensive, but the delicious vegetable makes a perfect company dish.

One medium lemon will yield approximately 3 tablespoons fresh lemon juice. You can store leftover lemon juice in the refrigerator for 2 to 3 days.

For variety, sprinkle the baked endive with 2 tablespoons chopped, toasted pecans or almonds in the place of the paprika and/or parsley.

You can make the chicken broth using instant chicken bouillon granules and water. Or, use canned broth or homemade, if you have it on hand.

To braise is to cook food slowly in a small amount of liquid in a tightly covered pan.

Nutrition Analysis (*Per Serving*): Calories: 32 / Cholesterol: 8 mg / Carbohydrates: 1 g / Protein: 0 g / Sodium: 176 mg / Fat: 3 g (Saturated Fat: 2 g) / Potassium: 58 mg.

UNCOMMON SIDE DISH

Commonly served cold in salads or as appetizers, Belgian endive is also a delicious hot side dish
when it is braised in butter and broth.

CURRIED CORN

1 Sauté the corn, green sweet pepper and onion in the butter or margarine for 5 to 7 minutes or until the vegetables are tender.

2 Stir in the sour cream, curry powder, salt and pepper. Heat the mixture slowly, stirring constantly; do not allow the mixture to boil or the sour cream may curdle.

 TIPS FROM OUR KITCHEN

If you love curry, try increasing the curry powder to ¾ teaspoon.

If you make this dish with canned corn, you may want to omit the salt.

For a subtle taste variation and more color contrast, try substituting red sweet pepper for the green.

To grate the onion, rub the cut surface of a peeled onion across the smaller holes of a shredder.

To ensure their freshness, buy your spices in small quantities and replace them once a year. To determine the freshness, check the color and aroma. When fresh, spices usually have a bright, rich color and a strong aroma when you open the container.

Nutrition Analysis *(Per Serving):* Calories: 202 / Cholesterol: 28 mg / Carbohydrates: 22 g / Protein: 4 g / Sodium: 476 mg / Fat 13 g (Saturated Fat: 7 g) / Potassium: 164 mg.

INDIAN ACCENT

A meat-and-potatoes meal calls for an exotic vegetable such as Erma Keller's Curried Corn. The spicy blend of curry powder, onion and green bell pepper, combined with the cool smoothness of sour cream makes this vegetable dish wonderfully intriguing, bite after bite.

RATATOUILLE

Makes 6 Servings

1	large onion, chopped
1	small sweet green pepper, chopped
2	stalks celery, finely chopped
¼	cup margarine *or* butter
2	medium zucchini, cut into ¼-inch thick slices
½	medium eggplant, peeled and cut into ½-inch strips
1	cup sliced fresh mushrooms *or* one 4-ounce can sliced mushrooms, drained
1	small clove garlic, minced
1	bay leaf
⅛	teaspoon dried oregano, crushed
2	tomatoes, peeled and cut into wedges *or* one 16-ounce can tomato wedges, drained
¼	cup grated Parmesan cheese

◆   ◆   ◆

Recipes travel! This one—a variation of a classic Mediterranean dish—can be traced from an Indian cook in Kuwait to Colombia, South America, then to Florida. World-class delicious!

June Richcreek
Paths of Sunshine
Florida Federation of Garden Clubs
Winter Park
FLORIDA

1 Preheat oven to 350°. In a large skillet, cook the onion, green pepper and celery in *2 tablespoons* of the margarine or butter until tender.

2 Drain the vegetables, if necessary, and place in a 8x8x2-inch baking dish.

3 Add the remaining margarine or butter to the skillet. Cook and stir the zucchini, eggplant, mushrooms, garlic, bay leaf and oregano over medium heat until the vegetables are tender.

4 Drain the vegetables, if necessary. Remove the bay leaf.

5 Layer the eggplant mixture on top of the onion mixture in the baking dish. Sprinkle with the tomatoes. Top with the Parmesan cheese.

6 Bake, uncovered, in the 350° oven for 30 to 40 minutes or until the vegetables are very tender.

 TIPS FROM OUR KITCHEN

To bring out the flavors of the vegetables, lightly salt each layer as you add it to the baking dish.

For an extra-special presentation of this garden-fresh vegetable dish, transfer it to a pretty serving dish.

Nutrition Analysis (*Per Serving*): Calories: 136 / Cholesterol: 3 mg / Carbohydrates: 11 g / Protein: 4 g / Sodium: 187 mg / Fat: 9 g (Saturated Fat: 2 g) / Potassium: 471 mg.

VEGETABLE CASSEROLE EXTRAORDINAIRE

A delicious Florida variation of the traditional Mediterranean side dish, this casserole is
a savory assortment of vegetables including eggplant, zucchini, tomatoes,
mushroom, onions and green sweet peppers.

VEGETABLES

PEAS WITH MINT AND ORANGE PEEL

Makes 6 Servings

2	pounds fresh peas (3 cups shelled)
½	cup water
⅛	teaspoon salt
¼	cup butter *or* margarine, cut up
3 to 4	teaspoons finely shredded orange peel
2	tablespoons snipped fresh mint *or* ½ teaspoon dried mint, crushed

Dash salt
Dash pepper

◆　◆　◆

When we spoke with Terry Robinette's daughter, Mary Beth Windsich, she told us about her fond memories of the Robinette's traditional Sunday dinners. Mary Beth said that her mother "always made something nice." Peas with Mint and Orange Peel was one of Terry's special dishes. Mary Beth told us that she believes the recipe came from a relative in Kentucky on her father's side of the family.

Terry Robinette
Madonna Heights Ladies
Auxiliary Favorite Recipe
Collections
Madonna Heights Ladies
Auxiliary
Huntington
NEW YORK

1 Shell the peas and rinse in cold water.

2 In a medium saucepan, bring the water and salt to a boil. Add the peas and return to a boil. Reduce heat. Cover and simmer for 10 to 12 minutes or until the peas are crisp-tender.

3 Drain the cooked peas. Add the butter or margarine, orange peel and mint; toss to coat. Season to taste with the salt and pepper. Serve immediately.

 TIPS FROM OUR KITCHEN

When shopping for fresh peas, look for small, plump, bright green, shiny pods that are filled with medium-size peas. Refrigerate unshelled and unwashed peas in a plastic bag up to 2 days.

To micro-cook fresh peas: Place them in a microwave-safe casserole with 2 table-spoons *water*. Micro-cook, covered, on 100% power (high) for 4 to 6 minutes or until the peas are crisp-tender, stirring once.

If fresh peas aren't available, substitute one 16-ounce package frozen peas and cook according to the package directions.

Spearmint and peppermint are the two most widely used mints. Peppermint has a sharp, pungent flavor, while spearmint has a more delicate flavor.

Instead of trying to chop fresh mint with a knife, place the leaves in a glass measuring cup and snip with scissors.

If you are using dried mint, measure it, then crush it between your fingers to release the aromatic oils.

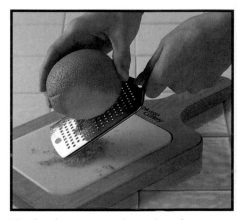

To shred orange peel: Push a clean orange across a fine shredding surface to make very fine strips.

Nutrition Analysis (*Per Serving*): Calories: 131 / Cholesterol: 21 mg / Carbohydrates: 12 g / Protein: 4 g / Sodium: 214 mg / Fat: 8 g (Saturated Fat: 5 g) / Potassium: 141 mg.

More Peas, Please

Garden fresh peas are always a treat. Fresh mint and shredded orange peel give these peas a cool,
citrusy boost in this simply delicious recipe from Huntington, New York.

PICKLED BEETS

Makes 6 Servings
10 to 12 small beets, roots and tops
    removed (2½ pounds
    before trimming)
1½ cups white vinegar
1½ cups water
 ½ cup sugar
 1 teaspoon whole allspice
 2 3-inch sprigs fresh tarragon
    or 1 teaspoon dried
    tarragon, crushed
 ½ teaspoon salt
 6 green onions, cut into
    ½-inch lengths (½ cup)

✦   ✦   ✦

Sharing the Bounty is a lovely
cookbook that features recipes
from St. Andrew's parishoners,
area restaurants, community
residents and people involved with
St. Andrew's Episcopal School.
Most of the recipes included in
this cookbook rely on ingredients
that are abundant in southeastern
Florida. The pages are envlivened
by a local artist's charming illus-
trations and a smattering of
sketches from students.

Avriett Grace
Sharing the Bounty
St. Andrew's Episcopal School
Scholarship Fund
Ft. Pierce
FLORIDA

1 Wash the beets under cold, running water. In a large saucepan, cook the beets, covered, in boiling salted water for 40 to 50 minutes or until just tender. Drain.

2 When the beets are cool enough to handle, slip the skins off. Discard the skins. Cut the beets into quarters or wedges and set aside.

3 Wash the saucepan in which you cooked the beets. In it, stir together the vinegar, water, sugar, allspice, the dried tarragon (if using) and salt. Bring to a boil, then reduce the heat and simmer, uncovered, for 10 minutes.

4 Carefully add the cooked beets to the simmering liquid. Return to a boil, then reduce the heat. Cover and simmer for 10 minutes.

5 Transfer the beets and liquid to a large nonmetal bowl. Add the onions and fresh tarragon (if using). Cool.

6 Cover and refrigerate overnight or up to 1 month.

TIPS FROM OUR KITCHEN

Fresh beets are most plentiful March through July, but are available year-round. Look for well-shaped, firm, small to medium beets with good color and smooth skins. Very large beets may be tough, pithy and less sweet. To store, trim the greens leaving one to two inches of stem. Do not cut the long, thin root. Refrigerate unwashed beets in an open plastic bag or a plastic bag

with holes in it, up to one week. When ready to cook, wash well and cut off all but 1 inch of stems and roots.

After cooking, the beet skins will slip off easily. To protect your hands from the red beet coloring when slipping off the skins, wear plastic gloves or put your hands inside plastic bags.

Allspice is a pungent, aromatic berry that has a flavor similar to cloves with hints of cinnamon and nutmeg. It is commonly found in pickling spice mixtures. Do not substitute ground allspice in this recipe as it will make the pickling liquid cloudy.

For a fancier shaped pickled beet, use a ridged cutter when cutting the beets into wedges or quarters.

Nutrition Analysis *(Per Serving)*: Calories: 49 / Cholesterol: 0 mg / Carbohydrates: 12 g / Protein: 1 g / Sodium: 141 mg / Fat: 0 g (Saturated Fat: 0 g) / Potassium: 354 mg.

LIVELY SIDE DISH

Allspice and tarragon join their aromatic forces with vinegar to transform beets into a tangy, colorful side dish. Pickled Beets, from Avriett Grace of Ft. Pierce, Florida, will certainly perk up any ho-hum meal.

VEGETABLES

427

FRESH ASPARAGUS WITH ORANGE HOLLANDAISE SAUCE

Makes 4 Servings

- 1 pound fresh asparagus spears
- 2 egg yolks
- 1 teaspoon grated orange peel
- 2 tablespoons orange juice
- Dash salt
- Dash pepper
- ¼ cup butter *or* margarine, cut into tablespoons
- ¼ cup dairy sour cream
- Finely shredded orange peel (optional)

◆　◆　◆

It's hard to improve the taste of perfectly prepared fresh asparagus, but Terri Brusco of Longview, Washington, gives us an inspired way to enjoy the tasty green spears. This orange-flavored variation of a traditional Hollandaise sauce served over asparagus is an unexpected treat for Terri's lucky dinner party guests.

Terri Brusco
Cabaret Cuisine
Longview Junior Service League
Longview
WASHINGTON

1 Snap off and discard woody bases from the fresh asparagus. If desired, scrape off scales. Cook, covered, in a small amount of boiling water for 8 to 10 minutes or until crisp-tender. Drain and set aside, keeping hot.

2 In a small saucepan using a wire whisk, combine the egg yolks, grated orange peel, orange juice, salt and pepper.

3 Over low heat, continue whisking, adding the butter, *one tablespoon* at a time, until the butter is melted and the sauce is thickened (about 7 minutes).

4 Remove the saucepan from the heat and stir in the sour cream. Return the sauce to the stovetop and heat through but *do not* boil.

5 Transfer the hot asparagus to a warm serving dish. Pour the sauce over the asparagus. Garnish with the finely shredded orange peel, if desired.

 TIPS FROM OUR KITCHEN

If you know you're going to be short on time, make this sauce ahead and store it, covered, in the refrigerator. Then, before serving, reheat the sauce over low heat just until warm.

Try this sauce over your favorite fish fillets or fish steaks too.

Nutrition Analysis *(Per Serving)*: Calories: 185 / Cholesterol: 144 mg / Carbohydrates: 5 g Protein: 4 g / Sodium: 164 mg / Fat: 17 g (Saturated Fat: 10 g) / Potassium: 292 mg.

SENSATIONAL CITRUS SAUCE

Here's a fabulous first course for your next candlelight dinner. The elegant, orange-flavored sauce is
simple to prepare and is the perfect counterpoint to crisp, steamed asparagus spears.

RED CABBAGE WITH APPLES

Makes 4 to 6 Servings

1 small head red cabbage, coarsely shredded (1¼ pounds)
¼ cup red wine vinegar
1 tablespoon brown sugar
½ teaspoon salt
½ cup finely chopped onion
1 tablespoon bacon drippings
⅛ teaspoon ground cloves
1 small bay leaf
¼ cup water
1 large cooking apple, peeled, cored and thinly sliced
2 tablespoons apple jelly
1 tablespoon lemon juice

◆　◆　◆

Sunday supper for Margaret Lauter's family always included savory pork chops and mother's Red Cabbage with Apples. "Rotkhol mit Apfeln" is a very traditional German dish and this particular version is exceptional. The deep crimson color contrasts nicely with many foods including roast turkey or goose, and the taste is sure to make it one of your family's favorite side dishes.

Margaret Lauter
Heart of the Rockies
Salida
COLORADO

1 In a large bowl, sprinkle the red cabbage with the red wine vinegar, brown sugar and salt. Toss the cabbage to coat it evenly. Set aside the red cabbage mixture.

2 In a large, deep skillet, cook the onion in the bacon drippings for 5 minutes or until the onion is tender, stirring frequently. Stir in the red cabbage mixture, cloves and bay leaf. Carefully pour in the water. Bring the mixture to a boil. Reduce the heat; cover the skillet and simmer for 30 minutes.

3 Add the apple slices, apple jelly and lemon juice to the skillet. Simmer, covered, for 5 minutes more or until the apple slices are tender. Remove the bay leaf. Transfer to a warm serving bowl.

TIPS FROM OUR KITCHEN

To shred cabbage, hold a quarter-head firmly against the cutting board. Using a sharp knife, slice the cabbage to make long, coarse shreds. Or, use the shredding disk of your food processor.

If you don't have apple jelly on hand, substitute 1 to 2 tablespoons of brown sugar, depending on how sweet you like your cabbage.

Red Cabbage looks lovely when served in a white bowl.

Nutrition Analysis (*Per Serving*): Calories: 126 / Cholesterol: 3 mg / Carbohydrates: 25 g / Protein: 2 g / Sodium: 281 mg / Fat: 4 g / (Saturated Fat: 1 g) / Potassium: 293 mg.

SWEET-SOUR SURPRISE

Served for generations in Germany, this beautiful, slightly crisp side dish will quickly become a
favorite with your family. The combination of sweet and sour flavors makes this a perfect
accompaniment to all cuts of pork, from loin roasts to broiled chops.

GOLDEN ZUCCHINI PANCAKES

Makes 12 Pancakes

3	medium zucchini, shredded (4 cups)
½	teaspoon salt
½	cup finely chopped onion
1	tablespoon butter *or* margarine
2	eggs, slightly beaten
¼	cup all-purpose flour
⅛	teaspoon pepper

Cooking oil

◆   ◆   ◆

When Nancy Griffin's organic gardener friends share their harvest, Golden Zucchini Pancakes are likely to appear on —and disappear from—Nancy's dining table. She says that her family likes them best served with tomato sauce as a side dish.

Nancy Griffin
Happiness is Anything
Homemade
Worcester Area Association for
Retarded Citizens, Inc.
Worcester
MASSACHUSETTS

1 Place the zucchini in a colander. Sprinkle with salt and set aside for 30 minutes.

2 Squeeze as much of the liquid as possible from the zucchini with your hands.

3 In a medium skillet, cook the onions in the butter or margarine over medium heat about 3 minutes or until tender, stirring occasionally.

4 Transfer the zucchini and onions to a large bowl. Stir in the eggs, flour and pepper.

5 Pour the cooking oil into a clean medium skillet to a depth of ⅛ inch. Heat over medium-high heat.

6 Drop slightly rounded tablespoons of the batter into the hot oil and flatten to 3-inch diameters with the back of a spoon.

7 Cook the pancakes over medium-high heat until golden, turning once (2 to 3 minutes on each side). Remove the pancakes with a slotted spatula and drain on paper towels. Add more oil to the skillet, if needed, and repeat until all of the batter is used.

 TIPS FROM OUR KITCHEN

When yellow summer squash is plentiful, substitute it for the zucchini.

Dress up these pancakes by adding ¼ cup shredded carrot to the batter.

If you like, drizzle the pancakes with your favorite cheese sauce.

Nutrition Analysis *(Per Pancake)*: Calories: 80 / Cholesterol: 36 mg / Carbohydrates: 4 g / Protein: 2 g / Sodium: 67 mg / Fat: 6 g (Saturated Fat: 1 g) / Potassium: 96 mg.

PANCAKE PANACHE

Pancakes aren't just for breakfast anymore! These savory vegetable flapjacks from Nancy Griffin of Worcester, Massachusetts, are a delightful summer side dish.

FRIED GREEN TOMATOES

Makes 6 Servings

1 egg, beaten
½ cup milk
½ cup cornmeal
¼ cup all-purpose flour
½ teaspoon salt
½ teaspoon pepper
4 medium green tomatoes, cut into ⅜-inch-thick slices
4 to 6 tablespoons cooking oil

◆ ◆ ◆

Gladys Norman has always enjoyed cooking and has been collecting recipes for years. She tells us that her family members—all tomato lovers—adore this southern recipe for Fried Green Tomatoes. We and the people putting together the Stinchcomb Sampler *are lucky—Gladys hasn't even given this recipe to anyone in her family!*

Gladys Norman
Stinchcomb's Sampler
Stinchcomb United Methodist Women
Stinchcomb United Methodist Church
Dewy Rose
GEORGIA

1 Combine the egg and milk in a shallow dish; set aside.

2 Stir together the cornmeal, flour, salt and pepper in another shallow dish. Dip the tomatoes into the egg-milk mixture, then into the cornmeal-flour mixture.

3 In a large skillet, heat *2 tablespoons* of the cooking oil over medium heat. Arrange a single layer of tomato slices in the skillet and cook about 2 minutes per side or until the tomato slices are golden brown on both sides.

4 Repeat with the remaining tomato slices, adding additional cooking oil to the skillet as needed.

 TIPS FROM OUR KITCHEN

Green tomatoes are immature, unripe tomatoes. You can find them at a farmer's market or, if you have a garden, pick the tomatoes while they are still green for this recipe. Choose tomatoes that are free of bruises and blemishes. Wash thoroughly under cool, running water to remove all traces of soil, fertilizers and pesticides.

This coating and cooking method also works well with sliced zucchini and yellow summer squash.

For added flavor, you can substitute garlic salt for the salt in this recipe. For flavor variety, you might add a pinch or two of dried herbs such as basil, oregano or thyme to the cornmeal-flour mixture.

Nutrition Analysis (*Per Serving*): Calories: 180 / Cholesterol: 37 mg / Carbohydrates: 18 Protein: 4 g / Sodium: 206 mg / Fat: 11g (Saturated Fat: 2 g) / Potassium: 249 mg.

UNRIPE, YET UNFORGETTABLE

Cornmeal adds a crispy crunch to this tasty, fried vegetable dish. Gladys Norman of Dewy Rose,
Georgia, gives us a perfect way to use unripe tomatoes from our gardens as the end of
the growing season approaches.

VEGETABLES

EGGPLANT CASSEROLE

Makes 6 to 7 Servings

1 pound ground beef
1 cup chopped onion
½ cup tomato paste
½ cup water
2 tablespoons margarine *or* butter
2 tablespoons snipped parsley
½ teaspoon salt
⅛ teaspoon pepper
⅓ cup fine dry bread crumbs
2 medium eggplants (about 1 pound each)
⅓ cup all-purpose flour
¼ cup olive oil
2 eggs, well beaten
¼ cup grated Parmesan cheese

✦ ✦ ✦

When Maria Dionyssopoulas's daughter gets married, Maria will be passing along her collection of recipes, including this one for Moussaka, which she received from her in-laws in Greece. Maria tells us that she sometimes leaves out the ground beef for a meatless version of this family-favorite dish.

Maria Dionyssopoulas
Grecian Delights
The Ladies of the Philoptochos of the Virgin Mary Greek Orthodox Church Plymouth MICHIGAN

1 Preheat the oven to 350°. Grease a 2-quart rectangular baking dish. Set aside.

2 In a large skillet, cook the beef and onion until browned. Drain the fat from the meat mixture. Add the tomato paste, water, margarine or butter, parsley, salt and pepper. Bring the mixture to a boil; reduce the heat and simmer, uncovered, for 1 minute. Stir in *2 tablespoons* of the bread crumbs.

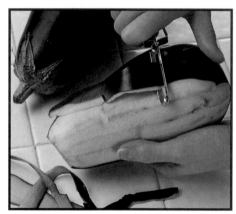

3 Using a vegetable peeler, peel the eggplants. Slice them crosswise into ¼-inch-thick slices. Coat each slice lightly with the flour. In a large skillet, cook the eggplant slices in the olive oil until golden brown on both sides. Add more oil to the skillet as necessary.

4 Sprinkle the prepared baking dish with *2 tablespoons* of the bread crumbs. Arrange *half* of the eggplant slices in the baking dish. Top with half of the meat sauce. Repeat with the remaining eggplant and meat sauce. Pour the beaten eggs over the top. Combine the Parmesan cheese and the remaining bread crumbs and sprinkle the mixture over the top of the casserole. Bake in the 350° oven for 25 to 30 minutes or until heated through.

TIPS FROM OUR KITCHEN

Western eggplant is the most common variety in the United States. It is large and usually pear-shaped—although it can be round—with a smooth, glossy, purple or white skin. White eggplant is smaller and firmer with a tougher, thicker skin and slightly sweeter flesh. Japanese eggplant is long, slender and purple with a mild flavor.

When shopping, choose eggplants that are plump, glossy and heavy for their size. Caps should be fresh-looking, tight and mold-free. Store eggplants in the refrigerator up to two days.

Nutrition Analysis (*Per Serving*): Calories: 398 / Cholesterol: 122 mg / Carbohydrates: 26 Protein: 21 g / Sodium: 411 mg / Fat: 24 g (Saturated Fat: 6 g) / Potassium: 804 mg.

MOUSSAKA VARIATION

Here is a flavorful casserole that features eggplant slices simmered in a lightly seasoned tomato sauce
and topped with eggs and cheese. A variation on the traditional Greek Moussaka,
this recipe comes to us from Plymouth, Michigan.

CHEDDAR-ALMOND-BROCCOLI CASSEROLE

Makes 6 Servings

1½ pounds broccoli *or* two
    10-ounce packages frozen
    broccoli spears
½   teaspoon salt
¼   cup margarine *or* butter
¼   cup all-purpose flour
1   cup milk
¾   cup water
1   teaspoon instant chicken *or*
    beef bouillon granules
1   tablespoon lemon juice
1 to 2 tablespoons dry sherry
⅛   teaspoon pepper
½   cup shredded cheddar
    cheese (2 ounces)
¼   cup toasted slivered
    almonds

◆   ◆   ◆

*Lynne Literski says that she loves
to cook and many of her friends
have even suggested she put
together her own cookbook. She,
like many of us, just needs to find
the time! In the meantime, Lynne
shared one of her favorite recipes
with the folks putting together*
Grazing Across Wisconsin, *and
they, in turn, shared it with us.*

Lynne Literski
Grazing Across Wisconsin
Telephone Pioneers of America
Wisconsin Chapter No. 4
Appleton
WISCONSIN

1 Preheat the oven to 375°

2 If using fresh broccoli, wash and cut into spears.

3 In a large saucepan, bring 1 inch of *water* to a boil. Add the broccoli and the salt. Cook, covered, for 8 to 12 minutes or until crisp-tender. (Or, cook the frozen broccoli according to the package directions.) Drain the broccoli and transfer to a 2-quart rectangular or oval baking dish.

4 Meanwhile, in a medium saucepan over medium heat, melt the margarine or butter. Blend in the flour, then add the milk, water and bouillon granules. Cook and stir until thickened and bubbly. Add the lemon juice, sherry and pepper.

5 Pour the sauce over the broccoli in the baking dish. Sprinkle with the cheddar cheese and almonds. Bake, uncovered, in the 375° oven for 15 to 20 minutes or until bubbly.

TIPS FROM OUR KITCHEN

Choose broccoli that has firm stalks and tightly packed heads. If the stalks seem tough, use a sharp knife to cut the tough outer portion away. Store fresh broccoli in a plastic bag in the refrigerator and use within four days for best flavor.

For a variation of this recipe, experiment with other cheeses, such as Swiss, Monterey Jack, Gouda, Muenster or provolone. Or, sprinkle with crushed cracker crumbs or buttered bread crumbs instead of cheese and almonds.

Nutrition Analysis *(Per Serving)*: Calories: 208 / Cholesterol: 13 mg/ Carbohydrates: 13 g /
Protein: 9 g / Sodium: 521 mg / Fat: 15 g (Saturated Fat: 4 g) / Potassium: 455 mg.

CHEDDAR MAKES IT BETTER

In this casserole from Appleton, Wisconsin, broccoli is lusciously surrounded by a creamy white sauce
and topped with cheddar cheese and almonds.

SPAGHETTI SQUASH TOMATO TOSS

Makes 8 Servings

1   3½-pound spaghetti squash
1   medium onion, coarsely chopped
1   tablespoon olive oil
5   medium tomatoes, peeled, seeded and coarsely chopped
½   cup snipped fresh basil
¼   cup snipped parsley
2   cloves garlic minced
¾   teaspoon salt
¼   teaspoon pepper
3   medium zucchini, sliced in ¼-inch pieces
    Parmesan cheese *or* parsley sprigs

◆   ◆   ◆

According to Carol Shepard, one of the editors of Heavenly Hosts, *Spaghetti Squash Tomato Toss is "a great alternative to spaghetti" and appeals to everyone, even those who aren't "true vegetable lovers." Carol adapted this recipe to suit her family's liking— especially her children's—and says the dish is an excellent way to use up surplus zucchini and tomatoes.*

Heavenly Hosts Committee
Heavenly Hosts
Presbyterian Women of The Bryn Mawr Presbyterian Church
Bryn Mawr
PENNSYLVANIA

1 Preheat the oven to 350°.

2 Using the tip of a sharp knife or the tines of a fork, pierce the squash in several places. Place in a 13x9x2-inch baking pan. Bake in the 350° oven for 1 hour and 15 minutes.

3 Meanwhile, in a large skillet, cook the onion in the olive oil until tender. Add the tomatoes, basil, parsley, garlic, salt and pepper. Bring to a boil. Add the zucchini and cook, covered, for 3 minutes. Uncover and cook for 8 to 10 minutes more or until the zucchini is crisp-tender. Keep warm.

4 Carefully slice the squash in half. Remove the seeds and discard. Use a fork to shred the squash into long strands into a bowl. Pour the sauce over the spaghetti squash; toss. Garnish with Parmesan cheese or parsley sprigs. Serve immediately.

TIPS FROM OUR KITCHEN

Spaghetti squash is a bright yellow, football-shaped vegetable with pale yellow, stringy flesh that resembles spaghetti when cooked. It has a mildly sweet flavor.

It's easier to "shred" the spaghetti squash if you use a hot pad to hold the halved squash at an angle. Use a fork to rake the stringy pulp from the shell into the bowl.

Store olive oil at room temperature up to 6 months, or in the refrigerator up to 1 year. When olive oil is chilled, it gets too thick to pour, so let it stand at room temperature for a few minutes or run warm water over the bottle before using.

Nutrition Analysis (*Per Serving*): Calories: 95 / Cholesterol: 1 mg / Carbohydrates: 16 g / Protein: 3 g / Sodium: 262 mg / Fat: 3 g (Saturated Fat: 1 g) / Potassium: 463 mg.

ALL-VEGETABLE EXCELLENCE

This wonderful recipe for spaghetti squash tossed with an herb-flavored tomato and zucchini sauce is from Bryn Mawr, Pennsylvania. Children especially love this "magic" vegetable.

CREAMED ONIONS

Makes 6 Servings

18	small white onions
3	tablespoons butter *or* margarine
3	tablespoons all-purpose flour
1½	cups milk
¼	teaspoon salt
¼	teaspoon Worcestershire sauce
2	tablespoons snipped parsley
¼	teaspoon paprika

◆   ◆   ◆

Kay Beasly tells us that a version of this recipe was often served at state dinners given for visiting ambassadors and dignitaries at Mount Vernon. She and her husband like to serve this dish at home with roast beef, turkey or a standing rib roast. In fact, when we spoke with Kay, she told us that she was planning to serve Creamed Onions at the upcoming Thanksgiving Dinner.

Kay Beasley
Renaissance Cuisine
The Fontbonne Auxiliary of
St. John Hospital
Detroit
MICHIGAN

1 In a medium saucepan, cook the onions in their skins in boiling water, about 20 minutes or until tender; drain. Cool slightly. Peel the onions by popping them out of their skins.

2 In a saucepan, melt the butter or margarine. Add the flour to the butter and stir with a wire whisk until blended.

3 Meanwhile, in another saucepan, bring the milk to boiling and add the salt and Worcestershire sauce. Add the milk mixture all at once to the butter-flour mixture, stirring vigorously with the whisk until the sauce is smooth and thickened.

4 Add the onions to the sauce and heat through. Transfer the onions to a warm serving dish. Sprinkle with the parsley and paprika.

TIPS FROM OUR KITCHEN

The flavorful cream sauce in this recipe is delicious served over cooked peas or broccoli. Use 2 cups of any type of cooked vegetables and you'll have a perfect amount of sauce.

Save on pan washing by cooking the onions first, then use the same pan to make the cream sauce.

To simplify the making of the sauce, you can add the cold milk, salt and Worcestershire sauce directly to the flour-butter mixture. Then, cook and stir the mixture over medium heat until the sauce is thickened and bubbly.

Nutrition Analysis *(Per Serving)*: Calories: 108 / Cholesterol: 20 mg / Carbohydrates: 9 g / Protein: 3 g / Sodium: 181 mg / Fat: 7 g (Saturated Fat: 4 g) / Potassium: 164 mg.

VERY VERSATILE

A delicate side dish, Creamed Onions are especially good with roasted meats and are a favorite at
holiday meals. This recipe—with its work-saving tips—is so easy, you shouldn't
wait for the next holiday to try it.

VEGETABLES

ONIONS AU GRATIN

Makes 6 Servings
  2   tablespoons butter *or* margarine
  5   medium onions, thinly sliced and separated into rings (5 cups)
  2   cups shredded cheddar cheese (8 ounces)
  ⅓   cup packaged biscuit mix
  ⅛   teaspoon pepper
  ½   cup shredded cheddar cheese (2 ounces) (optional)

When recipes for the Junior League of Rockford's cookbook were requested from league members and popular local restaurants, between 3,000 and 5,000 recipes were submitted. Each member taste-tested ten recipes, and then completed an evaluation for each one. The most popular recipes were then tested a second time. The result was a wonderful collection of super recipes such as this one for Onions au Gratin.

Brunch Basket
The Junior League of Rockford
Rockford
ILLINOIS

1 Preheat the oven to 350°. Grease a 1½-quart casserole dish; set aside.

2 In a large saucepan, melt the butter or margarine. Add the onions and cook, covered, over medium-low heat for 10 to 15 minutes or until tender, stirring occasionally. Remove from heat.

3 Stir the 2 cups cheddar cheese, the biscuit mix and pepper into the onion mixture. Transfer the mixture to the prepared casserole dish. Sprinkle with the ½ cup cheddar cheese, if desired. Bake the casserole, uncovered, in the 350° oven for 30 minutes. Serve immediately.

TIPS FROM OUR KITCHEN

The dry bulb onions that are available in most stores between April and August are generally milder, sweeter and less pungent than the so-called fall/winter onions. Dry bulb onions have thin, light outer skins and a high water and sugar content. They are fragile and bruise easily; they can be stored in the refrigerator for several weeks. The fall/winter, or storage, onions have a thicker, darker outer skin, a lower water content and a more pungent flavor. When they are stored in a cool, dry, well-ventilated spot, they will keep for several months.

If you want to cut the fat in this recipe, use only half as much butter or margarine to cook the onions. Add about ¼ cup *water* instead.

Use a fork or onion-holder to steady the onion when cutting it into slices. Transfer the slices to a large bowl or pan and use your fingers or a fork to separate them into rings. Or, if you don't mind half slices, use your food processor to slice the onions.

Nutrition Analysis (*Per Serving*): Calories: 255 / Cholesterol: 50 mg / Carbohydrates: 14 g / Protein: 11 g / Sodium: 353 mg / Fat: 17 g (Saturated Fat: 10 g) / Potassium: 199 mg.

A NATURAL COMPANION

Cheesy, browned and crisp, *au gratin* dishes are always popular, and this one—with biscuit mix substituting for the traditional bread crumbs—is no exception. Use red, yellow, white or Vidalia onions to make this natural companion for grilled or broiled burgers, steaks and chops.

VAGABOND PIES

Makes 8 Servings
- 4 carrots, thinly sliced (2 cups)
- 3 leeks, thinly sliced (1 cup)
- 1 cup finely chopped rutabaga
- 8 tiny new potatoes, chopped, *or* 2 cups chopped peeled potatoes
- ½ cup shredded fontinella *or* fontina cheese (2 ounces)
- ½ cup shredded mozzarella cheese (2 ounces)
- ½ cup snipped fresh parsley
- 2 teaspoons snipped fresh oregano
- 2 teaspoons snipped fresh marjoram
- 2 teaspoons snipped fresh thyme
- ¼ teaspoon salt
- ⅛ teaspoon pepper
- ¼ cup butter *or* margarine, melted
- ¼ cup olive oil
- 2 cloves garlic, minced
- 12 sheets phyllo dough (about 6 ounces)
- ¼ cup fine dry bread crumbs

♦   ♦   ♦

Dee Gaynor wanted to find a special dish to take to a party. While at the beauty salon, she and her hairdresser, Kathleen Samuels, came up with Vagabond Pies.

Dee Gaynor
Stanford University Medical Center Auxiliary Cookbook
Stanford University Medical Center Auxiliary
Stanford
CALIFORNIA

1 Place the carrots, leeks, rutabaga and potatoes in a steamer basket just above, but not touching, *boiling water.* Cover the pan and steam the vegetables for 10 to 12 minutes or just until the vegetables are tender; drain. Transfer the vegetables to a large bowl. Add the fontinella or fontina cheese, mozzarella cheese, parsley, oregano, marjoram, thyme, salt and pepper. Set aside.

2 Preheat the oven to 350°. In a small bowl, stir together the melted butter or margarine, olive oil and garlic.

3 Cut the phyllo dough sheets into 13½- to 14-inch squares; discard any unused portions of phyllo dough. Stack 6 sheets of phyllo, brushing *each* sheet with the butter or margarine mixture and sprinkling every other sheet lightly with the bread crumbs.

4 Cut *each* stack into *4* squares. Place *one-eighth* of the vegetable mixture (about ¾ cup) in the center of *each* square. Fold the sides of the dough toward the center to form a pouch. Pinch well to seal. Place the packets in a shallow baking pan. Brush the outsides with additional butter or margarine mixture. Repeat with the remaining phyllo sheets, butter or margarine mixture and vegetable mixture.

5 Bake in the 350° oven for 30 to 35 minutes or until the pouches are lightly browned. Serve immediately.

Nutrition Analysis (*Per Serving*): Calories: 290 / Cholesterol: 26 mg / Carbohydrates: 31 g / Protein: 8 g / Sodium: 290 mg / Fat: 16 g (Saturated Fat: 5 g) / Potassium: 360 mg.

BUNDLES OF FLAVOR

These individual "pies" are made of phyllo dough and are filled with a delectable assortment of
vegetables. Two kinds of cheese and a few fresh herbs flavor the bundles.

BRANDIED CANDIED YAMS

Makes 8 Servings

1 40-ounce can small whole yams *or* sweet potatoes, drained, *or* 5 to 6 (about 2½ pounds) fresh yams *or* sweet potatoes, cooked
½ cup packed brown sugar
¼ cup butter *or* margarine, melted
3 tablespoons brandy
2 tablespoons frozen orange juice concentrate
2 tablespoons water
1 teaspoon vanilla
½ teaspoon salt
2 eggs, slightly beaten

Topping:
½ cup packed brown sugar
2 tablespoons all-purpose flour
¼ teaspoon ground cardamom *or* ground cinnamon
2 tablespoons cold butter *or* margarine
¼ cup chopped pecans

♦   ♦   ♦

Ellen Letourneau, cookbook chairperson for Brunch Basket*, tells us that this recipe for Brandied Candied Yams is so delicious that even her brother—who strongly dislikes vegetables—loves it. Ellen dared him to taste the dish and now he requests it every Thanksgiving.*

Brunch Basket
The Junior League of Rockford
Rockford
ILLINOIS

1 Preheat the oven to 350°.

2 In a large mixing bowl, beat the yams or sweet potatoes with an electric mixer on medium speed about 4 minutes or until they are well mashed.

3 Add the ½ cup brown sugar, the melted butter or margarine, brandy, orange juice concentrate, water, vanilla and salt. Beat until combined. Add the slightly beaten eggs and beat until smooth.

4 Transfer the mixture to a 2-quart rectangular baking dish.

5 To make the topping: In a small bowl, combine the ½ cup brown sugar, flour and cardamom or cinnamon.

Using a pastry blender, cut in the cold butter or margarine until the mixture resembles coarse crumbs. Stir in the pecans.

6 Sprinkle the topping over the yam or sweet potato mixture. Bake in the 350° oven for 35 to 40 minutes or until the yams or sweet potatoes are heated through and the topping is crisp.

 TIPS FROM OUR KITCHEN

To cook fresh yams or sweet potatoes: Wash and peel 5 or 6 yams or sweet potatoes (about 2½ pounds). Cut off the woody portions and ends and discard. Then cut the yams or sweet potatoes into quarters or cubes. Cook, covered, in enough boiling, salted water to cover for 25 to 35 minutes or until tender.

The casserole can be assembled, covered and refrigerated up to 48 hours before baking. When taken directly from the refrigerator, bake in a 350° oven for 45 to 50 minutes or until the yams or sweet potatoes are heated through.

If desired, divide the yam mixture or sweet potato mixture among eight individual casserole dishes. Sprinkle on the topping and bake in a 350° oven for 20 to 25 minutes or until heated through.

Nutrition Analysis (*Per Serving*): Calories: 378 / Cholesterol: 76 mg / Carbohydrates: 61 g Protein: 5 g / Sodium: 321 mg / Fat: 12 g (Saturated Fat: 6 g) / Potassium: 601 mg.

FREQUENT FARE

Do you think of yams as a dish reserved for the holidays? This casserole just might change your mind. If the spice-flavored crumb and pecan topping doesn't convince you to serve Brandied Candied Yams frequently, then the smooth, richly flavored mashed yams will.

SOUFFLÉ POTATOES

Makes 8 Servings

3 cups mashed potatoes (5 or 6 potatoes)
1 cup cream-style cottage cheese
½ cup dairy sour cream
3 egg yolks, well beaten
3 tablespoons chopped onion
3 tablespoons chopped pimiento (optional)
2 tablespoons butter *or* margarine, melted
1 clove garlic, minced
½ teaspoon salt
Dash pepper
3 egg whites, stiffly beaten
1 tablespoon butter *or* margarine

◆   ◆   ◆

Phyllis Hallene tasted her sister-in-law's recipe for Soufflé Potatoes about twenty years ago and immediately requested the recipe. Phyllis suggests if you're a garlic lover, like she is, that you add a little extra to the dish. Although Soufflé Potatoes deflate slightly if not served immediately, Phyllis assures us that they'll still be absolutely delicious.

Phyllis Hallene
Return Engagement
The Junior Board of the Quad City Symphony Orchestra Association
Davenport
IOWA

1 Preheat the oven to 350°. Grease a 2-quart casserole; set aside.

2 In a large mixing bowl, stir together the mashed potatoes, cottage cheese, sour cream, egg yolks, onion, pimiento (if using), the 2 tablespoons melted butter or margarine, garlic, salt and pepper.

3 Beat with an electric mixer on medium speed until the mixture is light and fluffy, scraping the sides of the bowl. Gently fold in the beaten egg whites.

4 Carefully spoon the mixture into the prepared casserole. Dot with the 1 tablespoon butter or margarine.

5 Bake in the 350° oven about 1 hour or until the casserole is puffed and the top is golden. Serve immediately.

TIPS FROM OUR KITCHEN

For 3 cups mashed potatoes, peel and cut up 2 pounds potatoes. Keep the peeled and cut pieces immersed in cold water to prevent them from darkening. Cook, covered, in a small amount of boiling water for 20 to 25 minutes or until the potato pieces are tender, adding more water if necessary. Mash with a potato masher, slotted spoon or electric mixer.

If you want this to be a make-ahead dish, prepare the potatoes as directed up until the point of baking. Then, refrigerate the prepared potato mixture, covered, up to 4 hours. Uncover and bake about 1 hour or until the potatoes are puffed and the top is golden.

For a tangier flavor, use flavored sour cream dip such as garlic, chive or French onion in place of the sour cream in the recipe.

Nutrition Analysis (*Per Serving*): Calories: 224 / Cholesterol: 102 mg / Carbohydrates: 25 g / Protein: 8 g / Sodium: 331 mg / Fat: 11 g (Saturated Fat: 6 g) / Potassium: 478 mg.

FLUFFY SPUDS

While not a true soufflé, this dish is fluffy, light and full of flavor. Better still, it can be prepared ahead of time and baked just before serving.

Chapter Index

Nutrition Analysis

Keep track of your daily nutrition needs by using the information we provide at the end of each recipe. We've analyzed the nutrition content of each recipe serving for you. When a recipe gives an ingredient substitution, we used the first choice in the analysis. If it makes a range of servings (such as 4 to 6), we used the smallest number. Ingredients listed as optional weren't included in the calculations.

Recipe Index

O-P

Jul Grot, 141
Traditional Bread
Pudding, 139
Pumpkin Cake, 103

R-S

Raisin-Brown Sugar
Icing, 103
Raisins/currants
Carrot Walnut Cake, 97
Challah, 55
Chocolate-Almond
Bark, 147
Country Captain, 295
Curried Rice, 281
Hot Cross Buns, 65
Morning Glory Muffins, 79
Traditional Bread
Pudding, 139
Raspberries
Asparagus with Raspberry
Vinaigrette, 337
For The Glory Pie, 167
Fruit Pizza, 157
Raspberry Shrub, 43
Raspberry Shrub, 43
Ratatouille, 423
Red Snapper with Orange
Sauce, 171
Red Cabbage with
Apples, 431
Red Snapper Red Snapper
with Orange Sauce, 171
Reuben Casserole a' la
Orcas, 245
Rhubarb Cobbler with Oat
Dumplin's, 143
Rice Piedmont, 233
Rice
Arroz, 275
Baked Fish with Rice-Olive
Stuffing, 181
Chicken, Rice and Broccoli
Casserole, 317

Confetti Rice Salad, 353
Creole Black-eyed Peas and
Rice, 287
Curried Rice, 281
Green Rice Ring, 279
Jul Grot, 141
Mulligatawny Soup, 381
Northwoods Pilaf, 285
Simple Shrimp Creole, 205
Soubise, 277
Stuffed Chicken Breast with
Cherry Sauce, 307
Veal Rolls with Rice
Piedmont, 233
Ricotta Cookies, 113
Round steak
Backstage Special, 217
Beef Stroganoff, 223
Fajitas, 225
Ruby Date Bars, 127
Rum
Hazelnut Torte, 91
Raspberry Shrub, 43
Salad Niçoise, 367
Salads
24-Hour Salad, 346
Ashville Salad, 363
Asparagus with Raspberry
Vinaigrette, 337
Carrot Salad, 361
Cauliflower Salad, 351
Confetti Rice Salad, 353
Four Bean Salad, 357
German Hot Potato
Salad, 343
Layered Salad, 347
Marinated Coleslaw, 355
Orange-Kiwi-Avocado
Salad, 341
Salad Niçoise, 367
Snow Pea Splendor, 359
Special Occasion

Cranberries, 365
Spinach Salad Duo, 339
Tabouli, 349
Three-Lettuce Salad, 335
Salisbury Steak, 215
Salmon Hors D'oeuvres, 35
Salmon
Barbecued Salmon Steaks
with Avocado Butter, 193
Deep Dish Salmon Pie, 189
Salmon Hors D'oeuvres, 35
Salted Peanut Chews, 125
Sandwiches
Cucumber Sandwiches, 87
Monte Cristo
Sandwiches, 85
Super Dagwood
Sandwich, 83
Sausage
Chicago Pizza, 237
Creole Black-eyed Peas and
Rice, 287
Kale Soup, 407
Louisburg Chicken Pie, 319
Mini Calzones, 25
Super Dagwood
Sandwich, 83
Savory Grilled Chicken with
Mustard Sauce, 309
Scalloped Carrots with
Mustard-Cheese Sauce, 417
Scallops
Cioppino, 203
Ginger Scallops, 199
Hemenway's Seafood Pasta
Salad, 271
Seafood - See also individual
names
Manhattan Clam
Chowder, 409
Mildred Kemp's Secret
Ingredient Crab
Soup, 411
Sesame Seed Dressing, 369

RECIPE INDEX

Metric Cooking Hints

By making a few conversions, cooks in Australia, Canada, and the United Kingdom can use the recipes in *Better Homes and Gardens®* America's Best Loved Community Recipes with confidence. The charts on this page provide a guide for converting measurements from the U.S. customary system, which is used throughout this book, to the imperial and metric systems. There also is a conversion table for oven temperatures to accommodate the differences in oven calibrations.

Volume and Weight: Americans traditionally use cup measures for liquid and solid ingredients. The chart (top right) shows the approximate imperial and metric equivalents. If you are accustomed to weighing solid ingredients, here are some helpful approximate equivalents.
- 1 cup butter, caster sugar, or rice = 8 ounces = about 250 grams
- 1 cup flour = 4 ounces = about 125 grams
- 1 cup icing sugar = 5 ounces = about 150 grams

Spoon measures are used for smaller amounts of ingredients. Although the size of the tablespoon varies slightly among countries, for practical purposes and for recipes in this book, a straight substitution is all that's necessary.

Measurements made using cups or spoons should always be level, unless stated otherwise.

Product Differences: Most of the ingredients called for in the recipes in this book are available in English-speaking countries. However, some are known by different names. Here are some common American ingredients and their possible counterparts:
- Sugar is granulated or caster sugar.
- Powdered sugar is icing sugar.
- All-purpose flour is plain household flour or white flour. When self-rising flour is used in place of all-purpose flour in a recipe that calls for leavening, omit the leavening agent (baking soda or baking powder) and salt.
- Light corn syrup is golden syrup.
- Cornstarch is cornflour.
- Baking soda is bicarbonate of soda.
- Vanilla is vanilla essence.

Useful Equivalents

⅛ teaspoon = 0.5 ml	⅔ cup = 5 fluid ounces = 150 ml
¼ teaspoon = 1 ml	¾ cup = 6 fluid ounces = 175 ml
½ teaspoon = 2 ml	1 cup = 8 fluid ounces = 250 ml
1 teaspoon = 5 ml	2 cups = 1 pint
¼ cup = 2 fluid ounces = 50 ml	2 pints = 1 litre
⅓ cup = 3 fluid ounces = 75 ml	½ inch = 1 centimetre
½ cup = 4 fluid ounces = 125 ml	1 inch = 2 centimetres

Baking Pan Sizes

American	Metric
8x1½-inch round baking pan	20x4-centimetre sandwich or cake tin
9x1½-inch round baking pan	23x3.5-centimetre sandwich or cake
11x7x1½-inch baking pan	28x18x4-centimetre baking pan
13x9x2-inch baking pan	32.5x23x5-centimetre baking pan
2-quart rectangular baking dish	30x19x5-centimetre baking pan
15x10x2-inch baking pan	38x25.5x2.5-centimetre baking pan (Swiss roll tin)
9-inch pie plate	22x4- or 23x4-centimetre pie plate
7- or 8-inch springform pan	18- or 20-centimetre springform or loose-bottom cake tin
9x5x3-inch loaf pan	23x13x6-centimetre or 2-pound narrow loaf pan or paté tin
1½-quart casserole	1.5-litre casserole
2-quart casserole	2-litre casserole

Oven Temperature Equivalents

Fahrenheit Setting	Celsius Setting*	Gas Setting
300°F	150°C	Gas Mark 2
325°F	160°C	Gas Mark 3
350°F	180°C	Gas Mark 4
375°F	190°C	Gas Mark 5
400°F	200°C	Gas Mark 6
425°F	220°C	Gas Mark 7
450°F	230°C	Gas Mark 8
Broil		Grill

Electric and gas ovens may be calibrated using Celsius. However, increase the Celsius setting 10 to 20 degrees when cooking above 160°C with an electric oven. For convection or forced-air ovens (gas or electric), lower the temperature setting 10°C when cooking at all heat levels.

Appetizers, Beverages & Snacks

*E*ntertaining is easy with these appetizers, beverages, and snacks. Whether you're serving a few friends or a large crowd, preparation is a snap with savory treats like Spinach Quiche Appetizers and refreshing drinks such as Ginger Cranberry Punch. These recipes are simple to fix but sure to please. From the exotic Chinese Baked Pork Rolls and the elegant Salmon Hors D'oeuvres to the easy Cheddar Crisps, all are appropriate for any gathering.

STUFFED CHERRY TOMATO HALVES

Makes 40 to 60 Appetizers
20 to 30 cherry tomatoes
Cream Cheese Filling:
1   8-ounce package cream cheese, softened
¼   cup catsup *or* hot-style catsup
1   teaspoon dried dillweed
Guacamole Filling:
1   large ripe avocado, seeded and peeled
4   teaspoons lemon juice
1   tablespoon finely chopped onion
1   clove garlic, minced
Toppings:
½   of a 4½-ounce can whole tiny shrimp, drained
6   slices bacon, cooked and crumbled

◆   ◆   ◆

The Feingold Association is a support group that conducts research on the effects of certain foods and food additives on behavior and learning and provides information about its findings to members. <u>*Made with Love, Not Additives*</u> *was put together to raise funds for research and education, as well as to present delicious additive-free recipes.*

<u>*Made with Love, Not Additives*</u>
Feingold Association of the U.S.
Alexandria
VIRGINIA

1 Wash and stem the tomatoes. Cut each in half crosswise.

2 Using a melon baller or grapefruit spoon, scoop out the seeds and discard. Lay the tomatoes, cut side down, on paper towels. Let stand for 30 minutes.

3 To prepare the Cream Cheese Filling: In a small bowl stir together the cream cheese, catsup or hot-style catsup and dillweed until blended. Set aside.

4 To prepare the Guacamole Filling: In a small bowl, mash the avocado with a fork. Stir in the lemon juice, onion and garlic.

5 Using 2 spoons, pile about *1 teaspoon* of the desired filling in each

tomato half. Garnish each of the tomato halves stuffed with the Cream Cheese Filling with a shrimp. And, garnish the tomato halves stuffed with the Guacamole Filling with crumbled bacon.

6 Cover and refrigerate up to 4 hours. Drain, if necessary, and serve on chilled plates.

 TIPS FROM OUR KITCHEN

The number of tomatoes you need depends on which filling you want to use. Use about 30 whole tomatoes for the Cream Cheese Filling (makes 60 appetizers) and about 20 whole tomatoes for the Guacamole Filling (makes 40 appetizers).

Look for a very ripe avocado for the Guacamole Filling. To encourage fast ripening of a less-than-ripe avocado, place it in a clean brown paper bag or next to other fruit and check the ripeness in a day or two.

Both fillings can also be served as a dip with chips or as a spread on crackers or thinly sliced bread.

Canned crabmeat can be substituted for the shrimp.

To add extra zip, mix about ½ teaspoon of prepared horseradish into the Cream Cheese Filling, or a dash of hot pepper sauce into the Guacamole Filling.

Nutrition Analysis (*Per Appetizer*): Calories: 40 / Cholesterol: 10 mg / Carbohydrates: 1 g / Protein: 1 g / Sodium: 54 mg / Fat: 3 g (Saturated Fat: 2 g) / Potassium: 76 mg.

CHOICE APPETIZERS

Decisions, decisions! Would you like cherry tomatoes filled with flavored cream cheese and topped with a plump little shrimp? Or, would you rather have them heaped with homemade guacamole and topped with crisp bacon? Each of these recipes is quick and easy to make, so why not make both?

SIX-LAYER PARTY DIP

Makes 16 Servings

- 1 cup dairy sour cream
- 1 cup mayonnaise
- 1 1¼-ounce envelope taco seasoning mix
- 1 large avocado, peeled and seeded
- ¼ cup salsa
- 2 tablespoons lemon juice
- ¼ teaspoon bottled hot pepper sauce
- 1 16-ounce can refried beans
- ½ teaspoon bottled hot pepper sauce
- 1½ cups shredded cheddar cheese (6 ounces)
- 1 to 2 tomatoes, chopped
- 1 4½-ounce can chopped ripe olives, well drained

Tortilla chips

♦ ♦ ♦

Elaine Morris, chairperson for McAlpin's Department Store Christmas Charities, told us about one way that McAlpin's brings joy to people in need at Christmas. On Christmas morning, the store hosts a special breakfast for the area's needy, after which guests are treated to a pre-paid $50 to $100 shopping spree.

Grace R. Costanzo
Seasoned With Love
McAlpin's Crestview Hills
Crestview Hills
KENTUCKY

1 In a small bowl, stir together the sour cream, mayonnaise and taco seasoning mix. Set aside.

2 In another bowl, mash the avocado with a fork. Stir in the salsa, lemon juice and the ¼ teaspoon bottled hot pepper sauce. Set aside.

3 In another bowl, stir together the refried beans and the ½ teaspoon bottled hot pepper sauce.

4 In a 2-quart rectangular glass baking dish, spread the bean mixture. Layer with the avocado mixture and then the sour cream mixture.

5 Sprinkle the cheese over the sour cream mixture. Top with the chopped tomatoes and sprinkle with the olives. Cover and refrigerate overnight. Serve with tortilla chips.

 TIPS FROM OUR KITCHEN

For a dip with a less salty flavor, use only half of the taco seasoning mix.

For lower fat and fewer calories, use reduced-fat sour cream and mayonnaise.

To make your own tortilla chips, first stack corn or flour tortillas, then cut the tortilla stack into 6 wedges.

In a heavy saucepan or deep skillet, heat ½ inch *cooking oil* or *shortening.* Fry the tortilla wedges, a few at a time, until they are crisp and lightly browned (about 1 minute for corn tortillas or about 45 seconds for flour tortillas). Drain well on paper towels.

Nutrition Analysis (*Per Serving*): Calories: 388 / Cholesterol: 26 mg / Carbohydrates: 28 g / Protein: 8 g / Sodium: 744 mg / Fat: 29 g (Saturated Fat: 8 g) / Potassium: 324 mg.

LAYERS OF FLAVOR

Grace Costanzo of Crestview Hills, Kentucky, brings us a terrific make-ahead layered dip with a
south-of-the-border flavor. Guests tend to congregate around this dip, so you might want
to prepare two batches for your next gathering.

VEGETABLE MUSHROOM CAPS

Makes 8 Servings

- 24 large fresh mushrooms (about 1½ to 2 inches in diameter)
- 2 tablespoons butter *or* margarine
- ½ cup finely chopped onion
- ½ cup finely chopped celery
- 2 teaspoons Worcestershire sauce
- 1 tablespoon snipped regular *or* Italian parsley
- ¼ teaspoon salt
- ⅛ teaspoon pepper
- 2 tablespoons butter *or* margarine, melted

Regular *or* Italian parsley sprigs (optional)

♦ ♦ ♦

<u>*Thymes Remembered*</u> *presents an intimate portrait of food, drawn from the most cherished family occasions. This recipe for Vegetable Mushroom Caps is one example of the many unique delectables found in the cookbook compiled by The Junior League of Tallahassee. This dynamic group of women is committed to promoting volunteerism and community improvement.*

<u>*Thymes Remembered*</u>
The Junior League of Tallahassee, Inc.
Tallahassee
FLORIDA

1 Rinse the mushrooms and pat dry. Remove and chop the stems. Set the mushroom caps aside.

2 Melt the 2 tablespoons butter or margarine in a large skillet. Stir in the mushroom stems, onion, celery, Worcestershire sauce, parsley, salt and pepper. Cook and stir until the vegetables are tender.

3 Brush the mushroom caps with the melted butter or margarine and spoon in the vegetable mixture.

4 Place the caps, stuffed side up, in the skillet. Cover and cook over medium heat for 8 minutes.

5 Transfer the mushroom caps from the skillet to a warm platter. Garnish with parsley, if desired.

TIPS FROM OUR KITCHEN

If you want to enjoy your guests instead of being stuck in the kitchen, try baking these caps rather than frying them. Arrange the mushroom caps in a 15x10x1-inch baking pan. Bake in a 425° oven for 8 to 10 minutes or until heated through.

Nutrition Analysis (*Per Serving*): Calories: 85 / Cholesterol: 15 mg / Carbohydrates: 7 g / Protein: 3 g / Sodium: 149 mg / Fat: 6 g (Saturated Fat: 4 g) / Potassium: 473 mg.

MOUTH-WATERING MORSELS

These delicious morsels are so tasty, they will disappear as fast as you set them out.
Be prepared for rave reviews!

JEANNE'S EGGPLANT APPETIZER

Makes 5½ Cups (About 22 Servings)

1	large eggplant, washed, peeled and cut into ½-inch cubes (6 cups)
½	cup olive oil
1	cup chopped onion
1	cup chopped celery
1	cup chopped green sweet pepper
1	cup tomato puree
¾	cup red wine vinegar
½	cup chopped ripe olives
2	tablespoons sugar
½	teaspoon salt

◆   ◆   ◆

Judy Elbaum, a free-lance cooking instructor, said she likes to serve Jeanne's Eggplant Appetizer on toasted pita bread, toast points or crackers. She credits her friend, Jeanne Katz, as the originator of the recipe. Judy submitted this recipe to the Candle Lighters's cookbook to help support Stepping Stones, a learning program for developmentally delayed children.

Judy Elbaum
Our Favorite Quick & Easy Recipes
The Candle Lighters
Livingston
NEW JERSEY

1 In a 12-inch skillet over medium heat, cook the eggplant in the hot olive oil about 10 minutes or until it is lightly browned, stirring occasionally. Cover the skillet during the last 2 minutes of cooking to steam and soften the eggplant.

2 Add the onion, celery and green sweet pepper to the skillet. Cook and stir until the vegetables are crisp-tender. Stir in the tomato puree, red wine vinegar, olives, sugar and salt. Simmer, uncovered, for 10 minutes, stirring occasionally. Remove from the heat; cool.

3 Transfer the eggplant mixture to a covered container. Refrigerate overnight. Serve with toasted French bread rounds or toasted pita wedges.

 TIPS FROM OUR KITCHEN

This dish is also delicious served over chicken, pork or fish.

Store this eggplant appetizer in the refrigerator up to 1 week or in the freezer up to 3 months. For quick identification, be sure to label the covered containers.

Package the mixture in a decorative container to give as a gift along with a loaf of cocktail bread and instructions for storing and serving.

Nutrition Analysis (*Per Serving*): Calories: 69 / Cholesterol: 0 mg / Carbohydrates: 6 g / Protein: 1 g / Sodium: 120 mg / Fat: 6 g (Saturated Fat: 1 g) / Potassium: 163 mg.

CAPONATA VARIATION

Like the traditional Sicilian dish caponata, Jeanne's Eggplant Appetizer is best served at room temperature. Accompanied by thinly sliced cocktail bread, the dish makes a wonderful first course or a perfect party pass-around appetizer.

APPETIZERS, BEVERAGES & SNACKS

15

WORLD'S BEST DEVILED EGGS

Makes 24 Servings

12	eggs
½	cup mayonnaise *or* salad dressing
2	tablespoons finely chopped onion
1	teaspoon snipped fresh chives
1	teaspoon snipped parsley
1	teaspoon dry mustard
½	teaspoon paprika
½ to ¾	teaspoon dried dillweed
¼	teaspoon salt
¼	teaspoon pepper
¼	teaspoon garlic powder

Milk

♦ ♦ ♦

When the cookbook Cause to Cook *was being created, two very similar recipes for Deviled Eggs were submitted by Cindy Thury Smith and Marge Jacoboski. Cindy tells us that her version and Marge's often "turn up" at the same local parties. Cindy's grandmother passed down her recipe for deviled eggs to Cindy, who then adapted it to create* World's Best Deviled Eggs.

**Cindy Thury Smith and
Marge Jacoboski**
Cause to Cook
*Jerry's Friends
Lilydale
MINNESOTA*

1 Place the eggs in a large saucepan. Add enough cold water to cover. Bring the water to a rapid boil over high heat.

2 Reduce the heat so the water is just below simmering. (The water should have bubbles on the bottom of the pan with only a few rising to the top.) Cover and cook for 15 minutes.

3 Pour off the hot water; fill the pan with cold water and a few ice cubes. Let stand at least 2 minutes.

4 Pour off the water, then gently roll the eggs around by shaking the pan from side to side. This will crack the shells thoroughly and uniformly.

5 Remove the shells by starting to peel from the largest end of the egg. If the shell doesn't come off easily, hold the egg under running water while pulling away the shell.

6 Cut the eggs in half lengthwise and remove the yolks. Place the yolks in a shallow bowl and mash with a fork. Add the mayonnaise or salad dressing, onion, chives, parsley, dry mustard, paprika, dillweed, salt, pepper and garlic powder to the egg yolks. Stir. If necessary, stir in a little milk to achieve the desired consistency.

7 Spoon the yolk mixture into egg white halves. Cover and chill until serving time.

 TIPS FROM OUR KITCHEN

Don't be concerned if a greenish ring surrounds the yolk of a hard-cooked egg. This is a common, harmless occurrence caused by the formation of iron sulfide during the cooking process. To decrease the chances of this occurring, follow the above method of cooking.

When serving, do not leave eggs at room temperature for more than two hours. Deviled eggs may be kept in the refrigerator for up to one week.

Nutrition Analysis *(Per Serving)*: Calories: 73 / Cholesterol: 109 mg / Carbohydrates: 1 g / Protein: 3 g / Sodium: 80 mg / Fat: 6 g (Saturated Fat: 1 g) / Potassium: 38 mg.

DEVILISH DELIGHT

To *devil,* in culinary terms, is to make a food hot or spicy. Among the spices at work on this American picnic classic are dry mustard, paprika, dillweed and garlic powder. Try these unusual eggs and you'll agree this is indeed a world-class recipe.

APPETIZERS, BEVERAGES & SNACKS

SPINACH QUICHE APPETIZERS

Makes 60 Small Appetizers

10	eggs
½	cup all-purpose flour
1	teaspoon baking powder
1	10-ounce package frozen chopped spinach, thawed and well drained
¼	cup butter *or* margarine, melted
2	4-ounce cans green chilies, drained, seeded and chopped
2	cups small-curd cottage cheese
2	cups shredded cheddar cheese (8 ounces)
2	cups shredded Monterey Jack cheese (8 ounces)

◆ ◆ ◆

Sue Crouse, publicity chairperson for The Pleasure of Your Company, *tells us that Spinach Quiche Appetizers are "a favorite in our house. Frequently, I serve them for a brunch or a light supper, and, of course, as appetizers." This recipe is presented in the summer section of the cookbook, but we're sure the appetizers taste just as delicious any time of the year.*

The Pleasure of Your Company
The Auxiliary of St. Joseph
Riverside Hospital
Warren
OHIO

1 Preheat the oven to 400°.

2 In a large bowl, beat the eggs. Stir in the flour and baking powder. Stir in the spinach, melted butter or margarine, green chilies, cottage cheese, cheddar cheese and Monterey Jack cheese.

3 Pour the mixture into a 3-quart rectangular baking dish. Bake in the 400° for 15 minutes. Reduce the oven temperature to 350°; bake for 25 to 30 minutes more or until the quiche is puffed and the center is set. Remove from the oven and let the quiche stand for 15 to 20 minutes before cutting it into squares.

TIPS FROM OUR KITCHEN

It is important to drain the spinach well before adding it to the egg mixture. To do so, place the spinach in a strainer or colander and press a spoon against the spinach to force out the excess moisture.

To cut the quiche into even-size squares, allow it to cool for 15 to 20 minutes after removing it from the oven. Then, with a sharp knife, cut the long side into 10 rows and the short side into 6 rows.

To shred cheese, push the cheese across a shredding surface.

Nutrition Analysis (*Per Appetizer*): Calories: 61 / Cholesterol: 46 mg / Carbohydrates: 1 g / Protein: 4 g / Sodium: 118 mg / Fat: 4 g (Saturated Fat: 2 g) / Potassium: 41 mg.

EGG-CITING SNACK

Chopped green chili peppers join with spinach and three kinds of cheese to flavor this hot, egg-based

appetizer. No need to make a crust—this quiche forms it own during baking!

MARY'S CHEESE BALL

Makes 3½ cups

1 8-ounce package cream
   cheese, softened
4 ounces blue cheese, finely
   crumbled
½ cup finely chopped onion
2 tablespoons prepared
   mustard
1 to 2 tablespoons pickle relish
2 teaspoons Worcestershire
   sauce
1 teaspoon prepared
   horseradish
½ teaspoon salt
2 cups shredded Swiss cheese,
   (8 ounces)
1 cup shredded cheddar
   cheese, (4 ounces)
1 tablespoon chili powder
   or paprika (optional)
½ cup ground walnuts or
   pecans (optional)
⅓ cup snipped fresh parsley
   or dill (optional)

♦   ♦   ♦

*The call went out in Wilmington,
to help restore the Grand
Opera House. From the most
popular fund-raising events
sponsored by the Grand Opera
Guild—their catered opening-
night parties—came the superb
cookbook Grand Recipes.*

Jean M. Watkins
Grand Recipes
Grand Opera House Guild
Wilmington
DELAWARE

1 In a large bowl, combine the cream cheese with the blue cheese, onion, mustard, pickle relish, Worcestershire sauce, horseradish and salt. Beat the mixture with an electric mixer until it is light and fluffy. Fold in the Swiss and cheddar cheeses. Chill the cheese mixture for at least 2 hours.

2 Form the chilled cheese mixture into 1 large or 2 small balls.

3 Roll the cheese ball(s) in your choice of coatings: chili powder or paprika, walnuts or pecans, or parsley or dill. Wrap and chill until serving time, for up to 3 days.

 TIPS FROM OUR KITCHEN

To make the cheese ball(s) ahead of time, we suggest preparing the recipe through Step 2. Wrap the cheese ball(s) tightly in freezer-safe plastic wrap and freeze. The day before serving, place the ball(s) in the refrigerator to thaw. Just before serving, roll in the coating of your choice. This will keep the coatings nice and crunchy.

If you'd like, garnish with sprigs of fresh rosemary and whole strawberries. We suggest serving Mary's Cheese Ball with fresh cut-up fruit and vegetable crudités, breadsticks, flatbreads and a variety of crackers.

Nutrition Analysis *(Per Tablespoon):* Calories: 46 / Cholesterol: 12 mg / Carbohydrates: 1 g / Protein: 2 g / Sodium: 94 mg / Fat: 4 g (Saturated Fat: 2 g) / Potassium: 21 mg.

TAILORED TO YOUR TASTE

Make this unique cheese spread from Jean Watkins of Wilmington, Delaware, to suit your fancy. Just choose your favorite blue cheese, pair it with a zesty mustard, then roll the cheese ball in the coating of your choice—spicy, crunchy or colorful!

APPETIZERS, BEVERAGES & SNACKS

BARBECUED CHICKEN WINGS

Makes About 40 Pieces

- 4 pounds chicken wings (20 wings)
- ¾ cup catsup
- ¼ cup finely chopped onion
- 2 tablespoons water
- 4 cloves garlic, minced
- 1 tablespoon white vinegar
- 1 tablespoon brown sugar
- 1 tablespoon Worcestershire sauce
- 1 teaspoon chili powder
- ½ teaspoon dry mustard
- ½ teaspoon dried oregano, crushed
- 2 bay leaves
- Few dashes bottled hot pepper sauce

♦　♦　♦

Diane Lusich can't remember where she found this recipe, although she does remember what happened when she first made it. She added a little of this and a little of that, and when finally satisfied with the recipe, she found she had enough sauce to feed an army. Luckily, Diane's family and friends love Barbecued Chicken Wings!

Pete and Diane Lusich
What's Cooking With Harvey's Employees
That's What Friends Are For
Stateline
NEVADA

1 Preheat the oven to 375°.

2 Rinse the chicken wings and pat them dry. Cut off and discard wing tips. Cut each wing at the joint to make 2 sections. Arrange the chicken pieces in a single layer in an ungreased baking pan. Bake in the 375° oven for 25 minutes. Drain the fat from the baking pan.

3 Meanwhile, in a medium saucepan, combine the catsup, onion, water, garlic, vinegar, brown sugar, Worcestershire sauce, chili powder, dry mustard, oregano, bay leaves and hot pepper sauce. Bring to a boil; reduce the heat. Simmer, uncovered, for 2 minutes, stirring occasionally. Remove the bay leaves.

4 Pour the barbecue sauce over the partially cooked chicken in the baking pan. Bake for 10 minutes; then stir the chicken and bake for 10 minutes more. Transfer the chicken pieces to a lettuce-lined platter.

 TIPS FROM OUR KITCHEN

To make the sauce spicier, use hot-style catsup.

This sauce also can be used on boneless, skinless chicken breast pieces.

Use the less meaty chicken wing tips for making broth. Place them in a large saucepan and cover with water. Add chopped celery, carrot, onion, garlic, salt and pepper. Heat to boiling, then reduce heat. Cover and simmer for 1 hour. Remove the chicken wing tips; cut off any meat and discard the bones and skin. Strain the broth, discarding the vegetables.

After cutting up chicken or any other uncooked meat, scrub both the cutting board and knife thoroughly with hot soapy water before using them with any other food.

Nutrition Analysis *(Per Piece)*: Calories: 57 / Cholesterol: 15 mg / Carbohydrates: 2 g / Protein: 5 g / Sodium: 72 mg / Fat: 3 g (Saturated Fat: 1 g) / Potassium: 69 mg.

SASSY FINGER FOOD

Chicken wings join French fries and nachos at the top of the list of crowd-pleasing finger foods. In this recipe, Worcestershire sauce, vinegar, chili powder, dry mustard, onion and garlic give the catsup-based barbecue sauce its spicy personality.

MINI CALZONES

Makes About 30 Appetizers

- ¾ cup ricotta cheese
- ¼ cup grated Parmesan cheese
- 1 pound loaf frozen bread dough, thawed
- 1½ ounces thinly sliced pepperoni, cut in half
- 2 tablespoons milk
- 1 cup tomato sauce
- 1 teaspoon dried Italian seasoning

◆   ◆   ◆

The Benjamin F. Sullivan Unit #155—a unit of the American Legion Auxiliary—created and developed Cookbook Unit #155 to generate funds to help purchase supplies for the local homeless shelter. The organization is also involved with projects that benefit abused, missing and handicapped children, as well as with drug abuse prevention programs.

Gloria Schilling
Cookbook Unit #155
Benjamin F. Sullivan Unit #155
Pittsfield
MASSACHUSETTS

1 Preheat the oven to 375°. Grease 2 baking sheets and set aside.

2 In a small bowl, stir together the ricotta cheese and Parmesan cheese.

3 On a lightly floured surface, with a lightly floured rolling pin, roll the dough to slightly less than a ¼-inch thickness.

4 With a 2½-inch round cutter or drinking glass, cut out circles of the dough.

5 Place a generous *teaspoon* of the ricotta mixture and *½ slice* of pepperoni on half of each circle of the dough. Fold the circles in half and seal the edges by pressing with the tines of a fork.

6 Place the filled calzones on the prepared baking sheets. Prick the tops with a fork to allow steam to escape. Brush the tops with the milk. Bake in the 375° oven for 15 to 20 minutes or until golden.

7 Meanwhile, in a small saucepan, combine the tomato sauce and the Italian seasoning. Heat to boiling; reduce heat and simmer, covered, for 15 minutes.

8 Remove the calzones from the baking sheets. Serve immediately with the tomato sauce for dipping.

TIPS FROM OUR KITCHEN

Calzones are a type of Italian turnover. The filling may be meat, cheese or vegetables.

If you're in a hurry, use 2 tubes of refrigerator pizza dough instead of frozen bread dough. The pizza dough may open a little more during baking, but the filling won't ooze out and you'll save quite a bit of time. Both doughs will be easier to roll if you let them rest a few minutes occasionally during rolling. Likewise, before re-rolling the dough scraps, press them together and let the new ball rest a few minutes.

The dough will be easier to fold over the filling if the cut (straight) edge of the pepperoni half slice is at the fold line. It also may be necessary to stretch the dough a bit to cover the filling.

Nutrition Analysis: (*Per Appetizer*): Calories: 75 / Cholesterol: 4 mg / Carbohydrates 10 g / Protein: 3 g / Sodium: 163 mg / Fat: 3 g (Saturated Fat: 1 g) / Potassium: 62 m

ITALIAN TURNOVERS

What a great way to turn a gathering into a party! Pass around a tray of these Mini Calzones and some sauce for dipping and watch the conversations come alive.

LEA'S SWEDISH MEATBALLS

Makes 30 to 32 Appetizer Servings

1	pound lean ground beef
8	ounces ground pork
¾	cup fine dry bread crumbs
½	cup finely chopped onion
½	cup milk
1	egg
1	tablespoon snipped parsley
1	teaspoon Worcestershire sauce
1	teaspoon salt
⅛	teaspoon pepper
¼	cup cooking oil
1	8-ounce carton dairy sour cream
¼	cup all-purpose flour
½	teaspoon salt
⅛	teaspoon pepper
2	cups water

◆　　◆　　◆

Even though Linda Goode wasn't able to tell us who Lea was, she remembered that she received the recipe from her mother-in-law. Linda said that this was an hors d'oeuvre her mother-in-law "always served at our New Year's Day open house." She also noted that these meatballs are easy to make and they serve a crowd of people.

Linda Goode
Central Texas Style
Junior Service League of Killeen, Inc.
Killeen
TEXAS

1 In a large bowl, stir together the ground beef, ground pork, bread crumbs, onion, milk, egg, parsley, Worcestershire sauce, the 1 teaspoon salt and the ⅛ teaspoon pepper; mix well. Shape the mixture into 64 walnut-size balls.

2 In a 12-inch skillet, heat the cooking oil. Add *half* the meatballs and cook for 12 to 15 minutes or until no pink remains, turning the meatballs to brown them evenly. Remove the meatballs from skillet; set aside. Repeat. Reserve the drippings in the skillet.

3 In a small bowl, stir together the sour cream, flour, the ½ teaspoon salt and the ⅛ teaspoon pepper. Add the water; mix well. Stir the mixture into the drippings in the skillet; heat until the gravy is thickened and bubbly.

4 Add the meatballs to the gravy in the skillet and heat through.

 TIPS FROM OUR KITCHEN

Crumble 3 slices of bread in your food processor to make the bread crumbs for this recipe.

One medium onion chopped in a food processor will yield enough onion for this recipe.

To brown the meatballs evenly on all sides, use a 12-inch skillet and turn the meatballs constantly. This also helps to keep them evenly rounded.

You can also brown and bake the meatballs in the oven. To bake the meatballs: Place them in a single layer in a 15x10x1-inch baking pan. Bake in a 350° oven for 15 to 20 minutes or until no pink remains. Then, stir together the flour and sour cream in a skillet or chafing dish; stir in the water. Add the meatballs and heat through.

If you're serving these meatballs at a buffet, be sure to keep them hot to prevent bacteria from growing.

Nutrition Analysis (*Per Serving*): Calories: 89 / Cholesterol: 24 mg / Carbohydrates: 3 g / Protein: 5 g / Sodium: 147 mg / Fat: 6 g (Saturated Fat: 2 g) / Potassium: 76 mg.

EMBELLISHING A CLASSIC

Everything about Lea's Swedish Meatballs is traditional except for the size. An interesting blend of beef and pork, these appetizers are served in a tasty sour cream sauce. These are so terrific that Lea probably decided to break tradition by using large, rather than small, meatballs.

APPETIZERS, BEVERAGES & SNACKS

CHINESE BAKED PORK ROLLS

Makes 12 Servings
Marinade:
- 2 tablespoons soy sauce
- 2 tablespoons catsup
- 1 tablespoon sugar
- 1 tablespoon dry white wine
- 1 tablespoon vinegar
- 1 teaspoon cornstarch
- 1 teaspoon toasted sesame oil
- ⅛ teaspoon pepper
- 1 pound pork tenderloin

Stuffing:
- 6 dried mushrooms
- 4 whole scallions
- 8 water chestnuts

◆ ◆ ◆

Residents, staff and family members at the St. Cabrini Nursing Home had the opportunity to work together on a cookbook designed to raise funds for the Nursing Home. Madame Yee Yo, author of You Can Cook Anything Chinese, *contributed her recipe for Chinese Baked Pork Rolls to the cause because her parents, Mr. and Mrs. Wan Tze, were both residents of St. Cabrini for years.*

Madame Yee Yo
Cabrini Cares
St. Cabrini Nursing Home
Dobbs Ferry
NEW YORK

1 To make the marinade: In a medium bowl, stir together the soy sauce, catsup, sugar, white wine, vinegar, cornstarch, sesame oil and pepper.

2 Cut the pork tenderloin crosswise into 12 thin slices. With a meat mallet, pound each piece between sheets of heavy-duty plastic wrap to a ¼-inch thickness. Toss the meat in the marinade and let stand for 15 minutes.

3 Preheat the oven to 400°.

4 To make the stuffing: Soak the mushrooms in *boiling water* for 15 minutes. Drain; discard the water and the stems. Thinly slice the mushrooms lengthwise. Using a knife, cut the scallions into thin shreds. Chop the water chestnuts. Stir together the vegetables.

5 Remove the pork slices from the marinade and drain, reserving the marinade. Place *2 tablespoons* of the stuffing on each pork slice. Roll the slice of pork around the stuffing. Fasten each roll with a wooden toothpick. Arrange the rolls in a single layer in a baking dish. Pour the reserved marinade over the pork rolls. Bake in the 400° oven for 20 minutes.

 TIPS FROM OUR KITCHEN

To shred scallions or green onions: Trim off the root ends and tops, leaving about 4 inches of green. Place the trimmed scallions on a cutting board and thinly slice them lengthwise, then cut them crosswise into 4-inch lengths.

Use heavy-duty plastic wrap to cover meat before pounding it. Lightweight plastic wrap or waxed paper is likely to tear as you pound.

If desired, the mushroom mixture can be made a day ahead and refrigerated until ready to use.

If you prefer, marinate the pork slices in the refrigerator up to two hours.

Nutrition Analysis (*Per Serving*): Calories: 68 / Cholesterol: 27 mg / Carbohydrates: 27 g / Protein: 9 g / Sodium: 207 mg / Fat: 2 g (Saturated Fat: 0 g) / Potassium: 224 mg.

APPEALING APPETIZER

Madame Yee Yo of Dobbs Ferry, New York, presents us with this exciting new appetizer idea. Tender marinated pork slices are wrapped around a stuffing of scallions, mushrooms and water chestnuts.

AUSTRIAN CHEESE AND SHRIMP STRUDEL

Makes 16 to 18 Slices

½   17¼-ounce package
     (1 sheet) frozen puff pastry,
     thawed
1½   cups shredded Swiss cheese
     (6 ounces)
½   cup dairy sour cream
¼   cup thinly sliced green
     onion
4   ounces cooked shrimp (1
     cup), chopped *or* one 4½-
     ounce can shrimp, rinsed,
     drained and chopped
1   egg, beaten

◆   ◆   ◆

Lori Stenglein has quite a recipe collection. When traveling, she enjoys collecting regional community cookbooks and recipe clippings from magazines and newspapers. Lori said that if she doesn't use a recipe within a year, she discards it. This recipe for Austrian Cheese and Shrimp Strudel has endured, perhaps because of its simplicity; according to Lori, "This is from my easier and faster category."

Lori Stenglein
The Flavor & Spice
of Holy Cross Life
Holy Cross Parish
Batavia
ILLINOIS

1 Preheat the oven to 400°. On a lightly floured surface, roll the thawed puff pastry to an 18x10-inch rectangle.

2 In a medium bowl, stir together the Swiss cheese, sour cream, green onion, shrimp and *half* of the beaten egg (about 2 tablespoons). Spread the mixture lengthwise down half of the rectangle. Using a pastry brush, brush the edges of the pastry with some of the remaining beaten egg.

3 Carefully fold the dough over the filling and seal the edges with the tines of a fork. Transfer the strudel to an extra large baking sheet. Brush the top and sides of the strudel with the remaining beaten egg.

4 Bake in the 400° oven for 20 to 25 minutes or until golden. Remove from the oven. Cool the strudel for 20 minutes before slicing.

 TIPS FROM OUR KITCHEN

If your grocer doesn't have puff pastry in sheets, buy frozen patty shells. When thawed, they, too, can be pressed together and rolled flat to make a sheet.

Brushing the edges of the pastry with the beaten egg helps them to seal and thus reduces the chances of the filling leaking out during baking. Brushing the egg over the strudel helps it to turn a golden brown during baking.

Be sure to let the strudel cool for 20 minutes before slicing. This will give the cheesy filling a chance to set up.

Nutrition Analysis (*Per Slice*): Calories: 134 / Cholesterol: 40 mg / Carbohydrates: 6 g / Protein: 6 g / Sodium: 109 mg / Fat: 10 g (Saturated Fat: 3 g) / Potassium: 40 mg.

SAVORY PASTRY

If the word *strudel* conjures up thoughts of a complicated preparation resulting in a sweet dessert, think again. Lori Stenglein's wonderful Austrian Cheese and Shrimp Strudel is a surprisingly easy-to-make appetizer.

GRILLED BACON-WRAPPED SHRIMP

Makes 8 Servings

- 2 cups hickory, apple *or* cherry wood chips
- ¼ cup water
- ¼ cup soy sauce
- 1 tablespoon brown sugar
- 1 tablespoon dry sherry
- 1 large clove garlic, crushed
- Dash Worcestershire sauce
- Dash ground red pepper
- ½-inch piece fresh gingerroot, peeled and grated
- 24 large shrimp (about 1 pound), shelled with tails left intact and deveined
- 8 slices lean bacon

◆ ◆ ◆

Combine an avid interest in grilling, an area boasting the freshest seafood and a generous-with-her-recipes aunt from Alabama and what you get (if you're as lucky as we are) is Tricia Willis's Grilled Bacon-Wrapped Shrimp.

Tricia Willis
Thymes Remembered
Junior League of Tallahassee
Tallahassee
FLORIDA

1 Cover the wood chips with water and soak for 30 minutes. Drain.

2 In a medium saucepan, combine all the remaining ingredients, *except* the shrimp and bacon. Cover and stir over medium heat to blend the flavors. Remove from heat; set aside to cool.

3 Place the shrimp in a medium bowl. Pour the marinade over the shrimp. Cover and chill for 1 to 2 hours, stirring occasionally.

4 Remove the shrimp from the marinade and drain well. Discard the marinade.

5 In a large skillet, partially cook the bacon until just limp. Drain on paper towels and cool.

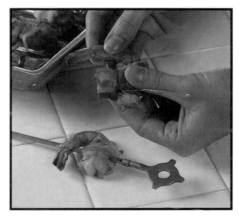

6 Cut each bacon slice into thirds. Wrap a piece of bacon around each shrimp and secure with a skewer.

7 Sprinkle wood chips over hot coals. Grill skewers of shrimp over hot coals for 6 to 10 minutes or until shrimp turns pink, turning once. Do not overcook.

TIPS FROM OUR KITCHEN

Because the bacon on these appetizers is only partially cooked, the dripping fat may cause some flare-ups during grilling. To combat flare-ups, raise the grill rack, cover the grill, space the coals farther apart or remove a few coals. If a large flare-up occurs, remove the appetizers from the grill and mist the fire with a pump-spray bottle filled with water. When the flare-up has died down, resume grilling.

To broil these appetizers, place the bacon-wrapped shrimp on a cold broiler rack. Cook 4 inches from the heat for 6 to 10 minutes or until done, turning once.

Nutrition Analysis (*Per Serving*): Calories: 95 / Cholesterol: 92 mg / Carbohydrates: 3 g / Protein: 12 g / Sodium: 716 mg / Fat: 4 g (Saturated Fat: 1 g) / Potassium: 139 mg.

GLORIOUS MENU STARTER

Hickory, apple or cherry wood chips add a subtle background flavor to these delicious bacon and shrimp morsels from Tallahassee, Florida.

SALMON HORS D'OEUVRES

1 In a medium mixing bowl, combine the salmon, celery, mayonnaise or salad dressing, lemon juice, onion powder, celery seed and pepper. (If desired, add *1 to 2 tablespoons* additional mayonnaise for a creamier mixture.)

2 On a serving plate, pat the mixture into the shape of a fish. Or, pat the mixture into a plastic wrap-lined 2- or 3-cup fish mold. Unmold onto a serving plate.

3 Decorate the fish, using the pimiento-stuffed green olive for the eye and the pitted black olive slices for scales. Sprinkle with the paprika.

4 Encircle the fish with lettuce and parsley. Garnish with twisted lemon slices. Cover and chill until ready to serve. Serve with crackers.

TIPS FROM OUR KITCHEN

To make the lemon twists: Cut halfway through a thin lemon slice, then twist one cut side. If desired, notch the peel before twisting and add a bit of red pimiento to the twist point.

If you're concerned about fat content, look for no-fat or low-fat labels on the mayonnaise or salad dressing. Check the fat content of your crackers as well.

If you don't have a fish mold or another fancy mold and don't want to hand shape the fish, you can use a 2-cup bowl lined with plastic wrap. Decorate the serving platter with ruffled lettuce, celery leaves, parsley and twisted lemon or lime slices.

Nutrition Analysis (*Per Serving*): Calories: 82 / Cholesterol: 13 mg / Carbohydrates: 1 g / Protein: 5 g / Sodium: 171 mg / Fat: 7 g (Saturated Fat: 1 g) / Potassium: 105 mg.

SPREADABLE BEGINNING

A decorative mold makes a party out of canned red salmon that has been subtly flavored with celery
seed, lemon juice and onion powder. Serve with crackers and embellish
with green and black olives, lemon twists, lettuce and parsley.

APPETIZERS, BEVERAGES & SNACKS

35

PARMESAN TWISTS

Makes 48 Twists

½   cup grated Parmesan cheese
¼   cup butter *or* margarine, softened
½   cup dairy sour cream
1   cup all-purpose flour
¼   teaspoon dried thyme, crushed
¼   teaspoon dried oregano, crushed
⅛   teaspoon dried basil, crushed
1   egg yolk, beaten with 1 tablespoon water
1   tablespoon sesame *or* poppy seed

♦   ♦   ♦

When Anne Bruno of Madison, Wisconsin created these twists, she never expected they'd be such a hit. Anne remembers being nervous, thinking her invention might be a failure. But, to her delight, Anne says, "The reaction was very, very good." Not only did her friends and family like these tasty treats, they have continued to request them year after year. Truly a culinary success story!

Anne Bruno
<u>Be Our Guest</u>
Madison
WISCONSIN

1 Preheat oven to 350°. Grease 2 baking sheets.

2 In a medium bowl, beat together the Parmesan cheese and the butter with an electric mixer until the mixture is fluffy. Beat in the sour cream.

3 In a small bowl, combine the flour with the thyme, oregano and basil. Beat the flour mixture into the cheese mixture. Knead the dough lightly and divide it in half.

4 On a lightly floured surface, roll out the dough into two 12 x 6-inch rectangles. Cut each rectangle into twenty-four 6 x ½-inch strips.

5 Before separating the strips, brush them with the egg yolk-water mixture and sprinkle them with the sesame seed or poppy seed.

6 Holding each strip by the ends, gently twist the pastry 2 or 3 times and place on the prepared baking sheets.

7 Bake the twists in the 350° oven for 10 to 12 minutes or until golden. Remove the twists and cool on wire racks.

TIPS FROM OUR KITCHEN

In a hurry? Cut the dough into 1-inch squares instead of strips to avoid the time and work of twisting the strips.

Nutrition Analysis *(Per Twist)*: Calories: 29 / Cholesterol: 9 mg / Carbohydrates: 2 g / Protein: 1 g / Sodium: 31 mg / Fat: 2 g (Saturated Fat: 1 g) / Potassium: 9 mg.

PREPARED FOR COMPLIMENTS

What a find! These "twists" on the usual breadstick are terrific served with salsa, dips, salads and soups and are a welcome addition to any meal. Anne Bruno of Madison, Wisconsin, likes to gather these savory treats into a pretty basket for serving.

CHEDDAR CRISPS

Makes 32 Crackers

1¾ cups all-purpose flour
½ cup yellow cornmeal
½ teaspoon baking soda
½ teaspoon sugar
½ teaspoon salt
½ cup butter *or* margarine
1½ cups shredded extra sharp cheddar cheese (6 ounces)
½ cup cold water
2 tablespoons white vinegar
Coarsely ground black pepper

◆ ◆ ◆

The Ladies Aid of St. John's Lutheran Church has compiled <u>Cooking with a Country Flair</u> *in order to raise funds for an addition to their church. The cookbook features over 700 excellent recipes, including Lucy King's Cheddar Crisps. Lucy told us that she likes to make these crackers to serve with soup or to munch as a snack.*

Lucy King
<u>*Cooking with a Country Flair*</u>
St. John's Lutheran Church
Amlin
OHIO

1 Preheat the oven to 375°. Grease a large baking sheet. Set aside.

2 In a large mixing bowl, stir together the flour, cornmeal, baking soda, sugar and salt. Using a pastry blender, cut in the butter or margarine until the mixture resembles coarse crumbs.

3 Using a fork, stir in the shredded cheese, cold water and vinegar just until the mixture forms a soft dough. If necessary, knead the mixture in the bowl until smooth. Shape the dough into a ball. Wrap the ball with plastic wrap and refrigerate about 1 hour or until it is firm enough to handle.

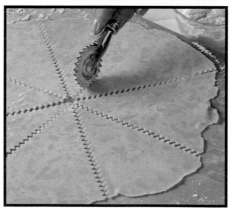

4 On a lightly floured surface, use a floured rolling pin to roll *one-fourth* of the dough into a paper-thin round approximately 13 inches in diameter (edges may be ragged). Keep the remaining dough refrigerated. Using a fluted pastry cutter or a pizza cutter, cut the round into 8 wedges.

5 Transfer the wedges to the prepared baking sheet. Sprinkle the crackers with the black pepper. Firmly press the pepper into the dough. Bake in the 375° oven for 8 to 10 minutes or until browned and crisp. Transfer the crackers to wire racks to cool. Repeat with the remaining dough. Store the cooled crackers in a tightly covered container.

 TIPS FROM OUR KITCHEN

For variety, sprinkle the crackers with sesame seed or poppy seed instead of pepper. Or, substitute pepper cheese for all or part of the cheddar cheese.

The crackers can be stored in the refrigerator or freezer, although they will lose some of their crispness.

For smaller wedges, divide the dough into 8 equal portions. Roll *one-eighth* of the dough into a paper-thin round, approximately 10 inches in diameter. Cut into 8 wedges. This will yield 64 crackers.

Nutrition Analysis (*Per Cracker*): Calories: 78 / Cholesterol: 13 mg / Carbohydrates: 7 g / Protein: 2 g / Sodium: 117 mg / Fat: 5 g (Saturated Fat: 3 g) / Potassium: 17 mg.

CHEESE CRUNCHERS

Make your own crackers? Sure! It isn't difficult and your efforts will yield a delicious reward. Cheddar
cheese and cornmeal are the main flavors in these crispy treats, which are topped with your choice
of coarsely ground black pepper, sesame seed or poppy seed.

Caramel Corn

6 quarts popped corn (no salt or butter)
1 cup butter *or* margarine
2 cups packed brown sugar
½ cup light corn syrup
½ teaspoon salt
½ teaspoon baking soda
1 teaspoon vanilla

◆ ◆ ◆

Cincinnati loves to celebrate! The Junior League of Cincinnati's first cookbook, Cincinnati Celebrates, *paid tribute to the city's festive spirit. Their second,* RiverFeast: Still Celebrating Cincinnati, *raises funds to support educational and charitable projects. We think this recipe for Caramel Corn is in keeping with this celebratory theme because it helps make any occasion special.*

RiverFeast: Still Celebrating Cincinnati
Junior League of Cincinnati
Cincinnati
OHIO

1 Preheat oven to 250°. Put the popcorn in a 17x12x2-inch roasting pan or large foil pan; set aside.

2 Melt the butter or margarine in a medium saucepan over medium heat. Add the brown sugar, corn syrup and salt. Stir until the mixture starts to boil. (The syrup should boil over its entire surface.) Boil for 5 minutes without stirring.

3 Remove from heat. Stir in the baking soda and vanilla, then pour the caramel mixture over the popped corn, stirring to coat.

4 Bake, uncovered, in the 250° oven for 1 hour, stirring every 15 minutes.

5 Remove the caramel corn from the oven and spread it out on a large piece of foil to cool. Break into clusters. Store in an airtight container.

 TIPS FROM OUR KITCHEN

Use a 2-quart saucepan to assure that the syrup will be just the right temperature and consistency after 5 minutes of boiling.

For a special touch, add nuts or candy-coated chocolate pieces to the caramel/popcorn mixture just before cooling.

Nutrition Analysis *(Per Serving):* Calories: 124 / Cholesterol: 23 mg / Carbohydrates: 11 g / Protein: 1 g / Sodium: 158 mg / Fat: 8 g (Saturated Fat: 5 g) / Potassium: 3 mg.

SNACK ATTACK

Munching on this sweet confection makes us all feel like kids again. Mix up a batch the next time you have the gang over for a night of movie-watching or board games. Or pack a bag in your children's lunchboxes for a special treat.

RASPBERRY SHRUB

Makes 4 Servings

    2 cups fresh *or* frozen
       loose-pack red
       raspberries
    2 cups water
1½ to 2 cups sugar
 1½ cups light rum *or*
       carbonated water
    1 tablespoon lime juice
Ice cubes, crushed
Mint sprigs, lime twists *and/or*
    fresh raspberries
    (optional)

◆   ◆   ◆

When we spoke with Garneta Bauerle, chairperson of 101 Years of Treasured Recipes, she told us about the wonderful response the United Methodist Women received when compiling their cookbook. By example, she cited the children of one woman who warned Garneta that their mother had even refused to give them any of her treasured recipes. But, when approached by Garneta, the woman agreed to contribute a recipe to the church's cookbook project.

Jody Brott
101 Years of Treasured Recipes
United Methodist Women
Champion
NEBRASKA

1 In a medium saucepan, combine the raspberries and water. Heat to boiling. Reduce heat and simmer, uncovered, for 20 minutes.

2 Strain the mixture, returning the juice to the saucepan and discarding the raspberry pulp. (You should have 2 cups juice.)

3 Add the sugar to the hot juice, stirring until the sugar is dissolved.

4 For each serving: Fill a tall glass with crushed ice. Add about *½ cup* of the raspberry syrup, *¼ cup* rum or carbonated water and *¾ teaspoon* lime juice.

5 Garnish with mint sprigs, lime twists and/or fresh raspberries, if desired.

 TIPS FROM OUR KITCHEN

Make specialty ice cubes by freezing whole raspberries and small mint leaves in water or ginger ale.

For variety, substitute lemon-lime carbonated beverage or ginger ale for the rum or carbonated water and omit the sugar.

If you are in a hurry and don't have time to crush the ice, you can leave the ice cubes whole.

Nutrition Analysis *(Per Serving)*: Calories: 329 / Cholesterol: 0 mg / Carbohydrates: 53 g / Protein: 3 g / Sodium: 5 mg / Fat: 0 g (Saturated Fat: 0 g) / Potassium: 66 mg.

BERRY REFRESHING

Welcome your family and guests to the table with this icy-cold fruit drink. You can make Raspberry Shrub with carbonated water or you can spike it with rum, as was the fashion during Colonial times. Either way, it's as good as a cool breeze on a hot summer day.

GINGER CRANBERRY PUNCH

Makes 16 (4-Ounce) Servings
Ginger Syrup:
   1   cup water
  ½   cup sugar
  ¼   cup chopped fresh
      gingerroot
Punch:
   1   1-liter bottle ginger ale,
      chilled
   1   32-ounce bottle cranberry-
      apple juice, chilled
   1   tablespoon grenadine
      (optional)
Ice ring
Fresh roses (optional)

◆   ◆   ◆

*Mary Yanko, President of the
Christ Child Society of Akron,
Inc., has served this refreshing
beverage to appreciative groups at
several gatherings, including a
going-away luncheon, a Ronald
McDonald House Tea and a
Women's dinner. Mary tells us
that the punch is always well
received and is so easy that once
she prepares the ingredients, she
can "delegate the responsibility of
mixing them up to my children."*

Mary Yanko
<u>*Savor the Flavors*</u>
*Christ Child Society of
Akron, Inc.
Akron
OHIO*

1 To make the Ginger Syrup: In a
small saucepan, stir together the water,
sugar and gingerroot. Simmer gently
for 30 minutes. Strain and chill.

2 To make the punch: In a chilled 12-
cup (or larger) punch bowl, stir
together the ginger ale, cranberry-apple
juice, *¼ cup* of the Ginger Syrup and
the grenadine, if using. Add the ice
ring. Garnish with the fresh roses or
fresh rose petals, if desired.

 TIPS FROM OUR KITCHEN

Gingerroot comes from a semitropical
plant and has been used in cooking
and baking for more than 4,400 years.
When shopping, select a piece that's
firm and heavy; avoid shriveled stems.
For short-term storage, wrap the root
in a paper towel and refrigerate. For
long-term storage, immerse peeled
slices in dry sherry, wine or oil and
refrigerate in a covered container up to
3 months. You can use the ginger-
flavored oil or sherry for cooking.
Unpeeled fresh gingerroot also can be
frozen in a moisture-proof and vaporproof bag. To use, grate or cut off the
amount needed.

The remaining Ginger Syrup can be
frozen to use in another punch. The
syrup isn't appropriate to use alone over
fruit; it's too spicy and bitter.

To make an ice ring, pour about ½
inch of water into a 3-cup ring mold.
Arrange fruit—such as sliced oranges,
lemons, cranberries, strawberries or
raspberries—on top and freeze until
solid. Carefully add water to fill the
mold; freeze again until solid. To
unmold, wrap the ring mold in a hot
towel, invert onto a plate and remove
the mold. Carefully slide the ring into
the punch bowl.

Edible flowers make an attractive
garnish for fruit punches. Choose from
roses, nasturtiums, pansies, geraniums
(*Pelargonium* species) and violets (*Viola*
species).

Nutrition Analysis (*Per Serving*): Calories: 87 / Cholesterol: 0 mg / Carbohydrates: 22 g /
Protein: 0 g / Sodium: 6 mg / Fat: 0 g (Saturated Fat: 0 g) / Potassium: 23 mg.

COLORFUL REFRESHER

This refreshing punch from Mary Yanko of Akron, Ohio, gets its wonderful flavor from the easy make-your-own, homemade Ginger Syrup.

MARDI GRAS PUNCH

Makes 14 Servings
1 6-ounce can frozen orange juice concentrate, thawed
1 6-ounce can frozen lemonade concentrate, thawed
1 cup water
Fruit pieces, such as cut-up oranges, strawberries, limes *and/or* whole blueberries
1 quart chilled apple juice
2 quarts chilled ginger ale

♦   ♦   ♦

The Artist's Palate Cookbook is a beautiful collection of contemporary adaptations of traditional Louisiana recipes. Recipe contributions by local chefs and artists and the volunteers and staff of the New Orleans Museum of Art are presented alongside color reproductions of artworks from the permanent collection of the museum. It is a unique venture that satisfies the epicure along with the art lover.

Artist's Palate Cookbook
New Orleans Museum of Art
New Orleans
LOUISIANA

1 Combine the orange juice and lemonade concentrates. Refrigerate *half* the concentrate mixture. To the remaining half, add the water. Make ice cubes with the pieces of cut-up fruit and the concentrate-water mixture.

2 To serve: In a large punch bowl, stir together the chilled juice concentrates and the apple juice.

3 Slowly pour the ginger ale down the side of the punch bowl. Add the fruit-filled ice cubes and serve.

 TIPS FROM OUR KITCHEN

To make ice cubes with a special touch, place bite-size pieces of fruit into each section of an ice-cube tray. Then pour in some of the orange juice-lemonade mixture. Freeze the ice cubes overnight.

Forgot to make the ice cubes ahead of time? No problem. Spoon scoops of your favorite sherbet into the punch instead.

To make this punch in advance of the party, combine all the ingredients except the ice cubes and ginger ale in a large punch bowl and chill the mixture until serving time. Then, add the ginger ale and ice cubes when you are ready to serve the punch.

Nutrition Analysis (*Per Serving*): Calories: 132 / Cholesterol: 0mg / Carbohydrates: 33 g / Protein: 1 g / Sodium: 16 mg / Fat: 0 g (Saturated Fat: 0 g) / Potassium: 210 mg.

MORE THAN A THIRST QUENCHER

Birthday, wedding shower, Mardi Gras—this sparkling beverage is ideal for any festive occasion. We love the tangy and refreshing combination of fruit flavors.

APPETIZERS, BEVERAGES & SNACKS

Breads, Muffins & Sandwiches

*T*here's nothing quite so cozy and homey as freshly baked bread and muffins. These recipes will bring back your fondest memories of Grandma baking in the kitchen. Perhaps you'll recall enjoying Challah (pronounced HA-lah) on the Sabbath. The Hot Cross Buns may remind you of Easter as a child. The sandwiches in this section range from the light, dainty classic Cucumber Sandwiches to the meal-in-a-bun Super Dagwood Sandwich. Whatever your background, you'll find comfort in many of these recipes.

VERMONT CHEDDAR CHEESE BATTER BREAD

Makes 1 Loaf (16 Servings)

1	package active dry yeast
1¼	cups warm water (105° to 115°)
2⅔	cups all-purpose flour
1	cup shredded sharp Vermont cheddar cheese (4 ounces)
2	tablespoons sugar
2	tablespoons shortening
1	teaspoon salt
1	teaspoon melted butter *or* margarine

♦   ♦   ♦

The Elizabeth H. Brown Humane Society provides animal care services including assisting in the placement of abandoned or unwanted animals. Deborah Hart's recipe for Vermont Cheddar Cheese Batter Bread comes to us from the society's fund-raising cookbook. Deborah tells us that she found a recipe for a cheese bread years ago and made little changes here and there to make it more her own. Delicious!

Deborah Hart
Elizabeth H. Brown Humane
Society Cookbook
Elizabeth H. Brown
Humane Society
Barton
VERMONT

1 In a large mixing bowl, dissolve the yeast in the warm water. Add *1⅔ cups* of the flour, the cheese, sugar, shortening and salt. Beat with an electric mixer on low speed for 30 seconds, scraping the bowl as needed. Beat on medium speed for 2 minutes, continuing to scrape the bowl.

2 Add the remaining *1 cup* flour, stirring until combined and scraping the batter from the sides of the bowl. Cover and let rise in a warm place for 30 minutes. Then, stir about 25 strokes.

3 Spread the batter evenly in a greased 1½-quart glass casserole. Cover and let rise in warm place about 45 minutes or until the batter has doubled in size.

4 Preheat the oven to 375°. Bake in the 375° oven for 40 to 45 minutes or until golden brown. Cover with foil the last 25 minutes of baking to prevent the top from overbrowning.

5 Remove the bread from the oven and brush the top with the melted butter or margarine. Remove the bread from the pan and cool on a wire rack.

 TIPS FROM OUR KITCHEN

This bread also can be baked in a greased 9x5x3-inch loaf pan or in two greased 7½x3½x2-inch loaf pans.

No-knead breads such as this batter bread generally have a more open, coarse texture than do kneaded breads.

If Vermont cheddar cheese is not sold in your area, feel free to substitute any variety of sharp cheddar cheese.

Nutrition Analysis *(Per Serving)*: Calories: 121 / Cholesterol: 8 mg / Carbohydrates: 16 g / Protein: 4 g / Sodium: 181 mg / Fat: 4 g (Saturated Fat: 2 g) / Potassium: 36 mg.

SAVORY SOUP COMPANION

Remember to make this savory loaf when you want an easy, delicious bread to serve at brunch or
lunch. Requiring only two short risings and 45 minutes in the oven, this bread is
as quick as it is tasty.

ONION TWIST BREAD

Makes 1 Loaf (16 Servings)

1 package active dry yeast
¼ cup warm water (105° to 115°)
4 to 4½ cups all-purpose flour
½ cup melted margarine *or* butter
½ cup milk
½ cup hot water (120° to 130°)
¼ cup sugar
1 egg, beaten
1½ teaspoons salt

Filling:
1 cup finely chopped onion
¼ cup margarine *or* butter
1 tablespoon grated Parmesan cheese
1 tablespoon sesame seed
1 tablespoon poppy seed
¼ teaspoon garlic salt
1 teaspoon paprika

♦ ♦ ♦

Debi says she doesn't often have the chance to give Onion Twist Bread loaves as gifts. "Everyone smells the bread baking and waits for it to come out of the oven. When it's cool enough to cut, it's half gone!"

Debi Maas
The Dollar a Month Club Anniversary Cookbook: A Collection of Recipes to Celebrate the Year
Jesuit Jamshedpur Mission
Baltimore
MARYLAND

1 To make the dough: In a mixing bowl, stir yeast into the warm water. Let the mixture stand for 10 minutes.

2 Stir in *2 cups* of the flour, the melted margarine or butter, milk, hot water, sugar, beaten egg and salt. Beat with an electric mixer on low speed until moistened; beat for 2 minutes more on medium speed. Stir in *2 cups* additional flour.

3 On a floured surface, knead in enough of the remaining flour to make a moderately stiff dough (5 to 8 minutes). Place in a greased bowl. Turn the dough once to grease the surface. Cover and let rise in a warm place until doubled in size, about 1 hour.

4 To make the filling: Cook and stir the onion in the ¼ cup margarine or butter until the onion is tender but not brown. Stir in Parmesan cheese, sesame and poppy seeds, garlic salt and paprika. Set aside.

5 Punch down the dough. If necessary, coat the dough lightly with flour until it is no longer sticky. Roll the dough into a 16x9-inch rectangle. Cut it lengthwise into 3 strips, each 16x4 inches.

6 Spread the filling down the center of each strip. Pull the dough up and around

the filling. Carefully seal the edges and ends and transfer the filled strips to a greased baking sheet, placing them about 1 inch apart. (Because this a long loaf, place the strips diagonally on the baking sheet.)

7 Gently pull the strips, stretching until each measures about 18 inches in length. Starting in the middle, loosely braid by bringing the left strip underneath the center strip; lay it down. Then bring the right strip under the new center strip; lay it down. Repeat to the end, keeping the seams inside the braid when possible. Press the ends together.

8 On the other end, loosely braid from the middle of the loaf by bringing the outside strips alternately over the center strip. Press the ends together.

9 Cover and let the braid rise in a warm place until nearly doubled in size. Preheat the oven to 350°. Bake in the 350° oven about 40 minutes or until golden brown.

Nutrition Analysis (*Per Serving*): Calories: 266 / Cholesterol: 14 mg / Carbohydrates: 27 g / Protein: 5 g / Sodium: 416 mg / Fat: 16 g (Saturated Fat: 3 g) / Potassium: 89 mg.

FLAVOR-FILLED BRAID

Onion Twist Bread really has that special "something." Hidden within a braided, tender dough is a
delicious filling made of onions, Parmesan cheese, sesame seed and poppy seed.
Caution: This loaf will disappear quickly!

CHALLAH

Makes 4 Loaves (48 Servings)

2	packages active dry yeast
¾	cup warm water (110° to 115°)
2	teaspoons sugar
½	cup margarine *or* butter
1	cup boiling water
½	cup sugar
¼	cup cooking oil
¼	cup honey
1	tablespoon salt
8	eggs
10	cups all-purpose flour
1	cup raisins
1	egg yolk, beaten
1	teaspoon water
¼	cup poppy seed

◆　　◆　　◆

To raise funds for their Hebrew School, the Sisterhood of Temple Beth-El compiled Cook & Tell, *"the best kosher cookbook ever written." Every year during Chanukah, the Sisterhood has a festival during which they cook and bake all day. This cookbook is a collection of the recipes that were prepared at their festivals.*

Bok Hurwich
Cook & Tell
Sisterhood of Temple Beth-El
Birmingham
ALABAMA

1 In a 1-cup measuring cup, dissolve the yeast in warm water. Stir in the 2 teaspoons sugar and set in a warm place until the mixture rises to the top of the cup.

2 Place the margarine or butter in a large mixing bowl and add the boiling water. After the margarine or butter melts, stir in the ½ cup sugar, cooking oil, honey and salt. Add the eggs, one at a time, beating well with an electric mixer after each addition.

3 Add the yeast mixture to the egg mixture. Beat in *5 cups* of the flour. Stir in *4 cups* of the remaining flour.

4 Turn the dough onto a well-floured board and knead, gradually working in the remaining *1 cup* flour. Shape into a ball and place in a large greased bowl. Cover and let stand in a warm place for 1½ to 2 hours or until doubled in size.

5 Turn the dough out onto a board and knead in the raisins. Divide the dough into 4 portions. Roll each portion into a 30-inch-long rope. Take one rope and hold down one end as you coil the free end of the rope around it counter-clockwise to form a round spiral or coil.

6 Place the round spiral loaf on a greased baking sheet. Repeat with the remaining ropes. Cover the loaves and let rise for 1 hour. Preheat the oven to 350°.

7 Stir together the egg yolk with the 1 teaspoon water; brush the mixture over the loaves. Sprinkle the loaves with the poppy seed. Bake in the 350° oven for 35 minutes. If necessary, cover the loaves with foil during the last 15 minutes of baking to prevent over browning.

 TIPS FROM OUR KITCHEN

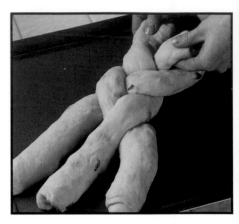

Traditionally, challah is a braided loaf. To make braided loaves: Divide the dough into four equal portions. Then divide each portion into thirds. Roll each into a rope about 14 inches long and place 3 ropes about 1 inch apart on a greased baking sheet. Starting in the middle, braid by bringing the left rope underneath the center rope; lay it down. Then bring the right rope under the new center rope; lay it down. Repeat to the end. Rotate the baking sheet. Beginning once again at the center, braid by bringing the outside ropes alternately over the center rope. Press the rope ends together to seal. Be sure to braid loosely so the bread has room to expand. Repeat with the remaining portions of dough.

Nutrition Analysis (*Per Serving*): Calories: 155 / Cholesterol: 40 mg / Carbohydrates: 25 g / Protein: 4 g / Sodium: 168 mg / Fat: 5 g (Saturated Fat: 1 g) / Potassium: 71 mg.

SABBATH BREAD

Pronounced HA-lah, this egg-rich yeast bread is traditionally eaten by Jews on the Sabbath and on
holidays. Most often, challah bread is braided, but in this recipe, Bok Hurwich of Birmingham,
Alabama, teaches us how to make a beautiful, coiled loaf.

NORTHERN MAINE OATMEAL BREAD

Makes 2 Loaves (32 Servings)

2	cups boiling water
1	tablespoon butter *or* margarine
1	cup rolled oats
1	package active dry yeast
½	cup warm water (110° to 115°F)
½	cup molasses
2	teaspoons salt
5¾ to 6¼	cups all-purpose flour

Melted butter

◆　◆　◆

When Joan moved with her husband from Massachusetts to Maine over 40 years ago, a friend gave her this old Maine recipe to take with her. It's a favorite with family and guests alike, sometimes even outshining the main dish. Joan's friend Millie shapes the dough into rolls, which she claims can transform a turkey sandwich into a gourmet creation.

Mrs. Joan Granger
<u>Merrymeeting Merry Eating</u>
Regional Memorial
Hospital Auxiliary
Brunswick
MAINE

1 In a large mixing bowl, combine the boiling water, butter and rolled oats and let stand for 1 hour (or for 30 minutes if you are using "quick" oats).

2 Dissolve the yeast in the ½ cup warm water. Add the yeast mixture, molasses, salt, and as much flour as you can stir into the oat mixture. Mix thoroughly.

3 On a lightly floured surface, knead the dough for 6 to 8 minutes, adding more flour, if necessary, to form a moderately stiff dough.

4 Place the dough in a greased bowl and turn the dough over once to grease the surface. Cover with a damp cloth and let rise in a warm place until doubled in size (about 45 minutes).

5 Punch the dough down. Divide the dough in half. Cover and let rest for 10 minutes. Shape each portion into a loaf. Place each loaf, seam side down, in a greased 8x4x2-inch or 9x5x3-inch loaf pan and let rise again until almost doubled in size (30 to 40 minutes). Preheat oven to 375°.

6 Bake in the 375° oven about 40 minutes or until bread tests done. Remove the loaves from the pans, brush the tops with melted butter to soften the crusts. Cool the loaves on wire racks.

 TIPS FROM OUR KITCHEN

If you like a rich molasses flavor, use dark molasses rather than light molasses.

There are two ways to shape bread into a basic loaf. One way, shown here, is to roll *each* half of the dough into a 12x8-inch rectangle and roll up tightly, starting at one of the short edges. Another way is to gently pull each half of the dough into a loaf shape and tuck the ends underneath.

For real down-home goodness, slather on the butter and your favorite jam or jelly.

Test for doneness by tapping the loaf with your finger. A hollow sound means the loaf is baked properly.

Nutrition Analysis *(Per Serving)*: Calories: 103 / Cholesterol: 1 mg / Carbohydrates: 21 g / Protein: 3 g / Sodium: 141 mg / Fat: 1 g (Saturated Fat: 0 g) / Potassium: 81 mg.

LOAVES OF GOODNESS

This five-generation recipe from Brunswick, Maine, impressed us with its good, old-fashioned flavor and homemade texture. It is the perfect loaf to cut into thick slices for morning toast or sandwiches.

BUBBLE BREAD

Makes 1 Loaf (12 Servings)
4½ to 5   cups all-purpose flour
2   packages active dry yeast
1   cup milk, scalded
½   cup shortening
½   cup sugar
1   teaspoon salt
2   eggs
1   cup sugar
½   cup finely chopped nuts
1   teaspoon ground cinnamon
½   cup margarine *or* butter, melted

◆   ◆   ◆

When Leola Stone attended her family reunion many years ago, she not only visited with relatives, she also discovered this recipe for Bubble Bread. The bread quickly became a regular feature at family breakfasts. Leola says, "It's easy to make and you don't even need to cut it; you can just pull off a piece." Bubble Bread is a perfect coffee companion and—as the Stone family testifies—a great way to start the day.

Leola Stone
<u>*Between Greene Leaves*</u>
Greene County Homemakers
Extension Association
Carrollton
ILLINOIS

1 Lightly grease a large bowl and grease a 10-inch tube pan; set aside.

2 In a large mixing bowl, stir together *2 cups* of the flour and the yeast. In a saucepan, heat and stir the milk, shortening, the ½ cup sugar and the salt until the mixture is warm (120° to 130°) and the shortening has almost melted. Add the milk mixture to the flour mixture along with the eggs. Beat with an electric mixer on medium speed until combined. Then beat on high speed for 2 minutes more. Using a wooden spoon, stir in as much of the remaining flour as you can.

3 Turn the dough out onto a floured surface. Knead in enough of the remaining flour to make a soft dough that is smooth and elastic (3 to 5 minutes). Shape into a ball.

4 Place the dough in the prepared bowl; turn once to grease the surface. Cover and let it rise in a warm place until the dough has doubled in size (about 1¼ hours). Punch the dough down. Turn it out onto a lightly floured surface. Cover and let rest for 10 minutes.

5 In a small bowl, stir together the 1 cup sugar, the nuts and cinnamon.

6 Divide the dough into 24 pieces. Shape each piece into a ball. Dip each ball in the melted margarine or butter, then roll in the sugar mixture.

7 Place the dough balls in the prepared pan in 3 layers, staggering each layer. Sprinkle the top layer with any remaining sugar mixture. Cover and let the bread rise in a warm place until nearly doubled in size (about 30 minutes). Preheat the oven to 350°.

8 Bake the bread in the 350° oven for 45 minutes or until done. If your pan has a removeable bottom, lift the bread from the bottom of the pan with large spatulas. (You may want to ask someone to lend you a hand.) If your pan does not have a removeable botom, simply invert the bread onto a serving plate. If desired, invert again.

Nutrition Analysis: (*Per Serving*): Calories: 449 / Cholesterol: 37 mg / Carbohydrates: 60 ; Protein: 7 g / Sodium: 303 mg / Fat: 21 g (Saturated Fat: 4 g) / Potassium: 141mg.

OLD-FASHIONED CINNAMON GOODNESS

For a delicious treat, pull off a "bubble" from this traditional, luscious loaf while it is still warm from the oven. Then pour yourself a cup of coffee or tea and settle in to enjoy a well-deserved break.

PETIT PAIN AU CHOCOLAT

Makes 24 Rolls

1	package active dry yeast
¼	cup lukewarm water (105° to 115°)
¾	cup milk
½	cup shortening
½	cup sugar
¾	teaspoon salt
3	eggs, beaten
4½ to 5	cups all-purpose flour
Cooking oil	
2	tablespoons butter *or* margarine, softened
6	milk chocolate bars (about 9 ounces total)
1	egg, beaten

♦   ♦   ♦

Libby Hopkins had pen pals in France and although many people often loose touch with their pen pals, Libby didn't. When she visited France, she met them for the first time and learned how to make this wonderful recipe. Libby is convinced that her French friends will be thrilled to know Petit Pain au Chocolat is featured in a cooking series.

Libby Hopkins
A Century of Good Cooking
Waldoboro Woman's Club
1890-1990
Waldoboro Woman's Club
Waldoboro
MAINE

1 Sprinkle the yeast over the lukewarm water. Stir until dissolved. Set aside.

2 In a small saucepan, heat the milk, shortening, sugar and salt to lukewarm (105° to 115°). Transfer the mixture to a large bowl. Stir in the 3 beaten eggs. Using a wooden spoon, beat in *2 cups* of the flour until the batter is almost smooth. Stir in the yeast mixture, then *2½ cups* of the flour. Form the dough into a ball.

3 Lightly brush the top of the dough with the cooking oil; cover with a clean towel. Let rise in a warm place (about 85°) until doubled in size (about 1 hour).

4 Punch down the dough. Turn the dough out onto a lightly floured surface. Knead in enough of the remaining flour to make a moderately soft dough that is smooth and elastic (3 to 5 minutes total). Cover and let the dough rest for 10 minutes.

5 On a lightly floured surface, roll *half* of the dough to a ¼-inch thickness. Using a 3½-inch round cutter, cut the dough into 12 circles. Pat or gently stretch each circle into a 4½-inch oval. Spread with the softened butter or margarine. Repeat with the remaining dough.

6 Divide the chocolate bars into 24 equal portions. Place *one* chocolate portion on *each* dough oval, breaking the chocolate pieces as necessary to fit. Pinch the long sides together to seal. Place the rolls, seam side down, on an ungreased baking sheet.

7 Cover the rolls and let rise in a warm place until doubled in size (about 30 minutes). Brush the rolls generously with the 1 beaten egg.

8 Preheat the oven to 375°. Bake the rolls in the 375° oven for 12 to 15 minutes or until the tops are golden. If desired, sprinkle the rolls with *powdered sugar* and serve either warm or cool.

 TIPS FROM OUR KITCHEN

If you don't have a 3½-inch round cutter, use an empty 6⅛-ounce tuna can to cut the circles.

To reheat the rolls, wrap them in foil. Then bake the rolls in a 350° oven for 15 to 20 minutes or until warm.

Nutrition Analysis (*Per Roll*): Calories: 213 / Cholesterol: 39 mg / Carbohydrates: 27 g / Protein: 4 g / Sodium: 102 mg / Fat: 10 g (Saturated Fat: 4 g) / Potassium: 92 mg.

A TASTE OF FRANCE

The name, Petit Pain au Chocolat (meaning Little Chocolate Breads) does little to describe the
delightful experience of biting into these seemingly ordinary, although appealing, rolls and finding a
pocket of gooey chocolate hidden within. Your family will be shouting, "Vive la France!"

CARROT CLOVERLEAF ROLLS

Makes 18 Rolls

4	medium carrots, peeled and sliced (2 cups)
1	cup milk
⅓	cup packed brown sugar
6	tablespoons butter *or* margarine
½	teaspoon salt
1	package active dry yeast
4½ to 5	cups all-purpose flour

Melted butter *or* margarine (optional)

♦　　♦　　♦

Vicky Kozel said that when her family was home, "there wasn't a week that went by that I didn't bake at least two to three times—baking was my first love." Vicky said that she had quite a few recipes, many of them for yeast breads. Carrot Cloverleaf Rolls were a part of her repertoire. Vicky told us that this particular recipe is similar to icebox rolls, but there's a surprise—carrots!

Vicky Kozel
Plum Good
The Christ Child Society of Cleveland
Chagrin Falls
OHIO

1 In a medium saucepan, cook the carrots, covered, in a small amount of *boiling water* about 25 minutes or until they are very tender; drain. Transfer the carrots to a pie plate. Using a potato masher, mash the carrots.

2 Transfer *1 cup* of the mashed carrot to the saucepan. Refrigerate the remaining mashed carrot in a covered container for another use.

3 Add the milk, brown sugar, the 6 tablespoons butter or margarine and the salt to the mashed carrots in the saucepan. Heat until the butter or margarine almost melts (120° to 130°), stirring constantly.

4 In a large mixing bowl, combine the yeast and *1½ cups* of the flour. Add the carrot mixture. Beat with an electric mixer on low speed for 30 seconds, scraping the sides of the bowl. Beat for 3 minutes on high speed. Using a wooden spoon, stir in as much of the remaining flour as you can.

5 Turn the dough out onto a lightly floured surface. Knead in enough of the remaining flour to make a moderately stiff dough (6 to 8 minutes). Place the dough in a greased bowl, turning once to grease the surface of the dough. Cover and let rise in a warm place until doubled in size (about 1 hour). Punch the dough down; let rest for 10 minutes.

6 Grease 18 muffin cups. Divide the dough into 18 equal portions. Shape *each* portion into 3 equal balls. Place *3* balls into *each* greased muffin cup. Cover and let the rolls rise for 30 to 45 minutes or until almost doubled in size.

7 Preheat the oven to 375°. Bake in the 375° oven for 20 to 25 minutes or until the rolls are browned and they sound hollow when lightly tapped.

8 If desired, while the rolls are still hot, brush the tops with the melted butter or margarine.

 TIPS FROM OUR KITCHEN

To freeze the rolls, cool them completely and then seal in a freezer bag or container; freeze. For the best quality, use within 3 months. Thaw in the package for 1 hour or reheat in foil in a 300° oven for 20 minutes.

Nutrition Analysis (*Per Roll*): Calories: 174 / Cholesterol: 13 mg / Carbohydrates: 28 g / Protein: 4 g / Sodium: 123 mg / Fat: 5 g (Saturated Fat: 3 g) / Potassium: 110 mg.

LOVE ME TENDER

Tender, golden Carrot Cloverleaf Rolls will add a little something special to your next soup-and-salad supper. Try serving them with an herb butter, such as one made with dill, marjoram or thyme.

HOT CROSS BUNS

Makes 20 Buns
Buns:

- 1 cup milk
- ⅓ cup sugar
- ⅓ cup shortening
- ½ teaspoon salt
- 2 packages active dry yeast
- ¼ cup lukewarm water
- 2 eggs, beaten
- ⅔ cup currants
- 1 teaspoon ground cinnamon
- 4½ to 5 cups all-purpose flour

Icing:
- ½ cup sifted powdered sugar
- ¼ teaspoon vanilla
- 2 to 3 teaspoons milk

◆   ◆   ◆

For four generations, women in Blanche Brobeil Spaulding's family have been making her grandmother's recipe for Hot Cross Buns during Lent. Blanche's children say that memories of their mom's baking are so strong that when they call her from Wichita, New York City and Chicago, they can smell Hot Cross Buns baking in the oven.

Blanche Brobeil Spaulding
The Thresher Table
Bethel College
Women's Association
North Newton
KANSAS

1 Scald the milk. While hot, transfer to a large mixing bowl and add the sugar, shortening and salt. Cool to lukewarm.

2 Dissolve the yeast in the lukewarm water and add to the milk mixture.

3 Add the eggs, currants and cinnamon. Stir in as much flour as you can with a wooden spoon.

4 On a lightly floured surface, knead in enough of the remaining flour to make a moderately soft dough that is smooth and elastic (3 to 5 minutes).

5 Place the dough in a greased bowl and turn once to grease the surface. Cover and let the dough rise until it is doubled in size (about 45 minutes).

6 Punch the dough down. Cover and let the dough rest for 10 minutes more.

7 Divide the dough into 20 portions. Shape into smooth balls. Place the balls 2 to 2½ inches apart onto large greased baking sheets. Cover and let rise until they are nearly doubled in size (about 20 minutes).

8 Preheat oven to 350°. Mark a crisscross on each bun with a sharp knife. Bake in the 350° oven about 20 minutes or until lightly browned. Remove from the baking sheets and cool on wire racks.

9 To make the icing: In a small bowl, stir together the powdered sugar, vanilla and enough milk to make the icing a piping consistency. When the buns are cool, pipe the icing along the crosses on top of the buns.

 TIPS FROM OUR KITCHEN

If you don't have a decorating bag to pipe the icing, make one from a plastic sandwich bag. Place the icing in the bag and force it into one corner. Then cut off a small tip from the corner.

Nutrition Analysis *(Per Bun)*: Calories: 175 / Cholesterol: 22 mg / Carbohydrates: 30 g / Protein: 4 g / Sodium: 67 mg / Fat: 4 g (Saturated Fat: 1 g) / Potassium: 110 mg.

Morning Welcome

The aroma of these tender, slightly sweet buns mingled with the scent of freshly brewed coffee will work better than an alarm clock to get your family to the breakfast table.

STUFFED FRENCH TOAST

Makes 10 Servings

10 1½-inch-thick slices French bread
1 8-ounce package cream cheese, softened
1 10-ounce jar apricot jam *or* orange marmalade
4 eggs
1 cup milk
2 tablespoons sugar
1 teaspoon vanilla
¼ teaspoon ground nutmeg *or* ground cinnamon
  Margarine, butter *or* cooking oil
  Maple-flavored syrup *or* maple syrup (optional)

◆ ◆ ◆

Very Innovative Parties is a source book for party inspiration. The cookbook includes sixty complete party ideas and 450 outstanding recipes, which range from quick and easy to gourmet. Profits from cookbook sales are used to help the Loma Linda University Dental Auxiliary in their efforts to support missionary work conducted by the health professions.

Very Innovative Parties
Loma Linda University Dental Auxiliary
Loma Linda
CALIFORNIA

1 Using a serrated knife, carefully cut a pocket in the middle of each bread slice, cutting ¾ of the way through.

2 Spread the cream cheese and jam or marmalade in each of the prepared pockets, dividing the full amount of both among the slices.

3 Place the stuffed slices, cut sides down, in a 13x9x2-inch baking pan.

4 In a small mixing bowl, beat together the eggs, milk, sugar, vanilla and nutmeg or cinnamon.

5 Pour *half* of the egg mixture over the slices and let stand until the bread has absorbed the mixture. Turn the slices over and pour the remaining egg mixture over the slices. Let stand until all of the egg mixture has been absorbed by the bread slices.

6 In a large skillet or on a griddle over medium heat, cook the stuffed bread in a small amount of hot margarine, butter or cooking oil for 2 to 3 minutes on each side or until golden brown. Add more margarine, butter or cooking oil as needed. Serve with syrup, if desired.

 TIPS FROM OUR KITCHEN

If you prefer to cook all the slices at once, try baking them. Place the soaked bread on a greased baking sheet. Bake in a 450° oven for 7 minutes. Turn the bread and bake 8 minutes more or until golden.

If desired, use reduced-fat cream cheese, skim milk and reduced-calorie syrup.

It may seem like the bread is stuffed with a lot of filling, but it won't be too much after the bread slices cook.

Pure maple syrup can be quite expensive because of the labor-intensive process involved in producing it. Maple-flavored syrup is less expensive because it is a combination of a less costly syrup, such as corn syrup, and a small amount of maple syrup. Pure maple syrup has a more subtle maple flavor, is thinner and is not as sweet as maple-flavored syrup.

Nutrition Analysis (*Per Serving*): Calories: 426 / Cholesterol: 112 mg / Carbohydrates: 60 g
Protein: 12 g / Sodium: 522 mg / Fat: 16 g (Saturated Fat: 7 g) / Potassium: 176 mg.

POCKET-FULL OF FLAVOR

Here's how to win the reputation for cooking the best breakfast in town. These yummy breakfast "sandwiches" will please family and guests alike. Just make a big pot of coffee and enjoy.

SPOON BREAD

Makes 6 to 8 Servings

1   cup cornmeal
3   cups milk
2   tablespoons shortening
1   teaspoon baking powder
1   teaspoon salt
3   egg yolks, beaten
3   egg whites

◆   ◆   ◆

Although Agnes Pearcy had never heard of Spoon Bread when she tried it for the first time at a luncheon in Oklahoma City in 1947, Spoon Bread was already an established favorite dish in that area. Since then, she has served it to many a skeptical friend—several who had not heard of Spoon Bread either— and always with success. Agnes suggests serving this bread with chicken, in place of potatoes or rice. We predict that your guests will return for seconds and thirds.

Agnes M. Pearcy
Charity's Cherished Recipes
DePaul Health Center
Auxiliary
Bridgeton
MISSOURI

1 Preheat the oven to 350°. Grease a 2-quart square baking dish. Set aside.

2 In a medium mixing bowl, stir together the cornmeal and *1 cup* of the milk.

3 In a 2-quart saucepan, over medium heat, warm the remaining 2 cups milk. Slowly stir the cornmeal mixture into the hot milk. Reduce the heat to low and cook, stirring frequently, for 10 minutes (mixture will be thick). Remove from heat.

4 In a clean, medium mixing bowl using an electric mixer, beat the egg whites until they hold stiff peaks (tips stand straight). Set aside.

5 Stir the shortening, baking powder and salt into the cornmeal-milk mixture. Stir in the beaten egg yolks. Fold in the beaten egg whites.

6 Turn the mixture into the prepared baking dish. Bake, uncovered, in the 350° oven for 40 to 45 minutes or until a knife inserted into the center comes out clean. Serve hot.

TIPS FROM OUR KITCHEN

It is necessary to stir the cornmeal-milk mixture frequently while it is cooking so that it thickens uniformly. Cook over low heat and be aware that the mixture will "pop" occasionally.

For variety, add 2 tablespoons sliced green onion or chopped green chili peppers, or ½ cup grated Parmesan cheese to the Spoon Bread batter.

For a boost in flavor, use margarine or butter in place of the shortening.

Nutrition Analysis (*Per Serving*): Calories: 227 / Cholesterol: 116 mg / Carbohydrates: 24 Protein: 9 g / Sodium: 503 mg / Fat: 10 g (Saturated Fat: 3 g) / Potassium: 257 mg.

COZY COMFORT FOOD

There is something about eating food with a spoon that brings many of us back to the comforting
feelings of childhood. To keep everyone at the table cozy and warm, serve this Southern
standard with a piping hot, hearty soup or stew.

ORANGE DATE-NUT BREAD

Makes 1 Loaf (18 Servings)

1	cup snipped dates
4	teaspoons finely shredded orange peel
⅔	cup boiling water
⅓	cup orange juice, freshly squeezed
¾	cup sugar
2	tablespoons shortening
1	beaten egg
1	teaspoon vanilla
2	cups all-purpose flour
1	teaspoon baking powder
½	teaspoon baking soda
¼	teaspoon salt
½	cup chopped nuts

♦ ♦ ♦

St. Melany's Byzantine Parish originally consisted of 35 families, and services were held in the homes of the parishioners. Eventually the growing parish found it necessary to move the services to a church. To help generate funds to purchase a building, the parishioners put together the Around the World Cookbook. *Chairperson Marcella Leight tells us that this project, "was a lot of hard work, but a lot of fun."*

Around the World Cookbook
St. Melany's Byzantine
Catholic Church
Tucson
ARIZONA

1 Preheat the oven to 350°. Grease a 9x5x3-inch loaf pan. Set aside.

2 In a large bowl, combine the snipped dates and shredded orange peel. Stir in the boiling water and orange juice.

3 Add the sugar, shortening, egg and vanilla, stirring until just mixed.

4 In a small bowl, stir together the flour, baking powder, baking soda and salt. Add the flour mixture to the date mixture and mix well. Stir in the nuts. Pour the batter into the prepared pan.

5 Bake in the 350° oven for 45 to 50 minutes or until a wooden toothpick inserted near the center comes out clean.

6 Cool the bread for 10 minutes in the pan. Then, remove the bread from the pan and cool thoroughly on a wire rack. Wrap and store the bread overnight.

 TIPS FROM OUR KITCHEN

Many quick-bread recipes suggest wrapping and storing the loaves overnight before slicing. This allows the flavors to mellow and also makes the loaves easier to slice. After baking, let the loaf cool completely on a wire rack, then wrap it in foil or plastic wrap and store at room temperature overnight.

Pre-chopped dates are available in many stores. They have a slight sugar coating to prevent them from sticking together in the package, but that won't affect the recipe. To snip the dates yourself, use kitchen shears. Dip the shears in water between snips.

Grease the loaf pan on the bottom and only 1 inch up the sides. This will eliminate a rim from forming around the edge of the baked loaf.

To make this recipe, you'll need one medium orange for the juice and peel. Choose an orange that feels heavy for its size and allow it to come to room temperature to get the most juice.

Nutrition Analysis: (*Per Serving*): Calories: 121 / Cholesterol: 12 mg / Carbohydrates: 21 g / Protein: 2 g / Sodium: 58 mg / Fat: 4 g (Saturated Fat: 1 g) / Potassium: 101 mg.

CAN'T WAIT

We won't blame you if you don't take our advice to store this bread overnight before eating it. While the
waiting period will make the loaf easier to slice and will help the flavors to mellow, it sure
isn't easy to resist digging into this delicious bread while it's still warm from the oven.

BREADS, MUFFINS & SANDWICHES

CRISPY CORNSTICKS

Makes 14 Cornsticks

1   cup yellow cornmeal
½   cup all-purpose flour
2½ teaspoons baking powder
1   teaspoon sugar
½   teaspoon salt
⅛   teaspoon baking soda
2   eggs
1   cup buttermilk
2   tablespoons cooking oil

◆   ◆   ◆

If you grew up in the South, muffins, biscuits, corn bread and cornsticks were a part of your everyday meal. Frances Jolley Syfan said that she makes her Crispy Cornsticks the old southern way—in a hot cornstick pan—"preheating the cornstick pan gives you more of a crispy crust, with a tender inside." She also said that when she has soup, it's just not complete unless she has Crispy Cornsticks with it.

Frances Jolley Syfan
Perennials: A Southern Celebration of Foods and Flavors
The Junior Service League of Gainesville, Georgia
Gainesville
GEORGIA

1 Preheat the oven to 450°. Heavily grease cornstick pans and place them in the oven to heat.

2 Meanwhile, in a medium bowl, stir together the cornmeal, flour, baking powder, sugar, salt and baking soda. Make a well in the center; set aside.

3 In a small bowl, mix together the eggs, buttermilk and cooking oil. Add the egg mixture to the dry ingredients all at once. Stir by hand just until smooth.

4 Transfer the mixture to a large sturdy plastic bag. Cut off one corner. Carefully squeeze the mixture into the hot cornstick pans.

5 Bake in the 450° for 10 to 12 minutes or until the cornsticks are golden.

 TIPS FROM OUR KITCHEN

For corn bread, you can bake this batter in a 9-inch square pan; bake in a 450° oven for 25 minutes.

To reheat the cornsticks: Place them on a plate and cover with paper towels. Micro-cook on 100% power (high) for 15 seconds for 2 cornsticks, or for 20 to 25 seconds for 4 cornsticks.

This recipe also can be baked in shaped iron bakeware pans to make cactus, fish, hearts or other shapes. Follow the directions provided for using the pan.

Nutrition Analysis (*Per Cornstick*): Calories: 88 / Cholesterol: 31 mg / Carbohydrates: 12 g / Protein: 3 g / Sodium: 117 mg / Fat: 3 g (Saturated Fat: 1 g) / Potassium: 57 mg.

HOT FROM THE OVEN

These southern-style breads are most delicious when eaten while they are still hot from the oven. You can enjoy them in many ways—plain with soups and stews, spread with honey butter or topped with creamed chicken or turkey.

SOUR MILK BISCUITS

Makes 24 Biscuits
4¼ cups all-purpose flour
1 tablespoon plus 1 teaspoon baking powder
1 teaspoon baking soda
¾ teaspoon salt
½ cup shortening
2 cups sour milk *or* buttermilk

♦   ♦   ♦

Back in 1819, the small town of Etna, New Hampshire, gathered for its very first community Chicken Pie Supper. Grandma Derby made her famous chicken pie and Bertha LaBombard contributed her light, flaky Sour Milk Biscuits—and the town had a bona fide annual hit on its hands. Rumor has it that people came from miles around—by horse and buggy, no less—just to get a taste. Today, 219,000 suppers later, Etna still gathers for their Chicken Pie Suppers, raising funds for their com-munity and satisfying hungry townsfolk in one grand feast.

Bertha LaBombard
Hanover Center Cooks
Etna
NEW HAMPSHIRE

1 Preheat oven to 400°. Lightly grease 2 baking sheets. Or, for soft-sided biscuits, lightly grease 2 round baking pans.

2 In a large bowl, stir together the flour, baking powder, baking soda and salt. Using a pastry blender or 2 knives, cut in the shortening until the mixture resembles coarse crumbs. Gradually stir in the sour milk or buttermilk until a soft dough forms.

3 Turn the dough out onto a lightly floured surface. Gently knead the dough for 10 to 12 strokes.

4 On a lightly floured surface, pat or roll the dough out to a ½-inch thickness. If necessary, add a little flour to the surface of the dough or rolling pin to keep the dough from sticking.

5 Using a 2½-inch biscuit cutter, cut out as many dough rounds as possible. Dip the biscuit cutter into flour between cuts to help prevent sticking. Press the cutter straight down to get straight-sided biscuits. Do not twist the cutter or flatten the biscuit edges.

6 Carefully transfer the cut biscuits to the prepared baking sheets or baking pans. For crusty-sided biscuits, place the rounds about 1 inch apart on the baking sheets. For soft-sided biscuits, place the rounds close together in the pans.

7 Bake in the 400° oven about 15 minutes or until the biscuits are puffed and golden. Serve the biscuits warm.

 TIPS FROM OUR KITCHEN

To make sour milk: In a 2-cup glass measure, place 2 tablespoons vinegar. Add enough milk to make 2 cups. Let the milk mixture stand at room temperature for 5 minutes before using.

Nutrition Analysis (*Per Biscuit*): Calories: 117 / Cholesterol: 1 mg / Carbohydrates: 16 g / Protein: 3 g / Sodium: 177 mg / Fat: 5 g (Saturated Fat: 1 g) / Potassium: 52 mg.

FLAKY AND FABULOUS!

These light, flaky biscuits are a terrific breakfast treat served with honey or your favorite jam or jelly.
They also make super snack-size sandwiches. Just split them in half and fill them with thinly
sliced roast beef, turkey or ham.

APPLE STREUSEL MUFFINS

Makes 18 Muffins

Muffins:

2	cups all-purpose flour
1	cup sugar
1¼	teaspoons ground cinnamon
1	teaspoon baking powder
½	teaspoon baking soda
½	teaspoon salt
2	eggs
1	8-ounce carton dairy sour cream
¼	cup margarine *or* butter, melted
1	cup finely chopped unpeeled apples

Streusel Topping:

¼	cup sugar
3	tablespoons all-purpose flour
¼	teaspoon ground cinnamon
2	tablespoons margarine *or* butter

✦   ✦   ✦

"You know how college kids are—they always love mom's cooking!" Mary Livelsberger often treated her children to Apple Streusel Muffins when they were home on college breaks, and the muffins were frequently part of a typical Livelsberger breakfast.

Mary Livelsberger
The Flavor and Spice
of Holy Cross Life
Holy Cross Parish
Batavia
ILLINOIS

1 Preheat the oven to 400°. Generously grease 18 muffin cups or line them with paper bake cups; set aside.

2 To make the muffins: In a large bowl, stir together the flour, sugar, cinnamon, baking powder, baking soda and salt.

3 In a small mixing bowl, beat the eggs. Stir in the sour cream and the ¼ cup melted margarine or butter. Add the egg mixture to the flour mixture along with the chopped apples. Stir just until moistened.

4 Spoon the batter into the prepared muffin cups filling them ⅔ full.

5 To make the Streusel Topping: In a small bowl, stir together the sugar, flour and cinnamon. Using a pastry blender, cut in the 2 tablespoons margarine or butter until the mixture resembles coarse crumbs. Sprinkle a portion of the topping on each muffin.

6 Bake the muffins in the 400° oven for 20 to 25 minutes or until the tops are golden.

 TIPS FROM OUR KITCHEN

To reduce some of the fat and calories in these muffins, use light sour cream instead of the regular sour cream.

To reheat room-temperature muffins, wrap one in a paper towel and micro-cook on 100% power (high) for 15 to 20 seconds. To reheat frozen muffins, wrap one in a paper towel and micro-cook on 100% power (high) for 30 to 45 seconds.

When making muffins, avoid over-stirring after the liquid ingredients are added; some lumps should remain. If you stir until the batter is smooth, the resulting muffins will have pointed tops, tunnels and a tougher texture.

Nutrition Analysis (*Per Muffin*): Calories: 176 / Cholesterol: 29 mg / Carbohydrates: 26 g / Protein: 3 g / Sodium: 142 mg / Fat: 7 g (Saturated Fat: 3 g) / Potassium: 50 mg.

TOP THIS!

The topping is what makes these muffins "tops" in our book. The word *streusel* comes from a German word meaning "something strewn" and refers to the crumbly mixture that is sprinkled over these down-home apple muffins.

MORNING GLORY MUFFINS

Makes 18 Muffins
- 2 cups all-purpose flour
- 1 cup sugar
- 2 teaspoons baking powder
- 2 teaspoons ground cinnamon
- ½ teaspoon baking soda
- ¼ teaspoon salt
- 2 cups finely shredded carrot
- 1 cup finely chopped apple
- ½ cup raisins
- ½ cup chopped nuts
- ½ cup shredded coconut
- 3 eggs
- ¾ cup cooking oil
- 2 teaspoons vanilla

❖   ❖   ❖

Ruth Matthews's recipe for Morning Glory Muffins is an old family favorite, given to her by her mother. Ruth tells us that she especially likes to serve the muffins around the holidays and to special visitors. We love this recipe just as it is, but if you'd like a different twist, try substituting shredded zucchini for all or part of the shredded carrot.

Ruth Matthews
What's Cooking at Northmont
Women's Christian Service
Organization, Northmont
United Presbyterian Church
Pittsburgh
PENNSYLVANIA

1 Preheat the oven to 350°. Lightly grease eighteen 2½-inch muffin cups or line them with paper bake cups.

2 In a large mixing bowl, stir together the flour, sugar, baking powder, cinnamon, baking soda and salt. Stir in the carrot, apple, raisins, nuts and coconut.

3 In a separate bowl, stir together the eggs, cooking oil and vanilla. Add the liquid ingredients all at once to the flour mixture and stir just until moistened.

4 Gently spoon the batter into the prepared muffin cups until each one is almost full.

5 Bake in the 350° oven about 30 minutes or until the top of a muffin springs back when lightly touched. Cool in the pan set on a wire rack for 5 minutes. Remove the muffins from the pan and cool on the rack. Serve warm or at room temperature.

 TIPS FROM OUR KITCHEN

The fastest way to get two cups of shredded carrot is to use a food processor fitted with a shredding blade. Follow the directions that came with your machine. The finer the shred, the more readily the carrot will become part of the batter.

This batter is naturally lumpy due to all of the extra ingredients. When adding the liquid ingredients to the flour mixture, do not overmix or your muffins will have peaked tops and a tough, heavy texture.

Nutrition Analysis *(Per Muffin)*: Calories: 231 / Cholesterol: 36 mg / Carbohydrates: 28 mg Protein: 3 g / Sodium: 101 mg / Fat: 12 g (Saturated Fat: 2 g) / Potassium: 132 mg.

OH, WHAT A BEAUTIFUL MORNING!

You'll be ready to climb a mountain, or at least speed through a day's worth of chores, after finishing just one of these energizing muffins. They are packed with shredded carrots and apples, raisins, nuts, coconut and—most of all—flavor.

BLUEBERRY-LEMON MUFFINS

Makes 12 Muffins

1¾   cups all-purpose flour
½   cup sugar
2½   teaspoons baking powder
¾   teaspoon salt
1 to 2   teaspoons grated lemon
       peel
1   egg, beaten
¾   cup milk
⅓   cup cooking oil
1   cup blueberries
2   tablespoons butter, melted

❖ ❖ ❖

In 1986, Minnesota school-children wondered: if they had a state food, what it would be? Wild blueberries? They grow all over northern Minnesota and are so popular. What about wheat? Many farmers in the state produce wheat. Among a growing population of "blueberry backers," 17 third graders from Carlton, Minnesota, "scored sweet political victory" when their blueberry muffin became law. We think these Blueberry-Lemon Muffins are fine examples of both democracy and flavor at their very best.

Janelle House
More Cooking in Minnesota
Minneapolis
MINNESOTA

1 Preheat oven to 400°.

2 Lightly grease or place paper liners in twelve 2½ inch muffin cups.

3 In a medium bowl, stir together the flour, *¼ cup* of the sugar, the baking powder and salt. Stir in the grated lemon peel.

4 In a large bowl, beat the egg with the milk and oil. Add the flour mixture to the egg mixture, stirring just to combine the ingredients. Be careful not to beat the batter too much; it should still have a few lumps.

5 Toss the blueberries with *2 tablespoons* of the sugar. Fold the blueberries into the batter. Spoon the batter into the prepared cups, filling them only ⅔ full.

6 Bake the muffins in the 400° oven for 20 to 25 minutes or until a wooden toothpick inserted in the centers comes out clean. While the muffins are warm, dip the tops in the melted butter, then in the remaining sugar.

TIPS FROM OUR KITCHEN

When grating lemon peel, be careful to remove only the yellow part of the rind. If you grate the white part of the peel, it will add a bitter taste.

If you're watching your sodium intake, we suggest you reduce the salt to ¼ teaspoon.

If fresh blueberries aren't in season, substitute frozen berries—you don't even have to thaw the berries before using them. We think these muffins taste great either way!

Nutrition Analysis *(Per Muffin):* Calories: 183 / Cholesterol: 24 mg / Carbohydrates: 24 g / Protein: 3 g / Sodium: 216 mg / Fat: 9 g (Saturated Fat: 2 g) / Potassium: 59 mg.

MINNESOTA TASTE TREATS

Muffins are not just for breakfast. They are also great snacks that can provide a quick boost of energy.
This yummy muffin recipe hails from Minnesota, where the state legislature named the blueberry
muffin the official State Muffin. You'll love the hint of lemon and the sugar-frosted topping.

SUPER DAGWOOD SANDWICH

Makes 8 Servings

1   1-pound loaf French bread
2   tablespoons butter *or mar-
    garine*, softened (optional)
8   ounces thinly sliced fully
    cooked ham
6   ounces sliced Provolone
    cheese
3   tablespoons Thousand
    Island dressing
4   ounces thinly sliced turkey
4   ounces thinly sliced salami
2   tablespoons butter *or
    margarine*, melted
1   tablespoon toasted sesame
    seed

❖   ❖   ❖

*Mae Louise Murnan told us that
when she's hosting a card party,
she often makes Super Dagwood
Sandwiches and refrigerates them
before her guests arrive. As they're
playing the last hand, Mae just
pops the sandwiches into the oven
and they're ready by the end of
the game. Mae also recommends
serving these sandwiches with a
tossed salad at lunch.*

Mae Louise Murnan
<u>Friends of Sappington
House Cookbook</u>
The Thomas Sappington House
Foundation
Crestwood
MISSOURI

1 Preheat the oven to 400°.

2 Using an electric or a serrated knife, slice the bread horizontally into 3 equal pieces.

3 Spread the first piece with *half* of the softened butter or margarine (if using). Top with the ham, Provolone cheese and *half* of the Thousand Island dressing.

4 Place the second piece of the bread on top. Spread with the remaining softened butter or margarine (if using).

5 Top with the turkey, salami, the remaining Thousand Island dressing and the top slice of bread. Place the loaf on a baking sheet.

6 Stir together the 2 tablespoons melted butter or margarine and the sesame seed. Brush the mixture over the top and sides of the loaf. Cover loosely with foil.

7 Bake in the 400° oven for 10 minutes. Remove the foil and bake for 5 minutes more. Slice to serve.

 TIPS FROM OUR KITCHEN

To toast sesame seed, spread in a thin layer in a shallow, ungreased baking pan. Bake in a 350° oven for 10 to 15 minutes, stirring once or twice. Sesame seed tends to become rancid quickly because of the high amount of oil it contains. Store sesame seed in the refrigerator or freezer.

This is a recipe that adapts well to individual creativity. You can substitute other regular, low-calorie and nonfat dressings, as well as other meat and cheese combinations.

If you prefer a cold sandwich, you can also add lettuce, sprouts and/or slices of tomato, onion and/or green sweet pepper.

Nutrition Analysis (*Per Serving*): Calories: 402 / Cholesterol: 56 mg / Carbohydrates: 31 g / Protein: 25 g / Sodium: 1218 mg / Fat: 20 g (Saturated Fat: 8 g) / Potassium: 283 mg.

HEAPED HERO

What's on the plate? It's a sub! It's a hoagie! No—it's a Super Dagwood Sandwich! Fuel hero-size
appetites with this magnificent giant sandwich—packed to the brim with
delicious ingredients.

MONTE CRISTO SANDWICHES

Makes 6 Sandwiches

Margarine *or* butter, melted
3 eggs, slightly beaten
⅓ cup milk
12 slices sandwich bread
6 slices Swiss cheese, cut in half
6 slices boiled ham
Powdered sugar (optional)
Currant jelly (optional)

◆ ◆ ◆

These Monte Cristo Sandwiches are Ann Elliott's adaptation of the popular sandwiches one finds in Midwestern restaurants. Ann's sandwiches are also quite popular. She tells us that a friend's husband always ordered Monte Cristos whenever he had a chance, so Ann gave his wife the recipe. Now he's able to have his favorite sandwich at home, too. Ann has several suggestions for those who are watching their fat intake, including eliminating the margarine or butter by cooking the sandwiches in a non-stick pan, and using skim milk and light cheese.

Ann Elliott
The Art of Cooking in the 80s
Mayfair Lioness Club
Chicago
ILLINOIS

1 Preheat the oven to 425°. Using a pastry brush, generously grease a 15x10x1-inch baking pan with the melted margarine or butter.

2 In a shallow dish, combine the eggs and milk.

3 For each sandwich, cover one slice of bread with a half slice of cheese, a slice of ham, then a second half slice of cheese. Top with a second slice of bread.

4 Dip each sandwich in the egg-milk mixture, taking care to coat each of the bread slices. Place the sandwiches in the prepared baking pan. Bake in the 425° oven for 15 minutes, turning once.

5 Transfer the sandwiches to a warm serving dish. If desired, sprinkle with powered sugar and serve with currant jelly.

 TIPS FROM OUR KITCHEN

Choose a firm-textured white or whole wheat bread. Both slices of the bread should be fairly well soaked in the egg-milk mixture so they remain soft beneath their crisply browned surfaces.

Another method of cooking these sandwiches is to grill them on a griddle or in a greased skillet. This is a higher-calorie option.

A thin slice of turkey can be added to the sandwich or substituted for the ham.

Spread the bread with Dijon-style mustard before adding the meat and cheese for a tangy variation.

Fresh fruit makes a tasty accompaniment to these sandwiches.

Nutrition Analysis (*Per Sandwich*): Calories: 357 / Cholesterol: 142 mg / Carbohydrates: 26 g
Protein: 22 g / Sodium: 736 mg / Fat: 18 g (Saturated Fat: 8 g) / Potassium: 238 mg.

ALL WRAPPED UP

Melted Swiss cheese and ham are enveloped in a French toast wrapper to create a rich and delicious meal-in-a-sandwich. Ann Elliott of Chicago, Illinois, gives us her unique time-and calorie-saving cooking method.

CUCUMBER SANDWICHES

Makes 10 to 20 Sandwiches

- ½ cup water
- ⅓ cup cider vinegar
- ½ teaspoon salt
- 1 small cucumber, peeled and sliced
- 10 slices day-old white bread *or* firm-textured bread
- 2 tablespoons butter *or* margarine, softened
- 4 ounces cream cheese, softened
- 2 tablespoons mayonnaise *or* salad dressing
- ½ teaspoon Worcestershire sauce
- ⅛ teaspoon pepper
- ⅛ teaspoon garlic salt

♦ ♦ ♦

Critics' Choice Chairperson Mrs. Carl Norwood says that she has been eating Mrs. Everett Meeks's Cucumber Sandwiches ever since she can remember. Mrs. Norwood tells us that she serves them to her guests at teas, garden club parties and at her Christmas buffet. She warns us that if we serve Cucumber Sandwiches, we shouldn't expect to have any leftovers.

Mrs. Everett Meeks
Critics' Choice
The Guild of Corinth
Theatre Arts
Corinth
MISSISSIPPI

1 In a medium bowl, stir together the water, vinegar and salt. Add the cucumber slices and soak for 30 minutes. Drain the cucumbers and pat dry.

2 Using a 1½-to 2-inch round cookie or hors d'oeuvre cutter, cut the bread into shapes. Spread each shape lightly with butter.

3 In a small bowl, stir together the cream cheese and mayonnaise. Add the Worcestershire sauce, pepper and garlic salt. Spread the mixture onto the buttered side of the bread. Using a butter knife, spread the mixture smoothly and evenly.

4 Place 1 cucumber slice on top of the cream cheese mixture on half of the bread shapes. Place one of the remaining cream cheese mixture covered bread shapes on top of each of the cucumber slices, cream cheese side down. Press each sandwich gently together.

5 Place the sandwiches on a cookie sheet that has been covered with a slightly damp towel. Cover the sandwiches with another slightly damp towel, then cover with plastic wrap. Chill for at least 3 hours before serving. Refrigerate leftover sandwiches for up to two days.

 TIPS FROM OUR KITCHEN

For a change of pace, cut these sandwiches into fanciful shapes, such as stars or diamonds. Just be sure to match the size of your cookie or hors d'oeuvre cutter to the size of your cucumber slices.

Use your imagination to decorate the sandwiches. Bits of fresh dill, pimiento and red pepper, and slices of fresh cucumber add flavor and color.

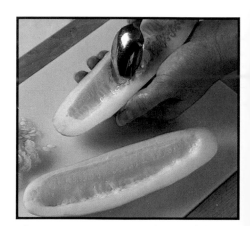

If you are using a cucumber with large seeds, cut the cucumber in half lengthwise and scoop out the seeds. Then slice the cucumber halves.

Nutrition Analysis *(Per Sandwich)*: Calories: 149 / Cholesterol: 20 mg / Carbohydrates: 14 Protein: 3 g / Sodium: 284 mg / Fat: 9 g (Saturated Fat: 4 g) / Potassium: 80 mg.

TEA TIME TREAT

Dust off your finest china teapot, cups and saucers and indulge in a bit of afternoon elegance.
Cucumber Sandwiches, cut into dainty shapes and garnished with pimiento, dill and
fresh cucumber. are as tasty as they are pretty.

Cakes & Cookies

*C*ompetition for the best cake and cookie recipes from community cookbooks is rigorous, but we've collected the cream of the crop. There's something here for any sweet tooth. Whoopie Pies, Sweet Potato Pound Cake, Blueberry Buckle, Mississippi Mud, and Peach Coffee Cake will all satisfy your desire for sweet treats. And chocolate lovers can take care of their cravings with Mom's Chocolate Roll, Peanut Butter-Chocolate Chip Cookies, or Chocolate-Molasses Lace Cookies.

HAZELNUT TORTE

Makes 12 Servings

Cake:
- 6 egg yolks
- 1 cup sugar
- ¼ cup all-purpose flour
- 1 teaspoon baking powder
- ¼ teaspoon salt
- 2 tablespoons rum *or* rum flavoring
- 3 cups ground hazelnuts (filberts)
- 6 egg whites
- ½ cup sugar

Filling:
- 1 cup whipping cream, whipped
- 2 tablespoons powdered sugar
- 1 teaspoon rum *or* rum flavoring

Frosting:
- 1 cup milk chocolate pieces, melted
- ½ cup dairy sour cream

♦ ♦ ♦

Over the years, Camp McCormick has been the source of fond memories for countless Girl Scouts. The Rock River Valley Council is committed to renovating, upgrading and expanding the camp facilities. Proceeds from the sale of <u>River Valley Recipes</u> sales are used for this purpose.

<u>River Valley Recipes</u>
Rock River Valley Council of Girl Scouts, Inc.
Rockford
ILLINOIS

1 Preheat the oven to 350°. Lightly grease three 8x1½-inch round cake pans. Line the bottoms of the pans with waxed paper. Grease the papers and set the prepared pans aside.

2 To make the cake: In a large mixing bowl, beat the egg yolks with an electric mixer on high speed about 4 minutes or until they are thick and light-colored. Gradually beat in the 1 cup sugar.

3 In a small bowl, stir together the flour, baking powder and salt. Stir the flour mixture into the egg mixture. Add the 2 tablespoons rum or rum flavoring. Fold in the hazelnuts; set aside.

4 In a clean, medium mixing bowl, using clean beaters, beat the egg whites until soft peaks form (tips curl). Gradually add the ½ cup sugar and beat until stiff peaks form (tips stand straight).

5 Stir about *one third* (one cup) of the egg whites into the yolk mixture to lighten it. Gently fold in the remaining egg whites.

6 Spoon the batter into the prepared pans, spreading evenly. Bake in the 350° oven for 25 to 30 minutes or until a wooden toothpick inserted near the centers comes out clean.

7 Use a sharp, narrow-bladed knife to loosen the layers from the sides of the pans. Remove the layers from the pans and carefully pull off the waxed paper. Cool the layers completely on wire racks.

8 To make the filling: Stir together the whipped cream, powdered sugar and the 1 teaspoon rum or rum flavoring. Place one cake layer on a serving plate. Spread it with *half* of the whipped cream mixture, then top with another layer. Spread with the remaining whipped cream mixture and top with the last cake layer.

9 To make the frosting: Stir together the melted chocolate and sour cream. Frost the top of the cake with the chocolate mixture allowing it to drizzle down the side of the cake.

Nutrition Analysis (*Per Serving*): Calories: 493 / Cholesterol: 140 mg / Carbohydrates: 42 g / Protein: 9 g / Sodium: 129 mg / Fat: 34 g (Saturated Fat: 8 g) / Potassium: 238 mg.

CELESTIAL CAKE

Ground hazelnuts are the basis for this delicious and beautiful torte, complete with a rum-flavored whipped cream filling and a chocolate-sour cream frosting. We think you'll adore this heavenly combination of flavors and textures.

FRESH ORANGE CAKE—PROPOSAL CAKE

Makes 12 Servings

Cake:

2¼	cups sifted cake flour
1½	cups sugar
2	teaspoons baking powder
½	teaspoon salt
¼	teaspoon baking soda
½	cup shortening

Grated rind of 1 orange (1 table-
        spoon or more)

¾	cup milk *or* water
¼	cup orange juice
2	eggs

Filling and Frosting:

1	cup milk
5	tablespoons sifted cake flour
½	cup shortening
½	cup butter *or* margarine, softened
1	cup granulated sugar
¼	teaspoon salt
1	teaspoon vanilla
1	cup finely chopped walnuts
½ to 1	cup sifted powdered sugar

♦   ♦   ♦

Elaine Holcomb's mom began making this cake in the late 1940s, and now Elaine makes it for special family get-togethers. The nickname, "Proposal Cake," comes from a spontaneous marriage proposal that was bestowed upon Elaine by a co-worker after he tasted the cake.

Elaine D. Holcomb
<u>Taste Tested Recipes from South United Methodist Church</u>
Manchester
CONNECTICUT

1 Preheat the oven to 350°. Grease and flour two 8-inch round baking pans. Set aside.

2 To make the cake: Sift the dry ingredients into a large mixing bowl. Add the shortening and the grated orange rind.

3 Add the milk or water and the orange juice to the dry ingredients and beat with an electric mixer on low speed until moistened. Beat for 2 minutes at medium speed. Add the eggs; beat for an additional 2 minutes.

4 Pour the batter into the prepared cake pans. Bake in the 350° oven about 25 minutes or until the cake tests done with a wooden toothpick.

5 Cool 10 minutes, then carefully remove the cake from the pans (may stick on bottom). Cool the layers on racks.

6 To make the filling and frosting: Blend the milk and cake flour in a saucepan. Cook over medium-low heat to a very thick paste, stirring constantly. Cool to lukewarm about 40 minutes.

7 Meanwhile, in small mixing bowl, cream the shortening and butter or margarine with the 1 cup granulated sugar and salt.

8 Add the lukewarm paste to the shortening mixture and beat with electric mixer on high speed until fluffy.

9 Stir in vanilla. Remove *¾ cup* of the mixture. (For its use, see tips below.) Fold the chopped nuts into the remaining mixture. Spread *1½ cups* of the mixture between the cake layers.

10 Add the powdered sugar to the remaining mixture and beat vigorously with a spoon to desired consistency. Frost top and sides of cake.

 TIPS FROM OUR KITCHEN

If the filling and frosting is a little soft, add some sifted powdered sugar until it is just the right spreading consistency.

If stray crumbs always seem to mess up the frosting on your cakes, try this tip. First, brush off as many crumbs as you can by hand. Then, spread the sides of the cake with a thin smooth coat of frosting. (This is where the reserved frosting is used.) This layer will help seal in any stray crumbs. Finally, spread a thicker layer of frosting over the thin layer, swirling the frosting decoratively.

Nutrition Analysis (*Per Serving*): Calories: 567 / Cholesterol: 59 mg / Carbohydrates: 67 g
Protein: 6 g / Sodium: 307 mg / Fat: 33 g (Saturated Fat: 10 g) / Potassium: 153 mg.

CITRUS SENSATION

Oranges and nuts turn this fine-textured cake into a dessert so special, it comes with a warning: "You just might get a marriage proposal when you serve this cake."

CAKES & COOKIES

MOM'S CHOCOLATE ROLL

Makes 10 Servings
Cake:
  1   cup sifted powdered sugar
  ¼   cup sifted cake flour
  ¼   cup unsweetened cocoa
      powder
  5   eggs, separated
  1   teaspoon vanilla
  2   tablespoons granulated sugar
Sifted powdered sugar
Cream Chantilly:
  ½   cup sifted powdered sugar
  1   teaspoon vanilla
  2   tablespoons Amaretto
      (optional)
  1   cup whipping cream, whipped

◆   ◆   ◆

*Denny Buckalew told us, "My
mom makes it; I just eat it." He
was talking about Mom's Chocolate Roll, a treat he has enjoyed
for about 25 years. Dale Crane,
Denny's mom, has been making
her acclaimed cake for Christmas
and birthdays ever since Denny
can remember. "She makes about
15 to 20 each time and gives some
as gifts and keeps some for the
family." Thanks, Mom!*

*Denny Buckalew
History Cookbook
Montgomery County Fair
Association
Conroe
TEXAS*

1 Preheat the oven to 400°. Grease a
15x10x1-inch baking pan, line it with
waxed paper and grease again. Set
aside. To make the cake: Sift together
the 1 cup powdered sugar, the flour
and cocoa powder; set aside.

2 In a large mixing bowl, beat the egg
yolks and vanilla about 5 minutes or
until thick and pale yellow.

3 Gradually add the flour mixture to
the yolk mixture, beating until combined.

4 In another bowl, using clean beaters,
beat the egg whites until soft peaks
form (tips curl). Gradually add the 2
tablespoons granulated sugar, beating
until stiff peaks form (tips stand
straight).

5 Stir about *one-fourth* of the stiffly
beaten egg whites into the yolk mixture
to lighten. Fold in the remaining egg
whites.

6 Spread the batter evenly in the
prepared pan. Bake about 10 minutes
or until the cake springs back when
pressed lightly. Remove from the oven
and loosen the edges of the cake with
a spatula.

7 Turn the cake onto a cloth that
has been generously sprinkled with
additional powdered sugar. Remove the
waxed paper and roll the cake and
towel together from a short side as for a
jelly roll. Cool on a wire rack.

8 To prepare the Cream Chantilly:
Fold the ½ cup powdered sugar, the
vanilla and, if using, the Amaretto into
the whipped cream.

9 Reserve *½ cup* of the Cream Chantilly
for a garnish. Unroll the cake and
spread with the remaining Cream
Chantilly to within ½ inch of the short
sides. Re-roll the cake without the
towel. Store the roll, seam side down,
in the refrigerator. To serve, sprinkle
with additional powdered sugar and
garnish with the remaining Cream
Chantilly.

 TIPS FROM OUR KITCHEN

Once assembled, this cake should be
served within 2 hours to prevent the
cream from dissolving.

Nutrition Analysis (*Per Serving*): Calories: 242 / Cholesterol: 139 mg / Carbohydrates: 28 g
Protein: 5 g / Sodium: 41 mg / Fat: 12 g (Saturated Fat: 6 g) / Potassium: 63 mg.

Birthday Tradition

Denny Buckalew shares with us a traditional family birthday cake recipe. Mom's Chocolate Roll
features a rich, chocolate cake and a flavored whipped cream filling.

CARROT WALNUT CAKE

Makes 12 to 16 Servings

3	cups all-purpose flour
2	teaspoons baking powder
1	teaspoon baking soda
1	teaspoon ground cinnamon
½	teaspoon salt
1	cup butter *or* margarine, softened
1	cup packed light brown sugar
1	cup granulated sugar
4	eggs
1	tablespoon grated orange peel
2	tablespoons orange juice
2	teaspoons grated lemon peel
2	tablespoons lemon juice
3	cups finely shredded carrots (1 pound)
1	cup coarsely chopped walnuts
1	cup raisins

Cream Cheese Frosting:

1	8-ounce package cream cheese, softened
1½	cups sifted powdered sugar
1	teaspoon grated lemon peel
1	tablespoon lemon juice
½	cup coarsely chopped walnuts (optional)

Whole walnuts (optional)

◆   ◆   ◆

Clara Rutledge
Katz Employee
Sunshine Cookbook
Katz Employee Sunshine Club
Honesdale
PENNSYLVANIA

1 Preheat the oven to 350°. Lightly grease and flour a 10-inch tube pan; set aside.

2 In a medium mixing bowl, stir together the flour, baking powder, baking soda, cinnamon and salt; set aside.

3 In a large mixing bowl, combine the butter or margarine, brown sugar and granulated sugar. Beat with an electric mixer on medium to high speed about 4 minutes or until light and fluffy, scraping the bowl occasionally. Add the eggs, one at a time, beating well (about 1 minute) after each addition.

4 Combine the orange peel, orange juice, the 2 teaspoons lemon peel and the 2 tablespoons lemon juice. Add the juice and the flour mixtures alternately to the butter-sugar mixture, beginning and ending with the flour mixture. After each addition, beat at low speed just until smooth.

5 Using a wooden spoon, stir in the carrots, walnuts and raisins. Mix well.

6 Pour the batter into the prepared pan, spreading evenly. Bake in the 350° oven for 60 to 65 minutes or until a wooden toothpick inserted near the center comes out clean.

7 Cool the cake in the pan on a wire rack for 20 minutes. Then, loosen the edge of the cake and remove it from the pan. Cool completely on the wire rack.

8 Meanwhile, to make the Cream Cheese Frosting: In a medium mixing bowl, combine the softened cream cheese, powdered sugar, the 1 teaspoon lemon peel and the 1 tablespoon lemon juice. Beat with an electric mixer on medium speed until smooth and creamy, scraping the sides of the bowl as needed.

9 When cool, carefully transfer the cake to a serving plate. Spread with the frosting. Decorate with the chopped walnuts and the whole walnuts, if desired. Store the cake, tightly covered, in the refrigerator until serving time.

TIPS FROM OUR KITCHEN

Use a fine—not coarse—grater for the carrots so the flavor and moisture are evenly distributed throughout the cake. A food processor also works well for this purpose.

If desired, for the garnish, sift the nuts after chopping them to remove the fine particles.

Nutrition Analysis (*Per Serving*): Calories: 659 / Cholesterol: 133 mg / Carbohydrates: 86 Protein: 10 g / Sodium: 457 mg / Fat: 33 g (Saturated Fat: 15 g) / Potassium: 398 mg.

WHOLESOMELY DELICIOUS

This moist and wholesome cake gets its character from the carrots, walnuts and raisins, while the
subtle flavoring comes from citrus and cinnamon. The cream cheese frosting completes
this absolutely delicious picture.

HUMMINGBIRD CAKE

Makes 12 Servings

Cake:

3	cups all-purpose flour
2	cups sugar
1	teaspoon ground cinnamon
1	teaspoon baking soda
½	teaspoon salt
1	8-ounce can crushed pineapple with juice
1	cup cooking oil
3	large eggs, well beaten
2	cups chopped banana (3 bananas)
½	cup finely chopped walnuts *or* pecans
1½	teaspoons vanilla

Glaze:

1	tablespoon melted butter *or* margarine
1	cup sifted powdered sugar

♦   ♦   ♦

This delicious Victorian cake recipe has been passed down to Bobbie Shinners from her friend, Mrs. Bonnie Wells. Bobbie says that she "just fell in love with it!" She loves the taste and says that it is a favorite dish to bring to gatherings because it freezes well and serves so many. Friends and family are always asking her for the recipe.

Bobbie Shinners
What's Cooking in Philadelphia
The Philadelphia Rotary Club
Philadelphia
PENNSYLVANIA

1 Preheat oven to 325°. Generously grease a 10-inch tube or fluted tube pan.

2 To make the cake: In a large mixing bowl, stir together the flour, sugar, cinnamon, baking soda and salt.

3 Remove *2 tablespoons* of the juice from the can of pineapple. Set aside for the glaze.

4 Add the pineapple, oil, eggs, banana, nuts and vanilla to the flour mixture. Stir until just blended (do not beat).

5 Pour the batter into the prepared pan. Bake in the 325° oven about 1 hour and 10 minutes or until a wooden toothpick inserted near the center comes out clean. Cool in the pan for 15 minutes. Invert the cake onto a wire rack and remove the cake from the pan. Cool completely.

6 To make the glaze: In a small mixing bowl, combine the melted butter or margarine and the powdered sugar. Add enough of the reserved pineapple juice to make a glaze of drizzling consistency. Drizzle the glaze over the cooled cake.

 TIPS FROM OUR KITCHEN

To evenly grease a fluted tube pan, use a pastry brush to coat the pan with shortening.

For a glaze with a whole new dimension, substitute rum for the pineapple juice.

Nutrition Analysis *(Per Serving)*: Calories: 516 / Cholesterol: 56 mg / Carbohydrates: 73 g Protein: 6 g / Sodium: 185 mg / Fat: 24 g (Saturated Fat: 4 g) / Potassium: 208 mg.

CAKE FOR A CROWD

We think that you'll be as attracted to this rich, sweet cake from Philadelphia as a hummingbird is to a flower. You'll wonder how something this easy can be so delicious!

SWEET POTATO POUND CAKE

Makes 16 Servings

Cake:
- 1 cup butter *or* margarine, softened
- 2 cups sugar
- 2 cups cooked, mashed and cooled sweet potatoes (2 medium)
- 1 teaspoon vanilla
- 4 eggs
- 3 cups all-purpose flour
- 2 teaspoons baking powder
- 1 teaspoon ground cinnamon
- ½ teaspoon baking soda
- ½ teaspoon ground nutmeg
- ¼ teaspoon salt

Glaze:
- 1 cup sifted powdered sugar
- 3 to 5 teaspoons orange juice
- Shredded orange peel (optional)

♦   ♦   ♦

During the colonial days, cakes were difficult and costly to make, and even the gentry reserved them for holidays and special occasions. Pound Cake, a timeless favorite in the South, was so named because it was made with one pound of each ingredient. Luckily for us, it's no longer so difficult or expensive to make a scrumptious cake!

<u>*Virginia Hospitality*</u>
Junior League of Hampton Roads, Inc.
Hampton
VIRGINIA

1 Preheat the oven to 350°. Grease and flour a 10-inch tube pan. Set aside.

2 To make the cake: In a large mixing bowl, beat together the butter or margarine and sugar with an electric mixer until light and fluffy. Add the sweet potatoes and vanilla and beat until well combined.

3 Add the eggs, one at a time, beating for 1 minute after each addition. (The batter will look curdled.)

4 In a large mixing bowl, stir together the flour, baking powder, cinnamon, baking soda, nutmeg and salt. Slowly add the flour mixture to the potato mixture. Beat on low speed until just combined.

5 Pour the batter into the prepared pan. Bake in the 350° oven about 1 hour and 20 minutes or until a wooden toothpick inserted near the center of the cake comes out clean.

6 Cool the cake in the pan on a wire rack for 20 minutes, then invert onto a serving plate.

7 To make the glaze: In a small bowl, stir together the sifted powdered sugar and 1 tablespoon of the orange juice. Add enough additional orange juice (1 to 2 teaspoons) to give the glaze a drizzling consistency.

8 Spoon the glaze over the warm cake. If desired, sprinkle with orange peel. Cool completely.

 TIPS FROM OUR KITCHEN

This cake can be made in loaf pans, if you prefer. Prepare batter as directed above *except* grease and flour four 7½x3½x2-inch loaf pans or six 4½x2½x1½-inch loaf pans. Pour the batter into the pans. Bake in the 350° oven for 40 to 50 minutes or until a wooden toothpick inserted near the center comes out clean. Cool the cakes in the pans on wire racks for 10 minutes. Invert and glaze as directed above.

To cook sweet potatoes: Wash, peel and cut off woody portions, then cut the potatoes into quarters. Cook, covered, in enough boiling water to cover, about 25 minutes or until tender. Drain and mash until smooth using a potato masher, fork, food mill, food ricer or electric mixer.

Nutrition Analysis (*Per Serving*): Calories: 348 / Cholesterol: 84 mg / Carbohydrates: 55 g / Protein: 5 g / Sodium: 258 mg / Fat: 13 g (Saturated Fat: 8 g) / Potassium: 112.

GREAT GIFTS

The next time you invite your friends or neighbors over for coffee and cake, treat them to this light, fine-textured cake. Then, as a special treat, surprise them with a wrapped miniloaf to take home.

PUMPKIN CAKE

Makes 9 Servings

½	cup shortening
1¼	cups sugar
2	eggs
1¼	cups sifted cake flour
1	tablespoon baking powder
½	teaspoon salt
½	teaspoon ground cinnamon
½	teaspoon ground ginger
½	teaspoon ground nutmeg
1	cup cooked and cooled fresh pumpkin *or* 1 cup canned pumpkin
¾	cup milk
½	teaspoon baking soda
½	cup chopped nuts
	Raisin-Brown Sugar Icing

◆   ◆   ◆

By the age of 12 in 1904, Elva McGahuey was cooking for the large wheat and apple harvest crews in Eastern Washington. Later, her daughter Hazel stood beside her with pen in hand as Elva prepared the meals on a woodstove using no recipes. Pumpkin Cake is one of the recipes that Hazel wrote down, enabling us to share in this extraordinary taste of history today.

Hazel DeLorenzo
Fiddlin' in the Kitchen
**The Chamber Music Society
of Oregon
Portland
OREGON**

1 Preheat oven to 350°. Grease and flour a 9x9x2-inch baking pan. Line the bottom with waxed paper. Set aside.

2 To make the cake: In a large mixing bowl, cream the shortening. Gradually add the sugar, beating until light and fluffy. Beat in the eggs.

3 In a medium bowl, sift together the cake flour, baking powder, salt, cinnamon, ginger and nutmeg.

4 Combine the pumpkin and milk. Stir in the baking soda.

5 Add the flour and pumpkin mixtures alternately to the shortening-sugar mixture, beating well after each addition. Fold in nuts. Turn the batter into the prepared baking pan.

6 Bake in the 350° oven for 50 minutes. Cool in the pan on a wire rack for 10 minutes. Turn the cake out onto the rack; remove the waxed paper and cool completely. Frost the top and sides with the Raisin-Brown Sugar Icing.

7 Raisin-Brown Sugar Icing: In the top of a double boiler, beat together 1 large *egg white*, 1 cup packed *light brown sugar* and 3 tablespoons *water* just until blended. Place the mixture over rapidly boiling water and beat with a rotary beater or an electric mixer for 5 to 7 minutes, or until the mixture is light and fluffy and holds stiff peaks.

8 Remove from the heat. Carefully fold in ½ cup *coarsely chopped raisins.*

 TIPS FROM OUR KITCHEN

Don't add the baking soda to the pumpkin-milk mixture until you're ready to combine it with the flour mixture. Otherwise, the soda will lose much of its leavening power.

Don't be surprised or worried if the icing thins a little when you add the raisins.

Nutrition Analysis (*Per Serving*): Calories: 430 / Cholesterol: 49 mg / Carbohydrates: 69 g / Protein: 5 g / Sodium: 301 mg / Fat: 17 g (Saturated Fat: 4 g) / Potassium: 244 mg.

MOIST AND SPICY TREAT

Here is a deliciously moist cake from Hazel DeLorenzo of Oregon City, Oregon. The spicy flavor
makes it a perfect autumn dessert, but don't hesitate to serve it any time of the year.

BLUEBERRY BUCKLE

Makes 12 to 16 Servings
Cake:
2   cups fresh *or* frozen
     blueberries
⅓   cup milk
1   teaspoon lemon juice
¾   cup sugar
¼   cup butter *or* margarine,
     softened
1   egg
1½   cups all-purpose flour
2   teaspoons baking powder
¼   teaspoon salt
Glaze:
2   tablespoons butter *or*
     margarine
¼   cup sugar
1   tablespoon lemon juice

◆ ◆ ◆

Sandra Miller says that this is a dish "everyone always raves about." Sandra often takes Blueberry Buckle to parties because it's so easy to make—all she needs to do is double the recipe. Although she occasionally uses frozen berries, more often Sandra picks her own fresh berries and, come summertime, she makes Blueberry Buckle every week!

Sandra Miller
<u>*Magnolia Cookery*</u>
Magnolia Mennonite Church
Macon
MISSISSIPPI

1 To make the cake: Rinse the fresh blueberries, discarding any stems or blemished berries. Or, thaw the frozen blueberries and drain.

2 Preheat the oven to 350°. Grease an 8x8x2-inch baking dish; set aside.

3 In a glass measuring cup, combine the milk and the 1 teaspoon lemon juice; set aside.

4 In a medium mixing bowl, combine the ¾ cup sugar, the ¼ cup softened butter or margarine and the egg. Beat with an electric mixer on medium speed until smooth. Continue beating while gradually adding the milk mixture.

5 In a small mixing bowl, stir together the flour, baking powder and salt. Add the flour mixture to the butter mixture, mixing well. Gently fold in the berries by hand.

6 Spread the batter in the prepared baking pan. Bake in the 350° oven about 40 minutes or until a wooden toothpick inserted near the center comes out clean. Just before the cake is done, prepare the glaze.

7 To make the glaze: In a small saucepan, melt the 2 tablespoons butter or mar-

garine. Stir in the ¼ cup sugar and the 1 tablespoon lemon juice. Cook and stir over low heat until the mixture is bubbly. Remove from heat.

8 When the cake tests done, pour the glaze over the top. Return the glazed cake to the oven and broil 3 inches from the heat for 1 to 2 minutes or until the glaze bubbles. Watch carefully to avoid overbrowning.

 TIPS FROM OUR KITCHEN

If the batter seems thick, stir in the last portion of the flour by hand.

To make the cake without using the broiler, pour the glaze over the top of the warm cake and return it to the 350° oven for 5 minutes more.

If desired, double the ingredients and bake two cakes at the same time. Bake the second in an aluminum foil pan. When the cake has cooled, seal it in a freezer bag and label; freeze. Thaw and use the cake within 3 to 6 months.

Nutrition Analysis (*Per Serving*): Calories: 190 / Cholesterol: 34 mg / Carbohydrates: 31 g / Protein: 2 g / Sodium: 115 mg / Fat: 7 g (Saturated Fat: 4 g) / Potassium: 50 mg.

EARLY-MORNING SPECIAL

This butter-sugar glazed delight from Sandra Miller of Brooksville, Mississippi, can be enjoyed as a delicious coffee cake or as a dessert with a generous dollop of whipped cream.

PEACH COFFEE CAKE

◆ ◆ ◆

When volunteers at The General Hospital Center found it necessary to raise funds for their new uniforms, Alice Bock and her co-volunteers wrote their favorite recipes on the backs of greeting cards and sold them in the hospital lobby. The recipes were later published in <u>Always by Your Side</u>. This Peach Coffee Cake had already been taste-tested—and enjoyed—by the group!

Alice Bock
<u>Always by Your Side</u>
The General Hospital Center
Passaic
NEW JERSEY

1 Preheat oven to 350°. Grease an 8x8x2-inch baking pan.

2 To make the cake: In a large bowl, cream the ½ cup butter or margarine, sugar and vanilla together with an electric mixer. Add the egg and beat well.

3 In a small bowl, stir together the dry ingredients. Add the dry ingredients to the butter-sugar mixture alternately with the milk.

4 Spread the batter into the prepared pan. Top with the sliced peaches. Sprinkle with the brown sugar and drizzle with the melted butter.

5 Bake in the 350° oven for 30 to 35 minutes or until done.

TIPS FROM OUR KITCHEN

If the batter starts to climb your beaters as you're putting together this recipe, add the rest of the flour mixture by hand.

Don't worry about leftovers. They're easy to heat in the microwave oven. Just micro-cook, one piece at a time, on 100% power (high) for 15 seconds.

Nutrition Analysis (*Per Serving*): Calories: 297 / Cholesterol: 66 mg / Carbohydrates: 37 g /
Protein: 4 g / Sodium: 287 mg / Fat: 16 g (Saturated Fat: 9 g) / Potassium: 105 mg.

TENDER HOMEMADE TREAT

This light and fruity coffee cake from Passaic, New Jersey, is great for breakfast or dessert.
It's especially good served warm.

CAKES & COOKIES

PEANUT BUTTER-CHOCOLATE CHIP COOKIES

Makes About 4 Dozen Cookies

½	cup butter *or* margarine, softened
½	cup creamy peanut butter
½	cup granulated sugar
½	cup packed light brown sugar
2	eggs
1	teaspoon vanilla
1⅓	cups all-purpose flour
1	teaspoon baking soda
¼	teaspoon salt
1¾	cups semisweet chocolate pieces

◆   ◆   ◆

Marie Young McFarland collects recipes from papers, magazines and friends—basically, "from everywhere!" When she was asked to submit her favorite recipe to the Home Cookin' Mount Zion Heritage Cookbook, *she chose this recipe for Peanut Butter-Chocolate Chip Cookies "because it's a recipe my grandchildren love."*

Marie Young McFarland
Home Cookin' Mount Zion
Heritage Cookbook
Mount Zion Cemetery
Association
Apple Springs
TEXAS

1 Preheat the oven to 350°. Lightly grease a cookie sheet; set aside.

2 In a large mixing bowl, combine the softened butter or margarine and peanut butter. Beat with an electric mixer on medium speed until the mixture is light and fluffy. Gradually add the granulated sugar and brown sugar. Beat in the eggs and vanilla until well combined; set aside.

3 In a medium bowl, stir together the flour, baking soda and salt. Add the flour mixture and chocolate pieces to the dough. Stir until the dough is well blended.

4 Drop the batter by tablespoonfuls onto the prepared the cookie sheet. Bake in the 350° oven for 9 to 12 minutes or until the edges of the cookies are lightly browned or a slight impression remains when the cookies are lightly touched with a fingertip. Transfer the cookies to a wire rack to cool completely.

TIPS FROM OUR KITCHEN

Don't use margarine to grease the cookie sheets; it's more likely to burn than shortening or a nonstick vegetable spray.

If you use margarine instead of butter, be sure to choose a product that's labeled "margarine," not "spread." If you use 100-percent corn oil margarine, the dough will be softer than it would be if you use other margarines.

For a peanuttier flavor, add ⅓ cup chopped peanuts to the cookie dough. Or, substitute peanut butter-flavored pieces (¾ cup) for part of the chocolate pieces.

Cool the cookie sheet between batches to keep the dough from flattening too much during baking. Light-colored cookie sheets are better than dark-colored cookie sheets; dark-colored cookie sheets can cause the cookies to overbrown on the bottoms and sides before the centers are baked.

Nutrition Analysis (*Per Cookie*): Calories: 91 / Cholesterol: 14 mg / Carbohydrates: 11 g / Protein: 2 g / Sodium: 71 mg / Fat: 5 g (Saturated Fat: 1 g) / Potassium: 51 mg.

SWEET DUET

Two all-time favorite flavors unite to create a wonderful, irresistible cookie. In the interest of
maintaining harmony, you might want to consider doubling the recipe, otherwise
these buttery, rich treats will be gone before you know it.

WHOOPIE PIES

Makes About 3 Dozen Whoopie Pies
Cookies:
2	cups all-purpose flour
1	cup granulated sugar
½	cup unsweetened cocoa powder
1	teaspoon baking soda
½	teaspoon baking powder
¼	teaspoon salt
½	cup sour milk
½	cup water
½	cup shortening
1	egg
1	egg yolk

Filling:
½	cup shortening
2	tablespoons all-purpose flour
1	tablespoon granulated sugar
2	teaspoons vanilla
2½	cups powdered sugar
3	tablespoons milk

◆ ◆ ◆

In a small community of about 500, the sales of the Harrington Homemaker's <u>Harrington Cooks</u> is quite impressive—over 850 copies. According to Chairman Linda Wagner, many cookbook owners say, "this is the only cookbook I use." Profits were targeted for Harrington School projects, park beautification and community needs.

<u>Harrington Cooks</u>
Harrington Homemakers
Harrington
WASHINGTON

1 Preheat the oven to 400°.

2 To make the cookies: In a medium mixing bowl, combine the 2 cups flour, the 1 cup granulated sugar, the cocoa powder, baking soda, baking powder, and salt. Add the sour milk, water and the ½ cup shortening. Beat with an electric mixer on low speed until combined.

3 Beat on medium speed for 2 minutes more. Add the whole egg and egg yolk; beat for 2 minutes more.

4 Drop the dough by rounded teaspoonfuls 2 inches apart onto an ungreased cookie sheet. Bake in the 400° oven about 6 minutes or until the top springs back when lightly touched in the center. Remove the cookies from the oven and transfer them to a wire rack to cool.

5 Meanwhile, to make the filling: In a small mixing bowl, combine the ½ cup shortening, the 2 tablespoons flour, the 1 tablespoon granulated sugar and the vanilla. Beat with an electric mixer on medium speed for 30 seconds.

6 Slowly add *1¼ cups* of the powdered sugar; beat well. Add the milk. Gradually add the remaining powdered sugar; beat well.

7 Spoon about *2 teaspoons* of the filling onto *half* of the cookies. Top with the remaining cookies and sandwich together.

 TIPS FROM OUR KITCHEN

To make a surprise filling, add ½ cup miniature chocolate pieces to the filling.

To make sour milk: Pour 1½ teaspoons *lemon juice* or *white vinegar* into a 1-cup glass measure. Add enough *milk* to make ½ cup. Let the mixture stand for 5 minutes before adding it to the remainder of the ingredients.

Nutrition Analysis (*Per Pie*): Calories: 136 / Cholesterol: 12 mg / Carbohydrates: 19 g / Protein: 1 g / Sodium: 53 mg / Fat: 6 g (Saturated Fat: 2 g) / Potassium: 17 mg.

SWEET TREATS

Folks of all ages will love these cream-filled chocolate cookies. Whether you take them to picnics
or send them to school or work, one thing is for sure—Whoopie Pies will
be gobbled up in a matter of seconds.

CAKES & COOKIES

RICOTTA COOKIES

Makes 5½ Dozen Cookies
Cookies:
- 2 cups granulated sugar
- 1 cup margarine *or* butter, softened
- 3 eggs
- 2 teaspoons vanilla
- 4 cups all-purpose flour
- 1 teaspoon baking soda
- 1 teaspoon salt
- 1 15-ounce carton ricotta cheese (2 cups)

Frosting:
- 1 3-ounce package cream cheese, softened
- ½ cup margarine *or* butter
- 1 teaspoon vanilla
- 1 cup sifted powdered sugar

Ground nutmeg (optional)

◆ ◆ ◆

The <u>Easter Seal of Approval Cookbook</u> is the result of the efforts of parents, relatives, staff, volunteers and friends of the Easter Seal Society Parents Auxiliary of the Bucks County Center. Profits from sales have been used to help provide services to the preschoolers, campers and outpatients who use the Bucks County Center.

Judy Manchester
<u>Easter Seal of Approval Cookbook</u>
Easter Seal Society
Levittown
PENNSYLVANIA

1 Preheat the oven to 350°.

2 To make the cookies: In a large mixing bowl, beat the granulated sugar and the 1 cup margarine or butter with an electric mixer on medium to high speed until combined.

3 Add the eggs and the 2 teaspoons vanilla; beat until creamy. Add *half* of the flour, the baking soda and salt; beat until well blended. Stir in the remaining flour and the ricotta cheese.

4 Drop the dough by rounded tablespoons, 2 inches apart, onto an ungreased cookie sheet.

5 Bake in the 350° oven about 12 minutes or until the bottoms of the cookies are browned. The cookie tops *should not brown*. Transfer the cookies to wire racks to cool.

6 To make the frosting: Beat together the cream cheese, the ½ cup margarine or butter and the 1 teaspoon vanilla until light and fluffy. Gradually add the powdered sugar; mix well. Spread the frosting on the cooled cookies. If desired, sprinkle with ground nutmeg. Store the frosted cookies, covered, in the refrigerator.

 TIPS FROM OUR KITCHEN

Unless you have refrigerator space for several plates of single-layered, frosted cookies, refrigerate the cookies unfrosted and frost them just before serving. Store the unused frosting in a covered container in the refrigerator. For freezer storage, freeze the frosted cookies in a single layer, then package them in layered stacks, if desired. Separate the layers immediately after removing the cookies from the freezer and thaw the cookies in a single layer.

Ricotta cheese is a fresh, moist, white cheese with a very mild, semisweet flavor and a soft, slightly grainy texture. It is made from whey—the thin, watery liquid formed when milk is coagulated to make other cheeses. Whole or skim milk is sometimes added.

Making cookies of equal size requires scooping equal amounts of dough. Use a rounded tablespoonful for each one.

Nutrition Analysis (*Per Cookie*): Calories: 109 / Cholesterol: 13 mg / Carbohydrates: 13 g / Protein: 2 g / Sodium: 110 mg / Fat: 5 g (Saturated Fat: 1 g) / Potassium: 22 mg.

SWEET SOLUTION

These yummy cookies have a cakelike texture, a tasty frosting and a rich, homemade flavor. A couple
of Ricotta Cookies are just the solution when you crave "a little something sweet."

CHOCOLATE-MOLASSES LACE COOKIES

Makes 3 Dozen Sandwich Cookies

- ⅔ cup butter
- 2 cups quick-cooking rolled oats
- 1 cup sugar
- ⅔ cup all-purpose flour
- ¼ cup molasses
- ¼ cup milk
- 1 teaspoon vanilla
- ¼ teaspoon salt
- 1 11½-ounce package milk chocolate pieces (2 cups)

♦ ♦ ♦

Nancy Tippett told us about her former holiday baking tradition: In October, she started baking cookies, and then froze them so that she was ready to prepare her special gift trays. As a result of her advance preparation, Nancy said that often she had dozens and dozens of cookies to arrange. She also said that Chocolate Molasses Lace Cookies were her favorite—"They were the ones that attracted the attention on the cookie tray."

Nancy Tippett
Angel Food
The Women's Minis-tree of the
Roxborough Presbyterian Church
Philadelphia
PENNSYLVANIA

1 Preheat the oven to 375°. Line baking sheets with foil. Set aside.

2 In a medium saucepan, melt the butter. Stir in the rolled oats, sugar, flour, molasses, milk, vanilla and salt.

3 Drop by rounded teaspoonfuls 3 inches apart onto the prepared baking sheets. With floured fingertips, press down until the dough is very thin.

4 Bake in the 375° oven for 5 to 7 minutes or until the cookies are lacy and golden. Cool completely, about 15 minutes. Peel the foil away from the cookies.

5 In a medium saucepan, melt the chocolate pieces over low heat, stirring constantly. Spread about *1 teaspoon* of the melted chocolate on the bottoms of *half* of the cookies. Top with the unfrosted cookies.

 TIPS FROM OUR KITCHEN

We recommend butter for this recipe because margarines vary in amounts of water and may cause the cookies to spread too thin.

About half a package (1 cup) of chocolate pieces is enough to sandwich the cookies together. To melt the chocolate in a microwave, place the pieces in a microwave-safe container and micro-cook on 100% (high) power for 1 minute, stirring once.

Instead of creating cookie "sandwiches," you can spread the melted chocolate on top of all of the cookies.

Instead of milk chocolate, try white chocolate, such as Alpine white bars, as filling for the cookie sandwiches.

Nutrition Analysis (*Per Cookie*): Calories: 129 / Cholesterol: 11 mg / Carbohydrates: 17 g / Protein: 2 g / Sodium: 60 mg / Fat: 6 g (Saturated Fat: 2 g) / Potassium: 72 mg.

YUMMY COOKIE SANDWICHES

If you think molasses and chocolate are unlikely companions, these cookies will convince you
otherwise. Two lacy-textured oat and molasses cookies surround a milk chocolate filling
to create a perfect sweet treat.

SOFT GINGER COOKIES

Makes 7 Dozen 2½- to 3-inch Cookies

1	cup butter *or* margarine
1	cup sugar
1	egg
1	cup molasses
1	cup sour milk *or* buttermilk
2	teaspoons baking soda
1	teaspoon ground cinnamon
1	teaspoon ground ginger
½	teaspoon salt
¼	teaspoon ground cloves
¼	teaspoon ground allspice
¼	teaspoon ground nutmeg
7	cups all-purpose flour

❖   ❖   ❖

Pearl Tabor Jones tells us that she made her Soft Ginger Cookies for over fifty years. Pearl always made them using a snowman cookie cutter—children told her that the cookies didn't taste the same unless they were made in the shape of a snowman! At Christmas, she would wrap each cookie individually and close the packages with a Christmas seal.

Pearl Tabor Jones
Grandmother's Recipes
For The Modern Cook
Havenwood-Heritage Heights
Concord
NEW HAMPSHIRE

1 Preheat the oven to 375°.

2 In a very large mixing bowl, beat the butter or margarine with an electric mixer on medium speed for 30 seconds. Add the sugar and beat until thoroughly combined. Then add the egg and beat well.

3 Add the molasses, then the sour milk. Stir in the baking soda, cinnamon, ginger, salt, cloves, allspice and nutmeg. Gradually stir in the flour. Divide the dough into *thirds* and wrap *each* piece in plastic wrap; chill thoroughly.

4 On a lightly floured surface, roll *one-third* of the dough at a time to ⅛-inch thickness. Cut the dough into desired shapes using cookie cutters.

5 Bake the cookies on an ungreased cookie sheet in the 375° oven for 6 to 8 minutes or until the edges are set. Cool the cookies on a wire rack. Repeat with the remaining dough.

 TIPS FROM OUR KITCHEN

To make 1 cup sour milk, measure 1 tablespoon lemon juice or vinegar into a 1-cup glass measure. Add enough milk to equal 1 cup and let it stand 5 minutes before adding it to the recipe.

Either dark or light molasses can be used in this recipe. Dark molasses is less sweet and gives a darker color and a more distinct molasses flavor than the milder flavored light molasses.

The two-part secret for success with cut-out cookies is making sure the dough is well chilled and rolling the dough out on a floured surface. Use one-third of the dough at a time and leave the remainder refrigerated. Using a floured pastry cloth and cloth-covered rolling pin helps to reduce dough-sticking problems.

Measuring the dough thickness with a ruler makes it easier to cut cookies that will bake evenly. If you want to bake both large and small cookies, group equal-sized cookies on separate cookie sheets so that all of the cookies on the same cookie sheet will be done at the same time.

Nutrition Analysis (*Per Cookie*): Calories: 75 / Cholesterol: 9 mg / Carbohydrates: 12 g / Protein: 1 g / Sodium: 58 g / Fat: 2 g (Saturated Fat: 1 g) / Potassium: 52 mg.

SEASONAL SWEETS

Don't wait for holidays and special occasions to make these delicious cookies. Serve them throughout the year—allowing the season to inspire the fanciful shapes. You might try flower shapes in the spring, sunbursts in the summer, leaves in the autumn and snowflakes in the winter.

CINNAMON TWISTS

Makes 24 Servings
1	8-ounce carton dairy sour cream
3	tablespoons granulated sugar
1	package active dry yeast
½	teaspoon salt
⅛	teaspoon baking soda
1	large egg
2	tablespoons shortening, softened margarine *or* softened butter
2½ to 3	cups all-purpose flour
⅓	cup packed brown sugar
1	teaspoon ground cinnamon
2	tablespoons margarine *or* butter, melted

◆　　◆　　◆

Mary Ann Johnston told us that she and her brothers grew up eating their mom's Cinnamon Twists. Her mom had enjoyed the recipe for over forty years, but about twenty-five years ago, she lost the recipe. As soon as she found it again, Mary Ann made sure she got a copy. She says that "Once you've made Cinnamon Twists, preparing them becomes second nature."

Mary Ann Johnston
Easy Elegant Edibles
Rogers-Bentonville Junior
Auxiliary
Rogers
ARKANSAS

1 Preheat the oven to 375°. Lightly grease 2 baking sheets. Set aside.

2 In a small saucepan, heat and stir the sour cream just until warm. *(Do not boil.)* Remove from heat; transfer to a large mixing bowl and stir in the granulated sugar, yeast, salt and baking soda until they are dissolved.

3 Using a wooden spoon, stir in the egg; the 2 tablespoons shortening, softened margarine or butter; and as much of the flour as you can.

4 Turn the dough out onto a floured surface and knead in enough of the remaining flour to make a moderately stiff dough that is smooth and elastic (6 to 8 minutes total). Cover and let rest for 10 minutes.

5 In a small bowl, stir together the brown sugar and the cinnamon. Set aside.

6 On a lightly floured surface, roll out the dough to a 24x6-inch rectangle. Brush the dough with the 2 table-spoons melted margarine or butter and sprinkle the brown sugar-cinnamon mixture over *half* of the dough (length-wise—a 24x3-inch area). Fold the area

of plain dough over the brown sugar-cinnamon mixture. Cut into twenty-four 1-inch-wide strips.

7 One at a time, hold the strips at both ends and twist in opposite directions. Place the twists on the prepared baking sheets, 2 inches apart, pressing both ends down. Cover and let the twists rise until almost doubled in size (45 to 60 minutes).

8 Bake in the 375° oven for 12 to 15 minutes or until lightly browned. Serve warm.

 TIPS FROM OUR KITCHEN

To reheat 1 twist, micro-cook on 100% power (high) for 10 to 12 seconds.

For easier rolling, divide the dough in half. Roll each half to a 12x6-inch rectangle.

Don't try to heat the sour cream in a microwave oven. It needs constant stirring during heating to avoid curdling.

Nutrition Analysis (*Per Serving*): Calories: 103 / Cholesterol: 16 mg / Carbohydrates: 14 g / Protein: 2 g / Sodium: 70 mg / Fat: 4 g (Saturated Fat: 2 g) / Potassium: 46 mg.

BREAKFAST TREATS

If breakfast foods are making your family yawn, maybe it's time to try Cinnamon Twists—rich, yeasty pastries twirled around a brown sugar-and-cinnamon filling. The scent of these treats baking is enough to make a "morning person" out of your most dedicated sleepyhead.

CAKES & COOKIES

ACORN COOKIES

Makes 48 to 60 Cookies

1	cup butter *or* margarine, melted
¾	cup packed light brown sugar
1¾	cups finely chopped pecans
1	teaspoon vanilla
2¾	cups all-purpose flour
½	teaspoon baking powder
1	cup (6 ounces) semisweet chocolate pieces

◆   ◆   ◆

A love of theater can quickly become an all-absorbing passion and the members of the Backers Volunteer Board of the Repertory Theater of St. Louis provide us with no exception to this rule. The energetic group supports their theater in every imaginable way, from making costumes to appearing on stage as extras. They created Cooking for Applause to be a recipe source for catered parties given for new subscribers and to raise money for the theater. Of course, Jacqui Thompson's Acorn Cookies are always in demand.

Jacqui Thompson
Cooking for Applause
Backers Volunteer Board
St. Louis
MISSOURI

1 Preheat oven to 325°.

2 In a large mixing bowl, beat the butter or margarine with the brown sugar until well blended. Stir in *¾ cup* of the pecans and the vanilla.

3 In a medium bowl, stir together the flour and baking powder. Beat the flour mixture into the butter mixture until combined.

4 Roll pieces of the dough into small (1-inch-diameter) balls. Place the balls 1 inch apart on ungreased cookie sheets.

5 To shape the cookies, gently press down on each cookie to flatten the bottom, then pinch up the top of the cookie to form the point of the acorn.

6 Bake the cookies for 12 to 15 minutes or until they are golden. Cool the cookies on wire racks.

7 Melt the chocolate in the top of a double boiler over warm water.

8 Dip the flattened bottoms of the cookies into the chocolate to make a "cap" for the acorn, then dip the chocolate cap into the remaining chopped pecans. Cool the cookies completely on waxed paper.

 TIPS FROM OUR KITCHEN

These cookies are so easy you don't even need a mixing bowl. You can mix them right in the saucepan you use to melt the butter.

If you don't own a double boiler, just melt the chocolate in a heavy saucepan over very low heat and watch it carefully. Or to melt the chocolate in your microwave: Place the chocolate pieces in a 2-cup glass measure. Cook the chocolate uncovered, on 100% power (high), for 1½ to 2½ minutes or until it is soft enough to stir smooth, stirring every minute of cooking.

Nutrition Analysis *(Per Cookie):* Calories: 122 / Cholesterol: 10 mg / Carbohydrates: 13 g / Protein: 1 g / Sodium: 47 mg / Fat: 8 g (Saturated Fat: 3 g) / Potassium: 63 mg.

NUTTY AND SWEET

Folks are drawn to these scrumptious cookies like squirrels to nuts, so be sure to keep your cookie jar well-stocked. These buttery acorn-shaped morsels, dipped in chocolate and chopped pecans, come from the kitchen of Jacqui Thompson of St. Louis, Missouri.

CAKES & COOKIES

MISSISSIPPI MUD

Makes 16 Servings

Cake:
- 1 cup margarine *or* butter
- 2 cups granulated sugar
- ½ cup unsweetened cocoa powder
- Pinch salt
- 4 eggs, beaten
- 1 teaspoon vanilla
- 1½ cups all-purpose flour
- 2 cups chopped pecans

Frosting:
- ½ cup margarine *or* butter, melted
- ⅓ cup unsweetened cocoa powder
- 1 1-pound box powdered sugar (4 to 4½ cups)
- ½ cup milk
- 1 6¼-ounce package miniature marshmallows (4 cups)

◆　　◆　　◆

Although Mississippi Mud isn't quite as southern as pecan pie, it is definitely favored in the south. Arlene Goldstein said that she first tasted this rich chocolate and marshmallow cake at a friend's house, where "everyone went crazy over it."

Arlene Goldstein
Cook & Tell
Sisterhood of Temple Beth-El
Birmingham
ALABAMA

1 Preheat the oven to 350°. Grease and flour a 13x9x2-inch baking pan.

2 To make the cake: In a large saucepan, melt the 2 sticks margarine or butter. Remove from heat. In a small bowl, stir together the sugar, the ½ cup cocoa powder and the salt. Add the sugar mixture to the melted margarine or butter. Stir in the beaten eggs and vanilla. Add the flour and pecans; stir until combined.

3 Spread the batter into the prepared 13x9x2-inch pan. Bake in the 350° oven for 35 minutes.

4 Meanwhile, to prepare the frosting: In a medium saucepan, melt the ½ cup margarine or butter. Stir in the cocoa powder. Stir in *2 cups* of the powdered sugar. Add the milk and stir until smooth. Stir in enough of the remaining powdered sugar to reach a spreading consistency.

5 Spread the marshmallows over the hot cake. Let the cake stand for 10 to 15 minutes. Then, spread the frosting on top of the marshmallows. When the cake is cool, cut it into squares to serve.

 TIPS FROM OUR KITCHEN

For a thinner, bar-type dessert, bake in a greased and floured 15x10x1-inch baking pan for 20 minutes. Continue as directed.

You'll need one pound of pecans if you're shelling them yourself. Store pecans in an airtight container in the refrigerator up to 1 year and in the freezer for at least 2 years.

Nutrition Analysis (*Per Serving*): Calories: 559 / Cholesterol: 54 mg / Carbohydrates: 75 g / Protein: 6 g / Sodium: 234 mg / Fat: 28 g (Saturated Fat: 4 g) / Potassium: 102 mg.

CHOCOLATE CAKE WITH MARSHMALLOWS

Soft, rich frosting envelops a moist and delicious cake, earning Mississippi Mud a spot among the best-loved desserts. The name doesn't come close to describing this delightful meal finale. If you are a chocolate lover, we think you'll enjoy this divine creation.

SALTED PEANUT CHEWS

Makes 36 Bars

1½ cups all-purpose flour
⅔ cup firmly packed brown sugar
½ cup butter *or* margarine, softened
2 egg yolks
1 teaspoon vanilla
½ teaspoon baking powder
¼ teaspoon baking soda
¼ teaspoon salt
3 cups miniature marshmallows
1 10-ounce package peanut butter chips (about 1¾ cups)
⅔ cup corn syrup
¼ cup butter *or* margarine
2 teaspoons vanilla
2 cups crisp rice cereal
2 cups salted peanuts

◆   ◆   ◆

The Holy Cross Parish is made up of people from a variety of ethnic origins and many different generations. Contributions to the Parish's cookbook, The Flavor & Spice of Holy Cross Life , directly reflect the diversity of the members of the Parish.

Marcia Konen
The Flavor & Spice
of Holy Cross Life
Holy Cross Parish
Batavia
ILLINOIS

1 Preheat the oven to 350°.

2 In a large mixing bowl, combine the flour, brown sugar, the ½ cup softened butter or margarine, the egg yolks, the 1 teaspoon vanilla, the baking powder, baking soda and salt. Beat the mixture with an electric mixer on low speed until crumbly.

3 Firmly press the mixture into the bottom of a 13x9x2-inch baking pan. Bake in the 350° oven for 12 to 15 minutes or until golden brown. Remove from the oven.

4 Immediately sprinkle the marshmallows over the surface. Return to the oven for 1 to 2 minutes more or just until the marshmallows begin to puff. Remove from the oven; cool while preparing the topping.

5 In a large saucepan, stir together the peanut butter chips, corn syrup, the ¼ cup butter or margarine and the 2 teaspoons vanilla. Cook over low heat, stirring constantly, until the chips are melted and the mixture is smooth. Remove from heat; stir in the rice cereal and peanuts. Immediately spread the cereal mixture over the marshmallow layer.

6 Cover and refrigerate about 2 hours or until firm. Cut into bars. Store in a covered container.

 TIPS FROM OUR KITCHEN

Line the pan with a piece of foil before pressing in the crumb mixture and baking. Then, you can easily lift out the bars to cut them up.

If you don't have miniature marshmallows, measure 3 cups (5¼ ounces) cut-up large marshmallows.

For a less salty flavor, substitute 1 cup salted peanuts mixed with 1 cup unsalted peanuts for the 2 cups salted peanuts in this recipe.

Nutrition Analysis (*Per Bar*): Calories: 195 / Cholesterol: 20 mg / Carbohydrates: 23 g / Protein: 3 g / Sodium: 118 mg / Fat: 11 g (Saturated Fat: 5 g) / Potassium: 78 mg.

MUNCH A BUNCH

Boxed lunches and snacks will never be the same once you try Marcia Konen's Salted Peanut Chews.
Crunchy, peanutty and chewy—these treats are destined for stardom.

RUBY DATE BARS

Makes 36 Bars

3	cups fresh *or* frozen cranberries
1	8-ounce package chopped, pitted dates
1½	cups water
¾	cup sugar
2	teaspoons finely shredded lemon peel
1	tablespoon lemon juice
1	cup packed light brown sugar
½	cup margarine *or* butter, softened
¼	cup shortening
½	teaspoon salt
½	teaspoon baking soda
½	teaspoon ground cinnamon
1½	cups all-purpose flour
1¼	cups quick-cooking oats

◆ ◆ ◆

The Women of Central Presbyterian Church put together the cookbook Central Cuisine to celebrate the 135th Anniversary of the founding of the church. The building was constructed in 1889, and is included in the National Register of Historic Places. Proceeds from cookbook sales help fund needed renovations.

Ardietta McClellan
Central Cuisine
Central Presbyterian Church
Saint Paul
MINNESOTA

1 In a large saucepan, combine the cranberries, dates, water, granulated sugar, lemon peel and lemon juice.

2 Bring the cranberry-date mixture to a boil over high heat, stirring frequently. Reduce the heat and simmer, uncovered, about 12 minutes or until the mixture is thickened, stirring occasionally. Cool slightly.

3 Preheat oven to 375°. Grease a 13x9x2-inch baking pan.

4 In a large mixing bowl, combine the brown sugar, margarine or butter, and shortening. Beat with an electric mixer until the mixture is light and fluffy. Add the salt, baking soda and cinnamon.

5 Add the flour, about *½ cup* at a time. Once the flour is incorporated, stir in the oats (the mixture will look crumbly). Set *2 cups* of the oat mixture aside for the topping. Press the remaining oat mixture evenly into the prepared pan.

6 Evenly spread the cranberry-date mixture on top of the oat mixture in the pan. Sprinkle with the reserved oat mixture. Bake in the 375° oven for 25 to 27 minutes or until the topping is lightly browned. Cool on a wire rack. Cut into 2x1½-inch bars.

 TIPS FROM OUR KITCHEN

To make chopping whole dates easier, dip your knife in water frequently. The water will keep the dates from sticking to the knife. Or, use kitchen shears, dipping them in water between snips.

Since cranberries are seasonal, stock up on them while you can. Double wrap a bag of cranberries with freezer wrap and freeze for up to 9 months. (It is not necessary to thaw the berries before using.)

These bars will be cholesterol-free if you use vegetable shortening in place of the butter or margarine.

Nutrition Analysis *(Per Bar)*: Calories: 123 / Cholesterol: 0 mg / Carbohydrates: 21 g / Protein: 1 g / Sodium: 73 mg / Fat: 4 g (Saturated Fat: 1 g) / Potassium: 86 mg.

DATE WITH A CRANBERRY

The tartness of cranberries and the sweetness of dates combine with the goodness of oatmeal and a
touch of cinnamon to make these chewy bars extra special.

Desserts

*T*his section is full of delightful desserts of all kinds—
decadent, down-home, and
delicious. If company's
coming, you'll impress them
with Snow Eggs, poached
meringues in custard. This
dessert originated in France
where it's known as "des
Oeuvre a la Neige." Looking
for something simpler,
but just as tasty? Try the Old-
Fashioned Strawberry
Shortcake. If you're partial
to pie, there's the classic
American Apple Pie. You'll
find an after-dinner delicacy
for any occasion here.

CHOCOLATE CHEESECAKE

Makes 10 to 12 Servings

Crust:

1	cup graham cracker crumbs
5	tablespoons butter *or* margarine, melted
2	tablespoons sugar

Filling:

3	eggs
1	cup sugar
3	8-ounce packages cream cheese, softened
1	12-ounce package semi-sweet chocolate pieces (2 cups)
1	cup dairy sour cream
¾	cup butter *or* margarine, melted
1	teaspoon vanilla
1	cup chopped pecans

♦   ♦   ♦

In 1989, Birmingham was named "The Most Livable City in America" by the U.S. Council of Mayors. After tasting this chocolate cheesecake, courtesy of Pearl Lewis, we can understand why! Birmingham's commitment to a progressive business environment, a vibrant cultural life and a rich heritage of Southern tradition make it a magical city indeed.

Pearl Lewis
What's Cooking In Birmingham
Temple Beth El Career Women
Birmingham
ALABAMA

1 To make the crust: combine the graham cracker crumbs with the 5 tablespoons melted butter or margarine and the 2 tablespoons sugar.

2 Press the crumb mixture over the bottom of a 9-inch springform pan. Place the pan in the refrigerator to chill.

3 Preheat oven to 325°.

4 In a large bowl, beat the eggs with the 1 cup sugar. Beat in the cream cheese until the mixture is smooth.

5 Melt the chocolate pieces in the top of a double boiler over warm water. Stir in the sour cream, the ¾ cup melted butter or margarine and the vanilla. Beat the chocolate mixture into the cream cheese mixture. Stir in the pecans.

6 Carefully pour the filling into the crust-lined pan. Then spread the filling with a rubber spatula to distribute the mixture evenly. Place the springform pan in a shallow baking pan to protect your oven in case any butter leaks out of the springform pan during baking. Place both pans in the oven.

7 Bake the cheesecake in the 325° oven about 1 hour or until the center is nearly set (a 1-inch area in the center will jiggle slightly when the cheesecake is done).

8 Cool the cheesecake on a wire rack for 10 minutes. Then use a thin metal spatula to loosen the sides of the cake from the pan as shown; this helps to keep the cheesecake edges from cracking. Cool the cheesecake on the rack for 3 hours before removing the sides of the pan. The cheesecake may fall in the center or the top may crack; this is normal. Remove the sides of the pan and chill the cheesecake thoroughly.

 TIPS FROM OUR KITCHEN

For perfect slices every time, we suggest using a very thin, sharp knife. Dip the knife into a glass of warm water before you make each cut and wipe the knife clean between cuts.

Nutrition Analysis *(Per Serving):* Calories: 833 / Cholesterol: 202 mg / Carbohydrates: 58 Protein: 11 g / Sodium: 503 mg / Fat: 65 g (Saturated Fat: 31 g) / Potassium: 395 mg.

DIVINE DECADENCE

This cheesecake, from the kitchen of Pearl Lewis of Birmingham, Alabama, is a real show-stopper, especially when presented with a garnish of mint leaves and fresh berries drizzled with chocolate. The blend of chocolate and cream cheese is so wonderfully delicious, your friends will shout, "Encore!"

OLD-FASHIONED STRAWBERRY SHORTCAKE

Makes 12 Servings
Shortcakes:

- 3 cups all-purpose flour
- ¼ cup sugar
- 3½ teaspoons baking powder
- ½ teaspoon salt
- ½ cup shortening, butter *or* margarine
- 1 cup milk
- 2 tablespoons melted butter *or* margarine
- 2 tablespoons softened butter *or* margarine (optional)

Topping:

- 2 quarts fresh strawberries, hulled, rinsed and sliced (8 cups) *or* three 10-ounce packages frozen strawberries, thawed
- 1 cup heavy whipping cream, whipped

♦   ♦   ♦

"In addition to the Derby, Kentucky is famous for its good cooks," says Irene Hayes, cookbook chairperson for <u>What's Cooking in Kentucky</u>. *Profits from the sale of the cookbook, now in its third edition, are given to a local church to help pay for needed renovations.*

Alice Hayes
<u>What's Cooking in Kentucky:</u>
<u>Treasured Old Recipes and the</u>
<u>Best of the New</u>
T.I. Hayes Publishing Company
Ft. Mitchell
KENTUCKY

1 Preheat the oven to 450°.

2 To make the shortcakes: In a large mixing bowl, stir together the flour, sugar, baking powder and salt. Using a pastry blender, cut in the shortening, butter or margarine until the mixture resembles coarse crumbs.

3 Add the milk to the flour mixture and stir just until moistened.

4 Turn the dough out onto a lightly floured surface and knead about 20 times.

5 Roll or pat the dough out to a ¼-inch thickness. With a 3-inch round cutter, cut the dough into circles. Place *half* of the circles on an ungreased baking sheet

and brush them well with the 2 tablespoons melted butter or margarine. Top with the remaining dough circles.

6 Bake the shortcakes in the 450° oven for 10 to 12 minutes or until golden brown. Remove from the oven.

7 To assemble: Separate the shortcake halves and spread them with the 2 tablespoons softened butter or margarine, if desired. Place the bottom halves on serving plates. Spoon *half* of the strawberries over the bottom halves of the shortcakes. Layer on the top halves of the shortcakes. Spoon on the remaining strawberries. Serve while the shortcakes are still warm, topped with the whipped cream.

 TIPS FROM OUR KITCHEN

If you don't have a round cutter, pat the dough into a rectangle and use a sharp knife to cut 3-inch squares.

You can make the shortcakes using an alternative method. Knead the dough and roll out or pat to a ½-inch thickness. Cut and bake the biscuits as directed. Before assembling, split the biscuits in half and proceed with the assembly.

For a juicier strawberry topping, combine the strawberries and 2 to 4 tablespoons *sugar* (depending on the natural sweetness of the berries) and let stand for 10 to 15 minutes to allow the mixture to become juicy. Lightly mash about half of the berries, then stir all of the berries together.

Nutrition Analysis (*Per Serving*): Calories: 349 / Cholesterol: 39 mg / Carbohydrates: 37 g Protein: 5 g / Sodium: 158 mg / Fat: 21 g (Saturated Fat: 9 g) / Potassium: 248 mg.

PERENNIAL DESSERT FAVORITE

Flaky, tender biscuits layered with juicy sweet strawberries and served with a dollop of whipped cream—is there a finer dessert? This recipe from Ft. Mitchell, Kentucky, will win the hearts of your family and guests alike.

SNOW EGGS

Makes 10 to 12 Servings
- 3 cups whole milk
- 1 vanilla bean, split lengthwise
- 6 eggs, separated
- ½ cup granulated sugar
- ⅛ teaspoon salt
- 2 teaspoons vanilla
- ½ cup powdered sugar
- Caramelized sugar *or* unsweetened cocoa powder (optional)

❖ ❖ ❖

While Adrianne Evans's husband was playing professional basketball in Europe, she was enjoying the rich culture. When they lived in Lyons, France, Adrianne "learned the fine art of cuisine" by taking cooking classes. One day while shopping at a deli, she saw a dessert that intrigued her. After she tried it, she "had to find the recipe." Luckily, she was able to learn how to make des Oeuvres à la Neige, and when she returned to the United States, she brought her recipe for Snow Eggs with her.

Adrianne Evans
<u>Dinner By Design</u>
Everywoman's Resource Center
Topeka
KANSAS

1 In a large saucepan, heat the milk and vanilla bean just to boiling.

2 Meanwhile, in a medium mixing bowl, beat the egg yolks and the granulated sugar with an electric mixer on medium to high speed about 2 minutes or until the mixture is smooth and lemon colored.

3 Stir about *1 cup* of hot milk into the egg yolk mixture. Return all of the egg yolk mixture to the saucepan and reduce heat to medium-low. Cook, stirring constantly, until the foam on the surface disappears and the mixture coats a metal spoon. *Do not boil.* Immediately pour the mixture into a large, flat dish or bowl. Remove the vanilla bean. Allow the custard to cool.

4 In a clean, large mixing bowl, using clean beaters, beat the egg whites and salt until soft peaks form (tips curl). Add the vanilla and continue beating. Gradually add the powdered sugar, beating until stiff peaks form (tips stand straight).

5 In a large Dutch oven, heat 7 to 8 cups *water* to a boil. Reduce heat; simmer.

6 Using 2 large spoons, drop the egg white mixture by mounds into the simmering water. *Do not try to cook too many meringues at once, or they will stick together.*

7 Simmer, uncovered, about 5 minutes or until the egg whites are set. Remove from the water and drain on a clean kitchen towel. Arrange the drained egg white mounds on the cooled custard and refrigerate.

8 If desired, before serving, drizzle with caramelized sugar or sprinkle with sifted cocoa powder.

 TIPS FROM OUR KITCHEN

To make enough caramelized sugar to drizzle over the mounds: Heat ¼ cup *granulated sugar* in a small heavy skillet over medium-high heat, shaking the skillet occasionally to heat the sugar evenly. When the sugar begins to melt, reduce heat to low and cook, stirring frequently, until the sugar is completely melted and golden brown (about 5 minutes more).

Nutrition Analysis *(Per Serving):* Calories: 151 / Cholesterol: 138 mg / Carbohydrates: 19 g Protein: 6 g / Sodium: 101 mg / Fat: 5 g (Saturated Fat: 2 g) / Potassium: 147 mg.

FANTASY DESSERT

Similar to a dessert known as Floating Island, this elegant, interesting dessert features poached
meringues resting on a sea of rich custard. As a finishing touch, the Snow Eggs are
drizzled with caramelized sugar or cocoa powder.

AUNT BENE'S INDIAN PUDDING

Makes 6 Servings

3	cups milk
⅓	cup molasses
¼	cup yellow cornmeal
1	egg, beaten
½	cup sugar
1	tablespoon butter *or* margarine
½	teaspoon ground ginger
½	teaspoon ground cinnamon
¼	teaspoon salt

Whipped cream
Ground nutmeg

◆ ◆ ◆

The Junior League of Birmingham is dedicated to sponsoring start-up programs. The League raises funds to support various organizations that are in need of assistance, concentrating on getting programs up and running. The successful results of their efforts are many, including the organization of a PTA for a local school, PATH (Partnership Assistance to the Homeless) and Adopt-a-School.

Edna Dexter Niederhauser
<u>Magic</u>
The Junior League of Birmingham
Birmingham
ALABAMA

1 Preheat the oven to 300°.

2 In a large saucepan, heat the milk until nearly bubbly. *(Do not boil.)*

3 In a small bowl, stir together the molasses and cornmeal. Carefully stir the molasses-cornmeal mixture into the hot milk. Cook, stirring constantly, over medium heat for 5 to 10 minutes or until the mixture is slightly thickened. Remove from heat.

4 Gradually stir about *1 cup* of the hot mixture into the beaten egg. Return all of the egg mixture to the saucepan. Stir in the sugar, butter or margarine, ginger, cinnamon and salt. Mix thoroughly.

5 Divide the mixture among 6 individual casseroles or six 6-ounce custard cups.

6 Bake in the 300° oven for 30 to 45 minutes or until bubbly around the edges. Serve warm or cool; dollop with whipped cream and a sprinkle of nutmeg.

 TIPS FROM OUR KITCHEN

Unlike some baked custard desserts, this pudding doesn't need to be put in a pan of water for baking. However, placing the individual casseroles in a 15x12x2-inch baking pan makes it easier to put them in and remove them from the oven.

This recipe is lower in fat than many other baked puddings or custards because it contains fewer eggs. You can lower the fat content even further by using low-fat milk.

Nutrition Analysis (*Per Serving*): Calories: 273 / Cholesterol: 73 mg / Carbohydrates: 39 g Protein: 6 g / Sodium: 266 mg / Fat: 11 g (Saturated Fat: 7 g) / Potassium: 387 mg.

REMINISCENT DESSERT

This outstanding version of a traditional New England dessert comes to us from Birmingham,
Alabama. Aunt Bene's Indian Pudding can be served warm or cool and features cornmeal,
molasses and a mixture of spices reminiscent of pumpkin pie.

DESSERTS

TRADITIONAL BREAD PUDDING

Makes 12 to 15 Servings

Custard Sauce:
- 4 eggs, beaten
- 1½ cups milk
- ⅔ cup granulated sugar
- 1 teaspoon vanilla

Hard Sauce:
- ½ cup butter *or* margarine
- 2 cups sifted powdered sugar
- 2 teaspoons vanilla

Bread Pudding:
- 8 cups dry bread cubes
- 1 cup raisins
- 1 cup flaked coconut
- 1 cup chopped pecans
- 4 eggs, beaten
- 2½ cups milk
- 2½ cups granulated sugar
- 2 cups half-and-half *or* light cream
- 2 tablespoons vanilla
- 1 teaspoon ground cinnamon
- 1 teaspoon ground nutmeg
- ⅓ cup butter *or* margarine, cut into small pieces

◆   ◆   ◆

Cooking New Orleans Style is a wonderful book filled with sights, culture and tastes. The successful cookbook features typical New Orleans food alongside photographs of local scenes.

Cooking New Orleans Style
The Women of All Saints' Episcopal Church
New Orleans
LOUISIANA

1 To make the Custard Sauce: In a heavy medium saucepan, stir together the 4 eggs, 1½ cups milk and ⅔ cup granulated sugar. Cook, stirring constantly, over medium heat until the egg mixture just coats a metal spoon.

2 Remove the saucepan from heat and stir in the 1 teaspoon vanilla. Quickly cool the custard by placing the saucepan in a bowl of ice water for 1 to 2 minutes, stirring constantly. (Be careful not to get any water in the sauce.) Pour the cooled custard into a bowl and cover the surface with plastic wrap. Refrigerate until ready to serve.

3 To make the Hard Sauce: In a small mixing bowl, beat the ½ cup butter or margarine and the powdered sugar with an electric mixer on medium speed for 3 to 5 minutes or until the mixture is well combined. (The mixture may still be crumbly.)

4 Beat in the 2 teaspoons vanilla and continue beating until the mixture is smooth. Cover and refrigerator to harden (about 1 hour).

5 To make the Bread Pudding: Preheat the oven to 350°. In a 3-quart rectangular baking dish layer *half* of the bread cubes, raisins, coconut and pecans. Repeat the layers; set aside.

6 In large bowl, stir together the 4 beaten eggs, 2½ cups milk, 2½ cups granulated sugar, half-and-half or light cream, 2 tablespoons vanilla, cinnamon and nutmeg.

7 Pour the milk mixture evenly over the ingredients in the baking dish. Dot with the ⅓ cup butter or margarine.

8 Bake the pudding in the 350° oven for 1 to 1¼ hours or until a knife inserted near the center comes out clean.

9 To serve: Spoon the warm Bread Pudding into serving dishes. Pass the Custard Sauce and Hard Sauce for spooning on top.

Nutrition Analysis (*Per Serving*): Calories: 690 / Cholesterol: 197 mg / Carbohydrates: 97 g
Protein: 11 g / Sodium: 318 mg / Fat: 31 g (Saturated Fat: 15 g) Potassium: 390 mg.

SWEET ABUNDANCE

Once a cook's solution for using up stale bread while utilizing abundant cream and eggs, today bread
pudding has become a special treat. Coconut and pecans enhance the traditional raisins
and spices to make this delicious New Orleans-style version.

JUL GROT

◆ ◆ ◆

Elna Dorothea Ingabourg Johanson Duncan's father immigrated from Sweden through Canada, eventually settling in New Sweden, Maine. Elna's mother also settled in New Sweden. She brought with her this recipe for Jul Grot that had been given to her by her mother in Sweden. We imagine the delicious holiday dessert was quite popular in the settlement, as we're sure it will be in your home.

Elna Duncan
(Jean Waters's mother)
<u>**Country Living Cookbook**</u>
Waterloo Area Historical Society
Stockbridge
MICHIGAN

1 Place the rice and salt in a heavy 3-quart saucepan. Add *4 cups* of the milk and the cinnamon sticks. Bring to boiling. Reduce heat and cook over low heat, uncovered, for 30 minutes, stirring occasionally with a wooden spoon. Gradually add the remaining milk.

2 Continue to cook about 30 minutes more or until the rice is tender. Add the ½ cup sugar and cook 5 minutes more.

3 Remove the saucepan from the heat. Remove the cinnamon sticks from the mixture and discard. Add the butter and stir until it has melted.

4 Pour the pudding into a warm serving dish or individual dishes. If desired, sprinkle with the ground cinnamon, sugar and raisins.

 TIPS FROM OUR KITCHEN

For the best consistency, allow the pudding to stand about an hour before garnishing and serving.

Swedish tradition calls for adding a whole almond to the pudding. Legend has it that the person who finds the almond in his or her serving will be married within a year. Secretly slip in the almond just before serving the pudding and see what happens.

A garnish of whipped cream and fresh strawberries helps to give this dish a festive flair. Or you may prefer to imitate the people of Finland and top it with a thickened fruit juice sauce.

Nutrition Analysis *(Per Serving)*: Calories: 176 / Cholesterol: 15 mg / Carbohydrates: 28 g Protein: 7 g / Sodium: 270 mg / Fat: 4 g (Saturated Fat: 3 g) / Potassium: 270 mg.

SCANDINAVIAN CHRISTMAS RICE PUDDING

This rich, custardy pudding laced with cinnamon is a traditional Christmas dessert in Scandinavia.
Jean Waters of Stockbridge, Michigan, generously shared her treasured family recipe with us
so that we might add it to our own holiday traditions.

RHUBARB COBBLER WITH OAT DUMPLIN'S

Makes 8 Servings
Fruit:
- ¾ cup sugar
- 2 tablespoons cornstarch
- 1 cup water
- ½ cup orange juice
- 1 pound fresh *or* frozen rhubarb, sliced into 1-inch pieces (4 cups)

Dumplin's:
- ½ cup all-purpose flour
- ½ cup rolled oats
- ⅓ cup sugar
- ¼ cup whole wheat flour
- 1½ teaspoons baking powder
- ½ cup milk
- 2 tablespoons cooking oil

Topping:
- 1 tablespoon sugar
- ¼ teaspoon ground cinnamon

◆ ◆ ◆

Toni Beach, a self-proclaimed rhubarb lover, makes this cobbler as a tasty, low-cholesterol dessert. By substituting skim milk and skipping the ice cream or whipped cream garnish, Toni proves to lucky guests that healthful can also be delicious.

Toni Beach
Cooking With Love
Helping Hands
Centerville
INDIANA

1 Preheat oven to 425°. To make the fruit: In a medium saucepan, stir together the sugar and cornstarch. Stir in the water and orange juice.

2 Cook and stir over medium-high heat until the mixture is thickened and bubbly.

3 Add the rhubarb pieces; cook and stir until mixture returns to boiling. Remove from heat. Cover the mixture to keep it warm.

4 To make the dumplin's: In a medium bowl, stir together the all-purpose flour, rolled oats, sugar, whole wheat flour and baking powder. In a small bowl, stir together the milk and cooking oil.

5 Add the milk mixture to the flour mixture; stir just until the flour mixture is moistened. *Do not over-mix.*

6 Transfer the warm rhubarb mixture to a 13x9x2-inch baking pan or a 2-quart casserole dish. *Immediately* spoon the dumpling batter into 8 mounds on top of the warm rhubarb mixture.

7 To make the topping: In a small dish, stir together sugar and cinnamon. Sprinkle the sugar mixture over the top of the dumplin's.

8 Bake, uncovered, in the 425° oven about 20 minutes or until done. Test for doneness by lifting a dumplin' to see if it is done underneath. Serve warm.

 TIPS FROM OUR KITCHEN

If you choose to use frozen rhubarb, be sure to run the frozen fruit under cold water to break up the fruit pieces before adding them to the hot orange mixture.

Nutrition Analysis (*Per Serving*): Calories: 227 / Cholesterol: 1 mg / Carbohydrates: 46 g / Protein: 3 g / Sodium: 67 mg / Fat: 4 g (Saturated Fat: 1 g) / Potassium: 268 mg.

DOWN-HOME DELIGHT

For real down-home flavor, serve this fruit-filled dessert from Toni Beach of Centerville, Indiana, with a dollop of whipped cream, a scoop of ice cream or a little light cream.

FRESH FRUIT TRIFLE

◆   ◆   ◆

Beckie Domanico and her husband are real fruit lovers, and they've been enjoying Beckie's recipe for Fresh Fruit Trifle for years. For a lower-fat version, Beckie suggests substituting low- or non-fat yogurt and sour cream. She also suggests varying the type of cookies used in the recipe.

Beckie Domanico
Seasoned with Love
McAlpin's Crestview Hills
Crestview Hills
KENTUCKY

1 In a very large bowl, gently stir together the pears, apples, strawberries, kiwi fruit, grapes and oranges.

2 In small bowl, stir together the yogurt and sour cream.

3 In a 3-quart serving bowl, place ½ cup of the broken cookies. Spoon *one-fourth* of the fruit mixture on top. Cover with *one fourth* of the yogurt mixture.

4 Repeat, layering the cookies, fruit and yogurt mixtures. Garnish with additional broken cookies, if desired. Serve immediately or within 1 hour.

TIPS FROM OUR KITCHEN

To break the cookies coarsely, place them in a self-sealing plastic bag. Partially seal, leaving one section of the seal open to allow air to escape. Gently roll a rolling pin over the bag until the desired texture is achieved.

This trifle can be made up to 2 hours before serving. If you plan to do so, however, dip the apples and pears in diluted lemon juice to prevent them from turning brown.

Amaretti (or amarettini) are crisp, almond-flavored macaroons usually imported from Italy. Look for them in specialty food shops.

For easier party serving, layer the cookies, fruit and yogurt mixtures in sherbet or plastic punch glasses. Garnish each with a small cookie or a sprig of fresh mint.

To section a peeled orange: Hold the orange over a bowl to catch the juices. Cut between one fruit section and the membrane, cutting to the center of the fruit. Turn the knife and slide it up the other side of the section next to the membrane; repeat. Remove any seeds from the fruit sections.

Nutrition Analysis (*Per Serving*): Calories: 213 / Cholesterol: 8 mg / Carbohydrates: 33 g / Protein: 4 g / Sodium: 35 mg / Fat: 8 g (Saturated Fat: 2 g) / Potassium: 393 mg.

A LITTLE BIT OF TEMPTATION

In this modern adaptation of the classic English dessert, fresh fruits are layered with crumbled cookies and a flavored yogurt-sour cream mixture. Even those not usually inclined toward desserts will be tempted by this fresh and not-too-sweet delight.

CHOCOLATE-ALMOND BARK

Makes Approximately 48 Pieces

- 2 cups semisweet chocolate pieces
- 1 tablespoon shortening
- ½ cup raisins
- ½ cup chopped toasted almonds

♦   ♦   ♦

Over 3,500 copies of <u>A Tasteful Collection</u> have been sold as one of the many fund-raising efforts of the Women's Auxiliary of the Hebrew Home of Greater Washington. The cookbook presents some of the greatest recipes from cooks in the Washington area. The 2,500 Auxiliary members are dedicated to raising money to help support the home. Originally established to provide care for twelve men who had no families, the now full-care home has been in operation for more than eighty years and currently provides services for 550 residents.

<u>A Tasteful Collection</u>
Women's Auxiliary of the Hebrew Home of Greater Washington
Rockville
MARYLAND

1 Line a 13x9x2-inch baking pan with waxed paper or foil. Set aside.

2 In a medium saucepan, melt the chocolate and shortening over low heat until the mixture is smooth, stirring constantly. Remove from heat and stir in the raisins and ¼ *cup* of the almonds.

3 Spread the chocolate mixture in the prepared pan. Sprinkle with the remaining almonds.

4 Refrigerate the bark for 30 minutes or until set. Then, break into pieces. Store in an airtight container in the refrigerator.

TIPS FROM OUR KITCHEN

If you like, you can substitute butterscotch or peanut butter pieces or a combination of semisweet and milk chocolate pieces for the semisweet chocolate pieces in the recipe as long as the total measurement equals 2 cups.

Because the chocolate pieces soften at room temperature, you'll have to store the bark in the refrigerator until serving time.

If you wish to store the candy at room temperature, you must quick-temper the chocolate. In a 4-cup glass measure, combine the chocolate and 2 tablespoons of shortening. Pour very warm tap water (100° to 110°) into a large bowl to a depth of 1 inch. Place the

measure with the chocolate in the bowl. The water should cover the bottom half of the measure. Add more water, if necessary. (Do not splash any water into the chocolate.) Stir the chocolate constantly with a rubber spatula until melted and smooth, about 15 to 20 minutes. Do not rush. If the water in the bowl begins to cool, replace it with more warm water. Do not allow any water to touch the chocolate. Just a drop can cause the chocolate to become thick and grainy. When the chocolate is melted and smooth, it is ready to use.

Nutrition Analysis *(Per Piece)*: Calories: 48 / Cholesterol: 0 mg / Carbohydrates: 6 mg / Protein: 1 g / Sodium: 0 mg / Fat: 3 g (Saturated Fat: 0 g) / Potassium: 43 mg.

AFFECTION FOR A SWEET CONFECTION

Chocolate lovers, rejoice! Here's a candy recipe that is easy and quick and doesn't require any special
equipment. Your children will love to participate in the preparation, and
they're sure to enjoy the tasting, too!

FROZEN ROCKY ROAD

Makes 8 or 9 Servings

1½	teaspoons unflavored gelatin
2	tablespoons cold water
¾	cup milk
¼	cup sugar
1	square (1 ounce) unsweetened chocolate, chopped
3 to 4	tablespoons coffee liqueur
1	cup whipping cream
1	cup tiny marshmallows
1	cup chopped pecans

◆   ◆   ◆

Witan is a self-sustaining, non-profit women's service organization dedicated to many worthwhile projects and programs that benefit women, children and the community. When Witan decided to publish its fund-raising cookbook, The Market Basket, the organizers were fortunate to receive Mary Jean Maglione's recipe for Frozen Rocky Road. Mary Jean tells us that she serves this delectable alternative to ice cream as a special company dessert.

Mary Jean Maglione
The Market Basket
Witan
Akron
OHIO

1 In a small bowl, stir together the gelatin and the cold water; set aside.

2 In a small saucepan, combine the milk, sugar and chocolate. Cook and stir over medium-low heat until the chocolate melts and the mixture is almost bubbly. If flecks of chocolate are visible, beat the mixture with a wire whisk or rotary beater to incorporate the chocolate completely.

3 Stir the gelatin mixture into the chocolate mixture. Cook and stir over low heat until the gelatin dissolves. Cool, then stir in the coffee liqueur. Cover and chill until partially set. (The mixture will have the consistency of unbeaten egg whites.)

4 In a medium bowl, whip the cream until soft peaks form (tips curl). Carefully fold the whipped cream into the gelatin mixture along with the marshmallows and pecans.

5 Carefully spoon the mixture into an 8x4x2-inch loaf pan or an 8x8x2-inch baking pan. Cover and freeze for 6 to 8 hours or until firm.

6 To serve: Let the frozen dessert stand at room temperature for 10 minutes. Cut into squares or slices.

 TIPS FROM OUR KITCHEN

If you wish, chill the mixture until it reaches the consistency of thick pudding before spooning it into the loaf pan or baking pan. At that time, give the mixture a light stir to distribute the marshmallows and pecans evenly.

If desired, use crème de cacao or strong, brewed coffee instead of the coffee liqueur. You may also substitute walnuts for the pecans.

For easier serving, instead of freezing the mixture in the loaf pan or baking pan, spoon the chilled mixture into individual dessert dishes. Cover the dishes with plastic wrap and set on a tray in the freezer.

Nutrition Analysis (*Per Serving*): Calories: 286 / Cholesterol: 42 mg / Carbohydrates: 19 g / Protein: 4 g / Sodium: 27 mg / Fat: 22 g (Saturated Fat: 8 g) / Potassium: 160 mg.

FROSTY CONFECTION

Serve this mocha confection studded with marshmallows and pecans to your loved ones and watch
them melt. For the ultimate indulgence, add a drizzle of hot fudge sauce on top.

CRANBERRY SORBET

Makes About 24 Servings
1 pound cranberries (4 cups)
3½ cups water
2 cups sugar
1 tablespoon unflavored gelatin (1 envelope)
1¼ cups orange juice
1 tablespoon lemon juice
⅛ teaspoon salt (optional)

◆ ◆ ◆

We asked Nancy Richards, General Manager of the Rapides Symphony Guild, what motivated the organization to create a cookbook as a fundraiser. Her response was that there weren't many cookbooks in Louisiana at the time and there were so many marvelous cooks in the area that it seemed like an excellent idea. And it definitely was—the cookbook was so well received that it was declared the "Official Cookbook of the World Fair" when the fair was hosted by New Orleans in 1984.

Thelma W. Green
Louisiana Entertains
Rapides Symphony Guild
Alexandria
LOUISIANA

1 In a large saucepan, combine the cranberries and water. Bring to a boil; reduce heat and cook, uncovered, about 5 minutes or until the cranberry skins have popped. Cool slightly.

2 Using a food processor, blender or food mill, puree the cranberries about *one-third* at a time. Strain the pureed mixture to remove the skins. Discard the skins; set aside the cranberry puree.

3 In another large saucepan, stir together the sugar and gelatin. Stir in the cranberry puree. Cook and stir over low heat until the sugar and gelatin are dissolved. Remove from heat. Stir in the orange juice, lemon juice and salt (if using). Cool for 30 minutes.

4 Transfer the mixture to a 13x9x2-inch baking pan. Cover and freeze about 4 hours or until *almost* firm.

5 Break the frozen mixture into small chunks. Transfer the chunks to a chilled, large mixing bowl.

6 Beat the frozen chunks with an electric mixer until the mixture is fluffy. (The mixture will lighten in color as it is beaten.) Return the mixture to the pan and freeze about 6 hours or until firm.

 TIPS FROM OUR KITCHEN

Sorbet is similar to sherbet, but since it's made with water instead of milk, it has an icier texture.

Refrigerate bagged fresh cranberries up to 4 weeks. Or, double-wrap the bag with freezer wrap and freeze the cranberries up to 9 months.

Cranberry color can vary from light to dark; color has no effect on quality. You should, however, discard any soft or bruised berries.

Nutrition Analysis (*Per Serving*): Calories: 80 / Cholesterol: 0 mg / Carbohydrates: 20 g / Protein: 0 g / Sodium: 2 mg / Fat: 0 g (Saturated Fat: 0 g) / Potassium: 48 mg.

FRUITY ICE IS NICE

Don't let a heavy meal bog you down! Serve this sweet-tart Cranberry Sorbet as a light dessert or between courses as a refreshing palate cleanser.

FROZEN RAINBOW DESSERT

Makes 16 Servings

2   cups heavy whipping cream
3   tablespoons sugar
1   teaspoon vanilla
3   cups coconut macaroon
    crumbs (about 15 cookies)
1   cup chopped walnuts
1   pint orange sherbet,
    softened
1   pint lime sherbet, softened
1   pint raspberry sherbet,
    softened

♦   ♦   ♦

This recipe for Frozen Rainbow Dessert has been in Bev Solheim's family for so long that she can't even begin to remember its origin. Bev tells us that the dessert is a nice, light ending to any meal and that children especially love it for its colorful presentation and fruity taste. For a change with a little bit of tang, Bev occasionally substitutes pineapple or lemon sherbet for one of the sherbets listed in the recipe.

Bev Solheim
Redeemer Lutheran Church
Favorite Recipes
Thief River Falls
MINNESOTA

1 Lightly oil an 11- to 12-cup mold. Invert the mold to drain the excess oil.

2 In a large mixing bowl, beat the whipping cream, sugar and vanilla with an electric mixer until stiff peaks form (tips stand straight). Combine the macaroon crumbs with the walnuts. Fold the crumb-nut mixture into the whipped cream.

3 Spread *half* of the whipped cream mixture evenly in the bottom of the mold. Freeze until firm. Refrigerate the remaining whipped cream mixture.

4 Layer the orange, lime and raspberry sherbets on top of the whipped cream layer. As necessary, place the mold in the freezer between adding the layers to prevent the layers from running together.

5 Top with the remaining whipped cream mixture.

6 Cover and freeze at least 6 hours. To unmold, briefly dip the mold in *hot* water and invert onto a platter.

TIPS FROM OUR KITCHEN

To soften the sherbet for easier spreading, place it in a chilled bowl. Working with a wooden spoon, press the sherbet against the sides of the bowl. Work quickly so the sherbet doesn't melt.

For nice, even layers that don't run together, freeze the dessert at least 20 minutes after adding each flavor of sherbet.

Using a cake pan with a removable bottom, such as as angel-food cake pan or a springform pan, makes unmolding this dessert easier.

To make slicing this frozen dessert easy, dip your knife in hot water between cuts.

Nutrition Analysis *(Per Serving)*: Calories: 346 / Cholesterol: 46 mg / Carbohydrates: 38 g / Protein: 3 g / Sodium: 51 mg / Fat: 21 g (Saturated Fat: 8 g) / Potassium: 217 mg.

COOL AND COLORFUL

The rainbow of pastel sherbets in this frozen dessert from Minnesota makes it a refreshing
summertime treat. You'll be delighted to learn how easy it is to make this
deliciously beautiful dessert.

APPLE DESSERT PANCAKE

Makes 6 to 8 Servings

5	tablespoons sugar
1	teaspoon ground cinnamon
2	tablespoons butter *or* margarine
2	medium apples, peeled, cored and thinly sliced
⅓	cup all-purpose flour
¼	teaspoon baking powder
⅛	teaspoon salt
2	eggs, separated
⅓	cup milk

Sour cream, whipped cream, vanilla ice cream *or* vanilla yogurt (optional)

◆   ◆   ◆

It took the Dallas SPCA about a year to put together their cookbook. When it was published, all of the volunteers who worked on it got together at the shelter to celebrate, and each made a dish from the cookbook. Proceeds from cookbook sales provide much-needed funds to care for the animals at the shelter, and the cookbook is an excellent source of delicious recipes for the SPCA's bake sales.

Joi Weffelmeyer
<u>Dallas SPCA Cookbook</u>
Dallas SPCA
Dallas
TEXAS

1 In a small bowl, combine *2 tablespoons* of the sugar with the ground cinnamon. Set aside.

2 In a 10-inch skillet, with an oven-safe handle, melt the butter or margarine. Swirl the skillet to coat the entire bottom with the melted butter or margarine. Sprinkle the cinnamon-sugar mixture evenly over the melted butter or margarine.

3 Add the apples, cover and cook over low heat for 5 minutes, stirring once. Remove from heat. Preheat the oven to 400°.

4 Meanwhile, in a medium mixing bowl, stir together the flour, baking powder, salt, egg yolks and milk. Beat with a whisk until smooth.

5 In another medium mixing bowl, using an electric mixer, beat the egg whites with the remaining sugar until soft peaks form (tips curl). Carefully fold the egg white mixture into the flour mixture.

6 Pour the batter over the apples in the skillet. Bake in the 400° oven, uncovered, for 10 to 15 minutes or until golden and puffed.

7 Remove the skillet from the oven. Loosen the edges of the pancake with a spatula. Invert a flat, round serving plate over the skillet. Hold the plate and the skillet together, then flip so that the plate is on the bottom. Lift the skillet away. Serve the Apple Dessert Pancake cut into wedges and topped with sour cream, whipped cream, vanilla ice cream or vanilla yogurt, if desired.

 TIPS FROM OUR KITCHEN

For this recipe, you need a skillet with a handle that can be placed in a 400° oven. Check carefully, because the handles of some ovenproof skillets cannot withstand temperatures over 350°.

For variety, you can substitute pear slices for the apple slices in this recipe.

Nutrition Analysis (*Per Serving*): Calories: 146 / Cholesterol: 82 mg / Carbohydrates: 21 g / Protein: 3 g / Sodium: 125 mg / Fat: 6 g (Saturated Fat: 3 g) / Potassium: 82 mg.

FABULOUS OVEN FLAPJACK

Pancakes for dessert? Absolutely! Especially when apples are sautéed in butter with a sprinkling of
cinnamon-sugar, then topped with a light batter and baked to sweet perfection. Add a
yummy topping for a perfectly fabulous dessert.

FRUIT PIZZA

Makes 2 Pizzas (24 Servings)
Sugar Cookie Crust:
   1 cup butter *or* margarine,
     softened
   1 cup sifted powdered sugar
  ⅓ cup granulated sugar
   1 egg
  ½ teaspoon vanilla
  ¼ teaspoon almond extract
2½ cups all-purpose flour
   2 teaspoons baking soda
   2 teaspoons cream of tartar
Orange Sauce:
  ½ cup granulated sugar
  ¼ teaspoon finely shredded
     orange peel
  ¼ teaspoon finely shredded
     lemon peel
   1 cup orange juice
   2 tablespoons lemon juice
   4 teaspoons cornstarch
Filling:
   2 8-ounce packages cream
     cheese, softened
   1 cup sifted powdered sugar
   1 teaspoon vanilla
   Fresh fruits of choice (about 7
     cups total): sliced peaches,
     nectarines, strawberries,
     kiwi fruit, bananas, grapes,
     apples, mandarin oranges
     and/or raspberries

◆   ◆   ◆

*Who says that too many cooks
spoil the broth? This delicious
dessert is the victorious outcome
of a recipe-by-committee!*

<u>*A Pinch of Salt Lake*</u>
*The Junior League of Salt Lake
City, Inc.
Salt Lake City
UTAH*

1 Preheat oven to 325°. Lightly grease two 12-inch pizza pans.

2 To prepare the crust: In a large mixing bowl, cream the butter or margarine, powdered sugar and granulated sugar until light. Add the egg, vanilla and almond extract, beating well.

3 Combine the dry ingredients and add to the creamed mixture, blending thoroughly.

4 Divide the dough in half. With lightly floured hands, pat the dough into the prepared pans. Bake in the 325° oven for 12 to 15 minutes or until golden; cool.

5 To prepare the orange sauce: Combine the sugar, orange and lemon peel, orange and lemon juice and cornstarch in a small saucepan. Cook and stir over medium heat until the mixture is thick. Cook and stir for 2 minutes more. Cover and cool the sauce without stirring.

6 Meanwhile, to prepare the filling: In a medium mixing bowl, beat the cream cheese, powdered sugar and vanilla with an electric mixer until fluffy.

7 Spread the cream cheese mixture over the cooled crusts. Decorate with fruit.

8 Glaze the fruit with the cooled sauce. Chill the pizzas until ready to serve.

 TIPS FROM OUR KITCHEN

When you only need one pizza, wrap and seal the extra crust in moisture-vapor-proof wrap and freeze the extra crust for another time; then make only half the filling and orange sauce.

The clusters of tiny grapes on top of the pizza in the photograph are known as champagne grapes. Look for them near the other grapes in the produce section of the grocery store.

Nutrition Analysis *(Per Serving)*: Calories: 267 / Cholesterol: 50 mg / Carbohydrates: 32 g / Protein: 3 g / Sodium: 207 mg / Fat: 15 g (Saturated Fat: 9 g) / Potassium: 168 mg.

Yummy, Nontraditional Dessert

Pizza for dessert? You bet—when the components are as sweet and flavorful as these: sugar cookie crust, fruit and sweetened cream cheese filling and orange sauce topping. We admit it's a little avant-garde, but even traditionalists can't argue with delicious.

AMERICAN APPLE PIE

Makes 8 Servings

- 2   tablespoons lemon juice
- 1   tablespoon cornstarch
- 1/3 cup packed light brown sugar
- 1/3 cup sugar
- 1   tablespoon butter *or* margarine, melted
- 1   teaspoon ground cinnamon
- 1/4 teaspoon ground nutmeg
- 1/4 teaspoon salt
- 6   cups peeled and sliced cooking apples
- Pastry for double-crust 9-inch pie
- 1   egg yolk, beaten with 1 teaspoon water
- Sugar

◆   ◆   ◆

When the supporters of Trinity Church in Bucks County, Pennsylvania, decided to create a cookbook to raise funds for the church, they just had to include Arlene Rumbold's American Apple Pie. Like so many good cooks, Arlene likes to take a recipe, add a bit of this and take out a bit of that to end up with her own creation. The original recipe for the pie was given to Arlene by her mother.

Arlene L. Rumbold
Bucks Cooks II
Solebury
PENNSYLVANIA

---

1 Preheat oven to 400°.

2 In a small bowl, stir together the lemon juice and cornstarch until well blended.

3 In a large bowl, combine the brown sugar and sugar, butter or margarine, cinnamon, nutmeg, salt and the cornstarch mixture. Add the apple slices and toss to coat the slices completely. Let the mixture stand for 10 minutes.

4 Roll out *half* of the pastry into an 11-inch circle on a pastry cloth or a lightly floured piece of waxed paper.

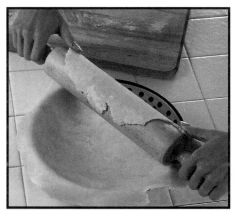

5 Wrap the pastry around the rolling pin by lifting the pastry cloth or waxed paper to guide the pastry onto the rolling pin; the pastry should slide easily onto the pin. Then slowly roll the pin to wrap the pastry around it. Loosely unroll the pastry onto the pie plate, being careful not to stretch the dough. To repair any tears in the pastry, moisten the edges with a little water and press together. Trim the pastry even with the rim of the pie plate.

6 Fill the pastry-lined pie plate with the apple mixture. Moisten the edges of the pastry with a little water.

7 Roll out the remaining pastry into a 12-inch circle on the pastry cloth or waxed paper. Follow Step 5 to transfer the pastry and place it over the filled crust. Trim the top crust ½ inch beyond the edge of the plate. Fold the top crust under the bottom crust; flute the edge. Cut several vents in the top crust and brush the whole top crust with the egg yolk mixture. Lightly sprinkle with sugar.

8 Bake the pie in the 400° oven about 40 minutes or until the crust is golden brown. If necessary, cover the edges of the crust with foil to prevent over-browning.

 TIPS FROM OUR KITCHEN

Get a jump on your next pie by making the pastry ahead and freezing it. Roll the pastry into rounds and stack them, 2 sheets of waxed paper between each layer. Seal the rounds in a large, freezer-safe plastic bag or container and freeze for up to 8 weeks. To use the frozen pastry, thaw the rounds, covered, while you make the filling.

Nutrition Analysis (*Per Serving*): Calories: 277 / Cholesterol: 34 mg / Carbohydrates: 41 g /
Protein: 2 g / Sodium: 168 mg / Fat: 13 g (Saturated Fat: 4 g) / Potassium: 115 mg.

SCRUMPTIOUS CLASSIC

Nothing is quite as American as apple pie—and this version from Arlene Rumbold of Solebury, Pennsylvania, is absolutely wonderful. Brought to this country by the Pilgrims, apple pie was originally served as a breakfast food. Today, we love to eat it anytime.

DESSERTS

CHOCOLATE CHESS PIE

Makes 8 Servings
- 1½ cups sugar
- 3 tablespoons unsweetened cocoa powder
- 2 eggs, beaten
- 1 5-ounce can (⅔ cup) evaporated milk
- ¼ cup margarine *or* butter, melted
- 1 teaspoon vanilla
- Dash salt
- 1 9-inch unbaked pie shell

◆　　◆　　◆

Mary Lynne collects recipes with an emphasis on minimum effort and fantastic results. For these reasons, she brings us Chocolate Chess Pie. For variety, Mary Lynne sometimes adds peppermint chips or peanut butter chips. At Christmastime, she uses this basic recipe to make tarts wreathed in whipped cream and garnished with green sugar sprinkles and red hots.

Mary Lynne Courtney
Potluck
The Women's Center
Raleigh
NORTH CAROLINA

1 Preheat oven to 325°.

2 In a medium mixing bowl, stir together the sugar and the cocoa. Add the eggs, evaporated milk, melted margarine or butter, vanilla and salt.

3 Carefully pour the mixture into a pastry-lined tart pan or pie plate. Bake in the 325° oven about 50 minutes or until puffed over the entire surface. Cool on a wire rack.

 TIPS FROM OUR KITCHEN

Prebaking the pastry will help make the crust deliciously flaky. Here's how to do it: Once you've positioned the pastry in the tart pan or pie plate, line the unpricked shell with a double thickness of heavy-duty foil. Bake it in a 450° oven for 5 minutes. Remove the foil. Bake for 5 to 7 minutes more or until the pastry is nearly done. Remove the pastry from the oven and reduce the oven temperature to 325°. Then add the filling and proceed according to this recipe.

For a lovely presentation, garnish each piece of the pie with some piped whipped cream and a little shaved milk chocolate.

For a dessert truly "made in heaven," top this brownie-like pie with a scoop of butter pecan or other nut-flavored ice cream.

Nutrition Analysis (*Per Serving*): Calories: 382 / Cholesterol: 59 mg / Carbohydrates: 53 g / Protein: 5 g / Sodium: 187 mg / Fat: 17 g (Saturated Fat: 5 g) / Potassium: 97 mg.

RICH AND FUDGY

Traditional chess pie relies on cornmeal and a lemony custard for its distinctive flavor and texture.
This unique variation from Raleigh, North Carolina, features a rich, chocolate-flavored custard.

PEANUT BUTTER PIE

Makes 6 to 8 Servings

Peanut Butter Mixture:
- ¾ cup sifted powdered sugar
- ½ cup crunchy peanut butter *or* smooth
- 1 9-inch pastry shell, baked

Filling:
- ¼ cup cornstarch
- ½ cup sugar
- ¼ teaspoon salt
- 2 cups milk, scalded
- 3 egg yolks
- 2 tablespoons butter *or* margarine
- ½ teaspoon vanilla

Meringue:
- 3 egg whites
- 3 tablespoons sugar

♦   ♦   ♦

Mrs. Fanning's aunts spent a great deal of time thinking of and preparing special dishes for their grandnieces and grandnephews. Fifteen years ago, these lovely ladies brought this pie and the recipe to Mrs. Fanning. The wise aunts knew it would become a Fanning family favorite. This is sure to be a hit in your home, too.

Mrs. Thomas Fanning
<u>*Winning Seasons*</u>
The Junior League of Tuscaloosa
Tuscaloosa
ALABAMA

1 Preheat the oven to 350°. To make the peanut butter mixture: In a medium bowl, cut the powdered sugar into the peanut butter until the mixture is well combined. Crumble *half* of the mixture into the bottom of the pastry shell.

2 To make the filling: Combine the cornstarch with the ½ cup sugar and the salt. Gradually stir in the scalded milk. In the top of a double boiler, beat the egg yolks until they are pale yellow. Slowly stir in the scalded milk mixture. Place the top of the double boiler over the bottom filled with boiling water. Cook, stirring, about 5 minutes or until the mixture is thickened and bubbly. Stir in the butter or margarine and vanilla. Remove from the heat. Wash the beaters.

3 To make the meringue: In a large mixing bowl, beat the egg whites until foamy. Gradually add the 3 tablespoons sugar, beating until stiff peaks form (tips stand straight).

4 Pour the hot filling over the peanut butter mixture in the pastry shell.

5 Spoon the meringue over the filling, first around the edges to seal the crust, then spreading toward the center to prevent shrinkage of the meringue during baking.

6 Crumble the reserved peanut butter mixture over the meringue.

7 Bake in the 350° oven about 15 minutes or until the meringue is lightly browned. Place on a wire rack and allow to cool 1 hour, then refrigerate.

 TIPS FROM OUR KITCHEN

If you don't own a double boiler, don't scald the milk. In place of Step 2: In a medium saucepan, combine the ½ cup sugar, cornstarch, and salt. Gradually stir in the milk. Cook and stir over medium-high heat until the mixture is thickened and bubbly. Reduce the heat; cook and stir for 2 minutes more. Remove the saucepan from the heat. Beat the yolks lightly with a fork. Gradually stir about *1 cup* of the hot filling into the yolks. Return all of the hot filling to the saucepan and bring to a gentle boil. Cook and stir for 2 minutes more. Remove the saucepan from the heat and stir in the butter or margarine and vanilla.

Nutrition Analysis (*Per Serving*): Calories: 433 / Cholesterol: 92 mg / Carbohydrates: 50 g Protein: 10 g / Sodium: 294 mg / Fat: 23 g (Saturated Fat: 7 g) / Potassium: 252 mg.

SOUTHERN CHARM IN A SLICE

This spectacular pie combines the irresistible flavor of peanut butter with a smooth, creamy filling
and a light, fluffy meringue. Mrs. Thomas Fanning of Tuscaloosa, Alabama, was given the recipe
for this now-famous pie by her two aunts who live in Kentucky.

LEMON LUSCIOUS PIE

Makes 8 Servings

 1 cup sugar
 3 tablespoons cornstarch
 1 tablespoon grated lemon
    peel
 ¼ cup lemon juice
 3 egg yolks
 1 cup milk
 ¼ cup butter *or* margarine,
    cut up
 1 cup dairy sour cream
 1 9-inch pie shell, baked
 1 cup whipping cream
 2 tablespoons sugar
 1 teaspoon vanilla

◆   ◆   ◆

Lucy Di Meglio tells us that she received this recipe for Lemon Luscious Pie from an old friend who was an excellent baker. Lucy is fortunate enough to have a large lemon tree in her backyard, and she believes that the combination of a homemade crust and fresh lemons gives her pies an extra-special touch.

Lucy Di Meglio
Around the World,
Around Our Town:
Recipes from San Pedro
Friends of San Pedro Library
San Pedro
CALIFORNIA

1 In a medium saucepan, combine the 1 cup sugar, the cornstarch and lemon peel. Stir in the lemon juice, egg yolks and milk until blended. Add the butter or margarine.

2 Cook the mixture over medium heat, stirring constantly until thickened and bubbly. Cook and stir for 2 minutes more. Cover the surface of the filling with plastic wrap and refrigerate for 30 minutes.

3 Remove the filling from the refrigerator. Fold in the sour cream. Spoon the filling into the pie shell. Cover the surface of the pie with plastic wrap and refrigerate for at least 2 hours.

4 In a small mixing bowl, beat the whipping cream with an electric mixer until thickened. Gradually beat in the 2 tablespoons sugar and the vanilla. Continue to beat until the whipped cream is fluffy. Spread the whipped cream over the top of the pie. Refrigerate for 1 to 2 hours.

TIPS FROM OUR KITCHEN

You'll need to buy one large or two medium lemons to have enough juice and peel for this recipe. Look for well-shaped fruits with smooth, evenly yellow skin.

For best results when whipping the cream, chill the bowl and the beaters in your freezer for 10 minutes before you begin. Be sure that your cream is very cold and whip it with an electric mixer

set on medium speed (not high) to avoid overbeating. (Overbeating will cause your cream to turn into butter.) When choosing your bowl, keep in mind that whipping cream doubles in volume when whipped.

To make a decorative edge on your pastry shell, roll out the pastry scraps until very thin. Use a knife or canapé cutter to cut the pastry into desired shapes. Brush the edge of the pastry shell with water. Arrange the cutouts on the edge of the pastry shell and press lightly to secure.

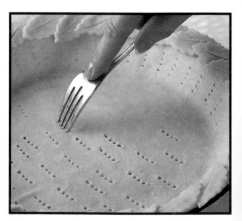

To prevent the crust from bubbling too much or shrinking while baking, use the tines of a fork to prick the unbaked pastry shell several times. Be sure to prick the bottom and the side.

Nutrition Analysis (*Per Serving*): Calories: 510 / Cholesterol: 151 mg / Carbohydrates: 48 g / Protein: 6 g / Sodium: 172 mg / Fat: 34 g (Saturated Fat: 17 g) / Potassium: 147 mg.

Ooo-la-la Lemon

A tribute to sweet indulgence! Gorgeous to behold, this lemony, rich and creamy pie is a
wonderful way to complete a special meal.

FOR THE GLORY PIE

Makes 8 Servings

1	9-inch unbaked pie shell
¾ to 1	cup sugar
1	8-ounce carton dairy sour cream
3	tablespoons all-purpose flour
¼	teaspoon salt
4	cups fresh blackberries
¼	cup fine dry bread crumbs
2	tablespoons sugar
1	tablespoon butter *or* margarine, melted

◆   ◆   ◆

When Huberta Young Manning moved into her new home about eight years ago, she found a patch of blackberries in her yard and began looking for recipes to use the berries. Her search resulted in the discovery of this delicious recipe for For the Glory Pie. Huberta tells us that she makes the pie every year during blackberry season and "always on the Fourth of July." She also freezes some of the fresh blackberries to enjoy throughout the year.

Huberta Young Manning
Cookin' with the Lion
Penn State Alumni Association
University Park
PENNSYLVANIA

1 Preheat the oven to 450°.

2 Line the bottom of a pastry-lined 9-inch pie plate with a double thickness of foil. Bake in the 450° oven for 5 minutes. Remove the foil and bake for 5 minutes more. Remove the pie shell from the oven and cool slightly. Reduce the oven temperature to 375°.

3 Meanwhile, in a small bowl, stir together the ¾ to 1 cup sugar, the sour cream, flour and salt until combined. Set aside.

4 Place the blackberries in the pre-baked pastry shell. Spread the sour cream mixture evenly over the berries.

5 In a small bowl, stir together the bread crumbs, the 2 tablespoons sugar and the melted butter or margarine. Sprinkle the bread crumb mixture on top of the sour cream mixture.

6 Cover the edge of the pie with foil and bake in the 375° oven for 25 minutes. Remove the foil. Bake for 20 to 25 minutes more or until the top of the pie is golden and the berry mixture bubbles slightly.

 TIPS FROM OUR KITCHEN

Use fresh blackberries for this recipe; frozen berries don't work well because they release too much juice as they thaw. However, you could substitute other fresh berries like blueberries or raspberries.

Fine dry bread crumbs are easy to make. For ¼ cup of crumbs, place one slice of dried or lightly toasted bread in a plastic bag and crush it with a rolling pin.

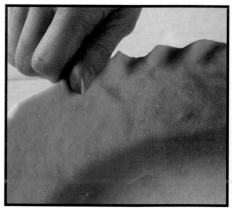

Pie crust edges are usually fluted by pressing the dough with the forefinger of one hand against the thumb and forefinger of the other hand. To make a rope-shaped edge, press the dough between the thumb and a bent forefinger.

An easy way to cover just the edge of the pie with foil is to cut a large circle out of the center of a 12-inch square of foil.

Nutrition Analysis (*Per Serving*): Calories: 353 / Cholesterol: 17 mg / Carbohydrates: 50 g / Protein: 4 g / Sodium: 187 mg / Fat: 17 g (Saturated Fat: 7 g) / Potassium: 210 mg.

IRRESISTIBLE DESSERT

Who could resist a fresh blackberry pie, especially one with a layer of sweetened sour cream and a
buttery crumb topping? Keep this recipe handy when fresh berries are in season.

Fish & Seafood

*T*here's hardly a healthier entrée than fish or seafood, and
freshness is the key to good
fish and seafood. So buy fresh
instead of frozen, if possible.
Ask when the fish arrived in
the market, and try to choose
the fish that came in the same
day. Fish and seafood should
have a clean, oceany—not
fishy—smell. Several of these
recipes come from places where
fish is certainly plentiful. For
example, we found Ginger
Scallops in *A Taste of Aloha* by
the Junior League of Honolulu.

RED SNAPPER WITH ORANGE SAUCE

Makes 6 Servings

1 ½	pounds red snapper fillets
¼	teaspoon salt
⅛	teaspoon pepper
½ to 1	teaspoon minced garlic
1	tablespoon butter *or* margarine
1	teaspoon grated orange peel
3	tablespoons orange juice

Orange Sauce:

1	whole clove garlic
2	tablespoons butter *or* margarine
3	tablespoons orange juice
⅛	teaspoon ground ginger
2	tablespoons snipped parsley

◆　　◆　　◆

Since its founding in 1894, the Greater Kansas City Section of the National Council of Jewish Women has been actively supporting many community services. Proceeds from <u>The Cook Book</u> *have gone to scholarship and literacy programs as well as programs for children, teens, the handicapped and the elderly.*

<u>The Cook Book</u>
Greater Kansas City Section
of the National Council
of Jewish Women
Kansas City
MISSOURI

1 Preheat oven to 400°.

2 In a large baking pan, arrange the red snapper fillets in a single layer. Sprinkle the fillets with the salt and pepper.

3 In a small saucepan over medium heat, cook the minced garlic in the 1 tablespoon butter or margarine for 30 seconds.

4 Sprinkle the garlic-butter mixture, the grated orange peel and the 3 tablespoons of orange juice over the fillets.

5 Bake the fillets, uncovered, in the 400° oven until the fish flakes easily when tested with a fork. (Allow 4 to 6 minutes per ½-inch thickness of fish.) Transfer the fillets to a platter and keep warm.

6 Meanwhile, to make the Orange Sauce: In a small saucepan over medium heat, cook the garlic clove in the 2 tablespoons butter or margarine until the garlic begins to turn golden; remove and discard the garlic clove. Stir in the 3 tablespoons orange juice and the ginger.

7 To serve, spoon some of the sauce over each fillet. Sprinkle with the parsley.

TIPS FROM OUR KITCHEN

Be sure to choose a baking pan that's large enough to allow the fish fillets to lie flat without touching. This will help the fish to cook more evenly.

To test fish for doneness: Poke the tines of a fork into the thickest portion of the fish at a 45-degree angle. Then, gently twist the fork and pull up some of the flesh.

Undercooked fish is translucent, with clear juices. The flesh is firm and does not flake. Properly cooked fish is opaque with milky-white juices. The flesh flakes easily. Overcooked fish is opaque and dry. It flakes into tiny pieces.

Nutrition Analysis (*Per Serving*): Calories: 173 / Cholesterol: 57 mg / Carbohydrates: 2 g / Protein: 24 g / Sodium: 198 mg / Fat: 7 g (Saturated Fat: 4 g) / Potassium: 510 mg.

DELECTABLE FISH DISH

In this recipe from Kansas City, Missouri, a tangy orange sauce really brings out the best in the red snapper. Although most people traditionally pair fish with lemon, we think this orange sauce with its hint of garlic and ginger is much more exciting.

CURRIED FISH-FILLED AVOCADO

Makes 4 Servings

8	ounces fish fillets, cooked and flaked into chunks (1½ cups)
½	cup finely chopped celery
¼	cup cooked green peas
¼	cup slivered almonds, toasted
¼	cup mayonnaise
1 to 2	tablespoons sugar *or* honey
2	teaspoons lemon juice
½	teaspoon salt
½	teaspoon curry powder
¼	teaspoon pepper
2	ripe avocados

Lemon juice *or* cut lemon
Lettuce leaves
Pimiento strips (optional)
Lemon wedges

♦   ♦   ♦

"Week of the Ocean" is a marine education program designed to promote an awareness of the ocean's vast resource of food, water and energy, as well as its historic and cultural influence on mankind. Recipes in Festival of Favorites *come from the organization's seafood cooking competition. We think you'll agree that Amber Ead's Curried Fish-Filled Avocado is a true winner.*

Amber Eads
Festival Favorites
National Week of the Ocean, Inc.
Fort Lauderdale
FLORIDA

1 In a medium bowl, stir together the cooked fish, chopped celery, cooked peas and toasted almonds. Set aside.

2 In a small bowl, stir together the mayonnaise, sugar or honey, lemon juice, salt, curry powder and pepper. Gently fold the mayonnaise mixture into the fish mixture.

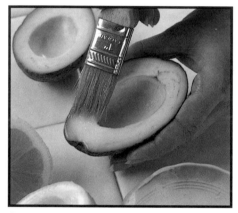

3 Halve and pit the avocados. Brush them with lemon juice or rub with a cut lemon to prevent them from darkening.

4 Fill the avocado centers with the fish mixture and place the filled avocados on lettuce-lined plates. Garnish with pimiento strips, if desired, and serve with lemon wedges.

 TIPS FROM OUR KITCHEN

You can use any type of firm-textured white fish such as cod or haddock for this recipe.

To micro-cook thawed or fresh fish: Place the fish in a single layer in a shallow, microwave-safe baking dish. Tuck under any thin edges of the fillets. Cover with vented microwave-safe plastic wrap. Micro-cook on 100% power (high). For 8 ounces of ½-inch-thick fillets, allow 3 to 4 minutes; for 1 pound of ½-inch-thick fillets, allow 4 to 7 minutes. For 1 pound of ¾- to 1-inch-thick steaks, allow 7 to 9 minutes. Chill the fish before flaking it into bite-size pieces.

To poach fish: In a large skillet, bring 1½ cups water, broth or wine to a boil. Add the fish and return to a boil. Reduce heat and simmer, covered, for 4 to 6 minutes for ½-inch-thick fresh or thawed fish. Allow 6 to 9 minutes for ½-inch-thick frozen fillets or steaks. Chill the fish before flaking it into bite-size pieces.

To pit an avocado, tap the seed with the blade of a sharp knife so it catches in the seed. Twist the knife from side to side to loosen the seed. Lift the knife and remove the seed.

Nutrition Analysis (*Per Serving*): Calories: 380 / Cholesterol: 39 mg / Carbohydrates: 14 g / Protein: 17 g / Sodium: 423 mg / Fat: 30 g (Saturated Fat: 4 g) / Potassium: 858 mg.

SUMMER SUPPER

Amber Eads of Fort Lauderdale, Florida, gives us the perfect answer to "What's for dinner?" on hot summer nights. The flavorful combination of cooked fish and avocado is married with a mild curry dressing. Almonds and celery add crunch, while peas and pimiento add color.

FISH & SEAFOOD

BAKED FISH WITH VEGETABLES

Makes 6 to 8 Servings

3	medium onions, cut up
3 or 4	medium zucchini, cut up
3	medium tomatoes
1	large green sweet pepper, halved and seeded
½	cup Italian parsley leaves
2 to 3	cloves garlic
½	teaspoon salt
¼	teaspoon pepper
¼	cup olive oil
1	15-ounce can tomato sauce
1½ to 2	pounds fresh *or* frozen fish fillets (1 to 1½-inches thick), thawed
1	lemon, thinly sliced

♦   ♦   ♦

On March 28, 1889, the Watch Hill Improvement Society was incorporated "to build up and beautify Watch Hill and to render it a still more inviting and desirable place of residence." Throughout the years, the organization has been responsible for town maintenance and theatrical extravaganzas, as well as many other projects.

<u>*Watch Hill Cooks*</u>
The Watch Hill
Improvement Society
Watch Hill
RHODE ISLAND

1 Fit a food processor work bowl with a coarse slicing disk. Slice the onions, zucchini, tomatoes and green sweet pepper, transferring them to a large mixing bowl as the work bowl gets full. *Or,* using a sharp knife, slice the vegetables by hand.

2 Replace the slicing disk with a steel knife. Add the parsley and garlic; process until chopped. *Or,* snip the parsley and mince the garlic by hand. Add the parsley mixture to the vegetables. Stir in the salt and pepper.

3 In a 12-inch skillet, heat *2 tablespoons* of the olive oil. Add the vegetable mixture; cook and stir over medium heat about 5 minutes or until the vegetables begin to soften. Carefully add the tomato sauce. Simmer, covered, for 10 minutes. Drain, reserving the liquid. Preheat the oven to 375°.

4 Coat the bottom of a 3-quart rectangular baking dish with the remaining olive oil; add the fish. Spoon the drained vegetables over and around the fish. Bake, uncovered, in the 375° oven for 35 to 40 minutes or until the fish flakes easily when tested with a fork.

5 While the fish is baking, return the reserved vegetable liquid to the skillet. Bring to a boil. Cook over medium heat about 5 minutes or until the liquid is reduced by half. Using a slotted spoon, serve the fish and vegetables. Spoon the sauce over each serving. Garnish with the lemon slices.

 TIPS FROM OUR KITCHEN

Lake trout, grouper, walleye pike, pike or bluefish (if available) work well for this recipe.

Italian parsley has larger, flatter, darker green leaves and a milder flavor than the more common curly-leaf parsley. To store, wash parsley and shake off the excess moisture. Wrap in paper towels and place in a plastic bag in the refrigerator up to 1 week.

Thaw frozen fish in the refrigerator overnight; do not thaw it at room temperature.

Nutrition Analysis (*Per Serving*): Calories: 349 / Cholesterol: 47 mg / Carbohydrates: 22 g / Protein: 32 g / Sodium: 670 mg / Fat: 16 g (Saturated Fat: 3 g) / Potassium: 1143 mg.

A HEALTHY COMBINATION

An assortment of fresh vegetables surrounds this catch in an easy-to-make, delicious dish. The flaky and colorful main-dish recipe is from Watch Hill, Rhode Island.

STUFFED FISH FILLETS

♦   ♦   ♦

The Mushroom Lover's Cookbook is a collection of recipes from the Wilmington, Delaware, branch of the American Association of University Women. Wilmington is near Kennett Square, Pennsylvania, the birthplace of mushroom growing in the United States.

The Mushroom Lover's Cookbook
The American Association of University Women, Wilmington, Delaware Branch
Wilmington
DELAWARE

1 Thaw the fish if frozen. Preheat the oven to 450°. Grease a 2-quart rectangular baking dish. Set aside.

2 To make the stuffed fish: In a medium skillet over medium heat, melt the margarine or butter. Add the celery and mushrooms and cook and stir until the vegetables are tender; remove from heat.

3 Stir in the stuffing mix, Parmesan cheese, garlic powder, dry sherry, ½ teaspoon lemon juice and beaten egg.

4 Divide the stuffing among the fillets. Wrap the ends of the fillets around the stuffing and place the rolls seam-side down in the prepared baking dish.

5 Bake, uncovered, in the 450° oven for 12 to 15 minutes or until the stuffing is hot and the fish flakes easily when tested with a fork.

6 To make the Lemon Sauce: In a small saucepan, over medium heat, melt the margarine or butter. Reduce the heat to medium-low, add the mushrooms and cook and stir for 2 minutes; remove from heat.

7 Stir in the 2 to 3 teaspoons lemon juice, garlic powder, salt and pepper. Spoon the sauce over *each* fish fillet just before serving. Sprinkle with the parsley.

TIPS FROM OUR KITCHEN

Sole and flounder are flat saltwater fish. Both have white flesh and are delicate to mild in flavor. Authentic sole is imported from Europe. The following are varieties of flounder commonly sold in the United States: gray sole, rex sole and lemon sole (also known as winter flounder). Other varieties of flounder include sand dab (also known as American plaice) and summer flounder (also called fluke).

Use your nose when shopping for fresh fish. Check for a mild smell, not a strong odor. Fillets should appear moist and freshly cut. Fresh fish is very perishable and is best cooked the same day that it is purchased. If this isn't possible, wrap fish in moisture/vapor-proof wrap and store in the coldest part of your refrigerator up to two days.

Nutrition Analysis (*Per Serving*): Calories: 238 / Cholesterol: 61 mg / Carbohydrates: 6 g / Protein: 23 g / Sodium: 380 mg / Fat: 13 g (Saturated Fat: 3 g) / Potassium: 424 mg.

SIMPLY DELICIOUS

In this simple-to-prepare recipe from Wilmington, Delaware, mild-flavored fillets of sole or flounder
are wrapped around an herb-seasoned mushroom stuffing. Top these with a tangy lemon sauce
for a simply delicious dish.

BLACKENED REDFISH

Makes 3 Servings

1   tablespoon paprika
1   teaspoon salt
1   teaspoon onion powder
1   teaspoon garlic powder
1   teaspoon ground red
    pepper
¾   teaspoon white pepper
¾   teaspoon black pepper
½   teaspoon dried oregano,
    crushed
½   teaspoon dried thyme,
    crushed
¼   cup margarine *or* butter
3   redfish fillets, ¾ inch thick
    (12 ounces)

◆   ◆   ◆

Debbie Espy first tasted Black-ened Redfish at a dinner given by a friend about five years ago. Debbie got the recipe, and when her friend came to her home for dinner, it was Debbie's turn to serve the delicious fish dish! It's very easy to make—"Cook, flip, cook and it's done!" Debbie suggests serving the redfish with steamed vegetables and French bread.

Debbie Espy
Our Daily Bread
Mountain View Baptist Church
Stone Mountain
GEORGIA

1 In a small dish, stir together the paprika, salt, onion powder, garlic powder, red pepper, white pepper, black pepper, oregano and thyme; set aside.

2 Melt the margarine or butter. Dip the fish in the margarine or butter, then sprinkle each side with about *1 teaspoon* of the spice mixture. Place the coated fish in single layer on a platter.

3 Outdoors, on a camping stove or a grill, heat an ungreased 10-inch cast-iron skillet directly on the hot coals until it is very hot; keep hot. Carefully place the coated fish in the skillet and cook approximately 2 minutes on each side or until the fish flakes when tested with a fork. Each side will look black. Serve immediately.

TIPS FROM OUR KITCHEN

Because a great deal of smoke is given off when you blacken fish, cooking outdoors is highly recommended.

To prepare the fish on a grill: Remove the grill rack and heat the coals until hot. Set an ungreased cast-iron skillet directly on the coals and heat for 5 minutes or until a drop of water sizzles when dropped in the skillet. Add the coated fish and cook about 2 minutes on each side.

Store any remaining spice mixture in a covered container.

Redfish is a saltwater fish with firm, white meat and a mild flavor; it is sometimes called red drum. Because so much was taken from the Gulf of Mexico in the 1980s, authorities banned the commercial redfish harvest. Black drum is a good substitute. This cooking method also works well with other types of fish such as croaker, carp, cod or haddock.

Cajun cooking is the cuisine of French-speaking south Louisiana. It features simple, one-pot dishes with French, Italian, Spanish, African, Indian and southern influences. The name *cajun* comes from *Acadian*, the name for the early French-Canadian settlers.

Nutrition Analysis (*Per Serving*): Calories: 261 / Cholesterol: 42 mg / Carbohydrates: 3 g / Protein: 24 g / Sodium: 704 mg / Fat: 17 g (Saturated Fat: 3 g) / Potassium: 531 mg.

CAJUN SPECIALTY

Yes, you, too, can make the Cajun specialty, blackened fish, at home! Just pull out your cast-iron skillet and follow Debbie Espy's method of outdoor cooking. Your family and guests will love this flavorful, tender fish.

BAKED FISH WITH RICE-OLIVE STUFFING

Makes 8 to 10 Servings

Rice-Olive Stuffing:

1	cup chopped onion
1	cup chopped celery
¼	cup olive oil
1	cup long grain rice
1	16-ounce can tomatoes, cut up
1	cup water
1½	teaspoon snipped fresh mint *or* 1 tablespoon snipped fresh oregano (optional)
2	tablespoons snipped parsley
1	tablespoon snipped fresh dill
¼	teaspoon freshly ground pepper
1	cup sliced black, green *or* stuffed olives

Fish:

1	5- to 6-pound whole bass, cod, haddock *or* sea trout
½	teaspoon salt
¼	teaspoon freshly ground pepper
1	cup thinly sliced onion
½	cup snipped parsley
1 to 1½	cups chicken broth
2	tablespoons cooking oil
2	tablespoons freshly squeezed lemon juice

♦ ♦ ♦

Popular Greek Recipes
Greek Orthodox Ladies
Philoptochos Society
Charleston
SOUTH CAROLINA

1 Grease a 1½-quart casserole dish. Set aside.

2 To make the stuffing: In a large skillet, cook and stir the onion and celery in the olive oil about 5 minutes or until tender. Add the rice, tomatoes, water, mint or oregano (if desired), parsley, dill and pepper.

3 Simmer, covered, about 25 minutes or until the rice is just tender. Stir in the olives.

4 To prepare the fish: Sprinkle the fish, inside and out, with the salt and pepper. Stuff the fish with the Rice-Olive Stuffing.

5 Preheat the oven to 500°. Meanwhile, place the onions and parsley in the prepared pan and place the stuffed fish on top. Pour in *1 cup* of the chicken broth.

6 In a small bowl, combine the cooking oil and lemon juice. Brush the fish with oil-lemon juice mixture.

7 Bake in the 500° oven for 10 minutes. Then, reduce the oven temperature to 375°; cover and bake for 30 minutes, adding more chicken stock as needed.

8 Uncover and bake about 15 minutes more or until the fish is done (fish flakes easily when tested with a fork).

 TIPS FROM OUR KITCHEN

Serving a whole fish is easy when you know the best way to remove the bones. First, position the cooked fish with the backbone toward you. Use a table knife and fork to remove the head and tail. Then make a lengthwise cut just above the backbone from the head to the tail of the fish. Next, gently loosen the top skin of the fish and peel the skin toward the stomach and away from the fish. Remove and discard the skin. Now, carefully lift the top fillet of fish away from the backbone onto a serving plate. Finally, pull up and discard the backbone and lift the bottom fillet away from the bottom skin.

Nutrition Analysis *(Per Serving)*: Calories: 339 / Cholesterol: 45 mg / Carbohydrates: 27 g / Protein: 24 g / Sodium: 496 mg / Fat: 16 g (Saturated Fat: 2 g) / Potassium: 611 mg.

A Taste of Greece

This traditional Greek dish was originally made with flavorful Calamata olives, but it is delicious
made with milder flavored olives, too. Garnish with lemon wedges and fresh mint
for an added touch of color.

FILLET OF SOLE PARMESAN

Makes 6 Servings
½ cup grated Parmesan cheese
¼ cup butter *or* margarine, softened
3 tablespoons mayonnaise *or* salad dressing
3 tablespoons chopped scallions *or* green onions
Dash bottled hot pepper sauce
1½ pounds skinless sole fillets *or* any fresh white fish such as orange roughy *or* red snapper
2 tablespoons lemon juice
Sliced scallions (optional)

♦   ♦   ♦

When the Junior League of Kansas City, Missouri, requested recipes from their 1,800 members, they received over 1,000. Then, they began the taste-testing and recipe-selection process. Each recipe was tested a minimum of three times by a committee and the recipes that passed were given to another committee who tested again for taste and presentation. Fillet of Sole Parmesan is clearly one of those that passed with flying colors!

<u>Beyond Parsley</u>
The Junior League of Kansas City
Kansas City
MISSOURI

1 Grease the rack of a broiler pan; set aside.

2 In a small bowl, stir together the Parmesan cheese, butter or margarine, mayonnaise or salad dressing, scallions or green onions and hot pepper sauce. Set aside.

3 Measure the thickness of the fish fillets, then place them in a single layer on the prepared rack of the broiler pan. Brush the fillets with the lemon juice and let stand for 10 minutes.

4 Allow 4 to 6 minutes of broiling time per ½-inch thickness of fillet. Broil the fillets 3 to 4 inches from the heat for 4 to 5 minutes. Spread the cheese mixture over the fillets. Broil for 2 to 3 minutes more or until the fish flakes easily when tested with a fork and the topping is golden. Garnish each fillet with additional sliced scallions, if desired.

 TIPS FROM OUR KITCHEN

Scallions are also called green onions. You can use as much of the green part as you want—just remove any wilted, brown or damaged tops. One green onion yields about 2 tablespoons sliced.

This buttery cheese topping is also good when spread on sliced French bread, and then broiled.

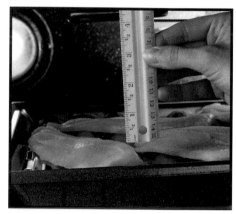

Use a ruler to check the distance from the heat source to the top of the fish—not to the top of the pan. Being too close or too far away from the heat will affect the length of broiling time.

Nutrition Analysis (*Per Serving*): Calories: 260 / Cholesterol: 92 mg / Carbohydrates: 1 g / Protein: 25 g / Sodium: 365 mg / Fat: 17 g (Saturated Fat: 8 g) / Potassium: 327 mg.

QUICK-FIX FISH

Not much time to prepare dinner, but still want to serve a scrumptious, impressive main dish? Fillet
of Sole Parmesan is just the answer! Mild-flavored sole fillets are treated to a mouth-watering,
golden brown cheese topping that cooks up in a flash.

FISH & SEAFOOD

183

FILLET OF SOLE WITH BACON AND SCALLIONS

Makes 6 to 8 Servings

1½ to 2 pounds sole fillets
⅛ teaspoon salt
¼ teaspoon pepper
2 tablespoons lemon juice
¼ teaspoon dried dillweed
4 slices bacon, cooked, drained and crumbled
½ cup chopped scallions *or* green onions
½ cup peeled, seeded and finely chopped tomato

◆   ◆   ◆

The Junior League of Wichita has lovingly prepared The Sunflower Sampler to assist in their fund-raising efforts that benefit many community projects, including the Sedgwick County Zoo, Cowtown Museum and Heritage Square Park. Proceeds from cookbook sales have also helped Wichita to become the first city in the world to have two Ronald McDonald houses.

Sunflower Sampler
Junior League of Wichita
Wichita
KANSAS

1 Preheat broiler. Lightly grease the broiler rack.

2 Arrange the sole fillets on the prepared broiler rack, tucking under any thin portions of fish. This makes the fillets about the same thickness so they cook evenly. Sprinkle the fillets with the salt and pepper.

 TIPS FROM OUR KITCHEN

We also like this vegetable-bacon topping served over flounder or pike fillets.

For a special presentation, arrange scallion tops in a grid pattern on a white plate. Place the cooked fillets on top. Thinly slice a lemon and fan the lemon slices alongside the fish. To really impress your guests, finish the dish off with a sprig of fresh dill.

3 In a small bowl, combine the lemon juice and dillweed. Brush the lemon juice mixture evenly over the fillets.

4 In another small bowl, combine the bacon with the scallions or green onions and tomato; spoon the bacon mixture over the fillets.

5 Broil the fillets 4 to 5 inches from the heat for 3 to 5 minutes or until the fish flakes easily when tested with a fork.

Nutrition Analysis *(Per Serving):* Calories: 132 / Cholesterol: 64 mg / Carbohydrates: 1 g / Protein: 23 g / Sodium: 206 mg / Fat: 3 g (Saturated Fat: 1 g) / Potassium: 371 mg.

WICHITA SOUL

This luscious fish dish comes to us from the Junior League of Wichita, Kansas. The colorful
vegetable-bacon garnish makes this a perfect choice for entertaining, but we also suggest serving this
quick and easy dish to your family.

TROUT MEUNIÈRE

Makes 6 Servings

6   dressed trout or 6 freshwater bass fillets
½   cup fine saltine cracker crumbs (15 crackers)
¼   cup butter *or* margarine
1   2-ounce package slivered almonds
½   cup dry white wine
2   tablespoons lemon juice
2   tablespoons snipped parsley
Lemon twists (optional)
Parsley sprigs (optional)

◆   ◆   ◆

Hearts & Flours is now in its third printing, continuing to fulfill its purpose of funding special projects of the Junior League of Waco, Texas. The League is known for its innovative and effective volunteer programs, and its current focus is on the city's youth. Proceeds from cookbook sales will help to fund programs aimed at reducing teenage pregnancy and encouraging high school graduation, among others.

Hearts & Flours
Junior League of Waco
Waco
TEXAS

1 Rinse the fish; do not pat dry. Roll each piece of fish in the cracker crumbs.

2 In a large skillet, melt *2 tablespoons* of the butter or margarine. Add the fish pieces and gently cook for 2 to 3 minutes on each side or until the fish flakes when tested with a fork. Do not overcook.

3 Using a spatula, carefully remove the fish from the skillet and transfer to a serving platter. Keep warm.

4 Melt the remaining 2 tablespoons butter in the skillet. Add the almonds and cook and stir until the almonds are lightly browned. Spoon the almonds over the fish.

5 Add the wine, lemon juice and snipped parsley to the skillet. Simmer for 2 minutes. Pour the sauce over the fish and almonds.

6 Garnish the fish with the lemon twists and the parsley sprigs, if desired.

 TIPS FROM OUR KITCHEN

If you're watching your sodium intake, use low-sodium saltine crackers.

For added flavor, add a pinch of fresh or dried herbs to the cracker crumbs. Basil, dillweed or savory would work well with the flavor from the almonds.

Here's how to make sure the fish you buy is fresh. First, use your nose. Fresh fish in any form has a fresh, mild odor.

Next, take a good look. For whole, drawn or dressed fish, look for shiny, taut and iridescent skin and clear, bright eyes. The gills should be bright red or pink and not slippery.

Fillets should have a moist appearance with clean cuts. Ragged edges and discoloration indicate poor quality.

Buy equal-sized fish or pieces of fish to ensure uniform doneness.

Nutrition Analysis *(Per Serving)*: Calories: 433 / Cholesterol: 152 mg / Carbohydrates: 7 g / Protein: 49 g / Sodium: 234 mg / Fat: 21 g (Saturated Fat: 7 g) / Potassium: 1228 mg.

CATCH OF THE DAY

Delicately flavored fish fillets are dredged in cracker crumbs, panfried, showered with toasted almonds and then finished with a wine-lemon sauce. Good eating!

DEEP DISH SALMON PIE

Makes 4 to 6 Servings
Creamed Salmon:
  3   tablespoons butter *or* margarine
  2   small onions, chopped (⅔ cup)
  1   medium green sweet pepper, chopped (¾ cup)
  5   tablespoons all-purpose flour
  ½   teaspoon salt
  2⅔ cups milk
  1   14¾-ounce can salmon, drained, flaked and skin and bones removed
  1   tablespoon lemon juice
Cheese Rolls:
  1½ cups all-purpose flour
  1   tablespoon baking powder
  ½   teaspoon salt
  3   tablespoons shortening
  ½   cup milk *or* water
  ¾   cup shredded cheddar, mozzarella, Swiss, American *or* hot pepper cheese (3 ounces)
  ¼   cup chopped pimiento (optional)

◆ ◆ ◆

The recipes in this wonderful cookbook were contributed by the staff, board members and volunteers of the center.

Sue M. Young
Novato Human Needs Center Cookbook
· Novato Human Needs Center
Novato
CALIFORNIA

1 Preheat the oven to 425°. Grease a 2-quart baking dish. Set aside.

2 To make the Creamed Salmon: In a saucepan, melt the butter or margarine. Add the onion and green sweet pepper to the saucepan; cook until the vegetables are tender. Stir in the flour and the ½ teaspoon salt. Slowly add the 2⅔ cups milk. Cook and stir until the mixture is thickened and bubbly. Stir in the salmon and lemon juice. Pour the mixture into the prepared baking dish.

3 To make the Cheese Rolls: In a medium bowl, mix together the flour, baking powder and the ½ teaspoon salt. Using a pastry blender, cut in the shortening. Add the ½ cup milk or water. Stir just until the dough clings together.

4 Turn the dough out onto a lightly floured surface. Knead the dough gently for 10 to 12 strokes. Roll the dough out to a 12x8-inch rectangle. Sprinkle the cheese and pimiento (if using) over the dough. Roll up from a long side.

5 Cut into 8 slices. Using a rolling pin or your hand, slightly flatten the slices. Place the spirals on top of the salmon mixture.

6 Bake the casserole in the 425° oven about 25 minutes or until brown. Let stand for 10 minutes before serving.

 TIPS FROM OUR KITCHEN

If desired, substitute two 6½- or 7-ounce cans of tuna for the salmon.

If you use milk instead of water in these rolls, they will be more tender.

This casserole is very hot when it first comes out of the oven. So before serving, be sure to let it stand for the full 10 minutes specified in the recipe.

Nutrition Analysis (*Per Serving*): Calories: 679 / Cholesterol: 90 mg / Carbohydrates: 57 g / Protein: 40 g / Sodium: 1339 mg / Fat: 32 g (Saturated Fat: 14 g) / Potassium: 845 mg.

YUMMY FAMILY SUPPER

Cheesy browned rolls rest on top of a mouth-watering creamy sauce in this delectable Deep Dish Salmon Pie. Use your favorite cheese in the rolls, and we bet your family will be asking for seconds.

TUNA FISH SOUFFLÉ

Makes 4 Servings

1½ cups soft bread crumbs
(2 slices)
1 6½- or 7-ounce can water-packed tuna, drained and flaked
1 teaspoon lemon juice
½ teaspoon paprika
¾ cup milk
3 egg yolks, beaten
3 egg whites
Paprika (optional)

◆ ◆ ◆

In order to raise funds for needed church renovations, the Adult Fellowship class from the Good Shepherd's United Church of Christ worked together to create Good Shepherd's Favorite Recipes. *Contributions were requested from friends and members "willing to share recipes and helpful hints." Dot Fleming answered the call with her family favorite, Tuna Fish Soufflé.*

Dot Fleming
Good Shepherd's Favorite Recipes
Good Shepherd's United Church of Christ
Boyertown
PENNSYLVANIA

1 Preheat the oven to 350°. Grease a 1- to 1½-quart baking dish. Set aside.

2 In a large bowl, combine the bread crumbs, tuna, lemon juice and the ½ teaspoon paprika; set aside.

3 In a small saucepan, heat the milk until it is very warm. Pour the warm milk over the bread crumb mixture. Stir in the egg yolks.

4 In a clean, large bowl, beat the egg whites using an electric mixer until stiff peaks form. Gently fold the beaten egg whites into the bread crumb mixture.

5 Carefully transfer the mixture into the prepared baking dish. If desired, sprinkle with paprika. Set the baking dish in a 13x9x2-inch pan and add hot water to the pan to a 1-inch depth.

6 Bake in the 350° oven about 30 minutes or until a knife inserted near the center comes out clean.

TIPS FROM OUR KITCHEN

This recipe also works well with canned salmon.

Two slices of bread will give you the right amount of soft bread crumbs. Tear the bread by hand into small pieces. Or, tear the bread into pieces and place in a blender container or a food processor work bowl with a steel blade. Blend or process until coarsely chopped.

Setting the baking dish in a pan of water during baking eliminates the potential problem of overcooking or curdling the eggs.

Cheese sauce or creamed peas are perfect accompaniments to this dish.

Nutrition Analysis (*Per Serving*): Calories: 188 / Cholesterol: 182 mg / Carbohydrates: 11 g
Protein: 20 g / Sodium: 337 mg / Fat: 6 g (Saturated Fat: 2 g) / Potassium: 273 mg.

PUFF THE MAGIC TUNA

While not a true soufflé—there is no white sauce used—this dish is light, fluffy and satisfying, and will have as much impact as a soufflé. Better still, it is ready to eat in less than 45 minutes.

BARBECUED SALMON STEAKS WITH AVOCADO BUTTER

Makes 6 Servings

  6 salmon steaks, cut 1 inch thick (about 3 pounds)

Marinade:
- ½ cup cooking oil
- 3 tablespoons lemon juice
- 2 teaspoons barbecue spice
- ¼ teaspoon dried basil, crushed
- ¼ teaspoon dried marjoram, crushed
- ¼ teaspoon pepper
- Dash salt

Avocado Butter:
- ½ cup butter *or* margarine, softened
- ¼ cup mashed avocado
- 4 teaspoons lemon juice
- 1 tablespoon snipped parsley
- 1 teaspoon Worcestershire sauce
- ¼ teaspoon garlic salt
- Parsley sprigs (optional)
- Lemon slices (optional)

◆   ◆   ◆

Over thirty-five years ago, Jo-Anne Brown received this recipe from a cook on a yacht in California. Although she has altered the recipe over the years, one ingredient—the avocado—has endured. Jo-Anne says emphatically, "The more avocado, the better."

Jo-Anne Brown
Mark Twain Library Cookbook
The Mark Twain Library Association
Redding
CONNECTICUT

1 Thaw the salmon steaks, if frozen. Place the fish steaks in a single layer in a 13x9x2-inch baking dish.

2 To make the marinade: In a glass jar with a tight-fitting lid, combine the cooking oil, the 3 tablespoons lemon juice, the barbecue spice, basil, marjoram, pepper and salt. Shake well and pour the marinade over the salmon. Cover and refrigerate for 1 hour, turning the fish once.

3 To make the Avocado Butter: In a blender container or food processor bowl, blend or process the butter or margarine, avocado, the 4 teaspoons lemon juice, the snipped parsley, Worcestershire sauce and garlic salt until smooth. Refrigerate the mixture in a covered container until ready to serve.

4 Drain the fish, reserving the marinade. Place the fish on a greased grill rack. Grill, uncovered, directly over medium-hot coals for 5 minutes. Using a wide spatula, carefully turn the fish over and brush with the reserved marinade. Grill for 3 to 7 minutes more or until the fish flakes easily when tested with a fork. Arrange the fish on a serving platter. Dollop each fish steak with Avocado Butter. Garnish with parsley sprigs and lemon slices, if desired.

 TIPS FROM OUR KITCHEN

Try swordfish or halibut steaks in place of the salmon.

You'll need 2 lemons for this recipe. Use 1½ lemons for the juice and the remaining for the optional slices.

One hour is long enough for marinating fish when the marinade contains an acid such as lemon juice. Marinating any longer will toughen the fish.

To broil the fish: Grease the rack of a broiler pan. Drain the fish, reserving the marinade. Place the fish on the prepared broiler rack and broil 4 inches from the heat for 5 minutes. Using a wide spatula, carefully turn the fish over and brush with the reserved marinade. Broil for 3 to 7 minutes more or until the fish flakes easily when tested with a fork.

Nutrition Analysis (*Per Serving*): Calories: 402 / Cholesterol: 82 mg / Carbohydrates: 1 g / Protein: 33 g / Sodium: 521 mg / Fat: 29 g (Saturated Fat: 12 g) / Potassium: 389 mg.

FISH-ON-THE-GRILL

A smooth-and-rich homemade Avocado Butter embellishes grilled fish steaks in this recipe from
Jo-Anne Brown of Redding, Connecticut. An herb-and-barbecue spice marinade flavors the fish.

SKEWERED SWORDFISH AND SHRIMP

Makes 8 Servings

½	cup olive oil
½	cup lemon juice
1 to 2	teaspoons dried thyme, crushed
½	teaspoon paprika
¼	teaspoon salt
⅛	teaspoon pepper
1	pound swordfish, skinned, cut in bite-size pieces
1	pound shrimp, shelled and deveined
16	small onion wedges
1	cup green sweet pepper pieces
1	cup red sweet pepper pieces

◆   ◆   ◆

The Hospital Auxiliary and Women's Association of Providence, Rhode Island, decided to publish a cookbook to raise funds for the hospital. Mrs. Harriet Samor, an association member for over 37 years, tells us of the countless kitchen parties in which they made, tested, tasted and remade over 2,000 recipes. Two years down the road, 600 recipes were chosen to represent "the best of the best."

<u>Simply Delicious</u>
Miriam Hospital Women's Association
Providence
RHODE ISLAND

1 To make the marinade: In a medium bowl, beat the oil with *¼ cup* of the lemon juice, the thyme, paprika, salt and pepper.

2 Toss the swordfish and shrimp with the marinade; cover and refrigerate for 4 hours, stirring occasionally.

3 Preheat the charcoal grill or broiler.

4 On eight 12-inch skewers, thread the swordfish and shrimp, alternating with onion wedges and sweet pepper pieces.

5 To grill, place the kabobs on an uncovered grill directly over *medium-hot* coals for 8 to 10 minutes on each side, turning frequently. Or, to broil, place the kabobs on a broiler pan. Broil 4 inches from the heat for 8 to 10 minutes or until the fish flakes easily and shrimp turns pink, turning frequently. Before serving, sprinkle the kabobs with the remaining lemon juice.

 TIPS FROM OUR KITCHEN

If you're in a hurry, marinate the swordfish and shrimp at room temperature for 30 minutes rather than in the refrigerator for 4 hours.

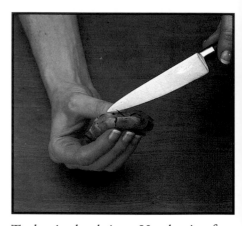

To devein the shrimp: Use the tip of a knife to gently make a shallow cut along the back of each shrimp and lift out the black vein.

Nutrition Analysis (*Per Serving*): Calories: 153 / Cholesterol: 80 mg / Carbohydrates: 4 g / Protein: 18 g / Sodium: 340 mg / Fat: 7 g (Saturated Fat 1 g) / Potassium: 295 mg.

SENSATIONAL SEAFOOD KABOBS

A year-round delight from Providence, Rhode Island, these flavorful
swordfish and shrimp kabobs can be either grilled or broiled. Serve these savory skewers with sliced
tomatoes and nutty brown rice.

EASTERN SHORE CRABCAKES

Makes 4 to 6 Servings

¼	cup butter *or* margarine
1	medium onion, chopped
¼	cup snipped parsley
½	cup all-purpose flour
1	cup milk
2	eggs
12 to 16	ounces fresh, frozen *or* canned cooked crabmeat, thawed, if frozen
¼	teaspoon salt
⅛	teaspoon pepper
1	cup cracker crumbs
3	eggs, beaten
¼	cup cooking oil

✦ ✦ ✦

Mary Bushey says that she reads her collection of cookbooks from her friends from all over the country like others read novels. This recipe, she reports, came to her from a "little grandmother" in Maryland. She sometimes makes Eastern Shore Crabcakes as hors d'oeuvres by forming the mixture into smaller cakes.

Mary W. Bushey
<u>*Critics' Choice*</u>
The Guild of Corinth
Theatre Arts
Corinth
MISSISSIPPI

1 In a large skillet, melt the butter or margarine. Add the onion and parsley and cook until the onion is tender. Add the flour and stir until blended.

2 In a small bowl, beat together the milk and 2 eggs; add to the hot mixture. Cook, stirring constantly, until the mixture is thick and coming away from the sides of the pan.

3 Add the crabmeat and mix well. Season with the salt and pepper. Cool.

4 Form the mixture into 8 to 12 flat cakes ½ to ¾-inch thick. Dip the cakes into the 3 beaten eggs and then roll in cracker crumbs.

5 In a large skillet, fry the crabcakes in hot oil over medium heat about 2 minutes per side or until golden brown. Using a slotted spatula, remove the crabcakes from the pan and drain on paper towels.

 TIPS FROM OUR KITCHEN

The crab mixture is easier to form into even patties if you let it cool slightly before shaping. Moistening your hands before you shape each patty helps, too.

Nutrition Analysis (*Per Serving*): Calories: 580 / Cholesterol: 392 mg / Carbohydrates: 31 g / Protein: 29 g / Sodium: 1045 mg / Fat: 37 g (Saturated Fat: 13 g) / Potassium: 356 mg.

PERFECT PATTIES

This very old Maryland recipe comes to us from Mary Bushey of Corinth, Mississippi. You are sure to enjoy these crisp, light patties as an entree or made into smaller portions as hors d'oeuvres.

GINGER SCALLOPS

Makes 4 to 6 Servings

   5   tablespoons butter *or* margarine
  ⅓   cup finely chopped scallions *or* green onion
1½ cups julienne-cut carrots
  ½   cup dry white wine
  1   tablespoon grated fresh gingerroot
  ¾   cup heavy whipping cream
  ¼   teaspoon salt
¼ to ½ teaspoon freshly ground pepper
  1   pound bay *or* sea scallops

♦   ♦   ♦

Food has always played an important role in Hawaiian tradition and custom, and feasting has often served both a religious and social function. As people of different nationalities arrived in Hawaii, they brought with them new crops and new methods of preparing foods which contributed to the developing culinary history of the islands. This recipe for Ginger Scallops provides us with an opportunity to sample the rich heritage of The Aloha State.

A Taste of Aloha
The Junior League of Honolulu
Honolulu
HAWAII

1 In a large skillet, melt *3 tablespoons* of the butter or margarine. Add the scallions or green onion; cook and stir for 1 minute. Add the carrots and cook for 2 minutes. Stir in the wine and gingerroot. When the mixture is thoroughly heated, add the cream, salt and pepper.

2 Cook and stir the sauce over medium-high heat about 5 minutes or until it is reduced by half.

3 Add the scallops to the sauce. Cook for 1 minute if using bay scallops or for 2 minutes if using sea scallops.

4 Stir in the remaining butter or margarine and serve.

TIPS FROM OUR KITCHEN

Serve this creamy dish over rice or in puff pastry shells.

If you're watching calories and fat, omit the 2 tablespoons of butter that are added to the sauce just before serving.

When choosing fresh gingerroot, select a piece that's firm and heavy; avoid shriveled stems. For short-term storage of fresh gingerroot, wrap the root in a paper towel and refrigerate. For long-term storage, immerse peeled slices of gingerroot in dry sherry, wine or oil and refrigerate in a covered container for up to three months. (The ginger-flavored sherry, wine or oil can be used in cooking.) Or, place the root in a moisture and vaporproof bag and freeze. Then, grate or cut off what you need from the unpeeled frozen root.

Nutrition Analysis *(Per Serving)*: Calories: 466 / Cholesterol: 167 mg / Carbohydrates: 9 g
Protein: 31 g / Sodium: 668 mg / Fat: 33 g (Saturated Fat: 19 g) / Potassium: 796 mg.

ALOHA GOOD TASTE!

From the beautiful islands of Hawaii comes this quick and creamy scallop dish. We suggest that you
stay with the tropical mood and serve a pineapple boat filled with colorful fruit for dessert.

ARTICHOKE AND SHRIMP CASSEROLE

Makes 4 Servings
1   9-ounce package frozen
    artichoke hearts
1   teaspoon salt
12 ounces fresh *or* frozen
    peeled and deveined shrimp
1½ cups sliced fresh mushrooms
4   tablespoons butter *or*
    margarine
1   8-ounce can sliced water
    chestnuts, drained
2   tablespoons all-purpose
    flour
1¼ cups milk
2   tablespoons dry sherry
1   teaspoon Worcestershire
    sauce
¼   teaspoon salt
⅛   teaspoon pepper
¼   cup grated Parmesan cheese
Dash paprika

◆   ◆   ◆

Barbara Wiedner, founder of Grandmothers for Peace, told us that the organization's purpose is to develop a society that enables children to "grow up as healthy, productive citizens." Founded eleven years ago, the organization has expanded internationally "through word of mouth."

Marjorie Welsch
<u>*Grandmothers for Peace*</u>
<u>*Cherished Recipes*</u>
Grandmothers for Peace
Sacramento
CALIFORNIA

1 Preheat the oven to 375°.

2 Cook the artichoke hearts according to the package directions; drain well. Cut any large artichokes in half. Place the artichoke hearts in a 1½-quart casserole dish.

3 Bring 1 quart *water* and the 1 teaspoon salt to a boil. Add the shrimp and bring to a second boil. Cook for 1 to 3 minutes or until the shrimp turn pink, stirring occasionally. Remove from heat and immediately rinse the shrimp under cold, running water. Drain well and arrange over the artichoke hearts.

4 In a medium saucepan over medium heat, cook and stir the mushrooms in *2 tablespoons* of the butter or margarine until tender. Pour the mushroom mixture over the shrimp. Sprinkle with the water chestnuts.

5 In the same saucepan, melt the remaining butter or margarine. Stir in the flour. Add the milk all at once. Cook and stir over medium heat until the mixture is thickened and bubbly. Cook and stir for 1 minute more.

6 Stir in the sherry, Worcestershire sauce, the ¼ teaspoon salt and the pepper. Pour the sauce over the water chestnuts. Sprinkle the Parmesan cheese and paprika over the top. Bake in the 375° oven for 20 to 25 minutes or until heated through.

 TIPS FROM OUR KITCHEN

If using fresh shrimp in shells, here's how to remove the shell. Using your fingers, open the shell lengthwise down the body. Hold the shrimp in one hand and carefully peel back the shell starting with the head end. Leave the last section of the shell and tail intact. Either cut the body portion of the shell off, leaving the tail shell in place, or gently pull on the tail portion of the shell and remove the entire shell. To remove the vein, make a shallow slit with a sharp knife along the back of the shrimp. Use the tip of the knife to scrape out the black vein.

For variety, add ½ teaspoon dried basil or thyme to the sauce before pouring it over the water chestnuts.

If you wish, bake this recipe in individual casseroles. Or, serve the baked casserole mixture in patty shells that have been baked according to package directions.

Nutrition Analysis: (*Per Serving*): Calories: 323 / Cholesterol: 172 mg / Carbohydrates: 23 Protein: 24 g / Sodium: 783 mg / Fat: 16 g (Saturated Fat: 9 g) / Potassium: 706 mg.

RICH AND YUMMY

This richly flavored dish from Marjorie Welsch of San Francisco, features artichokes, shrimp, water chestnuts and fresh mushrooms in a savory cream sauce.

CIOPPINO

❖ ❖ ❖

"This is absolutely the easiest dish to make for company!" recommends Jane Citron, who devised this delicious dish to instruct students in her cooking technique classes.

Jane Citron
The Best of the Best
Rodef Shalom Sisterhood
Pittsburgh
PENNSYLVANIA

1 Pour the oil into a large kettle. Add the onion and sweet green pepper. Cook and stir over low heat until the vegetables are tender.

2 Carefully add the *undrained* tomatoes, red wine, basil, tomato paste, oregano, thyme, pepper flakes and bay leaf. Bring to a boil; reduce heat and simmer, covered, for 1 hour.

3 Meanwhile, thaw the halibut or scrod, shrimp and scallops, if frozen.

4 Shell the shrimp, leaving the tails on. Clean the clams.

5 Uncover the sauce and return to a boil. Stir in the clams. Boil, covered, about 5 minutes or until the clams open. Discard any clams that do not open. Remove all of the clams from the sauce and set them aside.

6 Stir the halibut or scrod, shrimp, scallops and pepper into the sauce. Bring to a boil; reduce heat and simmer for 4 to 5 minutes more. Discard the bay leaf.

7 To serve, place the cooked clams (still in their shells) in shallow bowls. Ladle the stew mixture on top and garnish with parsley.

 TIPS FROM OUR KITCHEN

To clean clams: Use a stiff brush to scrub the clams under cold running water. In an 8-quart Dutch oven, combine 4 quarts *cold water* and ⅓ cup *salt*. Add the clams and soak for 15 minutes. Drain and rinse. Discard the water. Repeat twice.

The red wine will change the color of the seafood. For a lighter wine flavor, use 1 cup wine and 1 cup broth instead of the 2 cups wine. Or, eliminate all of the wine and substitute broth for the entire amount.

Nutrition Analysis (*Per Serving*): Calories: 280 / Cholesterol: 93 mg / Carbohydrates: 14 g / Protein: 37 g / Sodium: 449 mg / Fat: 6 g (Saturated Fat: 1 g) / Potassium: 1154 mg.

SAN FRANCISCO ORIGIN

Cioppino (pronounced *chu PEA no)* is a delicious stew that was first made in San Francisco,
California. This version from Pittsburgh, Pennsylvania, features a yummy variety of
fish, shellfish, vegetables and herbs in a tomato-wine sauce.

◀ FISH & SEAFOOD ▶

SIMPLE SHRIMP CREOLE

Makes 4 Servings

2	tablespoons butter *or* margarine
½	cup finely chopped onion
2	tablespoons all-purpose flour
3	cups water
1	6-ounce can tomato paste
½	cup finely chopped green sweet pepper
¼	cup finely chopped celery
1	teaspoon snipped parsley
½	teaspoon salt
¼	teaspoon bottled hot pepper sauce
Dash to ⅛	teaspoon ground red pepper
1	bay leaf
2	cups cooked shrimp
2	cups hot cooked rice

◆   ◆   ◆

After the parishoners of All Saints' Episcopal Church found themselves buying mimeographed copies of the recipes from a fund-raising dinner in 1974, they began to put together this wonderful cookbook.

La Bonne Cuisine: Cooking New Orleans Style
The Women of All Saints' Episcopal Church New Orleans
LOUISIANA

1 In a large heavy skillet over medium heat, melt the butter or margarine. Add the onion and cook until tender but not brown.

2 Stir in the flour. Add the water, tomato paste, green pepper, celery, parsley, salt, hot pepper sauce, ground red pepper and bay leaf.

3 Cook, uncovered, over medium-low heat about 30 minutes or until thickened, stirring occasionally.

4 Stir in the shrimp and heat through. Remove the bay leaf. Serve over the hot cooked rice.

 TIPS FROM OUR KITCHEN

To remove shells from fresh shrimp: Open the shell lengthwise down the body. Remove the legs. Hold the shrimp in one hand and carefully peel back the shell starting with the head end. Leave the last section of the shell and tail intact.

Either cut the body portion of the shell off, leaving the tail shell in place, or gently pull on the tail portion of the shell to remove the entire shell.

To devein shrimp: Make a shallow slit with a sharp knife along the back of the shrimp. Use the tip of the knife to scrape out the black vein.

To cook raw, shelled shrimp: In a large saucepan, heat 6 cups *water* and 2 tablespoons *salt* to boiling. Add the shelled shrimp. Reduce the heat and simmer for 1 to 3 minutes or until the shrimp turns pink. Drain.

Breaded fried okra makes a perfect accompaniment to this dish.

Nutrition Analysis *(Per Serving)*: Calories: 324 / Cholesterol: 163 mg / Carbohydrates: 44 g / Protein: 21 g / Sodium: 542 mg / Fat: 7 g (Saturated Fat: 4 g) Potassium: 715 mg.

GREAT NEW ORLEANS STYLE

This easy-to-prepare main course is a delicately seasoned classic. If you prefer a feistier flavor, add extra ground red pepper during cooking or pass the bottled hot pepper sauce at the table.

OYSTERS FRIED IN BEER BATTER

Makes 4 Servings
24	fresh oysters in shell *or* 1 pint shucked oysters
1	cup all-purpose flour
¼	teaspoon paprika
⅛	teaspoon salt

Dash of pepper
⅓ to ½ cup beer
Shortening *or* cooking oil for deep fat frying
Cocktail sauce or tartar sauce (optional)
Lemon wedges (optional)

◆   ◆   ◆

R.B. Taylor says that the three rules for cooking fish are, "Don't overcook it. Don't overcook it. Don't overcook it." His "forty or fifty" years of shipboard and company cooking make him an expert in our eyes! R.B., whose cooking specialty is Northwestern seafood, says that he developed this particular recipe by accident. He usually serves these oysters as hors d'oeuvres and sometimes includes a dipping sauce made from mayonnaise mixed with a dash of curry and a bit of finely chopped onion.

R.B. Taylor
Extraordinary Cuisine
Seattle Yacht Club
Seattle
WASHINGTON

1 Shuck the oysters, if necessary. Drain any excess liquid and pat dry with paper toweling.

2 In a medium mixing bowl, stir together the flour, paprika, salt and pepper. Gradually stir in ⅓ cup beer; stir until smooth. Add additional beer if the mixture seems too thick. Refrigerate until ready to use.

3 In a large heavy saucepan or deep-fat fryer, heat 2 inches of shortening or cooking oil to 375°. Dip the oysters, a few at a time, in the batter, allowing the excess batter to drip off into the bowl. Fry the batter-covered oysters in the hot fat, 5 or 6 at a time, about 1½ minutes or until golden brown. Drain on paper toweling. Repeat with the remaining oysters. Serve immediately with cocktail sauce or tartar sauce and lemon wedges, if desired.

TIPS FROM OUR KITCHEN

When shopping, look for live oysters with shells that are tightly closed, moist and unbroken. Ask when they arrived at the store and choose those that are not more than 2 days old. Shucked oysters should be surrounded by clear—not cloudy—liquid. Avoid oysters that have an off-odor.

Live oysters may be refrigerated up to 5 days if covered with a moist cloth in an open container. Tap any shells that open during storage and discard any oysters that don't close quickly. Shucked oysters that are covered with

their own juice may be refrigerated up to 5 days or frozen up to 3 months.

To shuck oysters: Put on a heavy oven mitt and hold the shell, flat side up, firmly against a cutting board. Using a strong-bladed oyster knife with a hand guard, insert the tip between the shells near the hinge, being very careful not to let the knife blade slip. Twist the blade and push it into the opening, prying the oyster open. Move the blade along the inside of the upper shell to free the muscle; remove and discard the top shell. Slide the knife under the oyster to cut the muscle from the bottom shell.

Nutrition Analysis (*Per Serving*): Calories: 418 / Cholesterol: 62 mg / Carbohydrates: 27 g / Protein: 11 g / Sodium: 195 mg / Fat: 29 g (Saturated Fat: 7 g) / Potassium: 298 mg.

SUCCULENT SHELLFISH

From Seattle, Washington, where fresh seafood abounds, comes a pearl of a recipe: Oysters Fried in Beer Batter. R.B. Taylor brings us a scrumptious way to enjoy the tasty mollusks.

Meats

*T*ired of meat and potatoes? These recipes really spice up the same old cuts of meat to make them truly special. Pot Roast Madeira, for example, takes plain pot roast and turns it into a terrific marinated meat with a superb sauce. Pork Chops Pacifica is a wonderful one-dish meal that's simple to fix and flavorful, too. The recipe for Tomato-Peach Barbecued Ribs provides a tasty twist on traditional grilled farc.

COMPANY MEAT LOAF

1 Preheat oven to 325°.

2 To make the meat loaf: Combine the beef, veal, crackers, eggs, onions, milk, parsley, celery, soy sauce, Worcestershire sauce, salt, pepper and garlic powder. Add more milk if texture is too stiff.

3 To shape the loaf: Pat meat mixture into an 8x4-inch baking dish, then invert into a shallow baking dish.

4 To make the topping: Cover the top of the meat with the catsup and the bacon slices.

5 To make the vegetables: Surround the meat loaf with the whole potatoes. Cover with foil. Bake in the 325° oven for 1 hour.

6 Uncover; carefully spoon off the drippings in the pan. Add the green sweet pepper on top of the potatoes. Bake in the 325° oven, uncovered, for 30 to 40 minutes or until the meat and potatoes are done.

7 To serve, arrange the meat and vegetables on a platter.

 TIPS FROM OUR KITCHEN

Using lean ground beef and precooking the bacon help to lower the fat content in this meat loaf.

To keep the skin on the new potatoes looking pretty, cut a wide strip around the middle of each potato with a sharp knife.

Nutrition Analysis *(Per Serving):* Calories: 338 / Cholesterol: 139mg / Carbohydrates: 32g / Protein: 28g / Sodium: 357 mg / Fat: 11g (Saturated Fat: 4g) / Potassium: 867mg.

An Old Favorite Made Special

Beef and veal team up with bacon and new potatoes to make this meat loaf extra special. We think this dish is a great way to treat your family like company.

MEATS

211

PASTIES

Makes 6 Servings

Filling:
- 1   pound ground beef, cooked and drained
- 1   pound potatoes, peeled and shredded (2½ cups)
- ½   cup finely chopped onion
- ½   cup shredded carrot *or* ¼ cup shredded carrot and ¼ cup shredded rutabaga
- ½   cup snipped parsley *or* ¼ cup dried parsley
- ¾   teaspoon salt
- ¼   teaspoon pepper

Pastry:
- 3   cups all-purpose flour
- ½   teaspoon baking powder
- ⅛   teaspoon salt
- 1   cup margarine *or* shortening
- 1   egg, slightly beaten
- 1   tablespoon vinegar *or* lemon juice
-     Water

♦   ♦   ♦

Pasties have endured throughout the years. Inez Gustafson told us that they were a popular lunch of the tin miners in Cornwall, England, during the 1700s and 1800s. She also said that this pocketlike meal is still quite popular—particularly in the upper peninsula of Michigan.

Inez Gustafson
Happy Cookin' Plus
The Bethphage Mission, Inc.
Axtell
NEBRASKA

1 To make the filling: In a large bowl, mix together the cooked ground beef, potatoes, onion, shredded carrot or carrot and rutabaga, parsley, the ¾ teaspoon salt and the pepper; set aside.

2 To make the pastry: In another large bowl, stir together the flour, baking powder and the ⅛ teaspoon salt. Using a pastry blender, cut in the margarine or shortening until the pieces are the size of small peas.

3 In a 1-cup glass measure, stir together the egg and vinegar or lemon juice; add enough water to equal *½ cup* liquid. Stir the egg mixture into the flour mixture just until it is moistened.

4 Preheat the oven to 450°. Form the dough into a ball and divide in half. On a lightly floured surface, roll *half* of the dough to slightly less than a ⅛-inch thickness. Using a 6-inch cardboard circle as a pattern, cut the dough into six 6-inch circles.

5 Place about *¾ cup* of the filling on 3 of the circles. Top with the remaining circles. Crimp the edges of the dough or seal with the tines of a fork. Place the filled dough circles on ungreased baking sheets. Repeat with the remaining dough and filling, re-rolling the scraps as necessary.

6 Bake in the 450° oven for 15 minutes. Reduce the oven temperature to 350° and bake about 15 minutes more or until the pastry is golden.

 TIPS FROM OUR KITCHEN

Pasties can be served with gravy, catsup, spaghetti sauce or pizza sauce.

Shred the potato in a bowl of cold water to prevent the cut surface from darkening. If desired, cover and refrigerate until ready to mix together the filling. Then before using, rinse the shredded potatoes and drain well, squeezing out excess water.

Nutrition Analysis (*Per Serving*): Calories: 716 / Cholesterol: 82 mg / Carbohydrates: 63 g / Protein: 23 g / Sodium: 730 mg / Fat: 41 g (Saturated Fat: 10 g) / Potassium: 601 mg.

MEAT-AND-POTATO TURNOVERS

If your family members are meat-and-potato lovers, try serving them Inez Gustafson's Pasties.
Pasties—short for Cornish pasties—are small pies or turnovers filled with ground
beef and shredded potatoes.

MEATS

SALISBURY STEAK

Makes 8 Servings
Patties:
  2 pounds lean ground beef
  1 medium onion
  ½ green sweet pepper
  1 stalk celery
  2 tablespoons snipped parsley
  1 clove garlic
  ½ teaspoon dry mustard
  ½ teaspoon dried marjoram, crushed
  ½ teaspoon dried thyme, crushed
  ½ teaspoon paprika
  ½ teaspoon salt
  ½ teaspoon pepper
Sauce (Optional):
  3 tablespoons margarine *or* butter
  4 ounces sliced fresh mushrooms (1 cup)
  ½ teaspoon all-purpose flour
  ⅓ cup chili sauce
  ¼ cup dry red wine
  1 teaspoon lemon juice
  1 teaspoon Worcestershire sauce
Dash bottled hot pepper sauce

♦   ♦   ♦

The railroad theme for The Utah Dining Car was chosen by the Junior League of Ogden because in 1869 the Union Pacific and Central Pacific railroads met near Ogden.

The Utah Dining Car Junior League of Ogden Cookbook
The Junior League of Ogden
Ogden
UTAH

1 To make the patties: Place the ground beef in a large bowl; set aside.

2 In a blender container or food processor bowl, combine the onion, green sweet pepper, celery, parsley and garlic. Blend or process until minced. *Or,* using a sharp knife, finely chop the onion, green sweet pepper, celery, parsley and garlic by hand. Add the vegetables to the bowl with the ground beef. *Do not stir.*

3 Add the dry mustard, marjoram, thyme, paprika, salt and pepper to the ground beef mixture; mix thoroughly.

4 Shape the meat mixture into 8 patties about ¾ inch thick. Place the patties on the unheated rack of a broiler pan. Broil the patties 3 to 4 inches from the heat for 12 to 14 minutes (for medium doneness) or until done, turning the meat halfway through cooking. *Or,* grill the patties directly over medium coals for 12 to 14 minutes, turning once.

5 To make the sauce, if desired: In a large saucepan, melt the margarine or butter; add the mushrooms. Cook for 4 to 5 minutes over medium-high heat until tender, stirring occasionally. Sprinkle with the flour; stir. Add the chili sauce, red wine, lemon juice, Worcestershire sauce and hot pepper sauce. Cook and stir until the mixture is bubbly. Cook for 1 minute more. If desired, serve the sauce over the meat patties.

 TIPS FROM OUR KITCHEN

To cook the patties evenly, use the same amount of meat for each one. To do this, lightly pat the meat mixture into a ¾-inch-thick square or rectangle and cut into 8 portions; shape into patties.

Handle ground beef as little as possible before and during cooking. Use a light touch when mixing in the vegetables and seasonings and when shaping the meat mixture into patties.

If grilling outside, be sure to use a clean plate to carry the cooked meat back to the table. Cooked meat should never be placed on a plate that previously held uncooked meat. Disease-causing micro-organisms that are killed during cooking can be transferred from the raw meat juices to the cooked meat if the plate has not been cleaned.

Nutrition Analysis (*Per Serving*): Calories: 224 / Cholesterol: 70 mg / Carbohydrates: 2 g / Protein: 22 g / Sodium: 202 mg / Fat: 14 g (Saturated Fat: 5 g) / Potassium: 326 mg.

ONE MAN'S PRESCRIPTION

Our research indicates that Salisbury Steak got its name from Dr. J.H. Salisbury, a 19th-century English physician who was a strong advocate of eating beef as a cure for a wide range of ailments. While we don't recommend this dish as a medical remedy, we do think it is a great cure for mealtime blues.

MEATS

BACKSTAGE SPECIAL

Makes 4 to 6 Servings

1	pound ground round steak
1	medium onion, chopped
1	clove garlic, minced
1	8-ounce can tomato sauce
½	cup tomato juice *or* water
1 to 2	tablespoons chili powder
¼	teaspoon dried oregano, crushed
1	15½-ounce can kidney *or* chili beans with juice
1	8-ounce bag corn chips
2	cups shredded lettuce
1	large tomato, chopped
½	cup chopped onion

◆ ◆ ◆

Ten years ago, Betty Jennings received this recipe from a family member in Florida, and she's been serving it ever since. She tells us that one theater director loved the dish so much that after he polished off three servings, he returned with a spoon to scrape the bottom of the pan! Betty suggests that if you should have any leftovers, sprinkle them with more corn chips before reheating to revive the crunchiness.

Betty A. Jennings
Gracious Goodness:
A Taste of Memphis
Memphis Symphony League
Memphis
TENNESSEE

1 Preheat oven to 350°. Grease a 2-quart square baking dish. Set aside.

2 In a large skillet over medium heat, brown the meat, onion and garlic. Drain the excess fat. Stir the tomato sauce, tomato juice or water, chili powder and oregano into the meat mixture.

3 Layer the meat mixture, beans and corn chips in the prepared baking dish, ending with corn chips.

4 Cover and bake in the 350° oven for 40 minutes. Just before serving, sprinkle with the lettuce, tomato and chopped onion.

 TIPS FROM OUR KITCHEN

It's also up to you to decide how thoroughly you want to drain the fat from the browned meat. One efficient way to drain the meat-onion mixture in this recipe is to drain it through a sieve.

Casseroles are one of the easiest types of recipes to adapt to your own style. To stylize this casserole, you might add chili peppers or snipped cilantro to the meat mixture and serve it with salsa and/or sour cream. Pass around the hot sauce for the more daring at your table.

Nutrition Analysis *(Per Serving)*: Calories: 630 / Cholesterol: 72 mg / Carbohydrates: 65 g / Protein: 39 g / Sodium: 1246 mg / Fat: 25 g (Saturated Fat: 5 g) Potassium: 1280 mg.

TACO CASSEROLE

Ever wonder what actors do in between afternoon and evening performances? At Theatre Memphis, they refuel with this easy-to-prepare casserole. You may not feel like a stage star when you eat it, but you are sure to receive plenty of applause when you serve it.

MEATS

PEPPERED CHUTNEY ROAST

Makes 8 to 12 Servings

Marinade:
- ½ cup unsweetened pineapple juice
- ⅓ cup steak sauce
- ¼ cup Worcestershire sauce
- ¼ cup port wine
- 3 tablespoons lemon juice
- 1½ teaspoons seasoned salt
- ¾ teaspoon pepper
- ¾ teaspoon lemon pepper seasoning
- ¾ teaspoon dry mustard

Roast:
- 1 2- to 3-pound beef tenderloin
- 1 teaspoon cracked black pepper
- 4 slices bacon
- ¼ cup chutney, snipped
- Chutney (optional)

♦ ♦ ♦

Every other year, the Independence Regional Health Center Auxiliary hosts a garden tour during which packed lunches are sold. Frequent requests for recipes used in the lunches inspired Bouquet Garni. *Profits from cookbook sales help benefit the Cliffview Center for Women's Health.*

Brenda Lewis
Bouquet Garni
Independence Regional Health Center Auxiliary
Independence
MISSOURI

1 To make the marinade: Stir together the pineapple juice, steak sauce, Worcestershire sauce, port wine, lemon juice, seasoned salt, pepper, lemon pepper seasoning and dry mustard.

2 To prepare the roast: Place the tenderloin in a large plastic bag. Pour the marinade over the meat and close the bag. Place the bag in a shallow baking dish. Refrigerate for 6 to 24 hours, turning the meat occasionally to distribute the marinade evenly. Drain the meat, reserving the marinade.

3 Preheat the oven to 425°. Sprinkle the meat with the cracked black pepper. Place the meat on a rack in a shallow roasting pan and arrange the bacon slices over the top.

4 Roast the meat, uncovered, in the 425° oven for 35 to 45 minutes or until a meat thermometer registers 135°. Baste the meat twice with the reserved marinade during roasting.

5 Remove the bacon slices from the meat and spoon the chutney evenly over the roast. Roast for 5 to 10 minutes more or until the meat thermometer registers 140° for rare.

6 Using 2 spatulas, transfer the roast to a serving platter and allow it to stand 10 minutes before slicing. Serve with additional chutney, if desired.

 TIPS FROM OUR KITCHEN

This marinade also works well with beef eye of round, boneless beef sirloin roast, beef tip roast, or 2 pork tenderloins. For these cuts, use a lower oven temperature (325°) and a meat thermometer. Allow 2 to 3 hours for the beef roasts to reach 160° (medium). Cook the pork tenderloin to 160° (medium well); start checking after 45 minutes.

Placing the bacon strips over the tenderloin is an example of *larding*. It's done to make the meat juicier and more flavorful.

You can purchase cracked black pepper, or crack the whole peppercorns yourself using a mortar and pestle.

Chutney is an East Indian specialty made from fruits or vegetables. It can range in texture from smooth to chunky, and in flavor from sweet to tart to spicy-hot.

Nutrition Analysis (*Per Serving*): Calories: 157 / Cholesterol: 44 mg / Carbohydrates: 8 g / Protein: 15 g / Sodium: 460 mg / Fat: 6 g (Saturated Fat: 2 g) / Potassium: 304 mg.

CHANGE OF PACE

An intriguing blend of flavors makes Peppered Chutney Roast a welcome change of pace from the usual beef and gravy. Before cooking, beef tenderloin is marinated in a spicy pineapple juice mixture, then sprinkled with cracked pepper. Finally, the meat is topped with chutney during the last few minutes of roasting.

MEATS

POT ROAST MADEIRA

Makes 10 Servings

1   cup chopped onion
1   tablespoon finely shredded orange peel
½   cup orange juice
½   6-ounce can (⅓ cup) frozen orange juice concentrate, thawed
⅓   cup water
1   teaspoon salt
1   teaspoon sugar
1   teaspoon ground coriander
½   teaspoon pepper
¼ to ½   teaspoon ground cloves
¼   teaspoon ground cumin
1   3½-pound beef chuck roast
1   tablespoon cooking oil
1   tablespoon butter *or* margarine
¼   cup water
2   tablespoons cornstarch
¼   cup Madeira
Orange slices (optional)

◆   ◆   ◆

Junior League of Pasadena members discovered an ingenious method for selecting recipes for their cookbook. All of their guests were served dishes under consideration, and the most popular were chosen.

The California Heritage Cookbook
Junior League of Pasadena
Pasadena
CALIFORNIA

1 In a blender container or food processor bowl, combine the onion, orange peel, orange juice, orange juice concentrate, ⅓ cup water, salt, sugar, coriander, pepper, cloves and cumin. Cover and blend or process until nearly smooth.

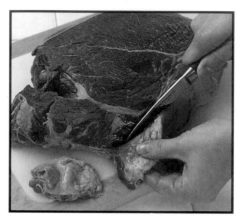

2 Trim the fat from the meat. Place the meat in a large bowl or shallow baking dish and pour the orange juice mixture over it. Cover and marinate in the refrigerator for 4 to 6 hours, turning the meat occasionally to distribute the marinade evenly.

3 Drain the meat, reserving marinade. Pat the meat dry with paper towels.

4 In a 4½-quart Dutch oven, heat the oil and butter or margarine over medium-high heat. Add the meat and brown well on all sides, about 4 minutes per side. Drain off the excess fat and discard.

5 Pour the reserved marinade over the meat and bring to a boil. Reduce the heat and simmer, covered, for 2 to 2½ hours or until the meat is tender. Transfer the pot roast to a warm serving dish and cover to keep warm.

6 Stir together the ¼ cup water and the cornstarch; stir the mixture into the cooking liquid. Add the Madeira. Cook, stirring constantly, until the sauce is thickened and bubbly. Cook and stir for 2 minutes more. Serve the sauce over the meat. Garnish with orange slices, if desired.

 TIPS FROM OUR KITCHEN

Be sure to shred the peel from the orange before juicing it. You'll need 1 large or 2 medium oranges for the peel and fresh juice. Before juicing the oranges, leave them at room temperature for 30 minutes. Then, roll the fruit on the counter under the palm of your hand a few times to encourage the juice to flow. For convenience, place the juicer on top of your measuring cup.

Cutting the meat for serving will be easier if you let the roast stand about 15 minutes after removing it from the oven. Place the meat on a non-wooden cutting surface and hold it steady with a carving fork. Using a long, sharp knife, cut slices across the grain.

Nutrition Analysis *(Per Serving)*: Calories: 275 / Cholesterol: 100 mg / Carbohydrates: 9 g / Protein: 33 g / Sodium: 284 mg / Fat: 11 g (Saturated Fat: 4 g) / Potassium: 400 mg.

ORANGE, BEEF AND WINE COMBINE

Pot roast gets new vitality and sophistication in this recipe from Pasadena, California. The beef is marinated in a mixture of orange juice and peel, coriander, pepper, cloves and cumin. Later the marinade is transformed into a delicious sauce with the aid of a splash of Madeira.

MEATS

BEEF STROGANOFF

Makes 6 Servings

1	pound beef round steak, cut into ¾-inch cubes
½	teaspoon paprika
¼	teaspoon salt
¼	teaspoon pepper
⅛	teaspoon garlic salt
¼	cup margarine *or* butter
1	small onion, chopped
1½	cups sliced fresh mushrooms
¾	cup beef broth
1	small bay leaf
2	teaspoons Worcestershire sauce
2	tablespoons all-purpose flour
1	8-ounce carton dairy sour cream
1	8-ounce package medium noodles, cooked (4½ cups dry noodles)

♦   ♦   ♦

Members of the Christian Women's Fellowship sell craft items and hold food sales at which they promote the sale of their fund-raising cookbook. These efforts contribute to the church's many outreach programs.

Diane Wright
First Christian Church Centennial
Commemorative Cookbook
First Christian Church
(Disciples of Christ)
Herington
KANSAS

1 Season the meat with the paprika, salt, pepper and garlic salt.

2 In a large skillet over medium-high heat, melt the margarine or butter. Add the meat and onion. Cook and stir until the meat is browned on all sides.

3 Add the mushrooms, beef broth, bay leaf and Worcestershire sauce to the skillet. Bring to a boil. Reduce heat, cover and simmer for 1 to 1¼ hours or until the meat is tender. Remove and discard the bay leaf.

4 In a small bowl, stir together the flour and sour cream. Add the sour cream mixture to the meat mixture in the skillet. Cook and stir over medium heat until the sauce is thickened and bubbly. Cook and stir for 1 minute more. Serve over the hot cooked noodles.

 TIPS FROM OUR KITCHEN

To season the meat cubes evenly, place the paprika, salt, pepper and garlic salt in a heavy plastic bag. Add the meat cubes and shake.

Sour cream that is tightly covered will keep in the refrigerator up to four weeks. Freezing is not recommended because the sour cream will separate as it thaws. If you notice any spots of mold on the surface of refrigerated sour cream, discard the entire container.

In this recipe, the sour cream is mixed with the flour before it is added to the skillet to prevent it from curdling when it is heated.

To reduce fat and calories, you can substitute "light" sour cream for the regular sour cream in the recipe.

Nutrition Analysis (*Per Serving*): Calories: 426 / Cholesterol: 65 mg / Carbohydrates: 35 g Protein: 25 g / Sodium: 392 mg / Fat: 20 g (Saturated Fat: 8 g) / Potassium: 461 mg.

STATELY SUPPER

This creamy, rich dish is believed to have been named after the 19th-century Russian diplomat,
Count Peter Stroganov. Beef round steak is simmered with mushrooms and seasonings,
then served in a sour cream sauce over noodles.

MEATS

FAJITAS

Makes 4 Servings

¼ teaspoon sugar
¼ teaspoon ground cumin
¼ teaspoon paprika
¼ teaspoon chili powder
¼ teaspoon dried oregano, crushed
2 tablespoons cooking oil
1 medium onion, sliced
1 medium green sweet pepper, seeded and cut into thin strips
1 clove garlic, minced
1 tablespoon snipped fresh cilantro (optional)
1 tablespoon lime juice
1½ pounds beef round steak *or* skinless, boneless chicken breasts (cut into thin strips)
8 7-inch flour tortillas
Condiments: shredded cheese, chopped tomatoes, shredded lettuce, grilled onions, sweet peppers, sour cream *and/or* salsa (optional)

♦   ♦   ♦

When Michele Liro Patterson's dinner group chose a Mexican theme for one of their parties, Michele discovered this recipe for Fajitas. She and her five-year-old daughter quickly adopted the dish as a special favorite.

Michele Liro Patterson
<u>*Heavenly Hosts*</u>
Presbyterian Women of the Bryn Mawr Presbyterian Church
Bryn Mawr
PENNSYLVANIA

1 In a small bowl, stir together the sugar, cumin, paprika, chili powder and oregano. Set aside.

2 In a large skillet or wok over medium-low heat, heat the cooking oil. Add the onion and green sweet pepper. Cook and stir until the vegetables are just tender.

3 Add the garlic, cilantro (if using), lime juice and the seasoning mixture. Continue cooking over medium-low heat for 2 minutes. Using a slotted spoon, transfer the vegetable mixture to a bowl; set aside.

4 Increase the heat to medium-high. Add *half* of the beef or chicken to the skillet or wok. Cook until the beef reaches the desired doneness or the chicken is tender and no longer pink. Transfer the beef or chicken to the bowl with the vegetable mixture. Repeat with the remaining beef or chicken.

5 Return all of the meat and vegetables to the skillet. Heat through. Serve the meat and vegetables rolled in the flour tortillas with the desired condiments.

 TIPS FROM OUR KITCHEN

To soften tortillas, wrap a stack of them in foil. Heat in a 350° oven for 10 minutes.

For 1 tablespoon fresh lime juice, you'll need half of a lime.

For optimum tenderness when using beef in this recipe, bias-slice it by cutting thinly across the grain. This is easiest to do when the meat is partially frozen and firm, but not hard. Hold a sharp knife at a 45-degree angle to the surface of the cutting board and cut thin, diagonal slices.

Cooking only half of the meat at one time helps ensure that it will all be cooked thoroughly. If all of the meat is cooked at once, it will steam instead of brown.

If you use a nonstick skillet, you can use less oil.

Cumin is a small amber-colored seed from a plant in the parsley family. It is used in making chili powder and curry powder.

Cilantro is the leaf of the coriander plant. If it's not available, use finely snipped parsley or celery leaves.

Nutrition Analysis (*Per Serving*): Calories: 540 / Cholesterol: 116 mg / Carbohydrates: 40
Protein: 44 g / Sodium: 291 mg / Fat: 22 g (Saturated Fat: 6 g) / Potassium: 526 mg.

ARTFUL DINING

This Tex-Mex/Mexican favorite was originally made with beef, but it is equally tasty when made with
chicken. Serve Fajitas with a variety of condiments so that each person at your table can
create his or her own individual culinary masterpiece.

MEATS

STUFFED FLANK STEAK

Makes 6 to 8 Servings
1   1½- to 2-pound beef flank
    steak
Salt
Pepper
¼   teaspoon dried marjoram,
    crushed
¼   teaspoon dried basil, crushed
¼   teaspoon dried parsley flakes
8   ounces fresh mushrooms,
    sliced
2   green onions, thinly sliced
    (¼ cup)
2   tablespoons butter *or*
    margarine
½   cup soft bread crumbs
2   tablespoons butter *or*
    margarine, melted
2   tablespoons Worcestershire
    sauce

♦   ♦   ♦

*Judy Chambers told us that
Stuffed Flank Steak is a family
favorite. She gave the recipe to
her daughter, who passed it along
to some of her friends. Judy
emphasizes that when you cook
Stuffed Flank Steak, you should
be sure to keep basting for a
tender, flavorful steak.*

Judy Chambers
<u>*VIP Cookbook: A Potpourri of
Virginia Cooking*</u>
*The American Cancer Society,
Virginia Division
Vienna
VIRGINIA*

1 Preheat the oven to 425°.

2 Pound the steak to a ¼-inch thickness. (It should be approximately a 12x8-inch rectangle.) Sprinkle the steak lightly with salt and pepper. Rub the marjoram, basil and parsley on 1 side of the meat.

3 Cook the mushrooms and onions in the 2 tablespoons butter or margarine until tender. Stir in the bread crumbs.

4 Spread the mushroom mixture over the herbs on the steak to within 1 inch of the edges.

5 Roll up the steak, jelly-roll fashion, starting from a short side. Tie with a string. Place the meat, seam side down,

on a rack in a roasting pan. Stir together the 2 tablespoons melted butter or margarine and the Worcestershire sauce; brush over the steak.

6 Bake in the 425° oven for 45 to 60 minutes or until the meat is tender, brushing occasionally with the butter-Worcestershire sauce mixture. Remove the strings; slice and serve.

 TIPS FROM OUR KITCHEN

When pounding the meat, first cover the steak with heavy-duty plastic wrap; lightweight plastic wrap or waxed paper is likely to tear as you pound. Pound from the center outward until the meat reaches the desired thickness.

If fresh marjoram, basil and parsley are available, use ¾ teaspoon of each instead of the dried herbs.

If you prefer your meat with gravy, serve this dish with bottled gravy or gravy prepared from a packaged mix.

The steak can be served with potatoes or rice. Or, for something a little different, try serving it with spinach noodles or orzo.

Nutrition Analysis (*Per Serving*): Calories: 257 / Cholesterol: 74 mg / Carbohydrates: 4 g / Protein: 23 g / Sodium: 247 mg / Fat: 16 g (Saturated Fat: 8 g) / Potassium: 493 mg.

Pinwheel of Beef

Presentation isn't all this recipe has to offer. Stuffed Flank Steak from Judy Chambers of Galax, Virginia, has exceptional flavor, too!

MEATS

227

GOLDEN STEAK FINGERS

Makes 4 Servings
1   pound boneless beef top
     round steak, cut ½-
     to ¾-inch thick
1   teaspoon lemon pepper
     seasoning
¼   teaspoon salt
½   cup buttermilk
1   cup all-purpose flour
¼   cup cooking oil

♦   ♦   ♦

*Judging from these highly
delectable Golden Steak Fingers,
it is no wonder why <u>Birthright
Sampler: A Melting Pot of Ethnic
Recipes</u> is in its third printing.
Florence Badowski tells us that
she sometimes substitutes sirloin
steak for the beef round in this
recipe for even more tender
Golden Steak Fingers. Her family
enjoys these served with a salad
for lunch.*

*Florence Badowski
<u>Birthright Sampler: A Melting
Pot of Ethnic Recipes</u>
Birthright of Johnstown, Inc.
Johnstown
PENNSYLVANIA*

1 Place the steak between 2 pieces of plastic wrap and pound to a ¼-inch thickness. Sprinkle the steak with lemon pepper seasoning and salt. Cut the pounded steak into 4x½-inch strips.

2 Dip the steak strips in the buttermilk and dredge in the flour.

3 In a large skillet over medium heat, heat *2 tablespoons* of the oil. Add *half* of the steak strips and brown on both sides (3 to 4 minutes total). Transfer the steak strips to paper towels. Place on a warm serving platter. Keep warm.

4 Repeat Steps 2 and 3 with the remaining steak strips and oil.

TIPS FROM OUR KITCHEN

If you don't have lemon pepper seasoning in your spice cabinet, substitute 1 teaspoon crushed dried basil, savory or thyme.

This recipe is ideal for pork loin strips, too.

Your family might enjoy being served a selection of sauces for dipping such as catsup, creamy Italian dressing, honey/mustard sauce and horseradish sauce.

Nutrition Analysis *(Per Serving)*: Calories: 360 / Cholesterol: 55 mg / Carbohydrates: 24 g
Protein: 24 g / Sodium: 477 mg / Fat: 18 g (Saturated Fat: 4 g) / Potassium: 365 mg.

QUICK AND TASTY MAIN DISH

Folks adore these tender strips of steak with a golden brown crust. Lemon pepper seasoning and
buttermilk give them their special tang. This superb recipe for Golden Steak Fingers
is from Florence Badowski of Windber, Pennsylvania.

MEATS

229

VEAL PARMIGIANA

Makes 6 Servings

1½ pounds veal leg roundsteak, cut ½ inch thick
2 eggs
½ cup fine dry plain *or* seasoned bread crumbs
½ cup grated Parmesan cheese
2 tablespoons cooking oil
1 medium onion, finely chopped
2 cloves garlic, minced
1 29-ounce can tomato sauce
1 16-ounce can whole tomatoes, undrained
¾ teaspoon dried oregano, crushed
¼ teaspoon dried thyme, crushed
8 ounces mozzarella cheese, sliced
¼ cup grated Parmesan cheese

◆ ◆ ◆

Betsy Worthington's husband loves veal parmigiana and always ordered it when they were out at restaurants. Fifteen years ago, he asked Betsy to find a recipe for it. Here is Veal Parmigiana, complete with Betsy's adaptations.

Betsy Worthington
<u>Virginia Seasons</u>
Junior League of Richmond
Richmond
VIRGINIA

1 Cut the veal into 6 pieces. Pound each piece between 2 sheets of plastic wrap or waxed paper to ¼-inch thickness.

2 In a small bowl, slightly beat the eggs with a fork. In a shallow bowl, combine the bread crumbs and the ½ cup Parmesan cheese.

3 Dip each piece of veal, first in the beaten egg, coating both sides, then in the bread crumb mixture, turning to coat evenly.

4 In a large skillet, brown the veal in hot oil about 1½ minutes per side or until lightly browned. Using a fork or tongs, transfer the veal to a 3-quart rectangular baking dish.

5 To make the sauce: Add the onion and garlic to the skillet and cook until the onion is tender but not brown. Carefully add the tomato sauce, *undrained* tomatoes, oregano and thyme. Simmer the sauce, uncovered, about 30 minutes or until thickened.

6 Preheat the oven to 375°. Spoon *half* the sauce over the browned veal. Sprinkle with mozzarella cheese. Spoon the remaining sauce over the cheese. Sprinkle with the ¼ cup Parmesan cheese. Bake, uncovered, in the 375° oven for 20 to 30 minutes or until bubbly.

 TIPS FROM OUR KITCHEN

You can use this same sauce and cooking method for boneless pork.

For a meatless meal, use eggplant that has been peeled and thinly sliced in place of the veal.

Nutrition Analysis *(Per Serving)*: Calories: 461 / Cholesterol: 194 mg / Carbohydrates: 23 g Protein: 45 g / Sodium: 1577 mg / Fat: 21 g (Saturated Fat: 9 g) / Potassium: 1176 mg.

ITALIAN RESTAURANT FARE

Don't wait until the next time you visit your favorite Italian restaurant—Veal Parmigiana is easy to prepare at home. Breaded veal is browned and then layered with fresh tomato sauce and cheese. Serve with pasta and a green vegetable for a stay-at-home treat.

MEATS

231

VEAL ROLLS WITH RICE PIEDMONT

Makes 8 Servings

Veal Rolls:

¼	cup snipped parsley
1½	teaspoons dried rosemary, crushed
1	teaspoon minced garlic
¼	teaspoon pepper
8	4-ounce veal scallopini *or* turkey steaks, pounded to ⅛-inch thickness
4	ounces very thinly sliced prosciutto *or* ham
2	tablespoons olive oil
½	cup dry Marsala *or* dry sherry
4	cups sliced fresh mushrooms

Rice Piedmont:

4	cups hot cooked rice
2	cups fresh *or* frozen peas, cooked
¼	cup butter *or* margarine, melted
	Dash ground nutmeg
¾	cup grated Parmesan cheese

♦ ♦ ♦

Rollini Di Vitella (veal rolls)
with Rice Piedmont comes to us
from Eugene, Oregon. This
delicious version of the classic
Italian dish is representative of
the rich cultural diversity of the
Oregon people.

A Taste of Oregon
The Junior League of Eugene
Eugene
OREGON

1 To make the rolls: In a small bowl, combine the parsley, rosemary, garlic and pepper. Lay the veal scallopini or turkey steaks on a flat surface. Sprinkle about *1½ teaspoons* of the herb mixture on *each* scallopini or turkey steak. Then top *each* scallopini or turkey steak with the prosciutto or ham, dividing it equally.

2 Starting from a short side, roll up each veal scallopini or turkey steak.

3 Fasten each veal or turkey roll with a wooden toothpick.

4 In a large skillet, quickly cook *half* of the veal or turkey rolls in *1 tablespoon* of the oil, lightly browning the rolls on all sides. Remove the rolls to a plate as they brown. Repeat with the remaining rolls and oil.

5 Remove the skillet from the heat, drain off any oil and carefully stir in the Marsala or sherry. Add the mushrooms and the meat rolls to the skillet and simmer, covered, for 15 to 20 minutes or until the veal is tender or the turkey is no longer pink, turning the rolls once during cooking. Remove the meat rolls and mushrooms to a warm platter and remove the wooden picks.

6 Bring the pan juices to boiling and boil until the juices are slightly thickened (or to the desired consistency). Spoon the juices over the meat rolls.

7 To make Rice Piedmont: In a large bowl, combine the rice, peas, butter and nutmeg. Gently fold in the Parmesan cheese being careful not to overmix the rice. Serve with the veal or turkey rolls and juices.

 TIPS FROM OUR KITCHEN

If veal scallopini isn't available, substitute ½-inch-thick pieces of veal round steak and pound them to a ⅛-inch thickness.

Nutrition Analysis (*Per Serving*): Calories: 523 / Cholesterol: 117 mg / Carbohydrates: 39 g Protein: 39 g / Sodium: 609 mg / Fat: 21 g (Saturated Fat: 8 g) / Potassium: 669 mg.

One-Dish Italian Classic

These delicious rolls of veal and prosciutto come to us from The Junior League of Eugene, Oregon. Seasoned with herbs and garlic and served on top of flavorful rice, this is an updated version of a traditional Northern Italian dish.

MEATS

233

BROILED EGGPLANT AND LAMB PATTIES

Makes 6 Servings

1	small eggplant (12 to 16 ounces)
1	teaspoon salt
1	egg
½	cup chopped ripe olives
⅓	cup fine dry bread crumbs
¼	cup grated Parmesan cheese
½	teaspoon dried oregano, crushed
1	clove garlic, minced
1½	pounds ground lamb
2	tablespoons olive oil
1	large tomato, cut into 6 slices (optional)
1	cup shredded Monterey Jack cheese (4 ounces)

◆　　◆　　◆

The Mothers' Guild of Our Ladies of Lourdes School have put together Our Culinary Treasures *in celebration of the twenty-fifth anniversary of the elementary school. Profits from cookbook sales are used to pur-chase supplies and to help the school maintain the lowest tuition in their Diocese.*

**Our Culinary Treasures
Our Ladies of Lourdes
Mothers' Guild
Taunton
MASSACHUSETTS**

1 Wash the eggplant; do not peel. Cut the eggplant into six ¾-inch-thick slices. Sprinkle each side of the eggplant slices with salt. Place them on paper towels; let stand for 20 minutes. Blot the surfaces of the eggplant slices with paper towels.

2 In a medium mixing bowl, beat the egg. Stir in the olives, bread crumbs, Parmesan cheese, oregano and garlic. Add the ground lamb and mix well.

3 Shape the lamb mixture into 6 patties equal to the diameter of the eggplant slices.

4 Brush the eggplant slices with the olive oil. Place the eggplant and lamb patties in a single layer on an unheated rack of a broiler pan.

5 Broil 4 to 5 inches from the heat. Broil the eggplant slices about 10 minutes or until the eggplant is tender. Broil the lamb patties for 15 to 18 minutes or until the lamb is no longer pink. Turn all slices and patties once during broiling.

6 Place an eggplant slice on top of each lamb patty. Layer on a tomato slice (if using) and the shredded cheese. Broil about 1 minute more or until the cheese melts.

 TIPS FROM OUR KITCHEN

If ground lamb isn't available, you can substitute ground beef in this recipe.

If desired, sprinkle the tomato-topped stack with shredded mozzarella cheese instead of Monterey Jack cheese.

You can buy commercially prepared dry bread crumbs, or you can make your own. To make your own: Place 1½ slices dry or toasted bread in a plastic bag and crush them with a rolling pin.

Sprinkling the eggplant slices with the salt helps draw out some of the moisture.

Nutrition Analysis (*Per Serving*): Calories: 355 / Cholesterol: 118 mg / Carbohydrates: 10 Protein: 23 g / Sodium: 384 mg / Fat: 24 g (Saturated Fat: 9 g) / Potassium: 414 mg.

COMPATIBLE DUET

The compatible flavors of lamb and eggplant form a delicious duet in this recipe from Taunton,
Massachusetts. Tomatoes, ripe olives and cheese are among the ingredients that
help make this dish sing.

MEATS

235

CHICAGO PIZZA

Makes 8 to 10 Servings
Pizza Dough:

2¾ to 3¼	cups bread flour *or* all-purpose flour
1	package active dry yeast
¼	teaspoon salt
1	cup warm water (120° to 130°)
2	tablespoons cooking oil

Cornmeal

Sauce:

1	pound bulk Italian sausage
1	14½-ounce can Italian-style plum tomatoes, cut up
1	cup water
¼	cup tomato paste
2	teaspoons dried oregano, crushed
2	teaspoons dried thyme, crushed
2	teaspoons dried basil, crushed
1	clove garlic, minced
½	cup sliced fresh mushrooms
½	medium onion, sliced and separated into rings
1	tablespoon olive oil
2	cups shredded mozzarella, Swiss, *and/or* cheddar cheese

♦   ♦   ♦

The Utah Dining Car Junior
League of Ogden Cookbook
The Junior League of Ogden
Ogden
UTAH

1 To make the pizza dough: In a large mixing bowl, combine *1¼ cups* of the flour, the yeast and salt. Add the warm water and cooking oil. Beat with an electric mixer on low speed for 30 seconds, scraping the sides of the bowl constantly. Beat on high speed for 3 minutes, continuing to scrape the bowl. Using a wooden spoon, stir in as much of the remaining flour as you can.

2 On a lightly floured surface, knead the dough for 6 to 8 minutes, adding enough of the remaining flour to make a moderately stiff dough that is smooth and elastic. Cover the dough and let rest for 10 minutes.

3 Preheat the oven to 375°. Grease a 12-inch cast iron skillet or deep-dish pizza pan; sprinkle with the cornmeal. With greased fingers, pat the dough into the bottom and halfway up the side of the prepared pan; cover and let rise in a warm place for 30 to 45 minutes or until nearly doubled in size. Bake in the 375° oven for 20 to 25 minutes or until lightly browned.

4 Meanwhile, to prepare the sauce: In a large skillet, brown the sausage. Drain and discard any fat. Add the *undrained* tomatoes, water, tomato paste, oregano, thyme, basil and garlic to the sausage. Bring to a boil; reduce heat. Cover and simmer about 12 minutes or until the sauce has thickened. Spread the sauce over the prebaked crust.

5 In a medium bowl, toss together the sliced mushrooms, onion rings and olive oil. Sprinkle the mixture over the top of the pizza. Top with the mozzarella, Swiss and/or cheddar cheese. Bake for 15 to 20 minutes more or until the topping is bubbly. Let the pizza stand for 5 to 10 minutes before cutting into wedges.

 TIPS FROM OUR KITCHEN

If you like, there are several meats you can substitute for the Italian sausage: pork sausage; turkey sausage; ground beef, pork or turkey; chopped ham; Canadian bacon; or pepperoni.

Prebaking the crust helps prevent it from becoming soggy under this saucy filling.

Nutrition Analysis (*Per Serving*): Calories: 449 / Cholesterol: 48 mg / Carbohydrates: 41 g / Protein: 22 g / Sodium: 676 mg / Fat: 21 g (Saturated Fat: 8 g) / Potassium: 448 mg.

IT'S IN THE PAN!

A golden, crispy crust and a thick, meaty sauce envelop fresh mushrooms and onions to
create this dazzling deep-dish delight.

TOMATO-PEACH BARBECUED RIBS

Makes 6 Servings

4 to 5	pounds pork ribs, cut into serving-size pieces
1	onion studded with 2 whole cloves
1	bay leaf
2	cups chopped, peeled peaches (1 pound)
1	10¾-ounce can condensed tomato soup
½	cup light corn syrup
½	cup cider vinegar
½	cup packed brown sugar
¼	cup cooking oil
1	tablespoon dry mustard
1	tablespoon Worcestershire sauce
1½	teaspoons paprika
½	teaspoon salt
½	teaspoon garlic powder
½	teaspoon pepper

◆　　◆　　◆

Years ago, Phyllis Knox created this recipe for Tomato-Peach Barbecued Ribs to enter a contest. The prizes included a barbecue grill and a grill accessory kit. In a hurry, she submitted the recipe without even tasting it. To her surprise, Phyllis won third prize and discovered a new family favorite.

Phyllis Knox
Teleco Cooks
Teleco Oilfield Services, Inc.
Meriden
CONNECTICUT

1 Place the ribs in a 5-quart Dutch oven or a kettle and add about 2 inches *water*. Add the onion and bay leaf and bring the water to a boil. Reduce heat; cover and simmer about 1 hour or until the ribs are tender.

2 Drain the ribs. In a covered grill, arrange *medium-hot* coals around a drip pan. Test for medium heat above the pan. Place the ribs, fat side up, on the preheated grill rack over the drip pan, but not over the coals. Lower the grill hood and cook for 1 hour.

3 Meanwhile, in a 2-quart saucepan, stir together the peaches, tomato soup, corn syrup, vinegar, brown sugar, cooking oil, dry mustard, Worcestershire sauce, paprika, salt, garlic powder and pepper. Bring the mixture to a boil, stirring constantly. Reduce heat and simmer, uncovered, about 20 minutes or until the sauce is slightly thickened, stirring occasionally.

4 After the ribs have grilled for 1 hour, brush them generously with the sauce and grill for 5 to 10 minutes more or until well-done, brushing occasionally with the sauce. Pass the remaining sauce with the ribs.

TIPS FROM OUR KITCHEN

Leftover sauce can be stored in the refrigerator for 2 weeks and enjoyed on pork chops, chicken or other poultry. To use, heat the sauce to boiling and brush it on the almost-cooked meat during the last 5 to 20 minutes of cooking.

Use your choice of pork ribs: spareribs, country-style ribs or back ribs.

Cut the pork into serving-size pieces before cooking.

Two cups frozen, unsweetened peach slices that have been thawed and chopped can be substituted for the fresh peaches in this recipe.

To grill ribs without precooking them, follow step 2, except use *medium* coals and grill the ribs for 2 hours.

To roast the ribs instead of grilling, place them fat side up in shallow roasting pan. Bake in a 350° oven about 2 hours or until well-done. Brush on the sauce during the last 5 to 10 minutes.

Nutrition Analysis (*Per Serving*): Calories: 742 / Cholesterol: 177mg / Carbohydrates: 28 g / Protein: 44 g / Sodium: 445 mg / Fat: 50 g (Saturated Fat: 18 g) / Potassium: 676 mg.

PEACHY DELICIOUS

As a surprising change from traditional barbecue sauce, peaches, tomato soup and other flavorings
combine to create a not-too-sweet coating for succulent pork ribs.

PORK CHOPS PACIFICA

Makes 6 Servings

6	1-inch thick pork chops
½	teaspoon salt
¼	teaspoon pepper
2	tablespoons olive oil
1¼	cups chicken broth
1	cup long-grain rice
1	14½-ounce can Italian tomatoes, cut up
1	cup chopped green sweet peppers
⅓	cup sliced scallions *or* green onions

♦　　♦　　♦

This recipe comes from the tiny town of Hingham in North Central Montana, which was settled in the early 1900s mainly by German and Scandinavian immigrants. Today residents of Hingham are a self-reliant community of 150 people. With the closest supermarket more than 35 miles away, Isabelle Devlin's creative one-dish dinner proves that using what's on hand can be delicious.

Isabelle Devlin
<u>*Wonderful Ideas in Farm Eating*</u>
Hingham
MONTANA

1 Preheat oven to 350°.

2 Trim any visible fat from the pork chops. Sprinkle the pork chops with the salt and pepper.

3 In a large skillet, heat the oil. Brown the pork chops, 3 at a time, for 2 to 3 minutes on each side.

4 Meanwhile, in a medium saucepan, bring the broth and rice to a boil. Stir in the tomatoes, green sweet peppers and scallions or green onions. Pour the mixture into a 13x9x2-inch baking dish.

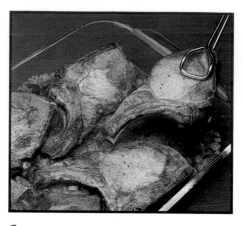

5 Arrange the pork chops on top of the rice mixture so the chops are not touching.

6 Bake the pork chops, covered, for 1 hour and 35 minutes to 1 hour and 45 minutes, or until the chops are cooked through and the rice is tender. When testing the chops for doneness, make a small cut in one of the chops; there should be no sign of pink.

 TIPS FROM OUR KITCHEN

Trimming the excess fat from the pork chops helps to keep the rice mixture from becoming too greasy and it also helps to reduce the total fat in the recipe.

This recipe requires a long baking time so that the rice will cook completely and the pork chops will be deliciously tender.

Nutrition Analysis (*Per Serving*): Calories: 522 / Cholesterol: 128 mg / Carbohydrates: 29 g / Protein: 41 g / Sodium: 552 mg / Fat: 26 g (Saturated Fat: 8 g) / Potassium: 824 mg.

MAGNIFICENT ONE-DISH MEAL

Here's a pork chop meal that is sure to become a favorite with your family and friends—and you!
Isabelle Devlin of Hingham, Montana, makes perfect pork chops in one dish. Just assemble the recipe,
pop it in the oven and you're free to enjoy the evening. To complete the meal, add a tossed salad.

SWEET-AND-SOUR PORK

1 Drain the pineapple, reserving ¾ *cup* of the juice. Set aside.

2 In a saucepan, partially cook the carrots in boiling *water* to cover for 5 minutes; drain, reserving ¾ *cup* of the cooking water (or add water, if necessary, to make ¾ cup). Set aside.

3 To make the sauce: In a 3-quart saucepan, stir together the sugar and the 2½ tablespoons cornstarch. Add the reserved water, the reserved pineapple juice, the catsup, rice vinegar and soy sauce. Cook and stir until thickened and bubbly. Cook and stir for 1 minute more; set aside.

4 In a small bowl, stir together the flour, the 1 tablespoon cornstarch, the salt and pepper. Add the egg, stirring until smooth. Add the pork cubes, stirring to coat.

5 In a heavy skillet or 4-quart Dutch oven, pour cooking oil to measure ½ inch deep. When the oil is hot, add the pork cubes, a few at a time. Cook about 2 minutes or until browned on all sides. Using a slotted spoon, remove the pork from the pan; drain on paper towels. Keep warm. Repeat until all the pork cubes are cooked.

6 Carefully add the onions, green sweet pepper and garlic to the oil in the skillet. Cook for 2 minutes. Using a slotted spoon, remove the vegetables and drain on paper towels. Repeat with the carrots, cucumber and mushrooms (if using).

7 Stir the drained vegetables and pineapple into the sauce and heat through. Stir in the pork. Serve with the rice.

TIPS FROM OUR KITCHEN

To keep the meat cubes warm, place the drained meat on a paper towel-lined baking sheet in a 300° oven.

Dried mushrooms should be soaked for 30 minutes in enough warm water to cover them. Rinse them well and squeeze to drain thoroughly. Remove and discard the tough stems.

Nutrition Analysis (*Per Serving*): Calories: 493 / Cholesterol: 70 mg / Carbohydrates: 74 g / Protein: 17 g / Sodium: 672 mg / Fat: 16 g (Saturated Fat: 3 g) / Potassium: 655 mg.

CHINESE ORIGINS

Homemade Sweet-and-Sour Pork is just a few steps away! Connie Dosen of Pinellas Park, Florida, shares her outstanding recipe for this colorful and delicious dish of Chinese origin.

REUBEN CASSEROLE Á LA ORCAS

Makes 6 to 8 Servings

8	ounces wide noodles, cooked and drained
3	tablespoons butter *or* margarine, softened
1	pound sauerkraut, drained
2	cups chopped corned beef
2	medium tomatoes, peeled and sliced
¼	cup Thousand Island salad dressing
2	cups shredded Swiss cheese (8 ounces)
4	crisp rye crackers, crushed
½	teaspoon caraway seed

♦   ♦   ♦

Patricia Jorgensen and her family love to ski—and they love Reuben sandwiches—so whenever they embark on a ski trip, Patricia is sure to bring along her Reuben Casserole. It is a quick, tasty winter dish that is perfect for those cozy dinners in the ski cabin. Patricia tells us that she frequently serves this casserole to dinner guests at home as well.

Patricia Jorgensen
Orcas Cuisine
Orcas Island Medical Guild
Eastsound
Orcas Island
WASHINGTON

1 Preheat the oven to 350°. Grease a 2-quart baking dish. Set aside.

2 While the noodles are still hot, place them in a bowl. Add the butter or margarine and stir to coat.

3 Layer the buttered noodles, sauerkraut, corned beef and tomatoes in the prepared baking dish. Dot with the Thousand Island salad dressing and sprinkle with the cheese.

4 Top the casserole with the crushed cracker crumbs and the caraway seed.

5 Bake, covered, in the 350° oven for 40 minutes. Uncover and bake for 15 minutes more or until bubbly.

TIPS FROM OUR KITCHEN

For easier serving, stir together the noodles, sauerkraut and *half* of the cheese before placing it in the baking dish. Layer the corned beef, tomato slices and Thousand Island salad dressing, then sprinkle the remaining cheese on top.

You may want to substitute caraway cheese for the Swiss cheese and caraway seed.

Corned beef is a beef product usually made from fresh beef brisket or beef round and cured with spices added to a salt brine. Corned beef tastes slightly salty and has a deep red color. You'll find ready-to-cook corned beef in the meat case.

An easy way to crush crackers is to place them inside a heavy plastic bag and then roll a rolling pin over them.

Nutrition Analysis (*Per Serving*): Calories: 530 / Cholesterol: 103 mg / Carbohydrates: 38 g / Protein: 26 g / Sodium: 1221 mg / Fat: 30 g (Saturated Fat: 14 g) / Potassium: 375 mg.

REUBEN REDEFINED

People are divided as to whether the originator of this casserole's namesake sandwich was Arthur Reuben, a New York City deli owner, or Reuben Kay, a grocer from Omaha, Nebraska. But we do know that this luscious variation on the theme comes from Patricia Jorgensen of Orcas Island in Washington State.

HAM ALEXANDRIA

Makes 10 Servings

- 6   tablespoons butter *or* margarine
- 8   ounces fresh mushrooms, sliced
- 2   14-ounce cans artichoke hearts, drained and quartered
- 3   tablespoons all-purpose flour
- 2   cups milk
- 1   cup shredded Swiss cheese
- 5   English muffins, halved and toasted
- 10 thin slices cooked ham
- 2   hard-cooked eggs, chopped
- 20 pimiento strips (one 2-ounce jar) (optional)

❖   ❖   ❖

Audrey Hammill found a recipe in the 1970s and made a few alterations to create this recipe for Ham Alexandria. Audrey, who loves to entertain casually, recommends serving the dish for brunch.

Audrey G. Hammill
Louisiana Entertains
Rapides Symphony Guild
Alexandria
LOUISIANA

1 In a large skillet, melt *2 tablespoons* of the butter or margarine. Add the mushrooms; cook and stir for 2 to 3 minutes. Add the artichoke hearts and continue to cook and stir for 3 minutes more. Transfer the mixture to a bowl.

2 In the same skillet, melt the remaining butter or margarine. Add the flour and stir until smooth. Add the milk all at once. Cook and stir until thickened and bubbly. Stir in the Swiss cheese and continue cooking until melted. Add the mushroom-artichoke heart mixture. Season with *salt* and *pepper* to taste; heat through.

3 Arrange the English muffin halves on a platter. Top with the ham slices, then cover generously with the sauce. Garnish with the eggs and, if desired, the pimientos.

 TIPS FROM OUR KITCHEN

If desired, use 10 ounces of presliced ham which should equal 10 thin slices. Fold the ham diagonally to fit on the muffin halves.

This dish will stay hotter if you "build" it under the broiler. Place the untoasted muffin halves on the rack of a broiler pan or on a baking sheet. Broil 4 to 5 inches from the heat for 1 to 2 minutes or until the muffins are toasted. Top with the ham slices and broil 1 to 2 minutes to heat through. Transfer to a plate and top with the hot cheese sauce. Garnish with the egg and pimiento, if desired.

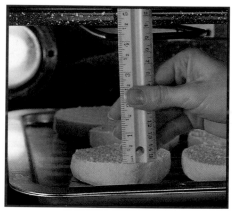

Before preheating the broiler, use a ruler to check the distance from the heat source to the top of the food being broiled. Don't just measure to the rack.

Nutrition Analysis (*Per Serving*): Calories: 310 / Cholesterol: 91 mg / Carbohydrates: 27 g / Protein: 16 g / Sodium: 826 mg / Fat: 16 g (Saturated Fat: 8 g) / Potassium: 629 mg.

KUDOS FOR YOU

Ham-topped English muffin halves are lavished with a mushroom- and artichoke-studded cheese
sauce. Try this dish for your next brunch and stand by for compliments.

MEATS

CORN DOGS

Makes 4 or 5 Servings

- 1   1-pound package frankfurters (8 to 10)
- 1   cup all-purpose flour
- ¾   cup yellow cornmeal
- 2   teaspoons sugar
- 1½ teaspoons baking powder
- ½   teaspoon salt
- 1   egg, slightly beaten
- ¾   cup milk
- 2   teaspoons melted shortening *or* cooking oil

Milk (if necessary)
Shortening *or* cooking oil
Catsup (optional)
Mustard (optional)

♦   ♦   ♦

Jessie Benge's three children grew up eating Corn Dogs for dinners and at picnics and birthdays. When the Mount Zion Cemetary Association printed the recipe, Jessie gave a cookbook to each of her children. And now her grandchildren are enjoying Corn Dogs too! The only change Jessie might make would be to add onions and jalapeño peppers.

Jessie Benge
<u>Home Cookin' Mount Zion</u>
<u>Heritage Cookbook</u>
Mount Zion Cemetary
Association
Apple Springs
TEXAS

1 Pat the frankfurters dry with paper towels. If desired, insert a wooden skewer into one end of each frankfurter; set aside.

2 In a medium bowl, stir together the flour, cornmeal, sugar, baking powder and salt; set aside.

3 In a small bowl, stir together the slightly beaten egg, milk and the 2 teaspoons melted shortening or cooking oil. Add the egg mixture to the flour-cornmeal mixture; mix well. The batter will be thick, but if it seems too thick, add a little additional milk (about 2 tablespoons).

4 In a large skillet, heat approximately ¾-inch shortening or cooking oil to 375°. Dip the frankfurters into the batter, coating all of the surfaces. Let any extra batter drip off.

5 Fry the frankfurters, about three at a time, turning them with tongs after 5 seconds to prevent the batter from sliding off. Fry for 3 minutes more; turn again after 1½ minutes. Serve the corn dogs with the catsup and mustard, if desired.

TIPS FROM OUR KITCHEN

The batter needs to be fairly thick to stay on the hot dogs. After mixing, transfer the batter to a shallow dish, such as a pie plate, for easier dipping. Then, set the dish of batter in a bowl of ice to keep the batter thick.

Nutrition Analysis (*Per Serving*): Calories: 747 / Cholesterol: 114 mg / Carbohydrates: 50 g / Protein: 21 g / Sodium: 1583 mg / Fat: 51 g (Saturated Fat: 17 g) / Potassium: 350 mg.

CARNIVAL ON A STICK

If you've only thought of Corn Dogs as carnival and fair food, think again. Jessie Benge's delicious
batter-coated frankfurters are easy to make at home.

MEATS

249

Pasta, Rice & Legumes

*T*hese dishes are good for filling hungry appetites in a nutritious *and* economical way. Your family will love Aunt Ella's Macaroni and Cheese, Grandma Nonie's Baked Beans, or the Classic Spaghetti and Meatballs. Entertain in style by serving Green Rice Ring or Pasta with Creamy Basil Sauce to your guests. Noodle Kugel and Soubise are both great substitutes for potatoes and go well with any meal.

LORI'S LINGUINE

Makes 6 to 8 Servings

1½	cups chopped onion
½ to ¾	cup chopped celery
¼ to ⅓	cup chopped green sweet pepper
½	cup chopped carrot
½	cup snipped parsley
1	small clove garlic, thinly sliced
1	tablespoon olive oil
1	16-ounce can whole Italian tomatoes, cut up
1	15-ounce can tomato sauce
2	teaspoons sugar
⅛	teaspoon salt
⅛	teaspoon pepper
⅛	teaspoon crushed red pepper flakes
⅛	teaspoon oregano
8	ounces packaged linguine *or* other pasta
⅓	cup grated Parmesan cheese

♦   ♦   ♦

Senator Lori Wilson is a self-proclaimed "mad scientist in the kitchen." Lucky for us, she concocted a wonderful sauce full of vegetables and flavor, yet low in calories and cholesterol. Vary the types of vegetables and pasta to create a new dish every time.

Senator Lori Wilson
<u>*Canopy Roads*</u>
Tallahassee Junior Woman's Club
Tallahassee
FLORIDA

1 In a large saucepan, cook and stir the onion, celery, green sweet pepper, carrot, parsley and garlic in the olive oil until the onion is tender. Add the *undrained* tomatoes, tomato sauce, sugar, salt, pepper, red pepper flakes and oregano. Reduce heat and simmer for 30 to 60 minutes or until the sauce reaches the desired consistency.

2 Cook the pasta according to the package directions. Drain.

3 Spoon the sauce over the cooked pasta, sprinkle with Parmesan cheese and serve immediately.

 TIPS FROM OUR KITCHEN

To save time, double the recipe for the sauce and freeze half for use at a later date.

If you prefer a meat sauce, brown a pound of lean ground beef, pork, turkey or Italian sausage. Add the meat to the sauce just before simmering.

To snip parsley, place it in a deep container, such as a 1-cup measure, and snip it with kitchen shears.

You may substitute 1 pound home-made pasta or fresh refrigerated pasta for 8 ounces of the packaged product.

Change the look of this pasta dish by changing the shape of the pasta.

Nutrition Analysis (*Per Serving*): Calories: 259 / Cholesterol: 4 mg / Carbohydrates: 45 g / Protein: 10 g / Sodium: 756 mg / Fat: 5 g (Saturated Fat: 2 g) / Potassium: 637 mg.

Pasta Power

It takes a lot of energy to live a senator's life. So it comes as no surprise that this linguine draped in a meatless tomato sauce is a specialty of Senator Lori Wilson of Tallahassee, Florida. Next time you need a delicious energy boost, pull out this recipe.

PASTA WITH CREAMY BASIL SAUCE

Makes 4 Servings

6	ounces radiatore *or* rigatoni
1	clove garlic, peeled
1¼	cups lightly packed fresh basil leaves
¾	cup low-fat cottage cheese
¼	teaspoon salt
⅛	teaspoon fresh ground pepper
1	medium tomato, chopped
1	ounce crumbled Gorgonzola *or* blue cheese (optional)
2	tablespoons pine nuts (optional)

◆   ◆   ◆

Diane Fortier combined two recipes to create this wonderful pasta dish. While her children prefer their pasta with a simple spaghetti sauce, she and her husband, Jacques, like the little extra zip that comes from the Gorgonzola cheese. Diane suggests serving this dish with a salad and garlic bread.

Diane Fortier
<u>**Wigh Cook?**</u>
**St. Gregory the Great Home &
School Association
Danbury
CONNECTICUT**

1 Bring 3 quarts *water* to a boil. Cook the radiatore or rigatoni according to the package directions.

2 Meanwhile, place the garlic in a food processor bowl; process until chopped. Add the basil and cottage cheese; process until smooth. Remove the cover and stir in the salt and pepper.

3 Drain the pasta. Return the pasta to the hot pan. Stir in the basil-cottage cheese sauce. Transfer to a warm serving dish and top with the chopped tomato. Sprinkle with the crumbled Gorganzola and pine nuts, if desired. Serve immediately.

 TIPS FROM OUR KITCHEN

Cooking pasta to the *al dente* stage requires frequent testing near the end of cooking time. The pasta should be tender but still slightly firm when it is bitten.

This sauce works best when prepared in a food processor. The use of a blender is not recommended.

While this sauce can be used on any pasta shape you choose, we found it clings especially well to ruffled or corkscrew pasta.

If fresh basil is not available, you can achieve a similar flavor by using 1¼ cups snipped fresh parsley or spinach plus 1 teaspoon dried basil, crushed.

Nutrition Analysis (*Per Serving*): Calories: 212 / Cholesterol: 4 mg / Carbohydrates: 37 g / Protein: 12 g / Sodium: 310 mg / Fat: 2 g (Saturated Fat: 1 g) / Potassium: 221 mg.

PRIMO PASTA

Looking for a delicious new sauce-and-pasta combination? Look no further—here's a fresh basil-
cottage cheese sauce that perfectly complements fancy-shaped pastas such as radiatore and rigatoni.
Top this dish with chopped tomatoes and crumbled Gorgonzola to add color and flavor.

Spinach and Pasta Casserole

Makes 16 to 20 Side-Dish or 8
Meatless Main-Dish Servings

1½	cups orzo pasta
1	cup chopped onion
2	tablespoons butter *or* margarine
2	10-ounce packages frozen chopped spinach, thawed and well drained
¼	teaspoon salt
¼	teaspoon pepper
3	eggs, beaten

Cream Sauce:

3	cups whole milk
1	medium onion, sliced
1	bay leaf
1	teaspoon whole black peppercorns
¼	teaspoon salt
¼	cup butter *or* margarine
⅓	cup all-purpose flour
2	eggs

Assembly and Topping:

1	cup grated Parmesan cheese
¼	cup butter *or* margarine, melted
1	cup fine dry bread crumbs

❖　◆　❖

Profits from the sale of <u>Continental Cuisine Cookbook</u> help to support Nick Triantafillis's philanthropic ventures, particularly his unselfish devotion to aiding the hungry.

Helen Paliouras
<u>Continental Cuisine Cookbook</u>
Nick's Cuisine
Burlington
NORTH CAROLINA

1 Preheat the oven to 350°. Grease a 3-quart rectangular baking dish; set aside. Cook the orzo according to the package directions; drain. Rinse with cold water; drain and set aside.

2 In a medium saucepan, cook the 1 cup chopped onion in the 2 tablespoons butter or margarine until the onion is tender and golden. Add the spinach, the ¼ teaspoon salt and the pepper; remove from heat. Stir in the 3 beaten eggs. Set aside.

3 To make the cream sauce: In a medium saucepan, stir together the milk, the sliced onion, the bay leaf, peppercorns and the ¼ teaspoon salt. Bring to a boil. Remove from heat. In another saucepan, melt the ¼ cup butter or margarine. Stir in the flour until smooth.

4 Strain the milk mixture; add the strained mixture, all at once, to the flour mixture. Cook, stirring constantly, until the sauce is thickened. In a small bowl, beat the 2 eggs. Stir *1 cup* of the sauce into the beaten eggs, then return all of the egg mixture to the saucepan. Cook and stir until the cream sauce is bubbly.

5 To assemble the casserole: Spread *half* of the orzo evenly into the bottom of

the prepared baking dish. Sprinkle *⅓ cup* of the Parmesan cheese over the orzo. Spoon the spinach mixture over the cheese and cover with the remaining orzo. Sprinkle with another *⅓ cup* of the cheese. Spread the prepared cream sauce over the top.

6 Stir together the ¼ cup melted butter or margarine, the bread crumbs and the remaining cheese; sprinkle over the casserole. Bake, uncovered, in the 350° oven for 40 to 45 minutes or until heated through.

Tips from Our Kitchen

Thaw the spinach by placing the packages in a bowl in the refrigerator overnight. Or, unwrap the packages and place the frozen blocks in a strainer. Hold the frozen spinach under warm, running water until it is thawed, using fork to help break up chunks. Drain the spinach thoroughly to prevent the casserole from becoming watery. If desired, place the thawed spinach in a clean nonterry towel and squeeze gently.

Nutrition Analysis (*Per Serving*): Calories: 257 / Cholesterol: 97 mg / Carbohydrates: 25 g / Protein: 11 g / Sodium: 380 mg / Fat: 13 g (Saturated Fat: 7 g) / Potassium: 256 mg.

COLORFUL SIDE DISH OR MAIN DISH

To add more color to this casserole, garnish with chopped tomato and snipped parsley. It is an
excellent choice served alongside roasted meat or poultry at a buffet or potluck. Or serve
it to your family as a special meatless main dish.

FETTUCCINE ALFREDO PRIMAVERA

Makes 4 Servings

4	ounces fettuccine
1	cup broccoli flowerets
1	cup cauliflowerets
1	cup sliced carrot
1	cup sliced yellow summer squash *or* zucchini
1	cup sliced fresh mushrooms
½	cup chopped onion
2	tablespoons margarine *or* butter
2	cloves garlic, sliced
1	cup half-and-half *or* light cream
1	egg, well beaten
1	cup grated Romano *and/or* Parmesan cheese
1	tablespoon snipped parsley

◆　　◆　　◆

Victims Services, Inc. is comprised of volunteers and professional counselors who provide educational services focusing on crime prevention. The group has approximately 700 programs directed toward 16,000 children from rural Pennsylvania. Profits from the <u>Country Cookbook</u> *are used toward the group's many essential programs.*

R. Ranallo
<u>*Country Cookbook*</u>
Victim Services, Inc.
Johnstown
PENNSYLVANIA

1 In a large saucepan or Dutch oven, bring 3 quarts *water* to a boil. Gradually add the fettuccine; reduce heat and continue to boil, uncovered, for 8 to 10 minutes or until the pasta is just tender. Drain; return the pasta to the hot pan.

2 Meanwhile, in a large saucepan, steam the broccoli, cauliflowerets and carrots for 4 minutes. Add the yellow summer squash or zucchini, mushrooms and onion. Steam for 4 minutes more. Set aside.

3 In a medium saucepan, melt the margarine or butter. Add the garlic and cook until tender. Stir in the half-and-half or light cream and cook over medium heat until the mixture is just ready to boil.

4 Stir about *half* of the hot mixture into the beaten egg. Return all of the egg mixture to the saucepan; cook and stir for 2 minutes.

5 Toss the vegetables and the Romano and/or Parmesan cheese with the hot cooked fettuccine. Transfer the mixture to a warm serving platter. Pour the sauce over the fettuccine mixture and sprinkle with the parsley. Serve immediately.

 TIPS FROM OUR KITCHEN

Steaming helps maintain the fresh flavor of the vegetables since they actually cook in the vapor given off by boiling water instead of in the water. If you don't have a special steamer, use a metal colander set inside a saucepan with a small amount of water. The vegetables should be above, not touching, the water.

Mince the garlic if you prefer smaller pieces.

You can use a purchased blend of Romano and Parmesan cheeses or make your own. Compared to Parmesan cheese, Romano cheese is slightly stronger in flavor and aroma. Freshly grated Romano cheese will have more flavor than what's typically available in a prepackaged container.

The variety of vegetables adds color and flavor. You can adjust the proportions of each to match your tastes.

Nutrition Analysis (*Per Serving*): Calories: 430 / Cholesterol: 106 mg / Carbohydrates: 38 Protein: 19 g / Sodium: 484 mg / Fat: 23 g (Saturated Fat: 11 g) / Potassium: 611 mg.

FRESH AS SPRING

Alla primavera, the Italian phrase meaning "spring style," usually refers in cooking terms to the use of
fresh vegetables with other ingredients. This tasty adaptation of the classic Fettuccine Alfredo
boasts a tempting variety of garden vegetables which adds color and flavor.

HOMEMADE LEMON PASTA

Makes 10 Servings

3	cups all-purpose flour
3	eggs
2	teaspoons grated lemon peel
½	teaspoon salt
½	cup lemon juice
1	tablespoon olive oil
¼	cup butter *or* margarine, cut up
⅓	cup pecan pieces

◆   ◆   ◆

The cookbook committee of the Junior League of Boise, Idaho, really had fun preparing <u>Bound to Please</u>. First, there was a contest to name the book; then they requested recipes from area restaurants as well as from League members. But the most fun of all was had by the testing teams. League members, their friends and husbands formed several teams, and each recipe was tested three times from start to finish. Then there were parties to eat the food! Guests were required only to eat well and comment on the recipes. Nice work—if you can get it!

Katie Gray
<u>*Bound to Please*</u>
The Junior League of Boise
IDAHO

1 In the bowl of a food processor, combine the flour, eggs, lemon peel and salt. Cover and process until the mixture forms fine crumbs about the consistency of cornmeal.

2 With the processor running, slowly pour the lemon juice and olive oil through the feed tube. Continue processing just until the dough forms a ball. If the dough is too dry, add a little water; if it is too sticky, add a little flour. Let the dough rest for 10 minutes.

3 Lightly sprinkle the work surface with flour. Turn the dough out onto the floured surface. Knead the dough by pushing down and away with the heel of your hand. Give the dough a turn, fold it over and knead again. Knead and turn until the dough is smooth and elastic, for 8 to 10 minutes. If the dough is sticky, add a little more flour. Cover the dough and let it rest for 10 minutes. Divide the dough into 6 pieces.

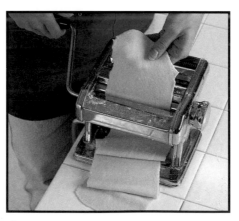

4 To machine-roll the dough: Pass the dough through a pasta machine until it is ¹⁄₁₆-inch thick, following the manufacturer's directions

5 Pass the dough through the pasta machine's cutting blades to cut it to the desired width. By hand, cut the strips into desired lengths.

6 To roll the dough by hand: On a lightly floured surface, roll out each piece into a 9-inch square that is about ¹⁄₁₆-inch thick. Let stand for 20 minutes. Cut the dough into desired widths and lengths.

7 Drop the noodles into boiling salted water and cook for 1 to 2 minutes or until the pasta is al dente (tender but firm to the bite). Drain the pasta. Toss with butter and pecans, if desired. Serve immediately.

 TIPS FROM OUR KITCHEN

If you don't own a food processor, here's how to mix the pasta dough by hand: In a large bowl, stir together only *2 ½ cups* of the flour, the lemon peel and salt. Make a well in the flour mixture. In a small bowl, combine the eggs, lemon juice and olive oil. Pour the egg mixture into the well in the flour mixture and stir until the dough forms a ball.

We found that a pizza cutter works very well for cutting strips of pasta by hand.

Garnish the pasta with sliced tomatoes, a lemon slice and fresh oregano leaves, if desired.

Nutrition Analysis (*Per Serving*): Calories: 204 / Cholesterol: 76 mg / Carbohydrates: 28 g Protein: 6 g / Sodium: 280 mg / Fat: 8 g (Saturated Fat: 4 g) / Potassium: 72 mg.

SIMPLY PERFECT PASTA

Few things can compare with the taste and texture of freshly made pasta. From the Junior League of
Boise, Idaho, this pasta has a delicate lemon flavor. Tossed with butter and toasted pecans, it makes
an elegant side dish for chicken, fish or veal. Or, try serving it with a white clam sauce.

CLASSIC SPAGHETTI AND MEATBALLS

Makes 6 Servings

1	egg, slightly beaten
¼	cup water
1	teaspoon salt
½	teaspoon dried basil, crushed
¼	teaspoon pepper
½	cup fine dry bread crumbs
¼	cup grated Parmesan cheese
1½	pounds lean ground beef
1	tablespoon olive oil
1	28-ounce can tomatoes, cut up
1	6-ounce can tomato paste
¼	cup chopped onion
2	tablespoons snipped parsley
2	cloves garlic, minced
1	teaspoon dried oregano, crushed
½	teaspoon salt
¼	teaspoon anise seed, crushed
12	ounces spaghetti, cooked and drained

Grated Parmesan cheese (optional)

◆　　◆　　◆

Patty Squires has had this recipe for Classic Spaghetti and Meatballs for years, and it's an old standby that she makes whenever she's in the mood for spaghetti. Patty added that sometimes she just makes the sauce—without the meatballs—to serve with other dishes.

Patty Squires
Sassafras!
The Junior League of Springfield
Springfield
MISSOURI

1 In a large bowl, stir together the beaten egg, water, the 1 teaspoon salt, the basil and pepper. Stir in the bread crumbs and the ¼ cup Parmesan cheese. Add the ground beef and mix well.

2 Shape the mixture into thirty-six 1-inch meatballs. In a 12-inch skillet, heat the olive oil. Add the meatballs and cook over medium-low heat, turning occasionally, until the meatballs are browned. Drain and discard the excess fat.

3 Meanwhile, in a medium bowl, stir together the *undrained* tomatoes, tomato paste, onion, parsley, garlic, oregano, the ½ teaspoon salt and the anise seed. Add the sauce to the meatballs in the skillet and bring to a boil. Reduce heat and simmer, covered, for 15 minutes. Uncover and simmer about 15 minutes more or until the sauce reaches the desired consistency.

4 Serve the meatballs and sauce over the cooked and drained spaghetti. Serve with additional grated Parmesan cheese, if desired.

 TIPS FROM OUR KITCHEN

To make even-size meatballs: Pat the meat mixture into a 6x6-inch square. Make 5 vertical and 5 horizontal cuts. Or, divide the meat mixture into thirds. Shape each third into a 12-inch roll and cut each roll into 12 pieces.

If you prefer, you can brown and bake the meatballs in the oven: Place the meatballs in a single layer in a 15x10x1-inch baking pan. Bake in a 375° oven about 20 minutes or until no pink remains. Drain. Add the meatballs to the sauce after uncovering.

Nutrition Analysis (*Per Serving*): Calories: 584 / Cholesterol: 109 mg / Carbohydrates: 65 g
Protein: 35 g / Sodium: 978 mg / Fat: 20 g (Saturated Fat: 7 g) / Potassium: 941 mg.

GENEROUS FAMILY SUPPER

Call your hungry ones to the table for a hearty, healthy pasta supper. This version of the classic dish, from Springfield, Missouri, features a generous six meatballs per serving.

AUNT ELLA'S MACARONI AND CHEESE

Makes 4 to 6 Servings

- 8 ounces elbow macaroni *or* assorted pasta, such as small shells, spirals and wagon wheels (2 cups)
- 1 tablespoon butter *or* margarine, softened
- 1 egg, well beaten
- 1 teaspoon dry mustard
- ½ teaspoon salt
- ⅛ teaspoon ground nutmeg
- 1 tablespoon boiling water
- 1 cup milk
- 3 cups shredded sharp cheddar cheese (12 ounces)
- ¼ cup grated onion
- Paprika

❖   ❖   ❖

"If it was Ella's, you knew it would be good." Who is Aunt Ella? If you lived in Wisconsin, you'd surely know—she's quite a famous lady there. In her day, Ella was a caterer in demand, an "effervescent organizer" whose peppy personality and popular menu caught on like wildfire. So, Aunt Ella opened Ella's Deli. Successful? "Everybody knows Ella's," says one of her many local admirers, "because everything she cooked was excellent!"

Sue Marcus
<u>The Best of Beth Israel</u>
Milwaukee
WISCONSIN

1 Preheat oven to 350°. Lightly grease a 1½-quart casserole dish.

2 Cook the macaroni or pasta in boiling water following the package directions until al dente (tender but firm to the bite). Drain the macaroni or pasta, then return it to the saucepan. Stir in the butter and egg.

3 In a large bowl, combine the mustard, salt and nutmeg with the tablespoon of boiling water. Stir in the milk, *2½ cups* of the cheese, the onion and macaroni or pasta.

4 Pour the macaroni mixture into the prepared casserole dish. Top with the remaining cheese. Sprinkle with the paprika.

5 Bake the casserole in the 350° oven for 1 hour or until a well-browned top crust has formed.

TIPS FROM OUR KITCHEN

If you'd like to lower the fat content a bit, substitute skim milk and low-fat cheddar or low-fat American cheese for the whole milk varieties. To lower the sodium content somewhat, use reduced-sodium cheeses and omit the ½ teaspoon of salt.

For an extra-crispy casserole, we baked this in a flat 1½-quart baking dish.

Fresh tomato wedges and a sprig of fresh thyme make a colorful garnish when set against the golden color of the casserole.

Nutrition Analysis *(Per Serving):* Calories: 651 / Cholesterol: 155 mg / Carbohydrates: 49
Protein: 32 g / Sodium: 871 mg / Fat: 36 g (Saturated Fat: 21 g) / Potassium: 266 mg.

Easiest, Cheesiest—and Best!

A new look at an old favorite, this extra-cheddar-cheesy casserole is from Sue Marcus of Milwaukee, Wisconsin. Not only is this dish quick and easy to put together, it also forms its own wonderful crust as it bakes. For extra-special dinners, try using a variety of different pasta shapes, as shown.

LASAGNA ROLL-UPS

Makes 6 to 8 Servings

12 lasagna noodles

Sauce:

- 1 tablespoon cooking oil
- 1 large onion, chopped
- 1 clove garlic, minced
- 2 16-ounce cans whole Italian-style (plum) tomatoes, cut up
- 1 6-ounce can tomato paste
- ⅔ cup water
- 3 tablespoons snipped parsley
- 1 tablespoon sugar
- 1 teaspoon salt
- 1 teaspoon dried oregano, crushed
- ¼ teaspoon pepper
- 2 15-ounce containers ricotta cheese
- 2 cups shredded mozzarella cheese (8 ounces)
- ½ cup grated Parmesan cheese
- 2 eggs, well beaten

❖   ❖   ❖

There's More to Lima than Beans is a wonderful cookbook compiled by the Lima and Allen County Medical Alliance to raise funds "to maintain current and future health education projects."

Charlotte Ditter
There's More to Lima than Beans
The Lima and Allen County Medical Alliance
Lima
OHIO

1 In a large saucepan, cook the lasagna noodles in boiling, *salted water* for 10 to 12 minutes or until tender; drain. Rinse with cool water and drain again. Set aside.

2 To make the sauce: In a large skillet, heat the oil. Add the onion and garlic and cook until tender. Carefully add the *undrained* tomatoes, tomato paste, water, *2 tablespoons* of the parsley, the sugar, salt, oregano and pepper. Simmer, uncovered, for 20 minutes.

3 Meanwhile, in a large mixing bowl, stir together the ricotta cheese, *1 cup* of the mozzarella cheese, the Parmesan cheese, eggs and the remaining parsley. Preheat the oven to 350°.

4 To assemble: Spread approximately *⅓ cup* of the cheese mixture evenly over *each* of the lasagna noodles.

5 Starting from a short side, roll up each of the lasagna noodles.

6 Pour *half* of the sauce into a 3-quart rectangular baking dish. Place rolled-up noodles seam side down in the baking dish. Top with the remaining sauce.

7 Cover and bake in the 350° oven for 45 minutes. Uncover and sprinkle with the remaining mozzarella cheese. Bake for 5 minutes more. Let stand for 10 to 15 minutes before serving.

 TIPS FROM OUR KITCHEN

Adding the cheese for the last 5 minutes only prevents it from sticking to the foil during baking.

This casserole adapts well to make-ahead preparation. Refrigerate the covered dish of roll-ups overnight. To serve: Bake in a 350° oven for 1 hour. Uncover and sprinkle with the remaining mozzarella cheese. Bake for 5 minutes more. Let stand for 10 to 15 minutes before serving.

Nutrition Analysis (*Per Serving*): Calories: 602 / Cholesterol: 143 mg / Carbohydrates: 56 g Protein: 39 g / Sodium: 1179 mg / Fat: 25 g (Saturated Fat: 13 g) / Potassium: 937 mg.

ITALIAN WITH A TWIST

It's true—everyone loves lasagna—and Charlotte Ditter's recipe for Lasagna Roll-Ups gives us a new variation of the old favorite. We predict this dish will be a big hit at your next potluck.

PARSLEY GNOCCHI

Makes 8 Servings

1   15-ounce container ricotta cheese
½   cup grated Parmesan cheese
½   cup snipped fresh parsley
1   small clove garlic, minced
1   egg, beaten
¾   cup all-purpose flour
½   teaspoon salt
All-purpose flour
3   tablespoons margarine *or* butter
3   tablespoons all-purpose flour
1½ cups milk
1   cup shredded fontina cheese (4 ounces)

♦   ♦   ♦

Denise Sartori loves to cook, and Italian cooking is her specialty. Denise told us that Parsley Gnocchi is a variation on the traditional Italian gnocchi. Usually, gnocchi is made with ground potatoes and water, but Denise warns that if you're not careful, the gnocchi can "come out like lead." Denise's variation, however, is much easier—the ricotta cheese makes it foolproof (and fantastic).

Denise Sartori
Lovin' Spoonfuls
Children's Hospital of Michigan
Detroit
MICHIGAN

1 In a large bowl, stir together the ricotta cheese, Parmesan cheese, parsley, garlic and beaten egg. Stir in the ¾ cup flour and the salt.

2 With floured hands, shape the mixture into 1-inch balls (about 1 tablespoon each). Roll each ball in the flour to coat lightly.

3 Cook *half* the balls in *boiling water*, uncovered, for 10 minutes. Using a slotted spoon, remove the gnocchi from the water. Drain on paper towels. Repeat with the remaining gnocchi.

4 Meanwhile, in a medium saucepan, melt the margarine or butter. Stir in the 3 tablespoons flour and cook for 1 minute. Add the milk all at once; cook and stir until the mixture is thickened and bubbly. Stir in the fontina cheese. Cook and stir until the cheese has melted. Remove from heat.

5 Preheat the oven to 500°.

6 Place approximately *½ cup* of the sauce in the bottom of a 2-quart square baking dish. Arrange the gnocchi on top of the sauce; pour the remaining sauce over the gnocchi. Bake, uncovered, in the 500° oven for 6 to 8 minutes or until the mixture is bubbly and browned.

 TIPS FROM OUR KITCHEN

If desired, prepare the gnocchi dough ahead of time and refrigerate in a covered container until ready to cook.

Cook only half of the gnocchi at a time to ensure that all of them are cooked evenly and that none are doughy or gummy.

The gnocchi in cheese sauce are baked in a very hot oven (500°). If you prefer to broil the gnocchi, place them in a skillet. Do not use a glass baking dish as it is not designed for use with a broiler.

Nutrition Analysis (*Per Serving*): Calories: 285 / Cholesterol: 68 mg / Carbohydrates: 18 g / Protein: 16 g / Sodium: 399 mg / Fat: 16 g (Saturated Fat: 5 g) / Potassium: 192 mg.

DELIZIOSO DUMPLINGS

Gnocchi (pronounced *NO key*) is an Italian dumpling usually made from potatoes, semolina flour or
puff pastry and frequently served in a savory sauce. Our Test Kitchen is still raving about Denise
Sartori's Parsley Gnocchi, claiming they were the best they had ever tasted!

HEMENWAY'S SEAFOOD PASTA SALAD

Makes 5 Servings

  6 ounces tri-colored rotini pasta (2½ cups)
 12 ounces seafood including small peeled shrimp, lump crabmeat *and/or* cooked bay scallops
  1 cup broccoli flowerets
  1 tomato, chopped (¾ cup)
  2 tablespoons finely chopped onion
  2 tablespoons sliced pitted ripe olives

Dressing:
 ⅓ cup red wine vinegar
 ¼ cup olive oil
  2 cloves garlic, minced
 ¼ teaspoon salt
 ¼ teaspoon sugar
 ¼ teaspoon dried thyme, crushed
 ¼ teaspoon dried oregano, crushed
 ¼ teaspoon dried basil, crushed
  1 small bay leaf
2 to 3 cups mixed greens

◆　　　◆　　　◆

Hemenway's Restaurant submitted this recipe to the organization, Keep Providence Beautiful, to help in the effort to beautify Providence "through education and awareness."

Hemenway's Restaurant
Pasta Challenge
Keep Providence Beautiful
Providence
RHODE ISLAND

1 Cook the pasta according to the package directions. Drain and rinse with *cold water*. Drain again.

2 In a large bowl, toss together the shrimp, crabmeat and/or scallops with the cooked pasta. Add the broccoli, tomato, onion and olives; toss.

3 To make the dressing: In a screw-top jar, combine the vinegar, olive oil, garlic, salt, sugar, thyme, oregano, basil and bay leaf. Cover and shake well to combine.

4 Pour the dressing over the salad and toss to coat. Cover and refrigerate for 4 to 24 hours, stirring occasionally. Remove the bay leaf. Serve the pasta salad over the mixed greens.

TIPS FROM OUR KITCHEN

To make broccoli flowerets, cut off the flower part from the stems and cut in half any flowers that are larger than bite size.

To cook fresh seafood: Bring a large saucepan of water to a boil. Add the shellfish and reduce heat to medium. Simmer the shrimp and/or scallops for 2 to 3 minutes or until the shrimp are pink and the scallops are opaque and firm. Simmer the fresh crabmeat for 25 minutes.

Rotini is also known as corkscrew pasta. In tri-colored pasta, a portion of the pasta is made in the usual manner, while some is flavored and colored with spinach and some with tomato.

When shopping for broccoli, look for firm stalks with deep green or purplish green, tightly packed heads. Store broccoli in a plastic bag in the refrigerator up to 4 days.

If fresh herbs are available, substitute ¾ teaspoon each for the dried thyme, oregano and basil in this recipe.

For a potluck or other large gathering this recipe can be doubled easily.

Nutrition Analysis (*Per Serving*): Calories: 324 / Cholesterol: 101 mg / Carbohydrates: 32 g Protein: 20 g / Sodium: 303 mg / Fat: 13 g (Saturated Fat: 2 g) / Potassium: 390 mg.

FEATURE PRESENTATION

An herb-flavored vinaigrette dressing allows the seafood flavor to shine through in this delightful salad. Your choice of seafood stars with a supporting cast of tri-colored pasta and vegetables.

PASTA, RICE & LEGUMES

271

NOODLE KUGEL

Makes 12 Servings

1	8-ounce package noodles (about 4 cups)
4	eggs
¾	cup sugar
1 to 2	teaspoons lemon extract
1	teaspoon vanilla
2	8-ounce cartons dairy sour cream
2	cups cottage cheese
1	cup milk
2	tablespoons butter *or* margarine
1½	teaspoons sugar
½	teaspoon ground cinnamon
2	tablespoons butter *or* margarine, cut into small pieces

◆   ◆   ◆

Jane Gold tells us that when she married, she was given this recipe for Noodle Kugel by her mother-in-law. Since then, Jane has passed the recipe along to her daughter and daughter-in-law. The Gold family enjoys this dish often, and always with pot roast. We think Noodle Kugel is destined to become a favorite of your family too!

Jane Gold
Tender Loving Care
The Auxiliary to the Broome County Medical Society
Vestal
NEW YORK

1 Preheat the oven to 350°.

2 Cook the noodles according to the package directions. Drain and set aside.

3 In a large mixing bowl, beat the eggs, ¾ cup sugar, lemon extract and vanilla. Add the sour cream, cottage cheese and milk and mix well. Stir in the cooked and drained noodles.

4 In a 13x9x2-inch baking pan, melt the 2 tablespoons butter or margarine. Add the noodle mixture to the baking pan.

5 In a small bowl, stir together the 1½ teaspoons sugar and the cinnamon. Sprinkle the mixture on top of the noodles, then dot with the 2 tablespoons butter or margarine.

6 Bake in the 350° oven for 1 hour to 1 hour and 15 minutes or until a knife inserted near the center comes out clean. The top should be nicely browned. Cool slightly before slicing into squares.

 TIPS FROM OUR KITCHEN

This recipe can be halved and baked in an 8x8x2-inch baking pan if you desire. Bake in the 350° oven about 1 hour or until the kugel tests done.

If you don't have lemon extract, increase the vanilla to 2 teaspoons.

If you're watching the amount of fat in your diet, choose reduced fat sour cream and cottage cheese for this recipe.

Use the knife test to check for doneness. Insert a knife near the center of the kugel. If it comes out clean, the kugel is done. To avoid having the browned topping "clean" the knife as it is pulled out, enlarge the hole slightly by moving the knife from side to side when you insert it.

Nutrition Analysis *(Per Serving)*: Calories: 309 / Cholesterol: 105 mg / Carbohydrates: 31 g Protein: 11 g / Sodium: 233 mg / Fat: 16 g (Saturated Fat: 9 g) / Potassium: 154 mg.

NOODLE NOSH

Cottage cheese, sour cream and lemon extract combine in a noodle casserole that is topped with cinnamon-sugar. This traditional Jewish dish is often served with the Sabbath meal.

ARROZ

Makes 6 Servings

1	tablespoon cooking oil
1	cup plus 2 tablespoons rice
½	cup sliced onion
1	14 ½-ounce can tomatoes, chopped and drained
1	4-ounce can chopped green chilies, drained
2 ¼	cups water
¾	teaspoon salt
½	cup thinly sliced potatoes
½	cup thinly sliced carrots
½	cup frozen peas

❖ ❖ ❖

In 1979, the Center for Latin American Studies at Western Kentucky University produced a cookbook to raise money for the Latin American Scholarship Fund. Violeta du Duran, studying art at the university at the time, submitted her mother's recipe for Arroz. The cookbook was a huge success, raising a great deal of money for the scholarship fund. We think if you serve this dish, your meal will be a huge success, too!

Violeta du Duran
From Guacamole to Rocambole
Bowling Green
KENTUCKY

1 In a 10-inch skillet, heat the oil over medium heat. Add the rice and onion to the skillet and cook and stir over medium heat for 2 to 3 minutes or until the rice is golden. (Use medium heat to assure that the rice won't stick to the skillet.)

2 Add the tomatoes and the chilies to the skillet and cook the mixture for 3 minutes. Stir in the water and salt.

3 Layer the potatoes, carrots and peas on top of the mixture in the skillet. Cover the skillet and simmer for 20 to 25 minutes or until the rice and vegetables are tender.

 TIPS FROM OUR KITCHEN

Arroz is such a colorful dish that you can make it in your prettiest skillet and bring it right to the table—no serving dish needed!

Nutrition Analysis (*Per Serving*): Calories: 196 / Cholesterol: 0 mg / Carbohydrates: 38 g / Protein: 5 g / Sodium: 444 mg / Fat: 3 g (Saturated Fat: 0 g) / Potassium: 317 mg.

SPICY SPANISH RICE

Arroz (ah-ROHS) is Spanish for rice—an understated name for this dish, which combines white rice with chilies, tomatoes, potatoes, carrots and peas. Violeta du Duran brought this recipe to Kentucky from her native Guatemala. We like this colorful rice dish with broiled steaks, chops or chicken.

SOUBISE

Makes 8 to 10 Servings

1½	cups water
½	cup long-grain rice
½	teaspoon salt
6 to 7	cups thinly sliced yellow onions
2	tablespoons butter *or* margarine, melted
½	teaspoon salt
½	teaspoon pepper
¼	cup heavy whipping cream
2	tablespoons butter *or* margarine
¼	cup shredded Swiss *and/or* cheddar cheese
1	tablespoon snipped parsley

◆　　◆　　◆

Cathie Oldham loved living in France for a year while her husband was conducting cancer research. While there, she lived in an apartment building where she always smelled wonderful dishes being cooked by the other residents. One of her neighbors gave Cathie this recipe for Soubise. Now, Soubise is such an Oldham family favorite that it's served every Christmas. The hearty side dish is a great substitute for potatoes.

Mrs. Cathie Oldham
<u>*Flaunting Our Finest: From Historic Franklin*</u>
Franklin Junior Auxiliary
Franklin
TENNESSEE

1 Preheat oven to 300°. In a medium saucepan, bring the water to boiling. Add the rice and the ½ teaspoon salt. Cook, uncovered, for 5 minutes. Drain.

2 In a 3-quart round casserole dish, stir together the onion and melted butter or margarine until the onion is coated with the butter. Bake, covered, in the 300° oven for 15 minutes. Remove the casserole from the oven.

3 Stir in the partially cooked rice, the ½ teaspoon salt and pepper. Bake, covered, in the 300° oven for 1 hour. Remove the casserole from the oven.

4 Stir the whipping cream and the 2 tablespoons butter or margarine into the rice mixture. Sprinkle with the cheese and parsley and serve immediately.

 TIPS FROM OUR KITCHEN

To reduce the calories and the amount of fat in this recipe, use light cream or half-and-half in place of the heavy whipping cream.

Save time by slicing the onions in a food processor. To achieve even slices, cut the onions in half before you slice them.

Nutrition Analysis *(Per Serving)*: Calories: 178 / Cholesterol: 29 mg / Carbohydrates: 20 g / Protein: 3 g / Sodium: 342 mg / Fat: 10 g (Saturated Fat: 6 g) / Potassium: 203 mg.

SAVORY RICE

Serve this delicious rice dish with roast turkey or chicken and skip the stuffing. Onions and cheese
give the baked casserole a distinctively different flavor.

GREEN RICE RING

- 6 cups hot cooked rice
- 2 cups shredded Monterey Jack *or* cheddar cheese (8 ounces)
- 1 4-ounce can chopped green chilies
- ½ to 1 teaspoon pepper
- 1 16-ounce carton dairy sour cream
- 1 pimiento, cut into strips

Celery leaves (optional)
Tomato wedges (optional)
Shredded lettuce (optional)

◆   ◆   ◆

When St. Albert the Great Newman Center & Parish members needed to raise funds, they put together a cookbook with the help of Maggie Gamboa, a local restaurateur and caterer. During her thirty years in the business, Maggie's clients have included the U.S. Congress, the U.S. Treasurer's office and a movie production company. We are delighted to have this opportunity to try one of Maggie's wonderful dishes, Green Rice Ring.

Maggie Gamboa
Recetas Del Valle
St. Albert the Great Newman Center & Parish
Las Cruces
NEW MEXICO

1 Preheat the oven to 350°. Grease an 8-cup ring mold. Set aside.

2 In a large bowl, combine the rice, cheese, chilies and pepper. Toss to mix well. Stir in the sour cream.

3 Spoon the cheese mixture into the prepared 8-cup ring mold, packing lightly with the back of a spoon. Bake in the 350° oven for 30 minutes. Cool the rice ring in the mold on a wire rack for 5 minutes.

4 Loosen the edges with a knife. To unmold onto a serving plate, cover the top of the mold with the serving plate, invert both and lift off the mold. Place pimiento strips over the top of the ring. If desired, fill the center with celery leaves and tomato wedges and frame the base of the ring with shredded lettuce.

 TIPS FROM OUR KITCHEN

To make 6 cups cooked rice, start with 2 cups raw long grain rice or 3 cups raw quick-cooking rice. Follow package directions for cooking and add 1 teaspoon salt.

Nutrition Analysis *(Per Serving)*: Calories: 287 / Cholesterol: 34 mg / Carbohydrates: 31 g / Protein: 9 g / Sodium: 167 mg / Fat: 14 g (Saturated Fat: 9 g) / Potassium: 118 mg.

RICE IN THE ROUND

Not many great cooks share recipes for their specialties as readily as New Mexico restaurateur Maggie Gamboa. Here, Maggie turns ordinary rice into an extra-special side dish by adding green chilies, cheese and sour cream, and baking the mixture in a ring mold.

CURRIED RICE

Makes 6 to 8 Servings

 3 tablespoons butter *or* margarine
1½ cups rice
1½ teaspoons curry powder
 3 cups chicken broth
 1 cup seedless raisins
 ½ cup chopped green onion
 ½ cup chopped green sweet pepper
 ½ cup chopped celery
 3 tablespoons chopped pimiento
 3 tablespoons pine nuts (optional)
1½ tablespoons vinegar
1½ tablespoons brown sugar
1½ tablespoons chutney, snipped
 ½ teaspoon seasoned salt

♦   ♦   ♦

One of the Junior League of Richmond's major fund-raisers is the cookbook Virginia Seasons. *The League is comprised of over 1,400 members who donate thousands of volunteer hours to community programs. Proceeds from cookbook sales are used to support projects that focus on children and education.*

Jane Helfrich
Virginia Seasons
The Junior League of Richmond
Richmond
VIRGINIA

1 In a 2-quart saucepan, melt *1½ tablespoons* of the butter or margarine. Add the rice and curry powder. Cook and stir over low heat for 5 minutes. Carefully add the chicken broth and bring to a boil; stir. Then, cover tightly and cook over low heat about 15 minutes or until all of the liquid is absorbed.

2 Meanwhile, in a medium skillet, melt the remaining butter or margarine. Add the raisins, green onion, green sweet pepper and celery. Cook and stir until the vegetables are tender. Add the pimiento, pine nuts (if using), vinegar, brown sugar, chutney and seasoned salt; toss lightly.

3 Transfer the hot rice to a serving platter. Spoon the raisin mixture over the top.

TIPS FROM OUR KITCHEN

Cooking the curry powder first in the butter or margarine eliminates its harsh, raw flavor, and lightly browning the rice gives it a nuttier flavor.

If you wish, serve the seasoned raisin mixture with cooked meat or poultry instead of the rice.

Chutney is an East Indian specialty that can range in flavor from sweet to tart and in texture from smooth to chunky. Commercially made chutney often contains mangoes, tamarinds, raisins and spices.

Pine nuts, also known as pignolia and piñon, have a sweet, faint pine flavor. Because of their high oil content, they can become rancid quickly. Store in an airtight container in the refrigerator up to 2 months or in the freezer up to 6 months.

Nutrition Analysis (*Per Serving*): Calories: 335 / Cholesterol: 16 mg / Carbohydrates: 62 g / Protein: 7 g / Sodium: 584 mg / Fat: 7 g (Saturated Fat: 4 g) / Potassium: 428 mg.

SIDE DISH WITH FLAIR

Spice up your rice! All it takes is a few special ingredients and less than 30 minutes in the kitchen
to turn your basic rice into a zesty side dish.

BARLEY BAKE

5 tablespoons butter *or* margarine
8 ounces fresh mushrooms, sliced
½ cup finely chopped celery
½ cup finely chopped green onion
1 cup quick-cooking barley
2 cups chicken broth
½ cup snipped parsley
¼ teaspoon salt
⅛ teaspoon pepper
½ cup slivered almonds

◆ ◆ ◆

When Barbara Jones Collins's six children were growing up, she was always on the lookout for a tasty, crowd-pleasing dish. Barley Bake certainly fits into this category. With her busy schedule and large family, we understand why this easy-to-prepare dish was one of Barbara's favorites.

Barbara Jones Collins
Sassafras
The Junior League of Springfield, Missouri, Inc.
Springfield
MISSOURI

1 Preheat the oven to 350°.

2 In a large skillet, melt the butter or margarine. Add the mushrooms, celery and green onion. Cook and stir over medium-high heat until the vegetables are tender.

3 Add the barley; cook and stir for 2 to 3 minutes or until the barley is golden.

4 In a 2-quart casserole, stir together the barley mixture, chicken broth, parsley, salt and pepper.

5 Cover and bake in the 350° oven for 50 to 60 minutes or until the barley is tender and the liquid is absorbed. Remove from the oven and stir in the almonds.

TIPS FROM OUR KITCHEN

If desired, garnish with green onions.

If you are concerned about your fat intake, use only *3 tablespoons* butter or margarine to cook the vegetables.

If desired, toast the almonds before adding them to the casserole.
  To toast almonds in a skillet: Place the almonds in a skillet over medium heat. Cook, stirring often, for 5 to 7 minutes or until the nuts are golden. Or, you can toast them in the oven while the casserole is baking.
  To toast almonds in the oven: Spread the almonds in a thin layer in a shallow baking pan. Bake in a 350° oven for 5 to 10 minutes or until light golden brown, stirring once or twice.

For a more colorful dish, add ⅓ cup shredded carrot to the vegetable mixture just before adding the barley.

Nutrition Analysis (*Per Serving*): Calories: 211 / Cholesterol: 19 mg / Carbohydrates: 22 g / Protein: 6 g / Sodium: 346 mg / Fat: 12 g (Saturated Fat: 5 g) / Potassium: 313 mg.

GREAT GRAIN

Your family will love this hearty side dish as a flavorful change of pace from potatoes. Sautéed barley, mushrooms, celery, onions and almonds give the dish its distinctive flavor and texture.

NORTHWOODS PILAF

Makes 8 Servings

- 1 cup wild rice
- 1¾ cups chicken broth *or* vegetable stock
- ⅓ cup vermouth
- 3 tablespoons butter *or* margarine
- 1½ cups sliced fresh mushrooms
- ¾ cup sliced celery
- ¾ cup julienned carrots
- 1 10-ounce package frozen artichoke hearts, thawed
- ⅓ cup sliced green onion
- 2 tablespoons chopped sweet red pepper
- 1 teaspoon grated lemon peel
- 1 tablespoon lemon juice
- ½ teaspoon dried thyme, crushed
- ¼ teaspoon salt
- ¼ teaspoon pepper

Snipped parsley (optional)

◆   ◆   ◆

Kathy Zokoych is originally from Northern Wisconsin, an area where wild rice is abundant. Now living in Illinois, she receives gifts of wild rice from her parents. Kathy developed this recipe for Northwoods Pilaf over the years, adding different ingredients until it reached its present perfection.

Kathy Zokoych
The Door To Incredible Edibles
Park Ridge Youth Campus
Park Ridge
ILLINOIS

1 Rinse the wild rice under running water for 1 minute; drain. Set aside.

2 Preheat the oven to 325°. Grease a 2-quart casserole; set aside.

3 In a medium saucepan, combine the chicken broth or vegetable stock, vermouth and wild rice. Bring to a boil. Reduce heat, cover and simmer for 30 minutes. Set aside. (*Do not drain.*)

4 In a large skillet, melt *2 tablespoons* of the butter or margarine. Add the mushrooms, celery and carrots. Cook and stir for 5 minutes.

5 Stir in the artichoke hearts, green onion, sweet red pepper, lemon peel, lemon juice, thyme, salt and pepper. Add the remaining *1 tablespoon* of the butter or margarine; remove from heat.

6 Stir the rice mixture into the vegetable mixture. Transfer the mixture to the prepared casserole. Bake, covered, in the 325° oven about 45 minutes or until the rice is done, stirring once. If desired, sprinkle with parsley before serving.

 TIPS FROM OUR KITCHEN

Instead of vermouth, you can use ⅓ cup more broth or substitute white wine, sherry or water.

Wild rice is not really rice. It is the seed of an annual marsh grass and is the only cereal grain native to North America. Before using, rinse wild rice to remove any particles left from processing. Because wild rice is expensive; you may want to substitute brown rice for part of the total amount.

Julienned means that the food has been cut into matchstick-thin strips about 2 inches long. To julienne carrots easily, first cut the carrots into slices about 2 inches long and ¼ inch thick. Stack the slices and cut them lengthwise to make thinner strips about ⅛ to ¼ inch wide.

Nutrition Analysis (*Per Serving*): Calories: 157 / Cholesterol: 12 mg / Carbohydrates: 22 g
Protein: 6 g / Sodium: 334 mg / Fat: 5 g (Saturated Fat: 3 g) / Potassium: 382 mg.

WILD RICE SIDE DISH

This sophisticated side dish from Park Ridge, Illinois, brings out the best in wild rice, North America's only native cereal grain. Wild rice combines with artichoke hearts, other vegetables, herbs and seasonings to make a delicious family-pleasing dish.

CREOLE BLACK-EYED PEAS AND RICE

Makes 5 Servings

1¼ cups dried black-eyed peas
¼ pound salt pork, chopped
1 pound fully cooked smoked sausage, sliced
1½ cups chopped onion
½ cup chopped green onion
½ cup chopped green sweet pepper
½ cup snipped parsley
½ cup tomato sauce
1 clove garlic, minced
1½ teaspoons Worcestershire sauce
¼ to ½ teaspoon pepper
⅛ teaspoon dried oregano, crushed
⅛ teaspoon dried thyme, crushed
Few dashes bottled hot pepper sauce
3 cups hot cooked rice (1 cup uncooked)

♦ ♦ ♦

Sylvia Moore believes this hearty dish originated in southern Louisiana. Creole Black-Eyed Peas and Rice is a perfect dish for casual company—simply serve it with a salad and a light dessert.

Sylvia Moore
Top Rankin' Recipes
Rankin General Hospital
Auxiliary
Brandon
MISSISSIPPI

1 Rinse the black-eyed peas and place them in a 4½-quart Dutch oven. Add 4 cups cold *water*. Bring to a boil; reduce heat and simmer for 2 minutes. Remove from heat. Cover and let stand for 1 hour. Drain and rinse the peas.

2 Return the peas to the Dutch oven. Add the salt pork. Add 3 cups *water* or enough to cover the peas. Cover and simmer for 45 minutes.

3 Stir in the sausage, onion, green onion, green sweet pepper, parsley, tomato sauce, garlic, Worcestershire sauce, pepper, oregano, thyme and hot pepper sauce.

4 Bring the mixture to a boil; reduce heat and simmer, covered, over low heat for 45 minutes. Serve over the hot cooked rice.

 TIPS FROM OUR KITCHEN

Use a sharp knife to cut away the rind on the salt pork before chopping it. You can substitute chopped bacon for the salt pork in this recipe.

Black-eyed peas are small, oval and cream colored, with a black oval "eye" that has a cream-colored dot in the center. Also known as cowpeas, black-eyed peas have a mealy texture and an earthy flavor. For this recipe, if you want the peas to retain their shape, don't soak them before cooking. Do rinse them, however, by placing the peas in a sieve and holding them under running water.

One cup uncooked rice will yield 3 cups cooked rice.

This recipe is easily doubled if you need to serve a crowd.

Nutrition Analysis (*Per Serving*): Calories: 804 / Cholesterol: 71 mg / Carbohydrates: 75 g / Protein: 37 g / Sodium: 1704 mg / Fat: 39 g (Saturated Fat: 14 g) / Potassium: 1015 mg.

FULL-FLAVORED, HEARTY DISH

This satisfying dish is full of flavor, yet not too spicy, thanks to the inclusion of smoked sausage and salt pork. We suggest accompanying the hearty, protein-packed stew with white rice and a crusty bread.

PASTA, RICE & LEGUMES

GRANDMA NONIE'S BAKED BEANS

Makes 8 Servings

2   cups dry navy beans
1   medium onion, chopped
⅓   cup light molasses
2   tablespoons butter *or* margarine, cut up
2   tablespoons catsup
1   tablespoon brown sugar
1   teaspoon salt
½   teaspoon prepared mustard
Dash pepper

◆   ◆   ◆

In the early 1900s, a young man of seventeen traveled from his home on Prince Edward Island, Canada, to Montana to work on the railroad. Later, he returned home to bring his seventeen-year-old bride, Elizabeth "Nonie" Trafton, back to Montana with him. Nonie carried with her a recipe for baked beans given to her by her mother. Recently, the recipe was submitted to Favorite Family Recipes by Nonie's niece, Maxine Trafton Feekins. We are happy to be able to share both the recipe and the story with you.

Maxine Trafton Feekins
Favorite Family Recipes
The Billings Alzheimer Family Support Group
Billings
MONTANA

1 Soak the beans in water overnight. Drain, discarding the soaking water. Place the beans in a saucepan with 8 cups fresh cold *water*. Bring to boiling. Cover and cook for 1¼ hours or until the beans are tender.

2 Preheat oven to 325°. Drain the beans, reserving *1 cup* of the liquid.

3 In a 2-quart casserole dish, combine the beans and reserved liquid. Stir in the onion, molasses, butter or margarine, catsup, brown sugar, salt, mustard and pepper. Bake, covered, in the 325° oven for 2 hours. Stir before serving.

 TIPS FROM OUR KITCHEN

When your time to cook is short, make this dish using canned navy beans. You'll need four 15- to 16-ounce cans. Drain them, reserving *1 cup* of the liquid. Then combine the beans and reserved liquid with the remaining ingredients in a 2-quart casserole and bake as directed in the recipe.

If you prefer your beans with meat, add cooked sausage or cooked pork to the beans during the last half hour of baking.

You can use another type or variety of dry beans in this recipe. Just make sure that the total equals two cups dry beans.

If you don't have molasses, substitute ½ cup brown sugar.

Nutrition Analysis *(Per Serving)*: Calories: 257 / Cholesterol: 8 mg / Carbohydrates: 46 g / Protein: 12 g / Sodium: 344 mg / Fat: 4 g (Saturated Fat: 2 g) / Potassium: 638 mg.

COOKOUT COMPANION

Nothing makes a grilled burger taste better than accompanying it with a mouth-watering mound of
homemade baked beans. These from Maxine Trafton Feekins of Miles City, Montana, are so good
that you'll probably be asked to bring them to every gathering.

Poultry

*P*oultry is wonderfully versatile, easy on the budget, readily available, and quick to fix. Who could ask for more? Year-round, nothing tops poultry for its ease and adaptability, whether you're cooking on the stovetop, in the oven, or on the grill. This section contains old favorites such as Buttermilk Fried Chicken and Biscuits and exotic innovations like Halikahiki Moa Curry.

BUTTERMILK FRIED CHICKEN AND BISCUITS

Makes 6 Servings

Chicken:
- 1 3- to 3½-pound broiler-fryer chicken, cut up
- ¾ cup buttermilk
- ½ cup all-purpose flour
- 2 tablespoons snipped parsley
- 1 teaspoon dried oregano, crushed
- ½ teaspoon salt
- ½ teaspoon pepper
- ¼ cup shortening
- ¼ cup margarine *or* butter

Melted margarine *or* butter
- ¼ cup chicken broth

Biscuits:
- 2 cups all-purpose flour
- 1 tablespoon sugar
- 2½ teaspoons baking powder
- ½ teaspoon baking soda
- ½ teaspoon salt
- ¾ cup buttermilk

❖　❖　❖

The Church of the Redeemer collected recipes from parish members and residents of the Camelot Nursing Home in Richmond, Virginia, for ...And These Thy Gifts. All profits from cookbook sales were donated to the Camelot Nursing Home to help purchase recreation equipment.

Cookie Suarez
...And These Thy Gifts
Church of the Redeemer
Mechanicsville
VIRGINIA

1 Rinse the chicken pieces; pat dry. Place the chicken pieces in a 3-quart rectangular baking dish. Pour the ¾ cup buttermilk over the chicken; cover and let stand for 30 minutes to 1 hour in the refrigerator.

2 About 10 minutes before removing the chicken from the refrigerator: In a shallow dish, stir together the ½ cup flour, the parsley, oregano, the ½ teaspoon salt and the pepper.

3 Remove the chicken from the baking dish, reserving the buttermilk. Coat the chicken with the flour mixture.

4 In a 12-inch skillet over medium heat, melt the shortening and the ¼ cup margarine or butter. Brown the chicken pieces in the skillet for 10 minutes, turning once. Drain and transfer the chicken to the baking dish, placing the pieces in the reserved buttermilk.

5 Strain the drippings from the skillet into a measuring cup. If necessary, add additional melted margarine or butter to make ⅓ cup. Reserve for the biscuits.

6 Preheat the oven to 375°.

7 Add the chicken broth to the skillet, scraping the bottom of the pan to loosen any browned bits. Pour the mixture evenly over the chicken in the baking dish. Bake, uncovered, in the 375° oven about 50 minutes or until the chicken is tender and no longer pink.

8 Meanwhile, to make the biscuits: In a medium bowl, stir together the 2 cups flour, the sugar, baking powder, baking soda and the ½ teaspoon salt. Add the reserved drippings and the ¾ cup buttermilk. Stir just until the dough clings together.

9 On a lightly floured surface, knead the dough gently for 10 to 12 strokes. Roll or pat the dough to ½-inch thickness. Using a 2-inch biscuit cutter, cut the dough into rounds. Transfer the biscuits to a baking sheet. Bake in the 375° oven for 15 to 20 minutes or until golden. Serve warm with the Buttermilk Fried Chicken.

 TIPS FROM OUR KITCHEN

To cut up a whole chicken: First remove the thighs and the legs by bending at the hip joints. Pull the wings away from the body and slit the skin between the wing and the body. Bend the wing back until the joint breaks. Using a sharp knife or kitchen shears, cut along the breast end of the ribs; bend the 2 halves apart and cut through the neck joints. Bend the 2 halves of the chicken back toward the skin side until the bones break. Cut in half and cut off the tail. Cut the breast in half lengthwise along the breastbone.

Nutrition Analysis (*Per Serving*): Calories: 573 / Cholesterol: 81 mg / Carbohydrates: 43 g Protein: 32 g / Sodium: 725 mg / Fat: 30 g (Saturated Fat: 7 g) / Potassium: 414 mg.

COUNTRY-STYLE SOUTHERN SPECIALTY

A hint of oregano flavors the crispy coating for this tender chicken. Accompanied by these mouth-watering biscuits, this recipe from Mechanicsville, Virginia, will bring a taste of southern country cooking to your table.

POULTRY

COUNTRY CAPTAIN

◆   ◆   ◆

*Mrs. Willaim Bullard of Warm
Springs, Georgia, needed a
special dish to serve at a dinner
for her famous neighbor,
Franklin Delano Roosevelt, so she
created this variation of a classic
chicken dish. Now we share this
dish with you courtesy of Mrs.
Bullard's daughter, Mrs. Leighton
W. McPherson.*

Mrs. Leighton W. McPherson
<u>*A Southern Collection*</u>
Columbus
GEORGIA

1 Preheat oven to 350°.

2 Sprinkle the chicken with the salt
and the ¼ teaspoon pepper. In a heavy
12-inch skillet, cook the chicken in the
oil about 5 minutes per side or until it
is browned. Transfer the chicken to a
13x9x2-inch baking pan.

3 Pour off most of the oil from the
skillet. Cook and stir the onion, sweet
pepper and garlic over low heat, until
the onion is translucent. Stir in the
curry powder. Add the tomatoes, *1
tablespoon* of the parsley, the thyme and
the ⅛ teaspoon pepper to the skillet.
Bring the mixture to a boil. Pour the
sauce over the chicken in the pan.

4 Cover and bake the chicken in the
350° oven for 45 minutes; uncover and
bake for 15 minutes more.

5 Place the chicken on a large warm
platter. Skim any fat from the sauce.
Stir the currants into the sauce and
pour some over the chicken. Sprinkle
the almonds and remaining parsley
over the chicken. Serve the remaining
sauce on the side.

 TIPS FROM OUR KITCHEN

To cut up canned tomatoes quickly
and easily, we use sharp kitchen scissors
and cut them right in the can.

In India, the spices that go into curry
depend on the cook and can be a blend
of as many as 16 different spices. If
you'd like to make your own, try the
following combination:

2   tablespoons ground coriander
5   teaspoons ground turmeric
1   tablespoon ground cardamom
1   tablespoon ground cumin
1   tablespoon ground fenugreek
1   teaspoon black pepper
1   teaspoon ground red pepper
½   teaspoon ground cinnamon
½   teaspoon ground cloves
½   teaspoon crushed fennel
½   teaspoon ground ginger.

We suggest you serve Country Captain
over fluffy rice and garnish with fresh
parsley.

Nutrition Analysis (*Per Serving,*): Calories: 437 / Cholesterol: 99 mg / Carbohydrates: 17 g /
Protein: 34 g / Sodium: 547 mg / Fat: 26 g (Saturated Fat: 6 g) / Potassium: 739 mg.

SPICY CHICKEN FAVORITE

Where the name of this spicy curried chicken dish came from has been lost along the way, but according to popular legend, it was introduced to the American South by a visiting sea captain. Generations of the McPherson family of Columbus, Georgia, have served this colorful dish.

POULTRY

DUCY'S BAKED CHICKEN AND YAMS

Makes 4 to 6 Servings

1	2½-pound broiler-fryer chicken, quartered
½	teaspoon salt
¼	teaspoon pepper
2	eggs, beaten
3	tablespoons water
¾	cup fine, plain bread crumbs
2	pounds yams *or* sweet potatoes, peeled and sliced ½ inch thick
⅓	cup butter *or* margarine, melted

✦   ✦   ✦

Hats off to "Ducy"—a baby name given to Lorraine Dupas by her aunt—and lovingly bestowed upon her award-winning chicken dish. Mrs. Dupas is the proud mother of three, a grandmother and a great-grandmother. In fact, when we spoke with her recently she was caring for her great-grandchild in Charlotte, North Carolina. Mrs. Dupas was just thrilled to hear that we were sharing her recipe (which was first created in 1949) with you.

Mrs. Curry Dupas
<u>*Foods á la Louisiane*</u>
Baton Rouge
LOUISIANA

1 Preheat oven to 350°. Lightly grease a 13x9x2-inch baking pan.

2 Sprinkle the chicken quarters with the salt and pepper. In a pie plate, stir together the eggs and water. In a second pie plate, spread the bread crumbs.

3 One at a time, dip the chicken quarters first in the egg mixture, then roll them in the bread crumbs, patting to cover the chicken well. Keep the wet and dry mixtures separate by using one hand for the egg mixture and the other for the bread crumbs.

4 Arrange the yam slices in the prepared pan. Drizzle with *half* of the melted butter or margarine. Arrange the chicken on top of the yams. Drizzle the remaining melted butter or margarine over the chicken.

5 Bake the chicken, uncovered, about 1 hour or until the yams are tender and the chicken is cooked through. Serve on a warm platter.

 TIPS FROM OUR KITCHEN

To quarter a chicken: Use a long, heavy knife or kitchen shears to cut through the center of the backbone to halve the chicken. Then cut the chicken halves crosswise through the breast and backbone, as shown, to make chicken quarters.

If you wish, you can substitute chicken pieces for the chicken quarters in this recipe.

For a change of taste, try substituting seasoned bread crumbs.

Nutrition Analysis *(Per Serving):* Calories: 775 / Cholesterol: 246 mg / Carbohydrates: 76 g / Protein: 40 g / Sodium: 702 mg / Fat: 34 g (Saturated Fat: 15 g) / Potassium: 1,818 mg.

SOUTHERN-STYLE SUPPER

Yams give this chicken dinner the special Southern touch. It's a home-style, easy-to-assemble supper dish straight from Mrs. Curry Dupas of Baton Rouge, Louisiana. Bake one hour for crisp, moist chicken and tender, buttery yam slices. Serve with a crisp green salad and cornbread.

BAKED CHICKEN WITH CIDER AND APPLES

Makes 6 Servings

3	pounds meaty chicken pieces
2	cups apple cider
½	cup all-purpose flour
1	teaspoon ground ginger
1	teaspoon ground cinnamon
½	teaspoon salt
⅛	teaspoon freshly ground pepper
1 to 3	tablespoons brown sugar
2	tablespoons applejack *or* apple cider
2	medium cooking apples, cored and cut into thin wedges

◆   ◆   ◆

The United Methodist Women's Gourmet Fellowship is a group of people from Nichols United Methodist Church who regularly get together in small groups for dinners. We agree with their philosophy, "There's no better way to get to know someone than to sit across a table from him or her."

United Methodist Women's Gourmet Fellowship
50th Anniversary Cookbook
Nichols United Methodist Women
Trumbull
CONNECTICUT

1 Wash the chicken pieces, pat dry and remove the skin and visible fat, if desired. Place the chicken pieces in a large nonmetal bowl or container and pour the cider over the chicken. Cover and refrigerate overnight, turning the pieces occasionally.

2 Preheat the oven to 350°. Remove the chicken from the cider, reserving the cider.

3 In a shallow bowl or plastic bag, combine the flour, ginger, cinnamon, salt and pepper. Coat the chicken pieces with the flour mixture. (If using a plastic bag, add the chicken pieces to the bag, a few at a time. Close the bag and shake to coat the pieces well.)

4 Place the chicken pieces in a single layer in a 3-quart rectangular baking dish. Bake in the 350° oven for 30 minutes.

5 Meanwhile, in a medium mixing bowl, combine *1½ cups* of the reserved cider, the brown sugar and applejack or apple cider. Stir in the apple slices.

6 After the chicken has baked for 30 minutes, pour the apple mixture over it, then continue to bake about 25 minutes more or until the chicken is tender and no longer pink, basting occasionally with the pan juices.

 TIPS FROM OUR KITCHEN

Many varieties of "cooking" apples are available throughout the year and each has a unique flavor. The following tend to be slightly to moderately tart: Baldwin, Cortland, Gravenstein, Grimes Golden, Jonathan, McIntosh, Rome Beauty and Wealthy. If you prefer a sweeter cooking apple, try Golden Delicious, whereas if you prefer a tarter cooking apple, try Winesap.

Nutrition Analysis (*Per Serving*): Calories: 362 / Cholesterol: 104 mg / Carbohydrates: 24 / Protein: 34 g / Sodium: 273 mg / Fat: 13 g (Saturated Fat: 3 g) Potassium: 424 mg.

APPLE ACCENTS

If you like apples, you'll love this entrée. Chicken pieces are marinated in apple cider and then coated in a yummy sauce featuring apple slices, cinnamon and ginger.

CHICKEN WITH ROSEMARY AND GARLIC

Makes 5 to 6 Servings

¼	cup olive oil
1	2½- to 3-pound broiler-fryer chicken *or* roasting hen
Several sprigs fresh rosemary	
1	tablespoon butter *or* margarine
½	teaspoon salt
⅛	teaspoon pepper
2	pounds small new red potatoes
30 to 40	cloves garlic, unpeeled
¼	teaspoon pepper

◆   ◆   ◆ .

Thirty-three local cooks and a small group of The Watch Hill Improvement Society family and friends served as the recipe selection committee for <u>Watch Hill Cooks</u>. *Each submission was prepared, tested and graded, with only the best recipes included in the cookbook. There is even an "Animal Fare" section—one of the taste testers for this section was Cassie, a committee member's dog!*

<u>Watch Hill Cooks</u>
The Watch Hill Improvement Society
Watch Hill
RHODE ISLAND

1 Preheat the oven to 375°.

2 Pour *2 tablespoons* of the olive oil in a 15½x10½x2-inch roasting pan; set aside.

3 Rinse the chicken inside and out; pat dry. Stuff a *few* sprigs of rosemary inside the cavity along with the butter or margarine. Sprinkle with *¼ teaspoon* of the salt and the ⅛ teaspoon pepper. Place the chicken in the prepared roasting pan, breast side up.

4 Scrub the potatoes, leaving them whole. Place the potatoes and the unpeeled garlic around the chicken. Sprinkle the potatoes with the remaining salt and the ¼ teaspoon pepper. Tuck rosemary sprigs all around the chicken among the potatoes and garlic. Drizzle the remaining olive oil over all.

5 Roast the chicken, uncovered, in the 375° oven for 10 minutes. Reduce heat to 350° and roast for 50 to 70 minutes more or until the chicken is no longer pink, turning the chicken and potatoes regularly so they crisp evenly. Transfer the chicken to a serving platter. With a slotted spoon, transfer the potatoes and garlic to the platter. Discard the baked rosemary and garnish with fresh rosemary, if desired.

 TIPS FROM OUR KITCHEN

Squeeze each roasted garlic clove with your fingers to free the garlic from its jacket.

Nutrition Analysis (*Per Serving*): Calories: 502 / Cholesterol: 78mg / Carbohydrates: 50g / Protein: 30g / Sodium: 304mg / Fat: 21g (Saturated Fat: 5g) / Potassium: 1079 mg.

POULET À L'AIR DE PROVENCE

Tradition suggests that this rosemary-flavored chicken be served with thick slices of fresh, warm bread and red radishes and that the roasted whole garlic cloves be popped from their jackets directly into the mouth. Alternately—and equally delicious— the garlic can be spread on the potatoes or accompanying bread.

POULTRY

HALIKAHIKI MOA CURRY

Makes 4 Servings

2	fresh pineapples
4	slices bacon, finely chopped
1/3	cup finely chopped onion
1/3	cup finely chopped green sweet pepper
1/3	cup all-purpose flour
1	tablespoon curry powder
1/2	teaspoon salt
1 1/2	cups chicken broth
1/2	cup whipping cream
2	cups chopped cooked chicken
1	cup frozen peas
1/2	cup sliced water chestnuts
2	tablespoons sliced pimiento

♦ ♦ ♦

Gladys Pavone tells us that she likes to prepare dishes a day ahead and refrigerate them to serve to company the next day. Halikahiki Moa Curry is the perfect recipe for her cooking style and it tastes even better if it's made a day ahead, says Gladys. She suggests substituting different meats or seafood for variety.

Gladys Pavone
Kona Kitchens Award-Winning Community Cookbook
Kona Outdoor Circle
Kailua-Kona
HAWAII

1 Preheat the oven to 350°.

2 Cut the pineapples in half lengthwise, leaving the crown and leaves intact. Remove the fruit, reserving the shells.

3 Remove the core from the pineapple. Cut up enough of the pineapple to make *2 cups* of bite-size pieces. Set aside. Refrigerate or freeze the remaining pineapple in a covered container for another use.

4 Place the pineapple shells on a large baking sheet or in a 15x10x1-inch baking pan. Wrap the crowns with aluminum foil. Bake the pineapples in the 350° oven for 20 minutes.

5 Meanwhile, in a 12-inch skillet or Dutch oven, fry the bacon about 4 minutes or until it is partially done, stirring constantly. Add the onion and green pepper. Cook and stir until the vegetables are limp and the bacon is crisp.

6 Stir in the flour, curry powder and salt until well combined. Add the chicken broth, blending well. Cook and stir the mixture until thickened and bubbly. Cook and stir for 1 minute more. Gradually stir in the whipping cream. Add the cooked chicken, the peas, water chestnuts, pimiento and pineapple pieces. Simmer, uncovered, for 5 minutes.

7 To serve, place the hot pineapple shells on serving plates and spoon in the curry-chicken mixture. Serve immediately.

 TIPS FROM OUR KITCHEN

If desired, substitute cooked lamb, turkey or ham for the chicken.

If you prefer a sweeter mixture, add up to 1 tablespoon of sugar along with the curry powder.

When shopping for fresh whole pineapple, look for one with a plump shape that is slightly soft to the touch and is heavy for its size. The stem end should smell sweet and aromatic, not heavy or fermented. Refrigerate and use within two days.

If desired, pass small bowls of green onion, toasted coconut and chopped tomato to sprinkle on individual servings.

Nutrition Analysis (*Per Serving*): Calories: 512 / Cholesterol: 114 mg / Carbohydrates: 51
Protein: 31 g / Sodium: 777 mg / Fat: 22 g (Saturated Fat: 10 g) / Potassium: 778 mg.

TROPICAL CHICKEN DISH

When a beautiful presentation and superb taste are in order, Gladys Pavone's Halikahiki Moa Curry is
the perfect dish to choose for your menu.

CHICKEN PICCATA

Makes 8 Servings

8   medium, boneless, skinless chicken breast halves (1½ pounds)
2   tablespoons lemon juice
2   tablespoons water
½   cup all-purpose flour
¼   teaspoon salt
¼   teaspoon pepper
2   tablespoons olive oil *or* cooking oil
1   tablespoon butter *or* margarine
¾   cup water
⅓   cup dry white wine
1   chicken-flavored bouillon cube *or* 1 teaspoon instant chicken bouillon granules
4   teaspoons all-purpose flour
1   lemon
Parsley
1   pound fettuccine, cooked and drained and kept warm

◆   ◆   ◆

The Junior Service League of Gainesville, Georgia, is involved in many community service programs. Perennials chairperson, Pat Hensley, reports that the cookbook project has generated over $200,000 toward their efforts.

Dee Lawson Morris
Perennials: A Southern Celebration of Foods and Flavors
The Junior Service League of Gainesville, Georgia
Gainesville
GEORGIA

1 Rinse the chicken and pat dry with paper towels.

2 Place the chicken breast halves, 1 piece at a time, between layers of heavy plastic wrap. Using the flat side of a meat mallet, pound to about ⅛-inch thickness. Remove the plastic wrap and place the chicken in a heavy plastic bag set in a deep bowl.

3 In a small bowl, combine the 2 tablespoons lemon juice and the 2 tablespoons water; pour over the chicken in the bag. Close the bag and marinate at room temperature for 30 minutes. Remove the chicken pieces and discard the marinade.

4 In a shallow dish, stir together the ½ cup flour, the salt and pepper. Dip the chicken in the flour mixture to coat.

5 In a 12-inch skillet, heat the oil and butter or margarine over medium heat. Cook the chicken, *half* at a time, for 6 to 8 minutes or until lightly browned and no pink remains, turning once. Transfer the chicken to a warm serving platter. Cover to keep warm.

6 In a small bowl, stir together the ¾ cup water, the white wine, bouillon cube or granules and the 4 teaspoons flour. Stir the mixture into the drippings in the skillet, scraping to loosen any browned bits. Cook and stir until the mixture is thickened and bubbly. Cook and stir for 1 minute more.

7 Squeeze the juice of *half* of the lemon (about 4 teaspoons) into the sauce in the skillet. Heat through. Pour sauce over the chicken.

8 Thinly slice the remaining lemon half and garnish the serving platter with the lemon slices and parsley. Serve with the hot cooked fettuccine.

 TIPS FROM OUR KITCHEN

If you want to debone and skin the chicken breasts yourself, buy 3 pounds of chicken breasts.

Because chicken is already tender, flatten it with the flat side of a meat mallet, not the ridged side which is designed for tenderizing.

If desired, serve the chicken with spinach noodles or vermicelli instead of fettuccine.

Nutrition Analysis (*Per Serving*): Calories: 398 / Cholesterol: 48 mg / Carbohydrates: 53 g Protein: 25 g / Sodium: 299 mg / Fat: 8 g (Saturated Fat: 2 g) / Potassium: 208 mg.

LEMONY ITALIAN CLASSIC

A classic dish from Italy, piccata usually features a sauce made from pan drippings and lemon juice.
This exceptionally tasty recipe hails from Dee Lawson Morris of Gainesville, Georgia.

STUFFED CHICKEN BREASTS WITH CHERRY SAUCE

Makes 8 Servings

Stuffing:

- ⅓ cup finely chopped onion *or* green onion
- 2 tablespoons finely chopped celery
- 3 tablespoons margarine *or* butter
- ⅔ cup long grain rice
- ½ teaspoon ground sage
- 1¼ cups chicken broth

Rolls:

- 4 whole medium chicken breasts (3 pounds total) skinned, boned and halved lengthwise
- 1 cup sauterne
- 1 small onion, cut into wedges

Whole cloves

Honey Glaze:

- ½ cup honey
- ⅓ cup orange juice
- ½ teaspoon ground ginger

Cherry Sauce:

- 1 16½-ounce can pitted dark sweet cherries
- 5 tablespoons sugar
- 3 tablespoons lemon juice
- 1 tablespoon cornstarch
- 1 tablespoon cognac

◆　　◆　　◆

Cynthia Yarin told us that she sometimes varies this recipe by using wild rice in the stuffing.

Cynthia Yarin
Cougar Delights
Melvin H. Kreps School
East Windsor
NEW JERSEY

1 To make the stuffing: In a medium saucepan, cook the ⅓ cup onion and the celery in the margarine or butter until the vegetables are tender. Add the rice and sage; cook and stir until the rice is golden. Carefully add the chicken broth. Bring the mixture to a boil; reduce heat and simmer for 20 to 25 minutes or until all of the liquid is absorbed and the rice is tender.

2 Meanwhile, to make the rolls: Rinse the chicken and pat dry. Place each breast half, boned side up, between 2 pieces of heavy-duty, clear plastic wrap. Working from the center to the edges, lightly pound the chicken with the flat side of a meat mallet to form ⅛-inch thick rectangles. Remove the plastic wrap. Preheat the oven to 325°.

3 For each roll, place *¼ cup* of the rice mixture on *each* chicken piece. Fold in the long sides of the chicken and roll up jelly-roll style, beginning at one of the short sides. Secure with wooden toothpicks. Place the chicken rolls in a 2-quart rectangular baking dish. Pour the sauterne over the rolls.

4 Stud each onion wedge with a whole clove and add them to the baking dish. Bake, uncovered, in the 325° oven for 30 minutes.

5 Meanwhile, to make the Honey Glaze: In a small bowl, stir together the honey, orange juice and ground ginger. Spoon the glaze over the chicken breasts. Continue baking about 10 minutes more or until the chicken is no longer pink.

6 To make the Cherry Sauce: Drain the cherries, reserving *⅔ cup* of the syrup. In a small saucepan, stir together the reserved syrup, sugar and lemon juice. Bring to a boil.

7 Stir together the cornstarch and 1 tablespoon *cold water*. Stir the corn-starch mixture into the hot mixture. Cook and stir until the mixture is thickened and bubbly. Cook and stir for 2 minutes more. Stir in the cherries and cognac.

8 Transfer the rolls to a serving plate. Serve the rolls with the Cherry Sauce.

Nutrition Analysis (*Per Serving*): Calories: 377 / Cholesterol: 45 mg / Carbohydrates: 54 g / Protein: 19 g / Sodium: 221 mg / Fat: 7 g (Saturated Fat: 2 g) / Potassium: 360 mg.

POULTRY ROLL-UP

Tuck sage-flavored rice inside rolled chicken breasts, then coat the rolls with a mixture of honey, orange juice and ground ginger before baking. Serve with sweet Cherry Sauce and you will have transformed chicken into an exceptional meal.

SAVORY GRILLED CHICKEN WITH MUSTARD SAUCE

Makes 4 Servings
Basil Butter:
- ¼ cup butter *or* margarine
- 1 teaspoon garlic powder
- 1 teaspoon snipped fresh basil *or* ¼ teaspoon dried basil, crushed
- ¾ teaspoon onion powder

Mustard Sauce:
- ⅓ cup mayonnaise
- 2 tablespoons Dijon-style mustard
- 1½ teaspoons Worcestershire sauce
- ¾ teaspoon dry mustard

Dash onion powder
Dash garlic powder
Dash ground white pepper
- 2 drops bottled hot pepper sauce
- 2 whole large chicken breasts (2 pounds total), skinned, boned and halved lengthwise

◆　◆　◆

As well as including many "ravishing" recipes, this cookbook also features a "Food for Fitness" section from the hospital staff physicians.

Stephen Leipre, Executive Chef
Lobster Shanty
<u>**Auxili-Ann and Andy's**</u>
<u>**Ravishing Recipes**</u>
Martin Memorial
Hospital Auxiliary
Stuart
FLORIDA

1 To make the Basil Butter: In small saucepan, melt the butter or margarine over low heat. Stir in the 1 teaspoon garlic powder, the basil and the ¾ teaspoon onion powder. Set aside.

2 To make the Mustard Sauce: In a small bowl, stir together the mayonnaise, Dijon-style mustard, Worcestershire sauce, dry mustard, dash onion powder, dash garlic powder, white pepper and hot pepper sauce. Refrigerate the sauce until serving. Or, if you prefer to serve the sauce hot, transfer the mixture to a small saucepan and cook and stir until heated through. Keep warm until serving.

3 Trim any fat from the chicken, rinse and pat dry. Place each breast half, boned side up, between 2 pieces of clear plastic wrap. Working from the center out to the edges, pound lightly with the flat side of a meat mallet to ¼-inch thickness. Remove the plastic wrap.

4 Grill the chicken directly over medium-hot coals for 10 to 12 minutes or until the chicken is tender and no longer pink. Halfway through grilling, turn over the breasts and generously brush each with the Basil Butter. Serve with the Mustard Sauce.

 TIPS FROM OUR KITCHEN

Instead of chopping fresh herbs with a knife, place the leaves in a deep container and snip with a scissors. Snip only the leaves, not the stems.

To avoid flare-ups, only brush the chicken with the Basil Butter once after turning.

Nutrition Analysis: (*Per Serving*): Calories: 370 / Cholesterol: 101 mg / Carbohydrates: 2 g / Protein: 23 g / Sodium: 482 mg / Fat: 30 g (Saturated Fat: 10 g) / Potassium: 225 mg.

POULTRY PIZZAZZ

Tired of plain, ol' grilled chicken? Try these tasty chicken breasts, brushed with basil-flavored butter during grilling, then served with a creamy mustard sauce for extra pizzazz. A green vegetable, fresh tomato wedges and a garnish of fresh basil perfectly complement the dish.

POULTRY

CHICKEN BOLOGNESE

Makes 4 Servings
- 4 chicken breast halves, skinned and boned
- Dash pepper
- ¼ cup all-purpose flour
- 1 tablespoon butter *or* margarine
- 1 tablespoon cooking oil
- 4 thin slices prosciutto
- 4 thin slices fontina *or* bel paese cheese (2 ounces)
- 1 tablespoon freshly grated Parmesan cheese
- 1 tablespoon chicken broth, *or* dry white wine

◆   ◆   ◆

<u>Sound Seasonings</u> *is the proud product of two years of work and untold hours of recipe testing by the enthusiastic members of The Junior League of Westchester on the Sound. Proceeds from the sale of this book help support the League's many community projects, which include helping to provide food and clothing to the area's needy and sponsoring Safe Place, a temporary haven for runaway and homeless youth.*

<u>*Sound Seasonings*</u>
The Junior League of Westchester on the Sound Larchmont
NEW YORK

1 Preheat oven to 350°.

2 Pound the chicken breasts between 2 sheets of waxed paper or plastic wrap to flatten. Remove the paper.

3 Sprinkle the chicken breasts with pepper. Dredge in the flour; shake off the excess.

4 In a heavy large skillet, melt the butter or margarine with the oil over moderate heat. Brown the chicken breasts about 2 minutes per side or until they turn a light golden color. Transfer the chicken to a shallow buttered baking dish.

5 Place a slice of prosciutto and a slice of fontina or bel paese cheese on each chicken breast. Sprinkle with the grated Parmesan cheese and drizzle the chicken broth over all.

6 Bake, uncovered, in the 350° oven for 10 to 20 minutes or until the cheese is melted and lightly browned and the chicken is no longer pink. Serve at once.

 TIPS FROM OUR KITCHEN

If you like to plan ahead, prepare and brown the chicken pieces. Then cover and chill until you are ready to bake them. Because the chicken pieces will be cold, be sure to use the high end of the baking time range.

There are several ways to vary this dish. Thinly sliced ham, corned beef or pastrami will work just as well in this recipe as the prosciutto. If you like, substitute slices of mozzarella or Monterey Jack cheese for the specified cheeses.

Because fontina and bel paese cheese are not sold in slices, use a cheese slicer to cut thin pieces from a larger wedge or block.

Nutrition Analysis (*Per Serving*): Calories: 293 / Cholesterol: 80 mg / Carbohydrates: 6 g / Protein: 30 g / Sodium: 469 mg / Fat: 16 g (Saturated Fat: 5 g) / Potassium: 195 mg.

CHICKEN ITALIAN-STYLE

You can prepare this elegant main dish for your guests in less than an hour. They will love the rich combination of cheese and prosciutto with the chicken.

CHICKEN STIR-FRY WITH VEGETABLES AND WALNUTS

Makes 4 or 5 Servings

- ½ cup water
- ¼ cup soy sauce
- 2 tablespoons dry sherry
- 4 teaspoons cornstarch
- 1 teaspoon ground ginger
- 3 tablespoons cooking oil
- ¾ cup walnuts
- 2 cloves garlic, sliced
- 8 ounces fresh mushrooms, sliced (3 cups)
- 2 whole chicken breasts, halved, skinned, boned and cut into ¾-inch pieces
- 1 medium red sweet pepper, cut into thin strips
- ½ medium green sweet pepper, cut into thin strips
- 1 bunch green onions, trimmed and sliced diagonally (½ cup)
- 2 cups fresh bean sprouts, rinsed and drained
- 2 to 2½ cups hot cooked rice

◆ ◆ ◆

Dorothy H. Lane says she loves Chicken Stir-Fry with Vegetables and Walnuts because it is a quick-to-cook, one-dish meal.

Dorothy H. Lane
<u>*Happiness is Anything Homemade*</u>
Worcester Area Association for Retarded Citizens, Inc.
Worcester
MASSACHUSETTS

1 In a small bowl, stir together the water, soy sauce, sherry, cornstarch and ginger until the cornstarch is dissolved. Set aside.

2 In a large heavy skillet or wok, heat *1 tablespoon* of the cooking oil. Add the walnuts and cook and stir over medium-low heat about 3 minutes or until the walnuts are slightly toasted. Using a slotted spoon, transfer the walnuts to a large bowl and set aside, reserving the oil in the skillet.

3 Add the garlic to the skillet. Cook and stir about 2 minutes or until the garlic is slightly browned. Remove the garlic from the skillet and discard.

4 Add *1 tablespoon* of the cooking oil to the skillet. Add the mushrooms. Cook and stir over medium-high heat for 3 to 4 minutes or until the mushrooms are lightly browned. Using a slotted spoon, transfer the mushrooms to the bowl containing the walnuts.

5 Add the remaining cooking oil to the skillet. Add the chicken. Cook and stir for 3 to 4 minutes or until the chicken is no longer pink. Using a slotted spoon, transfer the chicken to the bowl containing the walnuts and mushrooms.

6 Add the red sweet pepper, green sweet pepper and green onion to the skillet. Cook and stir about 1 minute or until the vegetables are just crisp-tender. Stir the cornstarch mixture, then add it to the skillet. Cook and stir until the mixture is thickened and bubbly. Cook and stir for 1 minute more.

7 Return the walnuts, mushrooms and chicken to the skillet. Add the bean sprouts. Stir gently to coat the mixture with the sauce; heat through. Serve with the hot cooked rice.

 TIPS FROM OUR KITCHEN

If fresh bean sprouts aren't available, you can substitute one 16-ounce can of bean sprouts. Before using, place the fresh or canned bean sprouts in a strainer and rinse under cold water.

If you use a deep skillet or wok, you will find it easier to stir and toss the foods without making a mess.

Nutrition Analysis (*Per Serving*): Calories: 530 / Cholesterol: 45 mg / Carbohydrates: 46 g / Protein: 26 g / Sodium: 1080 mg / Fat: 27 g (Saturated Fat: 4 g) / Potassium: 663 mg.

SKILLET TOSS

This tender-crisp stir-fry takes only minutes to cook once you've chopped and assembled all the ingredients. The toasted walnuts add crunch while the fresh red and green sweet peppers add color and flavor.

ENCHILADAS CON POLLO

Makes 5 Servings

2 cups shredded Monterey Jack cheese (8 ounces)

2 cups shredded, cooked chicken (10 ounces)

⅓ cup chopped tomatoes

⅓ cup chopped black olives

¼ cup chopped green chili peppers

¼ cup chopped onion

2 16-ounce jars taco sauce *or* salsa (3½ cups)

10 6- to 7-inch flour *or* corn tortillas

Chopped black olives (optional)

Chopped tomatoes (optional)

♦ ♦ ♦

Marcie Benne and her friends often have small dinner parties and pot lucks, and Marcie usually brings her specialty, Enchiladas Con Pollo. She tells us that this is a dish she can serve confidently, "They'll always be delicious." Marcie's sister gave her this recipe and we are happy to share in her generosity.

Marcie Benne
Dune Country Cookin'
Girl Scouts of Singing
Sands Council
Granger
INDIANA

1 Preheat the oven to 350°. Grease a 3-quart rectangular baking dish.

2 In a large bowl, stir together *1 cup* of the cheese, the chicken, tomatoes, olives, chili peppers and onion. Add *1 cup* of the taco sauce or salsa and mix well.

3 Place the remaining taco sauce or salsa in a shallow dish. Dip the tortillas in the sauce, one at a time.

4 Spoon *⅓ cup* of the chicken mixture down the center of *each* tortilla. Roll up and place, seam side down, in the prepared baking dish. Pour the remaining sauce over the tortillas.

5 Cover with foil and bake in the 350° oven for 30 minutes. Remove the foil. Sprinkle with the remaining cheese and return to the oven about 3 minutes or until the cheese melts. Garnish with chopped black olives and chopped tomatoes, if desired. Serve immediately.

TIPS FROM OUR KITCHEN

Shredded, cooked pork or beef can be used instead of the chicken in this recipe.

Taco sauce and salsa are purchased in jars that are labeled mild, medium or hot. Adjust the hotness of this dish by using a taco sauce that suits your preference.

To make six servings, use six 10-inch flour tortillas and fill *each* with ⅔ cup of the chicken mixture.

For a make-ahead dish, chill the remaining sauce separately and pour over the filled tortillas just before baking so the enchiladas won't become soggy.

Wheat tortillas are commonly used in northern Mexico, while corn tortillas are more common in southern Mexico.

Nutrition Analysis (*Per Serving*): Calories: 510 / Cholesterol: 91 mg / Carbohydrates: 43 g / Protein: 34 g / Sodium: 1,231 mg / Fat: 27 g (Saturated Fat: 10 g) / Potassium: 819 mg.

TORTILLAS ROLLED WITH CHICKEN

Mexican cooking combines Aztec and Mayan Indian traditions with Spanish influences for
incomparably delicious results. In this recipe, flour or corn tortillas are wrapped around
a filling of cheese, chicken and vegetables. Pass the salsa and enjoy!

POULTRY

315

CHICKEN, RICE AND BROCCOLI CASSEROLE

Makes 10 Servings

- 1 3½-pound broiler-fryer chicken, cooked *or* 3 cups cubed, cooked chicken *or* turkey
- 1¼ cups beef broth
- 1 cup long grain rice
- ¼ cup butter *or* margarine, cut up
- 1 10½-ounce can condensed French onion soup
- 1 4½-ounce jar sliced mushrooms, drained
- ¼ teaspoon garlic powder
- 2 10-ounce boxes frozen chopped broccoli *or* broccoli spears, thawed and drained
- 1 10¾-ounce can condensed cream of mushroom soup
- ⅔ cup milk
- ¼ cup mayonnaise *or* salad dressing
- ¼ teaspoon Worcestershire sauce
- 1 cup shredded cheddar cheese (4 ounces)

♦   ♦   ♦

Nell Abels told us that this casserole is loved by friends and family. In fact, her son "could eat the whole casserole himself." Nell enjoys preparing the dish, especially because "it smells so good baking!"

Nell Abels
Bravo
The Greensboro Symphony Guild
Greensboro
NORTH CAROLINA

1 Preheat the oven to 325°.

2 If using a roasting chicken, remove the meat from the bones and cut the meat into cubes; set aside.

3 Meanwhile, in a 3-quart rectangular baking dish, stir together the beef broth, uncooked rice, butter or margarine, undiluted French onion soup, mushrooms and garlic powder. Cover the baking dish tightly with aluminum foil. Bake in the 325° oven about 1 hour or until the rice is tender and the liquid has been absorbed. Remove from the oven. Increase the oven temperature to 375°.

4 Stir the rice mixture. Top with the drained broccoli and chicken or turkey.

5 In a medium bowl, stir together the undiluted cream of mushroom soup, milk, mayonnaise or salad dressing and Worcestershire sauce. Spoon the mixture evenly over the chicken or turkey. Sprinkle with the cheddar cheese. Bake the casserole, covered, in the 375° oven for 30 minutes. Uncover and bake about 10 minutes more or until heated through.

 TIPS FROM OUR KITCHEN

Homemade or purchased chicken broth can be used for the beef broth.

For a less salty flavor, use reduced-sodium condensed French onion soup and condensed cream of mushroom soup. Also use reduced-sodium cheddar cheese.

If you are taking this dish to a potluck or picnic, time the cooking so that the casserole is done just before it's time to leave. Then cover the pan with aluminum foil and wrap in several layers of newspaper, or place the pan in an insulated carrier to keep the dish hot. Afterwards, try to chill any leftovers within 2 hours because food safety experts recommend discarding cooked meat or poultry that sits at room temperature for 2 hours or longer. If you have questions about the safety of leftovers, call the U.S. Department of Agriculture's Meat and Poultry Hotline at 1-800-535-4555.

Nutrition Analysis (*Per Serving*): Calories: 419 / Cholesterol: 84 mg / Carbohydrates: 23 g / Protein: 25 g / Sodium: 857 mg / Fat: 25 g (Saturated Fat: 9 g) / Potassium: 371 mg.

POTLUCK OR FAMILY SUPPER

Whether you're looking for a dish to take to a potluck or to prepare for your family's weekday menu, Chicken, Rice and Broccoli Casserole is a terrific choice. A layer of rice, a layer of broccoli, a layer of chicken and an easy, cheesy, saucy topping all mount up to one delicious dish.

LOUISBURG CHICKEN PIE

Makes 8 Servings

2 pounds chicken breast *or* turkey breast portion

3 medium onions, coarsely chopped

3 stalks celery, coarsely chopped

6 black peppercorns

3 cups water

1 pound bulk pork sausage, coarsely crumbled, cooked and drained

2 cups cooked, cubed potatoes

2 cups sliced fresh mushrooms, cooked and drained

1 10-ounce package frozen peas and carrots, thawed

1 teaspoon minced garlic

½ teaspoon dried rosemary, crushed

½ teaspoon dried thyme, crushed

½ teaspoon salt

¼ teaspoon pepper

½ cup all-purpose flour

½ cup dry sherry

Pastry for a 2-crust pie

1 egg, beaten

♦　♦　♦

From the tiny town of Solebury, Pennsylvania, comes a superb cookbook, which was published to help fund the Trinity Church pre-school.

Dorothy M. Bidelman
Bucks Cooks II
Trinity Church
Solebury
PENNSYLVANIA

1 In a large saucepan or Dutch oven, combine the chicken or turkey with the onions, celery, peppercorns and water. Cover and simmer about 30 minutes or until the poultry is tender. Remove the poultry from the stock. Strain the stock and set aside to cool. (You should have about 3 cups.) Discard the onion, celery and peppercorns.

2 Skin and debone the poultry and cut the meat into bite-size pieces. Set aside.

3 Preheat oven to 375°. Place the chicken or turkey pieces in a 13x9x2-inch baking dish. Add the sausage, potatoes, mushrooms, and peas and carrots.

4 Skim the fat from the cooled stock and place the fat in a medium saucepan. If necessary, add enough margarine or butter to make a total of ¼ cup fat.

5 Melt the fat and stir in the garlic, rosemary, thyme, salt and pepper. Stir in the flour, then add the 3 cups stock and the sherry. Cook, stirring, until thickened and bubbly. Pour the sauce mixture over the poultry and vegetables in the baking dish.

6 On a lightly floured surface, roll out the pastry to extend about 1 inch beyond the edge of the baking dish. Fit the pastry over the dish and flute the edges, pressing the edges firmly on the rim of the dish. Cut several slits in the pastry and brush with the beaten egg.

7 Bake the pie in the 375° oven about 40 minutes or until the crust is golden and the mixture inside the crust is heated through. Let the pie stand 5 minutes before serving.

TIPS FROM OUR KITCHEN

If you're reluctant to make this main dish pie from scratch, here's a quicker version. Skip simmering the poultry (step 1) and start with 3 cups of cooked chicken or turkey meat and 3 cups canned chicken broth. (You can usually get cooked chicken at supermarket deli counters.) Then, instead of making your own pastry, use refrigerated pie crust.

For a fluted edge, press with your thumb from the inside of the pie against your thumb and forefinger of your other hand.

Nutrition Analysis *(Per Serving)*: Calories: 685 / Cholesterol: 110 mg / Carbohydrates: 47 g Protein: 34 g / Sodium: 906 mg / Fat: 38 g (Saturated Fat: 11 g) / Potassium: 791 mg.

OLD-FASHIONED GOODNESS

This meal-in-a-pie from Dorothy M. Bidelman of Solebury, Pennsylvania, boasts all the goodness of the filling farm meals of yesteryear. Here is familiar food at its warm and hearty best!

GRILLED TURKEY BREAST

Makes 8 Servings
¼ cup cooking oil
¼ cup lemon juice
¾ teaspoon salt
½ teaspoon paprika
½ teaspoon dried oregano, crushed
¼ teaspoon garlic powder *or* 1 clove garlic, minced
¼ teaspoon pepper
1 2½-pound boneless turkey breast half
Fresh thyme sprigs (optional)

♦   ♦   ♦

Marlene Tropper and a friend "from up north" were invited to a barbecue about eight years ago. As their contribution to the meal, the twosome decided to experiment with cooking turkey breasts. They brought their creation, Grilled Turkey Breast, to the barbecue, and everyone—including "some people who don't even like turkey"—loved it. We think you will too!

Marlene Tropper
Chef's EscOrt
Women's American Organization for Rehabilitation Through Training
Hollandale
FLORIDA

1 In a small saucepan, stir together the oil, lemon juice, salt, paprika, oregano, garlic powder or minced garlic and pepper. Bring to a boil. Reduce heat and simmer, covered, for 10 minutes. Cool.

2 Rinse the turkey; pat dry with paper towels. Place the turkey in a large plastic bag and set in a deep bowl. Pour the cooled marinade over the turkey in the bag, turning to cover all sides of the turkey. Seal the bag and refrigerate for at least 2 hours, turning occasionally.

3 In a covered grill, arrange coals around a drip pan. Test for medium heat above the drip pan.

4 Drain the turkey and discard the marinade. Place the turkey, skin side up, on the grill rack over the drip pan but not over the preheated coals. Close the grill hood.

5 Grill for 1 to 1¼ hours or until a meat thermometer inserted near the center of the turkey registers 170°. Let the turkey stand for 10 to 15 minutes before slicing. Garnish with fresh thyme, if desired.

 TIPS FROM OUR KITCHEN

To check the temperature of the coals: Hold your hand, palm side down, above the coals or drip pan, at the height the food will be cooked. Start counting the seconds, "one thousand one, one thousand two." If you need to remove your hand after three seconds, the coals are medium-hot; after four seconds, they're medium.

If you're starting with a frozen turkey, thaw it in the refrigerator, not on the counter or in a pan of water. Also, be sure that you thoroughly wash the bowl and any utensils that come in contact with the raw turkey before you use the utensils to lift, carry or cut the cooked turkey. *Do not*, under any circumstances, allow the cooked turkey to stand at room temperature for more than two hours. Keep the turkey hot (above 140°) or cold (below 40°).

Nutrition Analysis (*Per Serving*): Calories: 233 / Cholesterol: 85 mg / Carbohydrates: 0 g / Protein: 33 g / Sodium: 90 mg / Fat: 10 g (Saturated Fat: 3 g) / Potassium: 334 mg.

MARVELOUS MARINADE

A garlic-and-lemon marinade flavors this Grilled Turkey Breast from Marlene Tropper of Tamarac, Florida. The turkey is absolutely luscious served hot with rice and vegetables, and any leftovers will be a big hit in sandwiches or salads.

TURKEY MARENGO

1   tablespoon vegetable oil
2   onions, sliced and separated into rings
3   1¼- to 1½-pound turkey drumsticks, deboned and cut into pieces
2   apples, peeled, cored and chopped
1   tablespoon curry powder
¼   teaspoon salt
¼   teaspoon pepper
4   tomatoes, peeled and chopped
½   cup chicken broth
2   tablespoons lemon juice
2 to 3 cups hot cooked rice

♦ ♦ ♦

The Fontbonne Auxiliary was founded in 1947 by the Sisters of Saint Joseph of Nazareth to help support Saint John Hospital in Detroit. Today, the Auxiliary consists of nearly 1,300 people from all walks of life, who work to serve the physical, emotional and spiritual needs of the hospital community and surrounding areas.

Rosemary Zienger
Renaissance Cuisine
The Fontbonne Auxiliary of Saint John Hospital Detroit MICHIGAN

1 In a 12-inch skillet, heat the oil over medium heat. Add the onions and cook until they are soft. Push the onions to the edge of the skillet.

2 Add the turkey pieces and cook and stir until the turkey is brown. Stir in the apples, curry powder, salt and pepper. Cook the mixture for 2 minutes.

3 Stir in the tomatoes, chicken broth and lemon juice until the ingredients are well mixed. Cover the skillet and simmer the mixture for 45 to 60 minutes or until the turkey is tender.

4 Uncover the skillet and boil the stew gently for 15 minutes to reduce the liquid slightly. Serve with the hot cooked rice.

 TIPS FROM OUR KITCHEN

The liquid in the stew can be a bit thin. To thicken it quickly, transfer the turkey to a serving platter and keep it warm. In a small bowl, stir together 2 tablespoons *cornstarch* and 2 tablespoons *water*. Add the cornstarch mixture to the liquid in the skillet and stir over medium heat until the sauce is slightly thickened and bubbly. Cook and stir for 2 minutes more. Serve the sauce over the turkey.

To help eliminate some of the fat from this recipe, remove the skin from the turkey legs before you cut it into pieces.

If you'd rather use thighs to make this stew, substitute two 2-2½-pound thighs for the 3 turkey drumsticks.

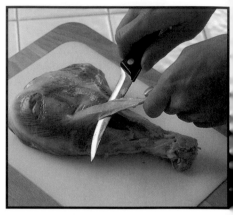

To bone a turkey drumstick, remove the skin so you can see the tendons. Remove the visible outer tendons using the tip of the knife to cut away.

Cut away portions of meat from the bone. To remove the long white inner tendons from the turkey pieces, pull on the end of a tendon with your fingers. At the same time, use a knife to scrape against the tendon, freeing the surrounding meat.

Nutrition Analysis (*Per Serving*): Calories: 654 / Cholesterol: 183 mg / Carbohydrates: 48 Protein: 67 g / Sodium: 418 mg / Fat: 20 g (Saturated Fat: 6 g) / Potassium: 1,180 mg.

TURKEY IN THE STEW

Here is a savory, slow-simmered stew that we love for its rich flavor and because it takes advantage of the packaged turkey parts now available in most supermarkets. This soul-warming turkey dish is offered to you by Rosemary Zienger of Detroit, Michigan.

POULTRY

TURKEY SCALOPPINE WITH PARMESAN CHEESE

Makes 4 Servings

4	3-ounce turkey breast slices, ¼ inch thick
¼	cup all-purpose flour
⅛	teaspoon salt
⅛	teaspoon pepper
1	egg
2	tablespoons water
1	cup fresh bread crumbs
½	cup freshly grated Parmesan cheese
¼	cup butter *or* margarine

Snipped parsley

◆   ◆   ◆

St. Thomas's Church parishoners are active in "The Country Cooks," a program in which participants provide large numbers of meals each week to Paul's Place, an urban soup kitchen located in Baltimore. Proceeds from the sale of Two and Company *help to support this program, as well as to provide funding for maintenance of the historic church and its grounds.*

Susan D. Baxter
<u>*Two and Company*</u>
St. Thomas's Church, Garrison Forest
Owing Mills
MARYLAND

1 Rinse the turkey slices and pat them dry.

2 Stir together the flour, salt and pepper in a shallow dish.

3 In a second shallow dish, beat together the egg and water.

4 In a third shallow dish, combine the fresh bread crumbs and Parmesan cheese. Dip each turkey slice first in the flour mixture, next in the egg mixture and finally in the bread crumb mixture.

5 In a 12-inch skillet over medium-high heat, melt the butter or margarine. Add the coated turkey slices to the skillet and cook for 2 to 3 minutes on each side or until no pink remains. Transfer the turkey to a serving platter. Garnish with the snipped parsley.

TIPS FROM OUR KITCHEN

To flatten turkey slices to ¼-inch thickness: Wrap each turkey slice in heavy-duty plastic wrap and pound from the center outward with a meat mallet or other heavy utensil.

Fresh Parmesan cheese varies in flavor from mild to robust depending on how long the cheese has been aged. To grate your own Parmesan, use a food processor or hand grater. If you use shaker-ready grated Parmesan cheese, you'll want to use less than the amount called for in the recipe. Close the shaker after each use and store in a cool, dry place.

Use a skillet with a non-stick coating to prevent the cheese from sticking to the skillet.

Nutrition Analysis (*Per Serving*): Calories: 261 / Cholesterol: 90 mg / Carbohydrates: 11
Protein: 19 g / Sodium: 309 mg / Fat: 15 g (Saturated Fat: 3 g) / Potassium: 211 mg.

SPEEDY SCALOPPINE

Discover moist turkey breast slices hiding beneath the golden crisp coating of this fast and easy main dish. Triple dipping gives the turkey its crispness, while Parmesan cheese adds flavor.

POULTRY

Turkey Fillet Kabobs

Makes 4 Servings
  1   pound turkey breast
      tenderloin *or* 1 pound
      skinless, boneless chicken
      breast halves
 ¼   cup soy sauce
 ¼   cup cooking oil
  2   tablespoons honey
  1   teaspoon ground ginger
  1   teaspoon dry mustard
  1   clove garlic, minced
  1   green sweet pepper, cut
      into 1-inch pieces
  8   pearl onions, peeled
  8   medium whole mushrooms
  8   cherry tomatoes
  2   cups hot, cooked rice

♦   ♦   ♦

In order to raise funds for scholarships and to purchase books and supplies for the Religious Education Program, St. Joan of Arc Catholic Church members decided to put together a cookbook in which "everyone could take a little ownership." The children involved in the program—preschool through high school—were asked to submit their favorite family recipes. Here is Travis Bode's favorite, Turkey Fillet Kabobs.

Travis Bode
<u>Sharing Family Fare</u>
St. Joan of Arc Catholic Church
Phoenix
ARIZONA

1 Rinse the turkey or chicken and pat dry with paper towels. Cut the turkey into 1-inch cubes or cut the chicken into 2-inch strips that can be folded to form 1-inch pieces.

2 In a small bowl, stir together the soy sauce, cooking oil, honey, ginger, dry mustard and garlic. Add the turkey or chicken, stirring to coat all sides. Marinate at room temperature for 30 minutes or cover and refrigerate overnight.

3 Drain, reserving the marinade. On four 15-inch skewers, alternately thread the turkey or poultry pieces with the peppers, onions and mushrooms. Place on an unheated broiler pan.

4 Broil the kabobs 3 to 4 inches from the heat for 6 minutes, brushing occasionally with the marinade. Turn the kabobs and brush on more marinade. Broil 6 to 8 minutes more or until no pink remains in the center of the turkey or chicken pieces. Add the cherry tomatoes to the ends of the skewers during the last 1 to 2 minutes of broiling to heat them through. Serve the kabobs with the hot, cooked rice.

Tips from Our Kitchen

Precooking the pearl onions makes peeling them easier. Place the onions in a pan of boiling water for 3 to 4 minutes. Drain. Trim off the root ends and gently press to slip off the skins.

Leave at least ¼-inch space between the meat and vegetables on the skewers so that all the pieces can cook evenly.

Soy sauce is a salty, brown liquid commercially made from fermented soybeans, wheat, water and salt. Many varieties of both Chinese and Japanese soy sauce are available. Soy sauce ranges in color from light to dark, in taste from sweet to extremely salty, and in texture from thin to very thick. If you prefer a less salty flavor or are concerned about your sodium intake, you may prefer to use a low-sodium or reduced-sodium soy sauce in this marinade.

If you use wooden skewers, soak them in water for a few minutes before threading on the meat and vegetables. This will prevent the skewers from burning under the broiler.

Nutrition Analysis (*Per Serving*): Calories: 412 / Cholesterol: 50 mg / Carbohydrates: 46 g
Protein: 27 g / Sodium: 827 mg / Fat: 13 g (Saturated Fat: 2 g) / Potassium: 582 mg.

POULTRY SKEWERS

In this tantalizing recipe from Phoenix, Arizona, boneless turkey or chicken pieces are soaked in a
flavor-packed, soy sauce marinade and then threaded on skewers along with tender vegetables.

CORNISH HEN WITH VEGETABLES

Makes 2 Servings

¼ cup sliced carrots
¼ cup chopped onion
¼ cup chopped celery
4 small whole mushrooms
2 teaspoons snipped parsley *or* 1 teaspoon dried parsley
½ teaspoon snipped fresh thyme *or* ⅛ teaspoon dried thyme, crushed
1 1- to 1½-pound Cornish game hen, thawed
2 tablespoons dry sherry *or* chicken broth
Paprika *or* salt and pepper
Brown Rice (optional)
Steamed Broccoli (optional)

◆ ◆ ◆

Paths of Sunshine, the Florida Federation of Garden Clubs, Inc.'s cookbook, is included in the Cookbook Hall of Fame. The Federation calls the cookbook a "history of Florida and its people," presented "through recipes for good Florida food." Recipes were submitted by federation members, as well as local chefs.

Paths of Sunshine
Florida Federation of Garden Clubs, Inc.
Winter Park
FLORIDA

1 Preheat the oven to 375°.

2 In a small saucepan, cook the carrots, onion and celery in a small amount of *boiling water* for 6 minutes. Drain the vegetables and return them to the saucepan. Stir in the mushrooms, parsley and thyme.

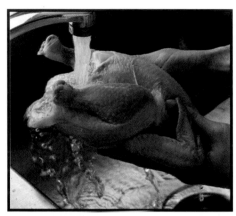

3 Rinse the Cornish hen under cold running water; reserve the giblets for another use.

4 Spoon the vegetable mixture into the cavity of the Cornish hen. Pour the sherry or broth over the vegetables in the cavity. Sprinkle the Cornish hen with the paprika or salt and pepper.

5 Place the Cornish hen on a rack in a shallow roasting pan. Cover the cavity with foil. Bake in the 375° oven for 1¼ to 1½ hours or until the meat is tender and no pink remains. Let the Cornish hen stand for 5 to 10 minutes before serving. Serve with brown rice and steamed broccoli, if desired.

TIPS FROM OUR KITCHEN

Thaw the Cornish hen on a plate in the refrigerator—not on the counter or in a pan of water. Rinse it thoroughly before adding the vegetables.

If desired, glaze the Cornish hen by brushing with apple or currant jelly about 5 minutes before the Cornish hen is done.

Precooking the carrot, onion and celery before stuffing them into the Cornish hen ensures that they will be tender when the Cornish hen is done.

If desired, substitute sage for part of the thyme or parsley.

Nutrition Analysis (*Per Serving*): Calories: 441 / Cholesterol: 134 mg / Carbohydrates: 9 g / Protein: 42 g / Sodium: 206 mg / Fat: 25 g (Saturated Fat: 6 g) / Potassium: 282 mg.

DINNER FOR TWO

Looking for a simply delicious dinner for two? You can end your search with this Cornish Hen with
Vegetables from Winter Park, Florida. Of course, feel free to double the recipe and invite
two more lucky people to your table.

OUR FAVORITE HONEY-GLAZED DUCK

Makes 6 to 8 Servings

- 2 medium onions, chopped
- 2 cloves garlic, minced
- ½ cup honey
- ½ cup dry sherry
- ¼ cup soy sauce
- Dash hot pepper sauce
- ½ teaspoon ground ginger
- ¼ teaspoon pepper
- 2 3- to 5-pound domestic ducklings
- Peel of 2 oranges

◆　◆　◆

Lynn and John Howard have served Our Favorite Honey-Glazed Duck to many of their dinner guests. Lynn says she likes the simple preparation and suggests that wild rice and a green salad make perfect accompaniments.

Lynn Howard
CordonBlueGrass
Junior League of Louisville, Inc.
Louisville
KENTUCKY

1 In a blender or food processor, thoroughly blend or process the onions, garlic, honey, sherry, soy sauce, hot pepper sauce, ginger and pepper until liquified. Set aside.

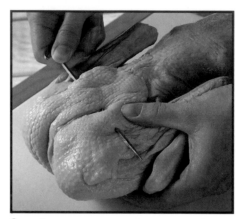

2 Preheat oven to 350°. Rinse each duckling and wipe inside and out with paper towels. Skewer the neck skin to the back and tie the legs to the tail. Snip off the wing tips and twist the wings under the back.

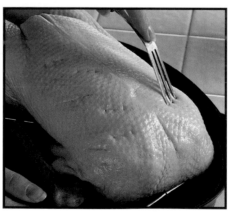

3 Place the ducklings, breast sides up, on a rack in a roasting pan. Prick the breast skin. Insert a meat thermometer into the center of one of the inside thigh muscles. Place the orange peel in the pan below the ducks.

4 Roast the ducks in the 350° oven for 2 to 2½ hours or until the meat thermometer registers 180°. Baste the ducks generously with the glaze after 1½ hours and then every 15 minutes until done.

 TIPS FROM OUR KITCHEN

To serve three or four people, halve this recipe.

Don't brush the ducklings with the glaze too soon or it will burn before the birds are done.

If you do not have a meat thermometer, cook the ducklings until the drumsticks move easily in their sockets and the duck is no longer pink.

For a holiday meal, try serving this duck with mashed sweet potatoes and whole cranberry sauce. A few orange slices will make a colorful garnish.

Nutrition Analysis *(Per Serving)*: Calories: 799 / Cholesterol: 165 mg / Carbohydrates: 29 g
Protein: 39 g / Sodium: 806 mg / Fat: 56 g (Saturated Fat: 19 g) / Potassium: 517 mg.

FANCY FEAST

This succulent duck recipe from the Junior League of Louisville is just what you want for an extra
special meal. How about serving Our Favorite Honey-Glazed Duck to dinner guests
that you want to impress?

POULTRY

Salads & Dressings

Salads are the perfect choice for a light and breezy lunch, dinner, or brunch, especially during the hot summer months. For a taste of the tropics, try the Orange-Kiwi-Avocado Salad from the Junior League of Phoenix cookbook, *Fiesta Under the Sun.* In the midst of a cold winter, you'll find paradise in the Snow Pea Splendor, and Special Occasion Cranberries are just right for the holidays.

THREE-LETTUCE SALAD

Makes 6 Servings

2 tablespoons olive oil *or* salad oil

2 tablespoons red wine vinegar

1 to 4 cloves garlic, minced

⅛ teaspoon salt

2 cups torn romaine lettuce

2 cups torn leaf lettuce

2 cups torn butter lettuce

1 11-ounce can mandarin oranges, drained

1 cup seedless red grapes, halved

Red onion, thinly sliced and rings separated

⅓ cup toasted slivered almonds

◆ ◆ ◆

When we spoke with Lorna Reay, she told us that she loves to experiment in the kitchen. Whenever she finds a new recipe, she makes little changes here and there to create her own dish. Such is the case with this recipe for Three-Lettuce Salad. When Lorna served this salad to her in-laws, they raved about it, and still do every time they see her.

The Reay Family

<u>**Johnston Schools**</u>

<u>**Cooking Up A Storm**</u>

Johnston PTO

Johnston

IOWA

1 In a screwtop jar, combine the olive oil or salad oil, vinegar, garlic and salt. Cover and shake until well blended. Chill until serving time.

2 In a large salad bowl, combine the romaine, leaf and butter lettuce. Add the mandarin oranges, grapes and as much red onion as you like.

3 To serve: Pour the dressing on top of the salad; toss to coat. Sprinkle with the almonds.

 TIPS FROM OUR KITCHEN

When you're in a hurry, substitute your favorite bottled Italian salad dressing for the homemade dressing used here.

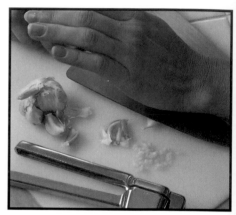

There are several ways to mince garlic: You can use a knife to cut it into tiny pieces, use a garlic press or crush the peeled garlic with the side of a French knife.

You can add some meat, poultry or fish to this recipe to make it a main dish. Smoked turkey would be especially delicious.

Try another oil in place of the olive oil for a subtle change of flavor. Consider using almond oil or walnut oil, and sprinkling the corresponding nuts on top.

For a change of pace, substitute toasted walnuts, pecans, pine nuts or cashews for the almonds.

Nutrition Analysis *(Per Serving)*: Calories: 126 / Cholesterol: 0 mg / Carbohydrates: 13 g / Protein: 3 g / Sodium: 51 mg / Fat: 8 g (Saturated Fat: 1 g) / Potassium: 329 mg.

LETTUCE SAMPLER

The flavor of green leaf, the crunchiness of romaine and the tenderness of butter lettuce are
complemented by mandarin oranges and seedless red grapes. This garden-fresh salad
will accompany many main dishes beautifully.

ASPARAGUS WITH RASPBERRY VINAIGRETTE

Makes 6 Servings
- 30 spinach leaves (about 3 cups)
- 30 asparagus spears, trimmed to 4½ inches
- 1 10-ounce package frozen raspberries with juice, thawed and drained
- ⅓ cup olive oil
- ¼ cup whipping cream
- 2 tablespoons vinegar
- ¼ teaspoon salt
- ⅛ teaspoon pepper
- Fresh raspberries (optional)
- Snipped fresh chives (optional)
- Cracked black pepper (optional)

◆ ◆ ◆

Since 1972, the Novato Human Needs Center has been providing human services to the North Marin community. The center's programs include providing food and clothing assistance for those in need, a child abuse hotline, a parental stress hotline, a phone-friend hotline for latchkey children, a senior transportation program and an employment service program, among others.

Sue Cummings
Novato Human Needs Center Cookbook
Novato Human Needs Center
Novato
CALIFORNIA

1 Wash and stem the spinach, then pat dry. Set aside.

2 In a Dutch oven, bring about 1 inch of *water* to a boil. Add the asparagus spears; cover and cook for 3 to 4 minutes or until the asparagus is crisp-tender. Place the asparagus in a colander and rinse with cold water. Set aside.

3 Place the raspberries in a blender container or food processor bowl. Cover and puree the berries. Strain the puree through a fine sieve into a bowl, discarding the seeds. Wash the blender container or food processor bowl.

4 Place the olive oil, whipping cream, vinegar, salt and pepper into the blender container or food processor bowl. Cover and blend or process until combined. Blend in the raspberry puree.

5 To serve: Arrange 5 spinach leaves on *each* of 6 plates. Arrange 5 asparagus spears on top of each bed of spinach. Pour about *2 tablespoons* of the raspberry vinaigrette mixture over the center of each serving. Garnish with raspberries, snipped chives and cracked pepper, if desired. Store any leftover dressing in the refrigerator up to 7 days.

TIPS FROM OUR KITCHEN

This recipe makes about ¾ cup extra vinaigrette dressing, enough to dress any extra ingredients you might add to the recipe. For example, you might add red onion rings, cooked chicken, cubed melon, pea pods or orange segments. As

an alternative, you might like to save any leftover dressing to dress a fruit salad.

Fresh asparagus is most readily available in April and May. Choose straight and firm spears with good color and tightly closed buds. The spears will cook more evenly if they are all about the same diameter. To store asparagus up to four days, wrap the stems in wet paper towels, then place in a tightly sealed plastic bag and refrigerate. Just before using asparagus, wash and cut or break off the stem ends.

Fresh spinach should have dark green leaves that are crisp and free of moisture and mold. Avoid buying spinach with broken or bruised leaves. Rinse fresh spinach thoroughly in cold water to remove any sand; pat dry and refrigerate in a plastic bag lined with a paper towel up to 3 days.

Nutrition Analysis (*Per Serving*): Calories: 190 / Cholesterol: 14 mg / Carbohydrates: 12 g / Protein: 3 g / Sodium: 121 mg / Fat: 16 g (Saturated Fat: 4 g) / Potassium: 289 mg.

TANGY TRIO

Asparagus, spinach and raspberries form a terrific trio of fresh flavors in this salad from Novato, California. The simple, but elegant, dish looks especially appealing garnished with a few fresh raspberries.

SPINACH SALAD DUO

Makes 6 to 8 Servings

Salad:
- 1   pound fresh spinach, rinsed and well dried (12 cups)
- 2   small apples, finely chopped
- ½   cup crumbled blue cheese
- ½   cup broken walnuts

Dressing:
- 1   cup mayonnaise *or* salad dressing
- ½   cup dairy sour cream
- ¼   cup crumbled blue cheese
- ¼   teaspoon salt
- ⅛   teaspoon coarsely ground pepper
- 6   slices bacon, crisply cooked and crumbled

◆   ◆   ◆

Using text, recipes, drawings and photos, From a Lighthouse Window succeeds in presenting a satisfying glimpse into Maryland's Eastern Shore "where crab is king and the oyster has a place in history." The bounty of the Chesapeake waters and fertile farmlands have contributed to a distinct culinary legacy, which survives today for all to enjoy.

From a Lighthouse Window
Chesapeake Bay Maritime Museum
St. Michaels
MARYLAND

1 To make the salad: Remove the tough stems from the spinach and discard. Tear the spinach into bite-size pieces.

2 In a very large bowl, toss together the spinach, apples, the ½ cup blue cheese and the walnuts. Cover and refrigerate until ready to serve.

3 To make the dressing: In a small bowl, stir together the mayonnaise or salad dressing, sour cream, the ¼ cup blue cheese, the salt and pepper. Cover and refrigerate until ready to serve.

4 Just before serving, pour the dressing over the spinach mixture. Gently toss. Sprinkle with the bacon and serve immediately.

 TIPS FROM OUR KITCHEN

Before you begin, make sure your salad bowl will hold at least 14 cups of salad mixture.

For a lighter version of the dressing, substitute ¼ cup *milk* and 1 table-spoon *honey* for the mayonnaise.

Don't add the dressing to the salad until just before serving. If you do, the spinach will become limp and the dressing will get watery.

If time is short, look for precleaned spinach. Otherwise, you can wash it thoroughly the day before you need to make the salad. To wash, rinse the spinach thoroughly in cold water to remove all of the sand from the crinkly leaves. Pat dry and store in a paper towel-lined plastic bag.

Toasting the walnuts will help to keep them crisp in the salad. To toast: Place the nuts in a small skillet and cook over medium heat for 5 to 7 minutes or until the walnuts are golden, stirring often. Let the walnuts cool before adding them to the salad.

The term *blue cheese* includes several varieties of blue-veined, semisoft cheeses. Gorgonzola is softer, creamier and less pungent than most blue cheeses. Roquefort is made from whole sheep's milk and is produced only within the city of Roquefort, France. Stilton is made only in England.

Nutrition Analysis (*Per Serving*): Calories: 488 / Cholesterol: 46 mg / Carbohydrates: 11 g / Protein: 10 g / Sodium: 674 mg / Fat: 47 g (Saturated Fat: 11 g) / Potassium: 611 mg.

FLAVOR-PACKED SALAD

The dynamic flavorful duo of apples and blue cheese adds a colorful twist to this spinach salad, while walnuts and bacon lend lively taste and crunch. The tangy, delicious dressing helps to make this dish a versatile family pleaser.

SALADS & DRESSINGS

ORANGE-KIWI-AVOCADO SALAD

Makes 6 to 8 Servings
  4   large oranges
      Lime juice
 ¼   teaspoon salt
  1   tablespoon honey
 ¼   walnut *or* salad oil
  2   large avocados
  4   kiwi fruit

◆   ◆   ◆

The Junior League of Phoenix, Arizona, which has been in existence since the 1930s, put together two cookbooks celebrating the eclectic cuisine of the Southwest. For each cookbook, they searched for recipes that would both reflect the local color and, of course, taste absolutely delicious. League member Polly Fitzgerald thinks the local efforts created a winning collection. Orange-Kiwi-Avocado Salad is one fabulous example.

<u>*Fiesta under the Sun*</u>
Junior League of Phoenix
Phoenix
ARIZONA

1 Peel the oranges. To section an orange, use a sharp paring knife to remove the white membrane. Working over a bowl to catch the juices, cut into the center of each orange between one section and the membrane. Turn the knife and cut along the other side of the section next to the membrane, as shown. Continue until all of the oranges are sectioned.

2 Measure the reserved orange juice. Add enough lime juice to make ½ cup. Add the salt, honey and oil. Beat the dressing with a wire whisk until it is combined.

3 Cut lengthwise through one avocado around the pit. With your hands, twist the avocado halves in opposite directions to separate them. Tap the pit with the blade of a sharp knife so that the knife catches in the pit. Carefully rotate the knife to loosen the pit. Lift the knife and remove the pit. Repeat with the second avocado. Slice the avocados. Peel and slice the kiwi fruit.

4 Arrange the orange sections and avocado and kiwi slices on salad plates. Drizzle *half* of the dressing over the salads. Serve the remaining dressing on the side.

 TIPS FROM OUR KITCHEN

For an extra-special touch, serve this fruit salad on a bed of greens. Kale, salad savoy or romaine lettuce would be especially effective.

Naval oranges result in prettier sections because you don't have to remove seeds.

Nutrition Analysis *(Per Serving):* Calories: 246 / Cholesterol: 0 mg / Carbohydrates: 20 g / Protein: 2 g / Sodium: 99 mg / Fat: 19 g (Saturated Fat: 2 g) / Potassium: 622 mg.

TROPICAL PLEASURE

The exotic flavors of this salad will transport you to a tropical paradise. Wonderfully refreshing, this colorful medley of fruits comes to us from Phoenix, Arizona.

GERMAN HOT POTATO SALAD

Makes 12 Servings

4	pounds whole tiny new potatoes
6 to 8	slices bacon
3	tablespoons minced onion
½	cup sugar
½	cup vinegar
1½	cups water
1	teaspoon salt
¼	teaspoon pepper
2	tablespoons cornstarch

◆   ◆   ◆

Eleanor Grishkowsky often makes this salad to bring to various gatherings. She says that she always receives compliments. The recipe came from her grand-mother who brought it from Russia. Eleanor's mother made it, and now Eleanor is planning to pass along the recipe to her son and daughter-in-law. Our thanks to her for letting us share in this delicious piece of family history.

Eleanor Grishkowsky
Zion Luthern Church Cookbook
Zion Luthern Church
Beulah
NORTH DAKOTA

1 In a covered saucepan, cook the potatoes in boiling water for 15 to 20 minutes or just until tender. Drain well. Cool slightly; then slice.

2 Meanwhile, in a large skillet, cook the bacon until crisp. Drain, reserving *¼ cup* of the bacon drippings. Return the reserved drippings to the pan. Brown the onion in the drippings.

3 Add the sugar, vinegar, *1 cup* of the water, the salt and pepper to the browned onions.

4 In a small bowl, dissolve the cornstarch in the remaining *½ cup* water. Add to the onion mixture and cook until the mixture is clear, thickened and bubbly. Cook and stir for 2 minutes more.

5 Pour the hot mixture over the sliced, cooked potatoes. Add the crumbled bacon and, if desired, additional salt and pepper to taste.

 TIPS FROM OUR KITCHEN

For easier slicing, slice the potatoes before cooking them.

Cover and refrigerate any leftover salad. Heat before serving.

If you're only serving a few people, cut this recipe in half.

Nutrition Analysis (*Per Serving*): Calories: 204 / Cholesterol: 3 mg / Carbohydrates: 45 g / Protein: 4 g / Sodium: 240 mg / Fat: 2 g (Saturated Fat: 1 g) / Potassium: 645 mg.

HOT AND TANGY SIDE DISH

Here is a satisfying side dish that is as perfect served alongside a succulent pork or beef roast as it is a
hot dog or your favorite sandwich. Don't wait for a special occasion to prepare this salad!

24-HOUR SALAD

Makes 16 Servings
- 2 eggs, beaten
- 2 tablespoons sugar
- 2 tablespoons orange juice
- 2 tablespoons vinegar
- 1 tablespoon butter *or* margarine
- Dash salt
- 2 8-ounce cartons dairy sour cream
- 1 cup seedless grapes, halved
- 1 cup dried bananas
- 1 15¼-ounce can pineapple tidbits, drained
- 1 cup pitted bing cherries
- 1 cup finely chopped orange
- 1 cup cantaloupe balls
- 2 plums, sliced
- 2 cups miniature marshmallows
- Lettuce leaves

✦   ✦   ✦

Betty Kracht said that she brings 24-Hour Salad to all of the Little Egypt Council's potluck dinners. She first tasted the salad at a potluck dinner hosted by a different organization when Ethel Porter, a fellow member, presented the unique treat.

Betty Kracht
Favorite Recipes of
Little Egypt Council
The Little Egypt Council
Telephone Pioneers of America
Centralia
ILLINOIS

1 In a small saucepan, stir together the beaten eggs, sugar, orange juice and vinegar. Cook and stir over medium heat just until thickened. Immediately remove from heat and stir in the butter or margarine and salt. Cool.

2 Place the sour cream into a medium bowl. Gently fold the cooled egg mixture into the sour cream. Cover and refrigerate the dressing while you prepare the fruits.

3 In a large bowl, stir together the grapes, dried bananas, pineapple, cherries, orange, cantaloupe balls, plums and marshmallows.

4 Pour the chilled dressing over the fruit mixture; stir to coat. Cover and refrigerate the salad overnight.

5 To serve, spoon the salad onto lettuce-lined plates.

TIPS FROM OUR KITCHEN

When you are cooking the dressing, watch carefully. When the mixture starts to thicken, immediately remove the pan from heat. If the dressing cooks too long, the egg will curdle.

You can substitute reduced-fat sour cream or vanilla yogurt for the sour cream, and pineapple juice for the orange juice.

If desired, omit the dried bananas. Just before serving, slice two medium bananas and add them to the salad.

Many kinds of plums are available—mainly from June through September. You may want to try one of the following in this salad recipe: Ace, Casselman, Friar or Queen Ann. Let the plums ripen at room temperature, then refrigerate them up to five days.

Nutrition Analysis (*Per Serving*): Calories: 160 / Cholesterol: 41 mg / Carbohydrates: 20 g / Protein: 3 g / Sodium: 43 mg / Fat: 9 g (Saturated Fat: 5 g) / Potassium: 220 mg.

FRUITY MAKE-AHEAD DISH

If you are looking for a delicious, make-ahead salad, 24-Hour Salad is the answer. A cooked, sweet-tart dressing coats a splendid variety of fruits. Refrigerate overnight to allow the flavors to mingle and mellow.

SALADS & DRESSINGS

LAYERED SALAD

Makes 12 to 15 Servings

1	large head iceberg lettuce, torn into bite-size pieces (6 cups)
¼	teaspoon salt
⅛	teaspoon sugar
⅛	teaspoon pepper
6	hard-cooked eggs, sliced
1	10-ounce package frozen peas
½	pound bacon, cooked until crisp, drained and crumbled (10 slices)
2	cups shredded Swiss cheese (8 ounces)
1¼ to 1½	cups mayonnaise *or* salad dressing
1 to 3	green onions, sliced

Paprika

♦   ♦   ♦

Dolly Johnson, Director of Volunteer Services at Northwestern Memorial Hospital, told us about the projects that have benefited from the sales of <u>First There Must Be Food</u>. One such project is bedside bingo. Through the use of closed-circuit television, patients are able to play bingo from their hospital beds.

Food Services Department
<u>First There Must Be Food</u>
Northwestern Memorial Hospital
Chicago
ILLINOIS

1 Place *3 cups* of the lettuce in a salad bowl. Sprinkle with *⅛ teaspoon* of the salt, the sugar and the pepper.

2 Stand some egg slices decoratively against the side of the salad bowl. Cover the lettuce with the remaining egg slices. Sprinkle with the remaining salt.

3 Sprinkle the frozen peas over the eggs. Top with the remaining lettuce.

4 Sprinkle the bacon over the lettuce, and the shredded Swiss cheese over the bacon.

5 Carefully spread the mayonnaise or salad dressing evenly over the salad. Top with the green onions and sprinkle with paprika. Cover and chill for 2 to 24 hours. Toss the salad at the table before serving.

 TIPS FROM OUR KITCHEN

This salad will completely fill a 3-quart casserole. Therefore, you'll need at least a 4-quart bowl to allow room for tossing the salad.

To tailor this recipe to suit your own preferences, try substituting or adding shredded carrots, alfalfa sprouts, sweet green or red pepper, onion, broccoli or cauliflower. You might also vary the kind of cheese you use or include a layer of julienned ham or turkey. Instead of the iceberg lettuce, try red-tipped leaf lettuce or fresh spinach.

The easy way to produce perfect egg slices is to use an egg slicer, a gadget specifically designed for this purpose.

To crisp-cook this amount of bacon with no fuss or spatter, place the slices on a rack in a shallow baking pan. Bake, uncovered, in a 400° oven about 20 minutes or until crisp. Or, if you wish to use your microwave oven, place the bacon on a microwave-safe rack or a plate lined with paper towels. Cover with paper towels. Cook on 100% power (high) until done. Allow 4 to 5 minutes for 6 slices.

You can flavor the mayonnaise dressing with ½ teaspoon crushed dried tarragon or basil or 2 to 3 teaspoons lemon juice.

Nutrition Analysis (*Per Serving*): Calories: 324 / Cholesterol: 142 mg / Carbohydrates: 5 g / Protein: 12 g / Sodium: 358 mg / Fat: 29 g (Saturated Fat: 8 g) / Potassium: 187 mg.

TERRIFIC TIERS

Easy to make and always welcome, layered salads are an adaptable basic that can be tailored to suit
your preferences. Here, bacon, hard-cooked eggs, Swiss cheese, iceberg lettuce and peas
are in the flavorful lineup.

TABOULI

◆   ◆   ◆

*Beth Yohe's recipe for Tabouli came
from several different recipes that
she combined to create one to
"suit her own tastes." Beth em-
ployed this recipe when she taught
a food preparation course at the
local Jewish Community Center.
She suggests serving the salad on
a bed of curly lettuce to enhance
the presentation of the dish.*

Beth Yohe
Best of Friends
Friends of the Maitland
Public Library
Maitland
FLORIDA

1 In a large bowl, combine the bulgur, cucumber, tomato, sweet green pepper and green onion. Set aside.

2 In a small bowl, stir together the parsley, olive oil, lemon juice, water, mint, salt and pepper.

3 Add the parsley mixture to the bulgur mixture and toss to mix. Cover and refrigerate for 4 to 24 hours. Serve the tabouli on a bed of leaf lettuce.

 TIPS FROM OUR KITCHEN

Bulgur (or bulghur) is a parched, cracked wheat product made by soaking, cooking and then drying whole wheat kernels. Five percent of the bran is then removed from the dried, hard wheat kernels, and the remaining kernels are cracked into small pieces. Bulgur is dark tan in color and has a nutty flavor. Store bulgur in an airtight container in a cool, dry place up to 6 months, or indefinitely in the freezer.

Be sure not to purchase cracked wheat breakfast cereal in place of bulgur.

Tabouli (or tabbouleh) is a Middle Eastern dish that can be served on pieces of pita, as an eat-with-a-fork salad or as a dip with celery or sweet green pepper wedges.

Use fresh lemon juice in this recipe, if possible. You'll need 2 medium lemons for ⅓ cup fresh lemon juice. Look for well-shaped fruits with smooth, evenly yellow skin. To get the most juice, choose fruits that are heavy for their size. Leave the lemons at room temperature for about 30 minutes, then roll gently under the palm of your hand. Or, cut the lemons in half and heat in microwave oven on 100% power (high) for 30 to 45 seconds before juicing.

An easy way to snip the parsley and mint is to place the fresh herbs in a deep container, such as a 1-cup glass measure, then snip with kitchen shears.

Nutrition Analysis: (*Per Serving*): Calories: 260 / Cholesterol: 0 mg / Carbohydrates: 23 g Protein: 4 g / Sodium: 55 mg / Fat: 19 g (Saturated Fat: 3 g) / Potassium: 321 mg.

WHOLE GRAIN SALAD

This classic Middle Eastern salad features bulgur (a precooked, cracked wheat product) and an assortment of garden vegetables in a minty lemon and oil dressing.

CAULIFLOWER SALAD

Makes 6 Servings

1 pound cauliflower, broken into flowerets and thinly sliced into bite-size pieces (4 cups)
1 cup thinly sliced radishes
1 bunch green onions, thinly sliced (½ cup)
½ cup sliced, pitted ripe olives
½ cup chopped watercress
1 8-ounce carton dairy sour cream
1½ tablespoons lemon juice
1 tablespoon grated Parmesan cheese
1 clove garlic, minced
¼ teaspoon salt
⅛ teaspoon pepper
Dash ground red pepper

♦   ♦   ♦

When Barbara Lewis lived in California, she and her husband attended a potluck Christmas party, where she tasted a fellow party goer's Cauliflower Salad. Barbara asked for the recipe. Now, when the Ladies of the Ribbon have their two annual cookouts, this is the dish Barbara brings every time!

Barbara Lewis
<u>**Pot Luck From Ladies**</u>
<u>**of the Ribbon**</u>
Ladies of the Ribbon
Bradenton
FLORIDA

1 In a large bowl, combine the cauliflower, radishes, onions, olives and watercress. Toss gently and set aside.

2 In a blender container, combine the sour cream, lemon juice, Parmesan cheese, garlic, salt, pepper and red pepper. Cover and blend well.

3 Pour the dressing over the vegetables, tossing to coat. Cover and refrigerate up to 2 hours.

 TIPS FROM OUR KITCHEN

To prepare fresh cauliflower: Rinse the entire head under cold water. Remove and discard the outer green leaves. Using a knife, remove and discard the woody stem. Break or cut the flowerets from the head.

If desired, you can use broccoli for all or part of the cauliflower in this recipe. If watercress isn't available, substitute finely snipped spinach.

The leaves and stems of watercress, while delicate in appearance, have a lively, peppery tang. When shopping, choose watercress with healthy-looking stems and bright green leaves. Clean watercress by dunking it in a large bowl of cold water. Repeat with fresh water until no more sand or dirt collects in the bowl. Pat dry. Store in a plastic bag with a paper towel.

This salad can be made up to 24 hours before serving. If you plan to do so, however, wait to add the watercress until just before serving since it has a tendency to release water into the salad.

Light sour cream can be used instead of regular sour cream.

Garnish the salad with radish roses or radish accordions and additional watercress. Or, try garnishing with a green onion brush. To make an onion brush, use just the green portion of green onion and make slashes at both ends of the onion to make fringes. Place in ice water to curl the ends.

Nutrition Analysis (*Per Serving*): Calories: 124 / Cholesterol: 18 mg / Carbohydrates: 7 g / Protein: 4 g / Sodium: 197 mg / Fat: 10 g (Saturated Fat: 5 g) / Potassium: 387 mg.

TAKE-ALONG DISH

Take Cauliflower Salad to your next potluck supper and watch it disappear. Radishes and watercress lend a peppery flavor to the salad while the sour cream-based dressing smooths out the taste.

CONFETTI RICE SALAD

Makes 6 Servings

⅔	cup long grain rice
¼	teaspoon salt
2	tablespoons snipped parsley
1 to 2	tablespoons snipped fresh dill
½	teaspoon finely shredded lemon peel
2	tablespoons lemon juice
2	tablespoons water
2	tablespoons olive oil
1	teaspoon Dijon-style mustard
⅛	teaspoon pepper
1	cup finely chopped yellow summer squash
1	cup small broccoli flowerets
3	radishes, thinly sliced
1	green onion, thinly sliced

◆　◆　◆

While visiting the Bahamas years ago, Gloria Pattison tried to prepare the original version of this dish but was unable to find several ingredients. To solve the problem, she substituted yellow squash and radishes—along with a few other ingredients—and the result was this tasty version of Confetti Rice Salad.

Gloria Pattison
<u>A Dunker Cookbook</u>
**The North County Church
of the Brethren
San Marcos
CALIFORNIA**

1 In a small saucepan, combine 1½ cups *water*, the rice and salt. Bring to a boil; reduce heat to low. Cover and cook for 20 minutes.

2 Transfer the cooked rice to a sieve. Rinse the rice under cold water. Drain and set aside.

3 In a large bowl, stir together the parsley, dill, lemon peel, lemon juice, the 2 tablespoons water, the olive oil, Dijon-style mustard and pepper.

4 Add the rice, yellow summer squash, broccoli, radishes and green onion. Toss until the mixture is well coated. Cover and chill for 4 to 24 hours, stirring occasionally.

 TIPS FROM OUR KITCHEN

For a change, substitute halved cherry tomatoes or chopped red sweet pepper for the radishes. Or, replace part of the yellow summer squash with chopped yellow sweet peppers.

If fresh dill isn't available, you can use 1 to 2 teaspoons dried dillweed.

To make fun and attractive individual serving bowls, wash and remove the stems and seeds from 3 large or 6 small green, red or yellow sweet peppers. Cut the larger peppers in half lengthwise. Spoon in the salad.

If desired, blanch the broccoli before adding it to the salad. Blanching makes the broccoli more tender and brings out the bright green color.

To get flowerets, trim the leaves from the broccoli and wash it under cold, running water. Cut off just the flowerets with a sharp knife. Reserve the stalks to use later in soups and casseroles.

Nutrition Analysis (*Per Serving*): Calories: 129 / Cholesterol: 0 mg / Carbohydrates: 19 g / Protein: 3 g / Sodium: 121 mg / Fat: 5 g (Saturated Fat: 1 g) / Potassium: 160 mg.

EASY, COLORFUL AND TASTY

It's no surprise that this colorful rice and vegetable salad is from sunny San Marcos, California. Cooked long grain rice is highlighted by yellow summer squash, broccoli and radishes. The lively flavors of lemon, Dijon-style mustard and fresh dill complete this easy and tasty dish.

SALADS & DRESSINGS

MARINATED COLESLAW

6 to 8	cups shredded cabbage
1	cup shredded carrot
½	cup chopped green sweet pepper (optional)
¼ to ⅓	cup sugar
½	teaspoon unflavored gelatin
¼	cup cider vinegar
2	tablespoons cold water
⅓	cup salad oil
1	teaspoon celery seed
¼	teaspoon salt
⅛	teaspoon pepper
¼	cup dairy sour cream

◆   ◆   ◆

Lorraine Stumbo and two of her neighbors had an annual Christmas cookie baking session during which they would bake, eat and "solve all the problems of the world." While they were baking, eating and solving, they were also sharing recipes. It was during one of the sessions, about ten years ago, that Lorraine was given the recipe for Marinated Coleslaw. Lorraine tells us that this salad is a great way for her to use up her garden's bounty.

Lorraine Stumbo
Country Collection
Bethel Church
Ogden
IOWA

1 In a large bowl, toss together the cabbage, carrot and, if desired, chopped pepper. Set aside.

2 In a small saucepan, stir together the sugar and gelatin. Add the vinegar and water. Bring to a boil, stirring constantly. Remove from heat and cool.

3 Pour the cooled dressing into a blender container. Add the salad oil, celery seed, salt and pepper; cover and blend well. Add the sour cream and blend just until combined.

4 Pour the dressing over the vegetables and toss to coat. Before serving, cover and refrigerate for several hours or overnight.

 TIPS FROM OUR KITCHEN

For a more colorful salad, try using a mixture of red and green cabbage and/or red, green and yellow sweet pepper.

There is no need to soften the gelatin in this recipe because mixing it with the sugar will ensure that the gelatin will not clump when the water is added.

This coleslaw is a perfect dish to take along on a picnic, but make sure that you keep it on ice in your cooler so that it doesn't spoil.

Nutrition Analysis *(Per Serving)*: Calories: 113 / Cholesterol: 3 mg / Carbohydrates: 10 g / Protein: 1 g / Sodium: 71 mg / Fat: 9 g (Saturated Fat: 2 g) / Potassium: 190 mg.

DUTCH TREAT

Although the term coleslaw comes from the Dutch word *oosla* meaning *cool cabbage*, shredded
vegetable salad has become an all-American favorite. Try this delicious version brought to
us by Lorraine Stumbo of Ogden, Iowa.

FOUR BEAN SALAD

1   medium green sweet
     pepper, seeded and thinly
     sliced into rings
1   medium onion, thinly
     sliced and separated into
     rings
1   16-ounce can green beans,
     drained
1   15-ounce can cut yellow
     wax beans, rinsed and
     drained
1   15½-ounce can garbanzo
     beans, rinsed and drained
1   15½-ounce can red kidney
     beans, rinsed and drained
Dressing:
½   cup white wine vinegar
⅓   cup salad oil
⅓   cup sugar
2   tablespoons snipped parsley
1   teaspoon dry mustard
1   teaspoon dried basil,
     crushed
½   teaspoon dried tarragon,
     crushed
¼   teaspoon salt
Romaine, washed, drained and
     separated into leaves

◆   ◆   ◆

*Dee Daniels says she discovered
this great recipe about twenty-
seven years ago when she was
living in California.*

Dee Daniels
<u>*There's More to Lima than Beans*</u>
The Lima and Allen County
Medical Alliance
Lima
OHIO

1 Cut the green sweet pepper and onion rings in half, reserving *2* whole pepper rings for a garnish.

2 In a large bowl, stir together the drained green beans, yellow wax beans, garbanzo beans, red kidney beans, the green sweet pepper ring halves and the onion ring halves.

3 To make the dressing: In a glass jar with a tight fitting lid, combine the wine vinegar, salad oil, sugar, parsley, dry mustard, basil, tarragon and salt. Cover and shake to blend the ingredients.

4 Drizzle the dressing over the bean mixture. Cover and refrigerate the salad for several hours or overnight, stirring once or twice.

5 Remove the bottom stems from the romaine leaves. Line a salad bowl with the romaine; set aside.

6 Before serving, stir the salad again; drain.

7 To serve, spoon the drained bean salad into the romaine-lined bowl. Garnish with the reserved green sweet pepper rings.

 TIPS FROM OUR KITCHEN

For a change of pace, you can use frozen Italian beans that have been cooked and drained or canned black beans that have been drained and rinsed in place of one of the beans in this recipe. As another variation, add canned whole kernel corn that has been drained to the salad.

Rinsing canned beans helps to remove some of the salt added during the canning process.

In place of the romaine, you can use leaf lettuce, butterhead, spinach or red cabbage to line the salad bowl.

Nutrition Analysis (*Per Serving*): Calories: 203 / Cholesterol: 0 mg / Carbohydrates: 27 g / Protein: 4 g / Sodium: 330 mg / Fat: 10 g (Saturated Fat: 1 g) / Potassium: 322 mg.

Potluck Salad Favorite

Dee Daniels brings us a delicious version of everybody's favorite picnic and potluck salad. Dried mustard, tarragon and basil flavor the tangy dressing that covers a delicious mélange of beans.

SALADS & DRESSINGS

SNOW PEA SPLENDOR

Makes 8 Servings
¼ cup sesame seed
½ cup salad oil
2 tablespoons lemon juice
2 tablespoons vinegar
2 tablespoons sugar
1 clove garlic, crushed
½ teaspoon salt
1 pound fresh pea pods
4 slices bacon
4 cups shredded lettuce
½ cup snipped parsley

✦   ✦   ✦

For a time, Faye Bullock and her husband ran a lodge in western United States. There, she gained a reputation as an innovative and inspiring cook who loved to try new things. We're sure you'll be inspired by her Snow Pea Splendor.

Faye Bullock
<u>Paths of Sunshine</u>
Florida Federations of Garden Clubs, Inc.
Winter Park
FLORIDA

1 To toast the sesame seed, spread them in a thin layer in a shallow ungreased baking pan. Bake in a 350° oven for 10 to 15 minutes or until golden, stirring once or twice. In a glass jar with a tight-fitting lid, combine the toasted sesame seed, salad oil, lemon juice, vinegar, sugar, garlic and salt. Cover and refrigerate.

2 Remove the stems from the pea pods. Steam 30 seconds. Cover and chill.

3 Fry the bacon until crisp. Drain on paper towels, then crumble.

4 In a large salad bowl, toss the lettuce, parsley, pea pods and bacon. Shake the dressing until well blended. Pour the desired amount of dressing over the salad; toss. Serve immediately.

 TIPS FROM OUR KITCHEN

If you have leftover dressing, store it in the refrigerator to use another day. It makes a delicious dressing for spinach salad or cooked green beans.

To make carrot cutouts, thinly slice a large carrot. Use a small canape cutter to make flower shapes.

Nutrition Analysis (*Per Serving*): Calories: 205 / Cholesterol: 3 mg / Carbohydrates: 10 g / Protein: 4 g / Sodium: 191 mg / Fat: 17 g (Saturated Fat: 3 g) / Potassium: 225 mg.

DELICIOUS SIDE DISH

Toasted sesame seed and bacon give this easy-to-prepare salad from the Sunshine State its robust flavor. Folks will surely ask for more.

CARROT SALAD

Makes 8 to 10 Servings

2 pounds carrots, thinly sliced (about 6 cups)
2 medium onions, thinly sliced and separated into rings
1 green sweet pepper, sliced into thin strips

Marinade:
1 10¾-ounce can condensed tomato soup
¾ cup vinegar
⅔ cup sugar
⅓ cup cooking oil
1 teaspoon Worcestershire sauce
1 teaspoon prepared mustard
¼ teaspoon salt

◆   ◆   ◆

Jean Farinacci has the recipe for Carrot Salad (also called Copper Pennies) tucked away in her files and occasionally she uses it for "salad suppers for a different and interesting tangy taste." She recommends that the salad accompany roast beef.

Jean Farinacci
The Market Basket
Witan
Akron
OHIO

1 In a large saucepan, cook the carrots in a small amount of *water* about 8 minutes or just until tender. Remove from heat; drain.

2 In a large mixing bowl or salad bowl, stir together the cooked carrots, onions and green sweet pepper; set aside.

3 To make the marinade: In a medium bowl, stir together the undiluted tomato soup, vinegar, sugar, cooking oil, Worcestershire sauce, mustard and salt.

4 Pour the marinade over the vegetables. Stir to coat the vegetables with the marinade. Cover and refrigerate for 4 hours or overnight, stirring occasionally. Drain and discard the marinade before serving.

 TIPS FROM OUR KITCHEN

Two pounds of carrots will yield about 6 cups of ¼-inch-thick slices. For faster slicing, use your food processor.

If desired, substitute yellow sweet pepper for half or all of the green sweet pepper in this recipe.

Either cider vinegar or white vinegar can be used in this recipe. You might also want to experiment with flavored vinegars, such as basil or garlic vinegar.

For party serving, chop the green sweet pepper and onion instead of slicing them. Then, serve the salad in halved and seeded green or yellow sweet peppers.

Nutrition Analysis (*Per Serving*): Calories: 107 / Cholesterol: 0 mg / Carbohydrates: 19 g / Protein: 2 g / Sodium: 143 mg / Fat: 3 g (Saturated Fat: 1 g) / Potassium: 315 mg.

CROWD APPEAL

This surefire crowd-pleasing dish will have everyone asking "Who made the Carrot Salad?" The next immediate question will be "Can I have the recipe?" But you don't have to tell anyone how easy it is—just smile and enjoy the compliments.

ASHVILLE SALAD

Makes 8 to 10 Servings

1	10¾-ounce can condensed tomato soup
1⅓	cups water
1	8-ounce package cream cheese, cut up
2	envelopes unflavored gelatin
½	cup cold water
1	cup mayonnaise
1½	cups finely chopped celery
¼	cup finely chopped sweet green pepper
3	large hard-cooked eggs, finely chopped
6	stuffed green olives, finely chopped
½	teaspoon dried minced onion
¼	teaspoon salt
⅛	teaspoon pepper

Watercress *or* shredded leaf lettuce
Hard-cooked eggs, finely chopped (optional)
Stuffed green olives, finely chopped (optional)

◆ ◆ ◆

<u>*Bell's Best*</u> *is the major fundraiser for many of the Telephone Pioneers' projects including Project Aware and Youths Against Drugs, among others.*

Evelyn Anderson
<u>*Bell's Best*</u>
Telephone Pioneers of America
Mississippi Chapter No. 36
Jackson
MISSISSIPPI

1 In a saucepan, combine the tomato soup and the 1⅓ cups water. Heat to boiling; reduce heat and add the cream cheese. Simmer, stirring constantly, until the cream cheese is softened and the mixture is almost smooth. Remove from heat. Beat with a wire whisk or a rotary beater until the mixture is thoroughly blended.

2 Soften the gelatin in the ½ cup cold water for 5 minutes. Add the gelatin mixture to the hot soup mixture, stirring until the gelatin is dissolved.

3 Cool for 15 minutes. Then, if necessary, place in the refrigerator until the mixture is partially set (the consistency of unbeaten egg whites).

4 Whisk in the mayonnaise. Carefully fold in the chopped celery, green pepper, chopped eggs, olives, dried onion, salt and pepper. Pour into a lightly oiled 1½-quart mold. Cover and refrigerate until firm, about 6 hours or overnight.

5 Line a serving plate with watercress or lettuce. Unmold the salad on top of the greens and garnish with additional chopped hard-cooked egg and chopped olives, if desired.

TIPS FROM OUR KITCHEN

Make this a keep-one, share-one salad by using two loaf pans or two 3-cup molds.

The flavor and texture of this salad nicely complement seafood.

Chopped vegetables or fruits will stay evenly distributed throughout a gelatin salad if you chill the gelatin mixture until it's partially set—a consistency similar to beaten egg whites—before adding the solid ingredients.

Nutrition Analysis (*Per Serving*): Calories: 370 / Cholesterol: 127 mg / Carbohydrates: 9 g Protein: 8 g / Sodium: 708 mg / Fat: 35 g (Saturated Fat: 10 g) Potassium: 301 mg.

MOLDED TO TASTE

The next time your menu calls for a tangy salad, try this one. Celery, green pepper, hard-cooked eggs, olives and onion add flavor and crunch to the tomato soup, cream cheese-gelatin base.

SPECIAL OCCASION CRANBERRIES

Makes 12 Servings

 1 8-ounce can crushed
    pineapple (juice packed)
Pineapple juice
 2 3-ounce packages *or* one 6-
    ounce package raspberry-
    flavored gelatin
 1 cup *boiling* water
 1 cup *cold* water
 1 cup whole berry cranberry
    sauce
 1 cup chopped walnuts *or*
    pecans
 ¾ cup finely chopped celery
 1 medium apple, cored and
    finely chopped (⅔ cup)
 ¾ cup seedless red grapes,
    quartered
Cream Cheese Sauce:
 1 3-ounce package cream
    cheese, softened
 2 tablespoons powdered sugar
 ½ teaspoon vanilla
Milk

◆   ◆   ◆

*Special Occasion Cranberries
provides a sampling of the wonderful finds in the <u>New Brighton
Sesquicentennial Cook Book
Sampler</u>.*

Mrs. George (Gladys) Preston
<u>*1838-1988 New Brighton*</u>
<u>*Sesquicentennial Cook Book*</u>
<u>*Sampler*</u>
*New Brighton Sesquicentennial
Committee
New Brighton
PENNSYLVANIA*

1 Drain the pineapple, reserving the juice. Add enough of the additional pineapple juice to make *1 cup*. Set aside.

2 In a large bowl, dissolve the gelatin in the boiling water. Stir in the 1 cup pineapple juice, the cold water and the cranberry sauce. Chill until the mixture is partially set (consistency of unbeaten egg whites), stirring occasionally.

3 Fold in the pineapple, walnuts or pecans, celery, apple and grapes. Pour into a 2- or 3-quart rectangular baking dish. Cover and chill about 4 hours or until firm.

4 To make the Cream Cheese Sauce: In a small bowl, stir together the cream cheese, powdered sugar, vanilla and enough milk to make a creamy consistency.

5 To serve, cut the gelatin-cranberry mixture into squares or spoon into individual glass dishes. Pass the Cream Cheese Sauce.

 TIPS FROM OUR KITCHEN

This gelatin salad has a high proportion of solids—too many to try to make it as a molded salad.

For a deep salad, use the 2-quart baking dish. For more surface area, use a 3-quart dish. If you are taking this salad to a potluck, prepare it in a 13x9x2-inch pan with a lid.

Place the bowl of gelatin in a large bowl of ice water to speed chilling to the partially set stage.

If the gelatin mixture gets too firm, before you fold in the nuts and fruit, place the bowl in a pan of hot water and stir the gelatin to melt it slightly.

Nutrition Analysis (*Per Serving*): Calories: 212 / Cholesterol: 8 mg / Carbohydrates: 32 g / Protein: 4 g / Sodium: 74 mg / Fat: 9 g (Saturated Fat: 2 g) / Potassium: 163 mg.

WHAT'S IN A NAME?

There's plenty "special" about this salad besides its name. The raspberry-flavored gelatin holds a scrumptious array of crunchy, sweet-tart ingredients. Topped with the cream cheese sauce for extra flavor, this cool refresher is a perfect addition to your next holiday dinner.

SALADS & DRESSINGS

365

SALAD NIÇOISE

Makes 8 Servings

- 8 tiny new potatoes (about ¾ pound)
- 2½ cups green beans, cooked to crisp-tender and drained (1 pound fresh)
- 1 small red onion, sliced
- ½ cup Niçoise olives *or* ripe olives
- ¼ cup snipped Italian parsley *or* regular parsley
- ½ teaspoon salt
- ½ teaspoon pepper
- ¼ cup red wine vinegar
- 1 tablespoon Dijon-style mustard
- 1 teaspoon sugar
- ¼ teaspoon salt
- ¼ teaspoon pepper
- 1 tablespoon finely snipped parsley *or* chives
- ½ cup olive oil
- 8 ripe Italian plum tomatoes, quartered
- 4 hard-cooked eggs, halved *or* sliced
- 1 12- or 13-ounce can water-packed tuna, drained

♦ ♦ ♦

Donna DeBoer says that she often makes Salad Niçoise for her family to take on their boat as delicious fare for hot summer nights.

Donna DeBoer
<u>*International Cookbook*</u>
Pamoja International Cultural Exchange, Inc.
Helena
NEW YORK

1 Cook the potatoes in salted boiling water about 10 minutes or until just tender. Drain. Cut the potatoes into quarters and place in a large bowl.

2 Stir in the green beans, onion, olives, parsley, the ½ teaspoon salt and the ½ teaspoon pepper.

3 To make the vinaigrette: In a small bowl, whisk together the vinegar, mustard, sugar, the ¼ teaspoon salt, the ¼ teaspoon pepper and the parsley or chives. Gradually whisk in the olive oil. Continue whisking until the mixture thickens slightly.

4 Pour about *half* of the vinaigrette over the vegetable mixture and toss gently.

5 Transfer the vegetable mixture to a large serving platter. Arrange the tomatoes and eggs around the edge of the platter. Flake the tuna and spoon it on top of the vegetable mixture. Drizzle the entire salad with the remaining vinaigrette. Serve immediately.

TIPS FROM OUR KITCHEN

Niçoise olives are dark brown, tiny, brine-cured and packed in olive oil.

Salad Niçoise is traditionally served at room temperature, although you can chill it if you prefer. Of course, be sure to refrigerate any leftovers.

To prepare the fresh green beans: Wash and remove the ends and strings. Cook, covered, in a small amount of boiling water for 20 to 25 minutes.

You can substitute two 9-ounce packages of frozen cut green beans for the fresh beans in the recipe. Cook them according to the package directions.

Hard-cooked eggs sometimes have a harmless, but unattractive greenish ring around the yolk or are difficult to peel. To minimize these possibilities, place the eggs in a single layer in a saucepan. Add cold water to a level 1 inch above the eggs. Bring to a boil over high heat. Reduce the heat so that the water is just below simmering. Cover and cook for 15 minutes. Drain the eggs immediately and cool them in an ice-water bath.

Nutrition Analysis (*Per Serving*): Calories: 301 / Cholesterol: 124 mg / Carbohydrates: 18 g Protein: 17 g / Sodium: 498 mg / Fat: 19 g (Saturated Fat: 3 g) / Potassium: 551 mg.

ONE-DISH LUNCH

Donna DeBoer of Suffern, New York, brings us a superb recipe for a one-dish lunch. New potatoes, fresh green beans, plum tomatoes, red onion and olives are teamed up with hard-cooked eggs and tuna. Drizzle with a tangy vinaigrette, add some crispy French bread and...c'est tout!

SESAME SEED DRESSING

Makes 2 Cups

2 to 4 tablespoons sugar
¼ teaspoon paprika
¼ teaspoon salt
¼ teaspoon Worcestershire sauce
⅛ teaspoon dry mustard
½ cup salad oil
¼ cup cider vinegar
1 teaspoon grated onion
2 tablespoons toasted sesame seed

♦   ♦   ♦

"Although in many ways we're an old-fashioned town, we're not old fashioned in our food tastes," writes Leslie Cannon of the Junior League. *"Cincinnati is a restaurant town. We have the Maisonette, which has been a 5-star restaurant for decades and the Gourmet Room, which is often a 5-star restaurant." Also there are funky little places like Mullanes, where they serve a delicious sesame dressing and have a tarot card reader come to your table! We don't know if this dressing is similar to the one they serve at Mullanes, but it's "in the cards" that you'll love it.*

Cincinnati Celebrates
The Junior League of Cincinnati
OHIO

1 In a small bowl, combine the sugar, paprika, salt, Worcestershire sauce and dry mustard.

2 Using an electric mixer beat constantly with an electric mixer, while alternately adding the oil and vinegar to the spice mixture.

3 Stir the onion and the toasted sesame seeds into the dressing.

TIPS FROM OUR KITCHEN

To toast sesame seed, spread them in a thin layer in a shallow, ungreased pan. Toast the seeds in a 350° oven for 10 to 15 minutes or until they are golden, stirring the seeds once or twice.

To save time and effort, make this dressing ahead and store it in a screw-top jar in the refrigerator. Then just shake the dressing well before pouring it over a salad.

To prevent the bowl from slipping while you mix, place a wet washcloth under the bowl.

Nutrition Analysis (*Per Tablespoon*): Calories: 96 / Cholesterol: 0 mg / Carbohydrates: 3 g / Protein: 0 g / Sodium: 46 mg / Fat: 10 g (Saturated Fat: 1 g) / Potassium: 13 mg.

DOUBLE-DUTY DRESSING

This versatile dressing, sweet to taste and fragrant with toasted sesame seeds, comes from the Junior League of Cincinnati. When topping vegetables, we suggest using only two tablespoons of sugar; if you want to sprinkle it over fruit, increase the sugar to four tablespoons. Either way, it's a winner!

EGG MUSTARD DRESSING

Makes 1 Cup

- 2 hard-cooked eggs
- 2 tablespoons cider vinegar
- 1 tablespoon Creole mustard
- 1 tablespoon mayonnaise *or* salad dressing
- ½ teaspoon garlic powder
- ½ teaspoon Worcestershire sauce
- ¼ teaspoon salt
- ¼ teaspoon celery salt *or* onion salt
- ½ cup safflower oil
- Slices of cooked crumbled bacon (optional)

◆   ◆   ◆

The Women's Volunteer Committee's purpose is to encourage community support for the New Orleans Museum of Art. In turn, the Museum provides educational programs, a superb art collection which is exhibited in its galleries and exhibitions of rare and precious objects from major collections in the USA and abroad. All proceeds from the sale of <u>Artist's Palate Cookbook</u> benefit the museum.

<u>*Artist's Palate Cookbook*</u>
Women's Volunteer Committee
New Orleans Museum of Art
New Orleans
LOUISIANA

1 Separate the hard-cooked egg whites and yolks. Finely chop the whites and refrigerate until needed to garnish the salad.

2 In a blender or food processor, combine the egg yolks, vinegar, mustard, mayonnaise, garlic powder, Worcestershire sauce, salt and celery salt or onion salt. Blend until the egg yolks are well mixed.

3 Slowly add the safflower oil. Process until thoroughly combined and the mixture has a smooth consistency. Serve immediately or cover and store in the refrigerator up to 3 days.

TIPS FROM OUR KITCHEN

If you prefer spicy dressings, you can substitute any spicy mustard for the Creole mustard.

When you dress a salad with this dressing, add a few slices of cooked, crumbled bacon to the salad just before tossing. Or, you might want to serve this dressing on the side. Just before serving, place the dressing in a serving bowl and sprinkle the reserved finely chopped hard-cooked egg white and some crumbled bacon on the top.

Try serving Egg Mustard Dressing on cooked, chilled asparagus; assorted mixed greens or spinach salad.

Nutrition Analysis *(Per Tablespoon)*: Calories: 77 / Cholesterol: 27 mg / Carbohydrates: 0 g / Protein: 1 g / Sodium: 85 mg / Fat: 8 g (Saturated Fat: 1 g) / Potassium: 14 mg.

ZESTY ADDITION

This smooth and tangy dressing from New Orleans, Louisianna, gives a flavorful touch of mustard to potato salad. The dressing also doubles as a sauce for meat, poultry, fish or vegetables.

Soups & Stews

*Y*our nose knows when soup's on. These recipes will fill your kitchen with all the aromas of good cooking, and your family will fill their tummies with flavorful, satisfying soups and stews. You'll find regional favorites like Manhattan Clam Chowder and Buck's Eastern Carolina Brunswick Stew. Several recipes have an ethnic background, such as Wonton Soup, Homemade Minestrone, and Tortilla Soup.

CAMP CHOWDER

Makes 4 Servings
- 4   slices bacon
- 1   cup chopped onions
- 4   potatoes (1¼ pounds) cooked, and cubed
- 2   6½-ounce cans minced clams, undrained
- ¼   teaspoon pepper
- 2   cups whole milk

✦   ✦   ✦

The mission of the Idaho Network For Children—a chapter of the National Committee for Prevention of Child Abuse—is to "acknowledge and prevent child abuse through the committed actions of Idaho's citizens." Carolyn Murphy, Executive Director, tells us education is the major focus of the organization. In addition to workshops, parenting groups and educational programs, the members of the Idaho Network have put together a cookbook designed to encourage a positive experience between parents and their children. Proceeds from cookbook sales are used to help support the organization's programs.

<u>Kids Edibles</u>
Idaho Network for Children
Boise
IDAHO

1 In a large saucepan, cook the bacon until crisp. Remove the bacon and place on paper towels to drain. Reserve *1 tablespoon* of the bacon drippings in the saucepan.

2 Crumble the bacon and set aside.

3 Cook the onion in the reserved drippings until the onion is tender but not brown. Add the potatoes, undrained clams and pepper. Heat just to boiling.

4 Add the milk and heat through; do not boil. Ladle the soup into individual soup bowls or mugs and sprinkle each serving with bacon.

TIPS FROM OUR KITCHEN

To make this chowder easier to prepare when camping, use one 15-ounce can of evaporated milk and ½ cup water instead of the whole milk.

If you are camping, you might want to save time and fuel by cooking enough bacon for the next day's breakfast at the same time you cook the bacon for the chowder. Allow the cooked bacon to cool; then wrap and store it in your cooler. Reheat in the morning.

For a flavor variation, you can add ¼ teaspoon of dried thyme with the potatoes, clams and pepper.

You can save time by not peeling the potatoes before cooking and cubing them. Just scrub thoroughly under running water.

Nutrition Analysis *(Per Serving)*: Calories: 312 / Cholesterol: 79 mg / Carbohydrates: 45 g / Protein: 17 g / Sodium: 220 mg / Fat: 8 g (Saturated Fat: 4 g) / Potassium: 992 mg.

Campfire Cuisine

Fill your home or campsite with the aroma of this easy-to-prepare clam chowder. Rich and satisfying,
it is a great way to end a day outdoors.

SOUPS & STEWS

375

PARMESAN CORN CHOWDER

Makes 6 to 8 Servings

2 cups chopped peeled potato
½ cup thinly sliced carrot
½ cup thinly sliced celery
¼ cup chopped onion
¼ teaspoon pepper
¼ cup margarine *or* butter
¼ cup all-purpose flour
2 cups milk
1 cup freshly grated Parmesan cheese
1 17-ounce can cream-style corn

◆   ◆   ◆

The All Saints' Episcopal Church began in the 1860s with a small group of individuals gathering for worship in local homes. About thirty years later, they were recognized as the All Saints' Episcopal Church. In 1969, the group merged with a small mission church and erected the present church; since that time, the congregation has grown to four hundred communicants. <u>The Churchmouse Cookbook</u> was created to raise funds for the church's many community projects.

Vera McIntosh
<u>The Churchmouse Cookbook</u>
All Saints' Episcopal Churchwomen
Concord
NORTH CAROLINA

1 In a large Dutch oven, stir together 2 cups *water*, the potato, carrot, celery, onion and pepper. Bring to a boil. Reduce heat; cover and simmer for 10 minutes.

2 Meanwhile, in a large saucepan, melt the margarine or butter. Stir in the flour. Add the milk all at once. Cook and stir over medium heat until the mixture is thickened and bubbly. Cook and stir for 1 minute more.

3 Add the cheese, stirring until it is melted. Carefully add the cheese mixture to vegetable mixture. Stir in the corn. Heat the soup through, stirring occasionally. *Do not boil.*

 TIPS FROM OUR KITCHEN

Freshly grated Parmesan cheese will melt better and give the soup a smoother texture than prepackaged Parmesan. You can use a food processor or grate it by rubbing a piece of cheese over a grater. A hand grater has tiny punched holes and rough, irregular edges, unlike the larger holes or smooth-edged slits of a shredder. For 1 cup of grated cheese, you'll need 4 ounces of ungrated Parmesan cheese.

Chowder usually designates a thick soup made with milk. Do the final heating over a medium to low heat to avoid boiling—and curdling—the milk.

To make preparation even easier and the soup lower in fat, omit the melting margarine step. Instead, combine the milk, flour and cheese; stir into soup.

If desired, sprinkle crisply cooked, crumbled bacon over the top of each serving.

Nutrition Analysis (*Per Serving*): Calories: 316 / Cholesterol: 19 mg / Carbohydrates: 36 g Protein: 13 g / Sodium: 720 mg / Fat: 15 g (Saturated Fat: 6 g) / Potassium: 492 mg.

HEARTY, HOMEMADE AND QUICK

Is there anyone who doesn't love digging into a big bowl of hearty, homemade soup? This chowder, from Vera McIntosh of Concord, North Carolina, is splendid because of its quick-and-easy preparation and its rich flavor.

SOUPS & STEWS

CREAM OF CARROT SOUP

Makes 8 to 10 Servings

2	tablespoons margarine *or* butter
1	small onion, chopped (⅓ cup)
5 to 6	medium carrots, peeled and chopped (3 cups)
1	large potato, peeled and cubed
2	14½-ounce cans chicken broth
1½	cups chopped fresh mushrooms
1	stalk celery, chopped
1	clove garlic, minced
½	teaspoon sugar
½	teaspoon salt
½	teaspoon dried thyme, crushed *or* 1½ teaspoons fresh snipped thyme
¼	teaspoon bottled hot pepper sauce
½	cup milk

Dairy sour cream (optional)
Fresh thyme sprigs (optional)

◆   ◆   ◆

Claire Bielawa tells us that her mother-in-law gave her this recipe. When Claire's family has their Easter dinners, this colorful and delicious soup is the dish that the children like best.

Claire M. Bielawa
<u>*The Mark Twain Library*</u>
<u>*Cookbook*</u>
The Mark Twain Library
Association
Redding
CONNECTICUT

1 In a large saucepan, melt *1 tablespoon* of the margarine or butter. Add the onion and cook until tender and light brown.

2 Add the carrots and potato. Cook and stir for 2 minutes. Carefully add the chicken broth, mushrooms, celery, garlic, sugar, salt, thyme and hot pepper sauce. Bring to a boil, then reduce the heat. Cover and simmer about 50 minutes or until the vegetables are very tender.

3 Let the soup mixture cool slightly, then transfer about *one-third* of the mixture to a blender container. Cover and blend until smooth. Repeat with the remaining mixture. Return the entire mixture to the saucepan.

4 Stir in the milk and the remaining margarine or butter. Heat the soup thoroughly, but do not boil. Season to taste with additional *salt* and *pepper*, if desired. Ladle the soup into individual bowls. Garnish with sour cream and fresh thyme, if desired.

 TIPS FROM OUR KITCHEN

Chopping the vegetables helps them to cook faster and blend into the liquid more smoothly.

Using a food processor is a quick way to chop the vegetables. You can also use a food processor to puree the cooked mixture. Process about *one-third* of the total mixture at a time.

For soup with a similar color but a different flavor, substitute 3 cups squash chunks for the carrots.

Nutrition Analysis (*Per Serving*): Calories: 101 / Cholesterol: 1 mg / Carbohydrates: 13 g / Protein: 4 g / Sodium: 569 mg / Fat: 4 g (Saturated Fat: 1 g) / Potassium: 391 mg.

BUNNY'S FAVORITE

What's brewing? How about a delicately seasoned, creamy soup that will please even your most
health-conscious family member? All it takes is a little over an hour of time, a few simple
vegetables and a couple of kitchen staples to make this colorful soup.

MULLIGATAWNY SOUP

Makes 6 Servings
2	tablespoons butter *or* margarine
2	stalks celery, finely chopped (¾ cup)
½	cup finely chopped onion (1 medium)
1	carrot, finely chopped (½ cup)
2	tablespoons all-purpose flour
2	teaspoons curry powder
4	cups chicken broth
1	bay leaf
½	cup raisins *or* snipped pitted prunes
¼	cup finely chopped apple
½	teaspoon shredded lemon peel
¼	teaspoon salt
¼	teaspoon pepper
¼	teaspoon dried thyme, crushed
½	cup cooked rice
½	cup finely chopped cooked chicken
½	cup milk *or* light cream

♦   ♦   ♦

Bill Dodge's mother gave him this recipe for Mulligatawny Soup. He says, "You can vary the ingredients, especially the dried fruits, without the recipe giving you trouble."

Bill Dodge
Cooking By Male
Greater Pittsburgh Commission
For Women
Pittsburgh
PENNSYLVANIA

1 In a large saucepan, melt the butter or margarine. Add the celery, onion and carrot. Cook until tender but not brown.

2 Stir in the flour and curry powder. Cook about 3 minutes. Add the chicken broth, bay leaf, raisins or pitted prunes, apple, lemon peel, salt, pepper and thyme. Simmer for 15 minutes.

3 Add the rice and chicken. Heat through. Just before serving, stir in the milk or light cream.

 TIPS FROM OUR KITCHEN

If you don't have leftover cooked rice, add 2 tablespoons uncooked rice to the broth with the bay leaf, raisins or prunes, apple, lemon peel, salt, pepper and thyme.

Curry powder is a blend of 16 to 20 ground spices, often including cumin, coriander, red pepper, fenugreek, turmeric, cinnamon, allspice, fennel, ginger and black or white pepper.

Cooking the flour-curry powder mixture in the butter or margarine before adding the chicken broth helps to mellow the flavors of spices.

For the cooked chicken, use your microwave oven to cook one 12-ounce chicken breast. Rinse and pat the chicken breast dry, then place it in a baking dish and cover with waxed paper. Micro-cook at 100% power (high) for 5 to 7 minutes or until the chicken is tender and no longer pink.

You can use a food processor to chop the celery, onion and carrot. First, cut the vegetables into 1-inch chunks and place them in the work bowl with a steel blade. Process with on/off turns until the vegetables are chopped to the desired size.

If you want to make this soup ahead of time, refrigerate or freeze it without the milk or light cream. Then, to serve, heat and stir in the milk or cream.

Nutrition Analysis: (*Per Serving*): Calories: 183 / Cholesterol: 24 mg / Carbohydrates: 23 g Protein: 9 g / Sodium: 702 mg / Fat: 6 g (Saturated Fat: 3 g) / Potassium: 452 mg.

EXOTIC EASTERN FLAVOR

Curry powder, a rich broth and a flavorful mixture of cooked chicken and fruits characterize
Bill Dodge's version of the traditional east Indian soup.

AUTUMN BISQUE

Makes 6 Servings

1 pound butternut squash, peeled, halved, seeded and cubed
2 tart apples, peeled, cored and cubed
1 medium onion, chopped
2 slices white bread, crusts removed and cubed
4 cups chicken broth
½ teaspoon salt
¼ teaspoon pepper
¼ teaspoon dried rosemary, crushed
¼ teaspoon dried marjoram, crushed
2 egg yolks, slightly beaten
¼ cup heavy whipping cream
Thin apple slices (optional)
Fresh rosemary (optional)

◆   ◆   ◆

Although Kim Button quadrupled her recipe for this hearty soup when she served it at a bazaar, there still wasn't enough to go around. Everyone loved it so much, it was gone within an hour! Kim makes this old family recipe every Thanksgiving and suggests that if you serve this to your guests, you should be prepared to share the recipe.

Kim Button
Kids Bowling for Kids Village Cookbook
Seattle
WASHINGTON

1 In a large saucepan, combine the squash, apples, onion, bread, chicken broth, salt, pepper, rosemary and marjoram. Bring to boiling. Reduce heat and simmer, uncovered, about 35 minutes or until the squash and apples are tender. Remove from heat; cool slightly.

2 Spoon *one-third* of the soup into a blender container or food processor bowl. Cover and blend or process until puréed. Repeat with the remaining soup.

3 Return all of the puréed mixture to the saucepan. Reheat the soup gently over very low heat.

4 In a small bowl, stir together the egg yolks and whipping cream. Beat in *1 cup* of the hot soup, then add the yolk mixture to the saucepan, stirring constantly. Heat and stir just until the soup begins to boil.

5 Transfer the soup to a tureen. Garnish with the apple slices and rosemary, if desired.

TIPS FROM OUR KITCHEN

Adding a small portion of the hot soup to the egg yolk and cream mixture warms the egg and cream so it will be less likely to form lumps when combined with the rest of the hot soup.

Depending on the variety of squash you choose, you might find the squash easier to handle if you first cut the squash into halves or quarters, then remove the seeds. Finally cut off the flesh from the peel and cube.

Instead of the butternut squash, experiment with other winter squashes such as acorn, banana, turban, hubbard and buttercup. When shopping, choose a squash that is heavy for its size and has a hard rind.

Nutrition Analysis *(Per Serving)*: Calories: 138 / Cholesterol: 49 mg / Carbohydrates: 17 g Protein: 5 g / Sodium: 746 mg / Fat: 6 g (Saturated Fat: 3 g) / Potassium: 386 mg.

SURPRISE SOUP

The secret ingredients in this hearty, cold-weather soup are the squash and apples. Richly satisfying
and gently seasoned with rosemary and marjoram, Autumn Bisque will help you take
the shivers out of the chilliest day.

SOUPS & STEWS

DANA'S CHEDDAR CHEESE SOUP

Makes 6 to 8 Servings

- 2 tablespoons butter *or* margarine
- ½ cup chopped carrots
- ½ cup chopped onion
- ½ cup chopped green sweet pepper
- ½ cup chopped celery
- 5 tablespoons all-purpose flour
- 4 cups chicken broth
- 3 cups sharp cheddar cheese, shredded (12 ounces)
- 1 12-ounce can evaporated milk
- Freshly ground pepper
- Bottled hot pepper sauce (optional)
- Toasted sunflower seeds (optional)

◆　　◆　　◆

According to Eleanor Donaldson, her daughter-in-law, Dana (the source of this recipe), is a "marvelous, natural cook." Eleanor has traditionally made Dana's Cheddar Cheese Soup on Christmas Eve. What a wonderful way to warm a special winter's evening!

Eleanor Donaldson
A Culinary Celebration
The Keynotes of Music for Mt. Lebanon
Mt. Lebanon
PENNSYLVANIA

1 In a large saucepan, melt the butter or margarine. Add the carrots, onion, green pepper and celery. Cook and stir over medium-low heat until the vegetables are tender.

2 Sprinkle the vegetables with the flour, adding it *1 tablespoon* at a time, stirring until the flour is blended in.

3 Add the chicken broth to the saucepan. Cook and stir over medium heat until the mixture comes to a boil.

4 Reduce heat; add the shredded cheese, stirring with a large whisk until the cheese is melted.

5 Slowly add the evaporated milk, stirring until the mixture is well blended and heated through.

6 Add enough freshly ground pepper to taste. If desired, add several drops of bottled hot pepper sauce and garnish with sunflower seeds.

TIPS FROM OUR KITCHEN

Melted natural cheeses commonly have a slightly grainy texture. For a smoother soup, use half American cheese and half cheddar cheese. For a different flavor, use Monterey Jack cheese.

If you're concerned about your sodium and/or fat intake, try using one of the reduced-sodium or reduced-fat cheeses for all or part of the total amount of cheese in this recipe. You might also want to consider using evaporated skim milk.

You can use homemade chicken broth or one of the following convenience products: canned chicken broth, canned condensed chicken broth, bouillon granules or bouillon cubes. Check the label on the condensed broth and bouillon to find the correct amount to use.

Nutrition Analysis (*Per Serving*): Calories: 409 / Cholesterol: 89 mg / Carbohydrates: 16 g Protein: 23 g / Sodium: 995 mg / Fat: 28 g (Saturated Fat: 17 g) / Potassium: 495 mg.

CHEESE-LOVER'S DREAM

Eleanor Donaldson of Richmond, Virginia, gives us a recipe for a terrific tummy-warming soup. The
rich, creamy and cheesy chicken broth base surrounds pieces of tender garden vegetables.
Pass the bottled hot pepper sauce to add your preferred amount of zip.

SOUPS & STEWS

385

CREAM OF CUCUMBER SOUP

4 large cucumbers (2 pounds)
3 tablespoons butter *or* margarine
½ cup finely chopped green onion
6 cups chicken broth (49½-ounce can)
¾ teaspoon dried dillweed
¼ cup farina (cream of wheat)
3 to 4 teaspoons tarragon vinegar
¼ teaspoon fresh ground pepper
1 cup light cream, half-and-half, dairy sour cream *or* crème fraîche
Sliced cucumbers, snipped fresh dill *or* parsley (optional)

✦   ✦   ✦

<u>More Than a Tea Party</u> was such a success that the members of the Junior League of Boston recently sold the last copy and now they are thrilled with having to decide whether or not to reprint it. The cookbook was created to raise funds for the League's thirty community service projects.

<u>More Than a Tea Party</u>
The Junior League of Boston
Boston
MASSACHUSETTS

1 Peel the cucumbers. Slice the cucumbers in half lengthwise. Using a spoon, scoop out and discard the seeds. Slice the cucumber halves thinly; set aside.

2 In a Dutch oven, melt the butter or margarine. Add the green onion and cook over low heat until the onion is tender but not brown. Add the cucumbers; cook and stir for 1 to 2 minutes. Add the chicken broth and dillweed; heat to boiling. Stir in the farina. Reduce heat and simmer the mixture, uncovered, for 20 to 25 minutes.

3 Puree the mixture, *one-third* at a time, in a blender container or food processor bowl. Pour the pureed mixture into a bowl or covered container. Stir the tarragon vinegar and pepper into the cucumber mixture.

4 Cover and refrigerate about 4 hours or until the mixture is cool. Stir in the light cream, half-and-half, sour cream or crème fraîche. Cover and chill for 2 more hours or overnight. Serve the soup in chilled bowls or glass mugs. If desired, garnish the servings with cucumber slices, snipped dill or parsley.

 TIPS FROM OUR KITCHEN

You'll want to use fresh cucumbers in this recipe. Fresh cucumbers are available year round. When shopping for cucumbers, look for those that are firm, without shriveled or soft spots. Smaller cucumbers of any type will be more tender. Fresh cucumbers can be stored in the refrigerator up to 2 weeks.

For a soup that is lower in calories and salt, reduced-calorie sour cream and reduced-sodium chicken broth can be substituted in this recipe.

To make Crème Fraîche: In a small bowl, stir together ½ cup *whipping cream* (not ultrapasteurized) and ½ cup *dairy sour cream*. Cover with plastic wrap. Let stand at room temperature for 2 to 5 hours or until the mixture is thickened. When thickened, cover and chill in the refrigerator until serving time or up to 1 week. Stir before serving.

Farina—also known as cream of wheat—is a mild-flavored wheat product. It is commonly found in hot breakfast cereals.

Nutrition Analysis (*Per Serving*): Calories: 150 / Cholesterol: 32 mg / Carbohydrates: 7 g / Protein: 6 g / Sodium: 641 mg / Fat: 11 g (Saturated Fat: 7 g) / Potassium: 410 mg.

BEAT-THE-HEAT

When the three H's—hazy, hot and humid—descend upon us, it's a pleasant change to try our
collection of summertime recipes. Refreshing Cream of Cucumber Soup is a delightful way
to enjoy fresh-from-the-garden cucumbers.

FARMERS' MARKET SOUP

Makes 10 to 12 Servings

2 10½-ounce cans condensed beef broth
1 28-ounce can crushed tomatoes, packed in puree
2 cups chopped onion
1 cup chopped celery
1 cup chopped carrot
1 medium potato, peeled and chopped (1 cup)
1 rutabaga, peeled and chopped (1 cup)
1 parsnip, peeled and chopped
½ cup shredded cabbage *or* lettuce
Additional vegetables: zucchini, okra, green beans, peas *and/or* corn (optional)
2 tablespoons snipped parsley
1 teaspoon dried oregano, crushed
1 teaspoon dried basil, crushed
1 clove garlic, minced
1 bay leaf
Dash bottled hot pepper sauce
Parmesan cheese (optional)

♦   ♦   ♦

Shirley Moyer often varies this soup by adding herbs from her own garden. She suggested adding "any leftover vegetables or whatever looks good at the market."

Shirley Moyer
Heavenly Hosts
Presbyterian Women of the Bryn Mawr Presbyterian Church
Bryn Mawr
PENNSYLVANIA

1 In a large Dutch oven, bring 6 cups *water* to a boil. Add the undiluted beef broth, *undrained* tomatoes, onion, celery, carrot, potato, rutabaga, parsnip and cabbage or lettuce. Add any additional vegetables, if using.

2 Stir in the parsley, oregano, basil, garlic, bay leaf, hot pepper sauce, ¼ teaspoon *salt* and ¼ teaspoon *pepper*. Return the broth to a boil.

3 Reduce heat and simmer about 20 minutes or until the vegetables are tender. Remove the bay leaf. If desired, sprinkle with the Parmesan cheese. Serve immediately.

TIPS FROM OUR KITCHEN

To use fresh tomatoes: Skin and chop enough washed tomatoes to measure about 3½ cups; use slightly less water in the broth.

Prepare any other vegetables you are using as you normally would. For example, wash zucchini, slice or seed it and chop it. If you're using okra, wash and slice it. Wash green beans and snip, break or cut them into 1-inch lengths.

If fresh oregano and basil are available, you can substitute 1 tablespoon of each fresh herb for the dried herbs in this recipe.

If you like, you can add leftover cooked chicken, turkey, beef, pork or ham to this soup.

To cube the rutabaga: Cut into strips that are ½ inch or more wide. Line up and stack the strips and cut lengthwise and crosswise through the stack to make even size pieces.

Store any leftover soup in individual microwave-safe containers for reheating later. Or, you can reheat the soup in a saucepan over low heat.

Nutrition Analysis (*Per Serving*): Calories: 117 / Cholesterol: 2 mg / Carbohydrates: 23 g / Protein: 5 g / Sodium: 710 mg / Fat: 1 g (Saturated Fat: 0 g) / Potassium: 621 mg.

LOVE THOSE VEGETABLES!

Are you someone who enjoys spending hours in the produce section of the supermarket? Then let us present Farmers' Market Soup. This is a hearty, full-of-veggies soup that provides an excellent base for your choice of ingredients. Have fun!

Fresh Mushroom Soup

Makes 6 to 8 Servings

¼	cup butter *or* margarine
12	ounces sliced fresh mushrooms (4½ cups)
1 to 2	cloves garlic, minced
¼	cup all-purpose flour
2	cups chicken broth
2	cups milk
½	cup snipped parsley
¼	teaspoon salt
⅛	teaspoon ground nutmeg
⅛	teaspoon pepper
3	tablespoons dry vermouth (optional)

◆ ◆ ◆

Tandy Sweeney Graves told us that her mother has always had a great influence on her cooking. In fact, it was when she and her mother were "playing around with different recipes" fifteen years ago that they created Fresh Mushroom Soup. Tandy likes to entertain, but says it's difficult to find the time to prepare the food. This dish is an easy and delicious solution.

Tandy Sweeney Graves
<u>Magic</u>
*The Junior League
of Birmingham*
Birmingham
ALABAMA

1 In a large saucepan, melt the butter or margarine. Add the mushrooms and garlic to the saucepan; cook and stir for 5 minutes.

2 Stir in the flour, blending well. Slowly add the broth, followed by the milk. Bring to a boil, stirring constantly.

3 Reduce the heat and simmer for 5 minutes. Add the parsley, salt, nutmeg and pepper. Add the vermouth, if desired, and cook until the mixture is heated through.

 TIPS FROM OUR KITCHEN

To reheat a single serving of the soup: Place 1 serving (¾ cup) in a microwave-safe bowl. Cover and micro-cook on 100% power (high) for 2 to 3 minutes or until heated through, stirring once.

Using whole milk will add richness. If you want an even richer flavor, use half-and-half. For a heartier soup, add 1 cup cooked wild rice.

You may want to experiment to find the flavor you like best by using different types of mushrooms. The common white, cream and brown mushrooms, with their familiar umbrella shape, have a mild flavor. The chanterelle (shant uh REL) has a golden to yellow-orange color and a delicate, meaty flavor. Oriental varieties

of mushrooms include: the enoki (ee KNOCK ee), a variety with a very mild flavor; the oyster with its pale cream to gray color and mild flavor; and the shiitake (shih TOCK ee) with its large floppy caps and rich, meaty flavor. (Shiitake stems are not used.)

Nutrition Analysis (*Per Serving*): Calories: 144 / Cholesterol: 22 mg / Carbohydrates: 11 g Protein: 6 g / Sodium: 472 mg / Fat: 9 g (Saturated Fat: 5 g) / Potassium: 454 mg.

SAVORY, EARTHY SOUP

Tandy Sweeney Graves of Birmingham, Alabama, has captured the incomparable earthy flavor of mushrooms in this easy-to-make creamy soup. Sprinkle with snipped parsley and serve as a first course at your next dinner party. Or, add a salad and sandwich to make a complete meal.

GAZPACHO

Makes 6 to 8 Servings

- 6 medium tomatoes
- 1 medium cucumber, peeled, seeded and chopped
- 1 medium onion, finely chopped
- 1 medium green sweet pepper, finely chopped
- 1 clove garlic, minced
- 1½ cups tomato juice
- ¼ cup olive oil
- 2 tablespoons vinegar
- 1 teaspoon salt
- ¼ teaspoon pepper
- Few drops of bottled hot pepper sauce
- Croutons

◆   ◆   ◆

"You always look for something easy with eight kids!" Edie Hellman tells us. All of her children love this dish and Edie finds herself preparing it in large batches. She suggests that you serve Gazpacho on hot summer days when you want something cool, refreshing and hassle-free.

Edie Hellman
Home on the Range
Home on the Range
Sentinel Butte
NORTH DAKOTA

1 Bring a medium saucepan of water to a boil. Carefully plunge the tomatoes into the boiling water for 30 seconds to loosen the skins.

2 Immerse the tomatoes in cold water to cool quickly. Remove the skins.

3 Coarsely chop the tomatoes and place them in a large bowl. Add the cucumber, onion, green pepper and garlic. Stir in the tomato juice, olive oil, vinegar, salt, pepper and hot pepper sauce.

4 Cover the gazpacho and chill it at least 4 hours. Serve cold and sprinkle with croutons.

For a zippier soup, substitute spicy tomato juice for the plain tomato juice.

Look for plump, well-shaped fresh tomatoes that are firm textured and bright colored for the variety. Avoid bruised, cracked or soft tomatoes. If fresh tomatoes need to ripen, store them at room temperature in a brown paper bag or in a fruit ripening bowl with other fruits. Don't stand them in the sun to ripen, or they will become mushy. When ripe, tomatoes will yield slightly to gentle pressure.

Nutrition Analysis *(Per Serving)*: Calories: 148 / Cholesterol: 0 mg / Carbohydrates: 16 g / Protein: 3 g / Sodium: 651 mg / Fat: 10 g (Saturated Fat: 1 g) Potassium: 539 mg.

REFRESHING SUMMER SOUP

Is there anything more refreshing on a hot day than cold gazpacho? While the origins of this soup are
in the south of Spain, this particular recipe comes to us from Sentinel Butte, North Dakota. Pass
the bottled hot sauce to those who want to add extra zip.

WONTON SOUP

1 In a medium bowl, stir together the ground pork, spinach, sherry, salt, sugar (if using) and pepper; mix well.

2 Place a generous ½ *teaspoon* of the pork mixture in the center of *each* wonton wrapper. Bring the opposite corners together in a fold. Seal the wonton by dotting the bottom edge with water and pinching it together firmly. Fold the other two corners toward each other and seal.

3 Cook the wontons in gently *boiling water* for 3 to 4 minutes or until the filling inside is no longer pink. Drain the wontons thoroughly and divide them among 4 or 5 individual soup bowls.

4 Bring the chicken broth or stock to a boil. Add the ⅛ teaspoon pepper. Divide the broth or stock among the soup bowls. Garnish each bowl with 3 snow peas and the sliced green onion. Add the crushed red pepper and Egg Sheet, if desired.

5 To make the Egg Sheet: Beat 1 *egg* with ½ teaspoon *dry sherry* and a dash *salt*. Heat 1 teaspoon *cooking oil* in a 10-inch skillet over medium heat. Pour in the egg mixture, rotating the skillet quickly so that the egg mixture covers the bottom of the skillet. Cook until lightly browned. Invert onto a cutting board and cut into thin strips.

 TIPS FROM OUR KITCHEN

The wontons can be assembled whenever convenient, then frozen in an airtight container.

Although you can cook the wontons directly in the broth, cooking them in plain water first will help keep the broth clear.

Here's an alternative method for folding the wontons. Spoon a generous ½ *teaspoon* filling just off-center of *each* wonton wrapper. Fold the nearest point of the wrapper over the filling, tucking the point under the filling. Roll toward the center, leaving about 1 inch unrolled at the top. Moisten the right-hand corner with water. Lap the right-hand corner over the left-hand corner, pressing them together to seal.

Wonton wrappers can be purchased prepackaged in most supermarkets and Chinese markets.

Nutrition Analysis (*Per Serving*): Calories: 132 / Cholesterol: 25 mg / Carbohydrates: 12 g / Protein: 11 g / Sodium: 928 mg / Fat: 4 g (Saturated Fat: 1 g) / Potassium: 352 mg.

TAKE-OUT COMES HOME

Carolyn Kramer of Bel Air, Maryland, brings us a great recipe for everyone's favorite Chinese-style
soup. Making wontons is really quite easy: Just stir together the filling and
fold the wonton wrapper around it.

SOUPS & STEWS

395

BUCK'S EASTERN CAROLINA BRUNSWICK STEW

Makes 6 to 8 Servings

1 4- to 5-pound chicken
3 pounds potatoes, peeled and cubed
4 16-ounce cans tomatoes, cut up
2 16-ounce cans midget-size butter beans *or* lima beans, drained
4 ounces salt pork, cubed
2 ounces smoked pork, cubed
1 red (hot) pepper pod
2 11-ounce cans white shoe peg corn (not yellow), drained

◆   ◆   ◆

Mary Hoffler's recipe for Brunswick Stew comes from her husband's family—in fact, it's been in his family so long, "no one remembers who stirred the first pot!" Mr. Hoffler (known by friends as "Buck") has been cooking this stew for forty or fifty years. He reminds us to be sure the fire isn't too hot, to stir often and to make enough to freeze for later.

Mary Hoffler
Bravo!
The Greensboro Symphony Guild
Greensboro
NORTH CAROLINA

1 In a covered Dutch oven, cook the chicken in 6 cups of *water* until tender (See Tip). Remove from heat. Transfer the chicken to a cutting surface. Cool slightly. Skim the fat from the surface of the stock. Discard the fat and reserve the stock.

2 Debone and cube the chicken.

3 Return the stock to the heat and bring to boiling. Add the cubed chicken, potatoes, tomatoes, butter beans or lima beans, salt pork, smoked pork and red pepper pod. Simmer slowly for 1 to 1½ hours or until the vegetables are tender, stirring occasionally to prevent the vegetables from scorching.

4 Add the white shoe peg corn to the stew. Cover and heat through, stirring occasionally.

TIPS FROM OUR KITCHEN

The cooking time for the chicken changes depending on whether you're using a stewing hen or a broiler-fryer. A stewing hen will cook in about 2 hours. A broiler-fryer will be done in about 50 minutes.

You can substitute bacon for the salt pork and ham for the smoked pork in this recipe.

To save time and add fiber to the meal, don't peel the potatoes.

You may substitute 4 to 5 cups cooked cubed chicken and four 14-ounce cans chicken broth, and eliminate the first step. Also omit the salt pork if you are using canned broth.

Nutrition Analysis *(Per Serving)*: Calories: 748 / Cholesterol: 112 mg / Carbohydrates: 89 g Protein: 47 g / Sodium: 1619 mg / Fat: 25 g (Saturated Fat: 8 g) / Potassium: 2142 mg.

SLOW-SIMMERING FAVORITE

The original Brunswick stew was created in 1828 in Brunswick County, Virginia, and included
squirrel meat among its ingredients. This version, which features chicken and pork,
hails from Greensboro, North Carolina.

EDINER'S CHICKEN NOODLE SOUP

Makes 6 Servings

8	cups water
1¾	pounds meaty chicken pieces
2	tablespoons instant chicken bouillon granules
1	teaspoon dried basil, crushed
1	bay leaf
½	teaspoon salt
¼	teaspoon pepper
2	cups chopped carrot
2	cups chopped celery
2	cups chopped onion
½	8-ounce package frozen noodles

◆   ◆   ◆

The Ediner Restaurant is quite popular in Edina, Minnesota, and with a dinerlike decor and marvelous food, there's no question why. This recipe for Chicken Noodle Soup is one of the most popular items on the menu— loved for its thick noodles and large chunks of chicken. In fact, Pat Meyers from the Concordia Language Villages told us that a quart of this soup is the perfect remedy for a sick friend!

The Ediner Restaurant
The Global Gourmet
Concordia Language Villages
Moorhead
MINNESOTA

1 In a Dutch oven, stir together the water, chicken pieces, instant bouillon granules, basil, bay leaf, salt and pepper. Bring to a boil; reduce heat and simmer, covered, for 20 to 30 minutes or until the chicken is done.

2 Using tongs, carefully remove the chicken from the broth. Set the chicken aside to cool slightly.

3 Add the carrot, celery and onion to the broth. Return to a boil. Add the noodles, stirring to separate them. Reduce heat and simmer, uncovered, for 20 minutes.

4 Meanwhile, cut the chicken into ½-inch pieces. Return the chicken to the broth. Simmer for 5 to 10 minutes more or until the noodles are tender. Remove the bay leaf and discard. To serve, ladle the soup into individual soup bowls.

TIPS FROM OUR KITCHEN

For a less fatty soup, use skinless chicken.

If you wish, substitute 1 tablespoon fresh basil for the dried basil in this recipe.

To shorten your chopping time, use your food processor. Start with 1 pound of carrots (6 to 8 medium); 5 stalks of celery; and 4 medium (or 2 large) onions.

Regular dried noodles can be substituted for the frozen noodles. Add the dried noodles about 10 minutes before serving.

Nutrition Analysis (*Per Serving*): Calories: 270 / Cholesterol: 77 mg / Carbohydrates: 24 g Protein: 24 g / Sodium: 1181 mg / Fat: 8 g (Saturated Fat: 2 g) / Potassium: 490 mg.

NOSTALGIC FAVORITE

This soup will bring you back to the days when nothing but your mother's homemade chicken soup
could make you feel better. This version from an Edina, Minnesota, diner is brimming
with flavor, vegetables and plump, tender noodles.

TORTILLA SOUP

1 In a large saucepan, stir together the chicken broth, chicken, onion, green chilies, chili powder and ground red pepper.

2 Bring the soup to boiling. Reduce heat and simmer the soup, uncovered, about 10 minutes or until the onion is tender.

3 Ladle the soup into individual bowls or a soup tureen. Add a *small handful* of the tortilla chips to each soup bowl or the entire 2 cups to the tureen. Sprinkle with the cheddar cheese and chopped tomato. Serve immediately.

TIPS FROM OUR KITCHEN

To lower the salt in this recipe, use low-sodium chicken broth and lightly salted or no-salt tortilla chips.

For added spiciness, increase the amount of chili powder to 2 tablespoons.

If you are using homemade chicken broth in this recipe you might like to try this method for clarifying the broth. Strain your broth into a large saucepan. Stir together one *egg white* and ¼ cup *cold water*. Add to the broth and bring the mixture to boiling. Remove from heat and let stand 5 minutes. Strain the broth through a large sieve or colander lined with several layers of damp cheesecloth for cooking. Your broth will now have a crystal-clear quality.

Nutrition Analysis *(Per Serving)*: Calories: 158 / Cholesterol: 34 mg / Carbohydrates: 10 g
Protein: 15 g / Sodium: 654 mg / Fat: 6 g (Saturated Fat: 1 g) / Potassium: 341 mg.

NEW MEXICO TASTE

New Mexico is known for its hot and spicy cuisine, and this recipe is no exception. A spicy chicken stock that can be adjusted for hotness surrounds corn chips and is topped with cheddar cheese and chopped tomato. You'll enjoy the flavor as well as the short preparation time.

HOMEMADE MINESTRONE

Makes 8 to 10 Servings

2	tablespoons margarine *or* butter
1	pound stew beef, cut into ½- to ¾-inch cubes
7	cups water
2	15-ounce cans tomato sauce
1	14½-ounce can tomatoes, cut up
1	medium onion, chopped (½ cup)
½	cup celery, chopped
4	beef bouillon cubes, crumbled *or* 4 teaspoons instant beef bouillon granules
2	tablespoons dried parsley flakes
½ to 1	teaspoon salt
½	teaspoon dried thyme, crushed
¼	teaspoon pepper
2	cups shredded cabbage
1	cup thinly sliced zucchini
1	cup thinly sliced carrots
1	15-ounce can garbanzo beans, drained
1	cup small macaroni, uncooked
3 to 4	tablespoons grated Parmesan cheese

♦   ♦   ♦

Carol Armbrust Fey
Georgia On My Menu: A Medley
of Southern Hits
Junior League of Cobb-Marietta
Marietta
GEORGIA

1 In a 6- or 8-quart Dutch oven over medium heat, melt the margarine or butter. Add the stew beef and cook until browned. Stir in the water, tomato sauce, tomatoes, onion, celery, bouillon cubes or granules, parsley flakes, salt, thyme and pepper. Bring the mixture to a boil, then reduce the heat to low. Cover and simmer for 1 to 1¼ hours or until the beef is tender, stirring occasionally.

2 Add the cabbage, zucchini, carrots, garbanzo beans and macaroni. Return the mixture to a boil, then reduce the heat to low. Cover and simmer for 20 to 25 minutes or until the vegetables are tender and the macaroni is done, stirring occasionally.

3 Ladle the soup into bowls and top each portion with a generous sprinkling of Parmesan cheese.

 TIPS FROM OUR KITCHEN

Soups are more adaptable than many other recipes. You can give this one your individual stamp by substituting rice for the pasta or using a different pasta shape such as ditalini, anelli, bow ties, stars or broken spaghetti. Or, you might try substituting canellini, kidney or great northern beans in place of the garbanzos.

Use a plastic cutting board when cutting uncooked meat or poultry. Scrub both the cutting board and knife thoroughly with hot soapy water before using them with any other food.

You may be able to save money by cutting your own stew beef rather than buying it precut. Choose a beef chuck pot roast or a beef round steak, then ask your butcher to cut a 1-pound slice. Or, if you prefer, buy the whole piece, cut off a 1-pound slice, and use the remainder as a roast for another meal. Cut the 1-pound slice into small cubes (½- to ¾-inch) to use in this recipe. Cutting the meat into small pieces spreads the beefy flavor throughout every serving.

For a twist on the soup topper, try spooning on pesto in place of the Parmesan cheese.

Nutrition Analysis *(Per Serving)*: Calories: 305 / Cholesterol: 43 mg / Carbohydrates: 35 g
Protein: 22 g / Sodium: 1693 mg / Fat: 9 g (Saturated Fat: 3 g) / Potassium: 949 mg.

SOUP BOWL CLASSIC

We think Georgia's Carol Armbrust Fey did a great job creating this recipe for a classic Italian soup,
but feel free to customize it to your own preferences. For a delicious, easy meal, serve the
soup with hot bread and a fruit salad.

LENTIL SOUP

Makes 6 Servings

8	cups water *or* chicken broth
3	cups lentils, rinsed (1¼ pounds)
1	teaspoon salt
1	cup chopped onion
1	cup chopped carrot
1	cup chopped celery
1	clove garlic, minced
1½	cups chopped tomatoes
2	tablespoons dry red wine
2	tablespoons lemon juice
1½	tablespoons brown sugar *or* cognac
1	tablespoon wine vinegar
½	teaspoon pepper

♦ ♦ ♦

The Fontbonne Auxiliary provides financial and other assistance to the St. John Hospital and Medical Center and to the Sisters of St. Joseph of Nazareth in Michigan. Through the Auxiliary's efforts, they contribute close to one-half million dollars yearly to the Hospital. Proceeds from the sale of Renaissance Cuisine *help them to achieve this worthwhile feat.*

Janice Hoski
Renaissance Cuisine
The Fontbonne Auxiliary of St. John Hospital
Detroit
MICHIGAN

1 In a 4½-quart Dutch oven, combine the water or chicken broth, lentils and salt. Cover and simmer for 20 minutes.

2 Meanwhile, steam the onion, carrot, celery and garlic over boiling *water* for 8 minutes. Add the steamed vegetables to the lentil mixture.

3 Add the tomatoes, red wine, lemon juice, brown sugar or cognac, wine vinegar and pepper to the Dutch oven. Simmer for 20 minutes. Ladle into soup bowls to serve.

TIPS FROM OUR KITCHEN

Transform water into chicken broth by adding 2 tablespoons *instant chicken bouillon granules* to 8 cups *water*.

If desired, add spicy smoked sausage or left-over ham to this soup.

You'll need 2 medium tomatoes to equal the 1½ cups chopped tomatoes.

Instead of steaming the vegetables, cook them in 2 tablespoons *butter* or *margarine*, if desired. Or, the uncooked vegetables can be added at the beginning of cooking along with the lentils. Cook as directed for 20 minutes before adding the tomatoes and other flavorings.

Thyme, oregano and/or basil can be added to the soup for additional flavor. Add 1 tablespoon snipped fresh or 1 teaspoon crushed dried herbs with the tomatoes.

Lentils are among the oldest known foods. They contain fewer of the gas-producing sugars than dried beans. To rinse lentils, place them in a strainer and hold under running water.

Nutrition Analysis (*Per Serving*): Calories: 371 / Cholesterol: 0 mg / Carbohydrates: 67 g / Protein: 26 g / Sodium: 572 mg / Fat: 1 g (Saturated Fat: 0 g) / Potassium: 1383 mg.

HEALTHFUL AND DELICIOUS

Serve your family this hearty, healthy soup for dinner and feel confident that, indeed, they have been well fed. Janice Hoski of Detroit, Michigan, brings us a soup that features lentils—an excellent source of vegetable protein—and tender vegetables in a delicious broth.

SOUPS & STEWS

405

KALE SOUP

Makes 6 Servings

3 slices bacon, cut up
4 large onions, sliced (6 cups)
6 cups water
8 cups washed, trimmed and cut up kale (approximately 8 ounces)
8 ounces linguisa sausage *or* kielbasa, thinly sliced
4 cups finely chopped potatoes (1½ pounds)
1 15½-ounce can kidney beans
1 teaspoon vinegar
½ teaspoon salt
¼ teaspoon pepper
Dash of bottled hot pepper sauce

♦   ♦   ♦

When Meredith De La Vergne's father, Charles, retired, he started cooking, often creating dishes from the bounty of his large garden. This recipe for Kale Soup comes from Charles's repertoire. It's a delicious, hearty soup that Meredith describes as "especially good."

Meredith De La Vergne
Recipes From Holly Hill
Holly Hill Mental Health Services
Raleigh
NORTH CAROLINA

1 In a Dutch oven, cook the bacon and onions until the onions are tender. Add the water, kale and sausage or kielbasa. Bring the mixture to a boil and reduce heat. Gently boil, covered, for 15 minutes.

2 Add the potatoes and *undrained* kidney beans. Bring to a boil. Cover and boil gently for 15 minutes more.

3 Stir in the vinegar, salt, pepper and hot pepper sauce. Cover and simmer the soup for 30 minutes.

 TIPS FROM OUR KITCHEN

Kale is most abundant in grocery stores during the winter. Look for small bunches with no yellow or limp leaves. Wash the leaves in cold water, pat dry, remove the stems and trim bruised leaves. Store kale in a paper towel-lined plastic bag in the refrigerator up to 3 days. Longer storage may cause the leaves to take on a bitter taste.

Linguisa is an uncooked, smoked sausage of Portuguese origin. It is made by coarsely grinding pork with garlic, cumin seed and cinnamon. The mixture is cured in brine before stuffing. Kielbasa is a cooked, smoked sausage also known as a Polish sausage. It is usually made from a combination of pork and beef, seasoned with coriander, garlic, marjoram, salt, pepper and sugar.

For easier preparation, use a food processor to slice the onions. Cut large onions in half vertically to fit them into a feed tube.

Leftover soup can be frozen in 2-cup containers. To reheat, transfer the frozen soup to a microwave-safe bowl and micro-cook on 70% power (medium-high) for 10 to 11 minutes, stirring occasionally.

Nutrition Analysis (*Per Serving*): Calories: 491 / Cholesterol: 34 mg / Carbohydrates: 51 g / Protein: 16 g / Sodium: 733 mg / Fat: 27 g (Saturated Fat: 6 g) / Potassium: 1016 mg.

CABBAGE COUSIN

Kale, a mild-flavored member of the cabbage family, is featured in this delicious, sausage-flavored soup from Meredith De La Vergne of North Carolina.

MANHATTAN CLAM CHOWDER

Makes 6 Servings

 2 cups chicken stock *or* broth
 1 cup cubed potatoes
 ½ cup cubed carrots
 ½ cup cubed celery
 ½ cup cubed onions
 ½ teaspoon minced garlic
 ½ teaspoon snipped parsley
 ¼ teaspoon dried thyme, crushed
 ¼ teaspoon dried oregano, crushed
 3 cups chopped, canned *or* fresh clams, with juice
 1 cup peeled and chopped fresh tomatoes
 1 8-ounce can tomato sauce
 1 tablespoon butter *or* margarine
 1 tablespoon olive oil

◆   ◆   ◆

Jerry Cegla, Executive Chef at the Edina Country Club Restaurant, told us that this chowder has been served in the restaurant for years. Although some chefs are protective about sharing recipes, Jerry said, "everyone can make soup from the same recipe and each one will come out a bit different. People will make little changes—it's just human nature."

**Jerry Cegla, CFBE
Edina Country Club Restaurant
<u>The Global Gourmet</u>
Concordia Language Villages
Moorhead
MINNESOTA**

1 In a large saucepan, stir together the chicken stock or broth, potatoes, carrots, celery, onions, thyme, garlic, parsley, and oregano. Bring to a boil. Reduce heat; cover and cook about 20 minutes or until the vegetables are tender.

2 Stir in the *undrained* clams, tomatoes, tomato sauce, butter or margarine and olive oil. Season to taste with *salt* and *pepper*. Heat until the soup is bubbly.

 TIPS FROM OUR KITCHEN

If you're using canned clams, you'll need approximately four 6½-ounce cans. For 3 cups chopped fresh clams, you'll need to buy 2 pints of shucked clams or about 36 clams in their shells. When buying shucked clams, look for plump ones with clear juices and no pieces of shell.

To clean and shuck the clams: Use a stiff brush to scrub the shells under cold running water. Then, soak the clams in salted water. To open the shells, hold the clam with the hinged

back side against a heavy cloth in the palm of your hand. Working over a plate to catch the juices, insert a sturdy, blunt-tipped knife between the shell halves. Hold the shell firmly and move the knife blade around the clam to cut the muscles that hold the shell together. Slightly twist the knife to pry open the shell. Cut the clam muscle free from the shell.

Cubed vegetables are all similar in size. To simplify cubing the vegetables: Cut the vegetables into strips that are ⅛ to ¼ inch wide. Line up and stack the strips and cut lengthwise and crosswise through the stack to make even size pieces.

Nutrition Analysis (*Per Serving*): Calories: 155 / Cholesterol: 82 mg / Carbohydrates: 15 g Protein: 13 g / Sodium: 614 mg / Fat: 6 g (Saturated Fat: 2 g) / Potassium: 616 mg.

SEASIDE SENSATION

The word chowder comes from the French *chaudière*, after the caldron in which fishermen once made their stews. You don't need a caldron and a seaside location to brew a batch of this delicious Manhattan Clam Chowder—just a large saucepan and a few simple ingredients will do.

SOUPS & STEWS

MILDRED KEMP'S SECRET INGREDIENT CRAB SOUP

Makes 4 Servings

- 4 medium tomatoes, peeled and chopped
- 1 large green sweet pepper, chopped
- 1 small onion, finely chopped
- 1 teaspoon dry mustard
- 12 ounces cooked crabmeat
- 1 tablespoon margarine *or* butter
- 1 tablespoon all-purpose flour
- ¼ teaspoon sugar
- ¼ teaspoon Worcestershire sauce
- 2 cups milk
- 1 cup half-and-half *or* light cream

◆   ◆   ◆

The Wades Point Farm is famous for its hospitality and cuisine, and guests return year after year to enjoy the ambiance of the charming inn. One of the house specialties is the crab soup that had an ingredient no one could quite figure out—and the cook would not divulge the secret. After asking several times, Inn Keeper Mildred Kemp hid in the kitchen to watch the cook prepare the soup and to discover the secret...sugar!

Mildred Kemp
From a Lighthouse Window
Chesapeake Bay Maritime Museum
St. Michaels
MARYLAND

1 In a medium saucepan, stir together the tomatoes, green sweet pepper, onion, 2 tablespoons *water* and the dry mustard. Bring to a boil; simmer, uncovered, for 15 to 18 minutes or until the vegetables are tender. Remove from heat. Stir in the crabmeat, ¼ teaspoon *salt* and ⅛ teaspoon *pepper;* set aside.

2 In a large saucepan over medium heat, melt the margarine or butter. Stir in the flour, sugar and Worcestershire sauce. Add the milk and half-and-half or light cream all at once. Cook and stir over medium heat until the mixture is slightly thickened and bubbly. Cook and stir for 1 minute more.

3 Stir the crabmeat-vegetable mixture into the milk mixture. Heat through but *do not boil.*

 TIPS FROM OUR KITCHEN

You'll need 2 to 2¼ pounds of crab legs for 12 ounces of crabmeat. To boil live crabs: In a 12- to 16-quart kettle, bring 8 quarts *water* and 2 teaspoons *salt* to a boil. Add the crabs and return the water to a boil. Reduce heat; cover and simmer for 15 minutes. Drain the crabs and refrigerate, or rinse the crabs under cold running water until they are cool enough to handle.

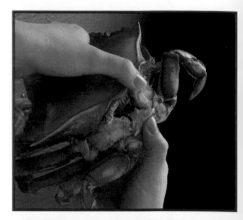

To crack a cooked crab: Turn the crab on its back. Use your thumb to pry up the tail flap or apron; twist it off and discard. Hold the crab with the top shell in one hand and grasp the bottom shell at the point where the apron was removed. Pull the top shell away from the body of the crab and discard. Use a small knife to remove the "devil's fingers" (spongy gills) from each side of the top of the crab. Discard the internal organs, mouth and small appendages at the front of the crab. To remove the meat, twist off the legs and claws using your fingers. Use a nutcracker to crack each joint, then pick out the meat. Break the body in half and remove the remaining meat.

Nutrition Analysis (*Per Serving*): Calories: 307 / Cholesterol: 104 mg / Carbohydrates: 22
Protein: 26 g / Sodium: 424 mg / Fat: 13 g (Saturated Fat: 6 g) / Potassium: 1066 mg.

A MYSTERY TO SOLVE

Full of succulent crab and tender vegetables, Mildred Kemp's Secret Ingredient Crab Soup hails from
the Eastern Maryland shore. The secret ingredient? See if you can figure it out before you
read the delightful story and discover the answer.

SOUPS & STEWS